# Worker Militancy and Its Consequences, 1965-75

# edited by
## Solomon Barkin

The Praeger Special Studies program—utilizing the most modern and efficient book production techniques and a selective worldwide distribution network—makes available to the academic, government, and business communities significant, timely research in U.S. and international economic, social, and political development.

# Worker Militancy and Its Consequences, 1965-75

## New Directions in Western Industrial Relations

PRAEGER SPECIAL STUDIES IN INTERNATIONAL ECONOMICS AND DEVELOPMENT

**Praeger Publishers**   New York   Washington   London

Library of Congress Cataloging in Publication Data
Main entry under title:

Worker militancy and its consequences, 1965-75.

(Praeger special studies in international economics
and development)
    Includes bibliographical references and index.
    1. Industrial relations—History—Addresses, essays,
lectures.   2. Trade-unions—History—Addresses, essays,
lectures.   3. Labor and laboring classes—History—
Addresses, essays, lectures.   I. Barkin, Solomon, 1907-
HD6971.W855        331'.09181'2       75-3745
ISBN 0-275-07410-2

PRAEGER PUBLISHERS
111 Fourth Avenue, New York, N.Y. 10003, U.S.A.
5, Cromwell Place, London SW7 2JL, England

Published in the United States of America in 1975
by Praeger Publishers, Inc.

© 1975 by Praeger Publishers, Inc.

Printed in the United States of America

To Elaine

This volume is an outgrowth of the editor's conviction that we must understand better and more thoroughly evaluate recent changes in the nature and character of trade unions and in the industrial relations systems of Western Europe. Too many commentators upon and participants in the daily events have treated these changes as routine. The country chapters that follow suggest that the strikes (both official and unofficial), the new demands, new gains, internal union controversy, the developments in the individual national trade unions, the new role of unionism, and the revisions in collective bargaining institutions augur a new era.

Trade unions have acquired fresh strength even where their following has not significantly increased. So strong, so powerful has their bargaining leverage become that they could negotiate sweeping improvements in the terms and conditions of employment, extend their rights and those of employees to participate in decision-making on an ever broadening range of subjects, and secure significant social gains for their constituency and for low-income groups in general. Some of the structural innovations affecting industrial decision-making may in time fundamentally alter the operation of the prevailing system of modern capitalism.

While continuing to voice the traditional slogans, trade union programs now include the humanistic values absorbed from the debates and propaganda of the leftist and student movements of the late 1960s. They are reinforcing, and in some countries for the first time, supporting, not only the messianic call for structural changes in economic and social institutions but also social tests of performance for all private and public economic institutions. Significantly, national union centers are becoming sufficiently self-confident to formulate their own programs and to urge political and social reform, a departure from past practice when labor parties preempted the initiative in this area. While remaining closely allied with labor or socialist and, in some cases Catholic democratic parties, they are less sectarian and increasingly inclined to press their positions on other political organizations. Their political influence has also grown, at times provoking the criticism that they are an extraparliamentary force negotiating directly with the central governments.

North American trade union movements did not share in this change of mood and outlook. They basically retained their older philosophies and positions, though the current ferment in Canada may betoken a departure in the direction found in Europe. Similar developments have not taken place in the United States, though one can suggest that the "time for reassessment" is here. If and when this country replaces reliance on the open market as economic regulator, the governmental refusal to provide positive direction, and the government alliance with big business interests, the trade union movement may become more disposed to reassess its own course. Now it is too integrated with the past patterns of thinking to venture on its own in new directions.

Observing developments in the industrial relations and trade union fields, the editor noted the "air of patience and moderation" that in the 1950s and 1960s overtook Western trade unionists. By the late 1960s and 1970s, however, a new dynamism began to develop abroad. But reports about it were primarily restricted to national boundaries. There were domestic polemical exchanges, but there were no integrated presentations of these events. This volume offers individual evaluations of events in each nation and their overall integration, thereby defining the nature of a new epoch.

Independent scholars were invited to analyze the evidence of unrest and changes in the industrial relations systems in the respective countries and project ahead their likely future. Each was supplied with a "checklist of issues to be considered for review in country papers"; the checklist raised questions on employee discontent and militancy, trade union dysfunctionalism, employer policies and their changes, bargaining mechanisms, the limitations of current collective bargaining procedures, and the changing relations between the industrial relations parties and the government. These questions defined the underlying query to which the editor was addressing himself--namely, does the upsurge in worker militancy reflect a temporary phenomenon, or is it rooted in deep-seated demands for structural changes in terms of employment, collective bargaining, and the economy? Generally, chapters were submitted in the native language of each contributor and, after being translated, were returned to him with questions from the editor. The chapter's final form was shaped by this exchange.

Each chapter reflects the contributor's views of the industrial relations scene in his country. Each offers a description of institutions involved in collective bargaining, respective national arrangements, the evidences of dysfunctionalism, extensions or changes being effected in the system, and the benefits enjoyed by employees; each also evaluates probable future developments. Since the Canadian collective bargaining system, like that in the United States, is built on local collective bargaining units, the chapter on Canada deals exclusively with the ferment occurring there. The United States chapter tells us about the static condition of its collective bargaining system and institutions and appraises the current role of trade unions in economic and political life, emphasizing the need for fresh thinking in this area.

The introductory chapter outlines the political, economic, and social setting in the third postwar decade (1965-75). This 10-year period evolved out of an era of political consensus, economic growth, and significant social progress enjoyed by employees. It was a decade characterized by an uneasy political balance, with an increasing emphasis on popular humanistic values and minority and coalition governments. Toward the end of the decade, the older postwar economic systems faced truly unprecedented problems owing to the immediate scarcity of materials, concentrated control of essential raw materials, inflation produced in part by oligopolistic price-setting, and the need for serious structural economic changes. Unemployment was rising to serious and threatening levels in most countries. In these last 10 years, moreover, governments have played an increasingly critical role in dealing with these issues and in a manner compatible with dominant national objectives, the newer expectations pervading the population, and greater equity sought in the distribution of benefits or the allocation of the costs of economic developments. They have also shaped the behavior of the private sector and in some instances even assumed entrepreneurial initiatives. Over this past decade, trade unions became the central force in the struggle for such values as equity, equality, and humanism, thereby helping to shape the course of the evolving democratic capitalistic society.

The concluding chapter summarizes the evidence offered in the chapters on individual countries. It also introduces other data, explores the forms and extent of unrest and protest, and defines the major new premises pervading the trade union movement and industrial relations systems. That the imperatives of the current crisis are compelling accommodations among the socioeconomic groups including the trade unions, employer associations, and individual employers is the underlying assumption. Complementing its traditional role of mediator the government has assumed a central function in facilitating new accommodations involving, not only the relations of the parties within the economic world, but also in defining their benefits and costs and rights and obligations. Truly new relationships are evolving in most Western countries.

The editor is highly indebted to the patient contributors whose continuing cooperation in following through the inquiries was needed to complete this book. He is most appreciative of the assistance of the translators, particularly Professors Frank Fata, Stowell Goding, and Vaclav Holesovsky and Mr. Roelof Wybrandus, all of the University of Massachusetts, Amherst. Many people read and offered advice respecting individual chapters. To them we extend our gratitude for their suggestions. The editor is particularly grateful to Professor Milton Cantor, to whom he turned on many occasions for counsel.  Bibliographical references have been severely reduced as they consist primarily of material in the author's native language.

The editor wishes to express his debt for the financial assistance of the Ford Foundation, which provided the resources for making possible this collaborative venture.  He is also appreciative for the aid provided by the University of Massachusetts, Amherst, Economics Department and its Labor and Research Center.

Solomon Barkin

# CONTENTS

# LIST OF TABLES

# LIST OF ABBREVIATIONS

Great Britain

| | |
|---|---|
| AUEW | Amalgamated Union of Engineering Workers |
| CIR | Commission on Industrial Relations |
| CBI | Confederation of British Industry |
| DE | Department of Employment |
| EEF | Engineering Employer's Federation |
| ETU | Union of Electrical, Electronic Telecommunication, and Plumbing |
| ICI | Imperial Chemical Industries LTD. |
| IT | Industrial Tribunals |
| NALGO | National and Local Officers' Association |
| NBPI | National Board for Prices and Incomes |
| NEDC (Neddy) | National Economic Development Council |
| NIRC | National Industrial Relations Court |
| NUGMW | National Union of General and Municipal Workers |
| NUM | National Union of Mine Workers |
| NUR | National Union of Railwaymen |
| TGWU | Transport and General Workers Union |
| TUC | Trade Union Congress |
| TUC-General Council | General Council of TUC |

Italy

## Industrial Relations

| | |
|---|---|
| CB | Committee of the Base (1968- ) |
| CD | Factory Councils (1919-20) |
| CG | Joint Management Councils (1943-45) |
| CGIL | Italian General Confederation of Labor (1944- ) |
| CGL | General Confederation of Labor (1906-27) |
| CI | Internal Commissions (1919- ) |
| CIL | Italian Confederation of Labor (1917-24) |
| CISL | Italian Confederation of Labor Unions (1950- ) |
| CISNAL | Italian Confederation of National Unions of Workers (1950- ) |
| CL | Chambers of Labor (now CGIL designation-- Local Federation of Unions of Confederation) |
| Confindustria | General Confederation of Italian Industry (1919- ) |
| ENI | Oil and Energy Corporations (state-owned) |
| FIM | Metal Workers Union of CISL |
| FIOM | Metallurgical Workers Federation (1918- ) (CGIL affiliate) |
| FLM | Federation of Metal and Mechanical Workers (1972- ) (Joint Three Confederations Agency) |
| FNDAI | National Federation of Managers of Industrial Enterprises (unaffiliated) |
| ICFTU | International Confederation of Free Trade Unions (1948- ) |

| | |
|---|---|
| INPS | National Institute of Social Security |
| Intersind | Public Corporations Collective Bargaining Association, particularly IRI affiliates (1960- ) |
| IRI | Institute for Industrial Reconstruction (state-owned) |
| LCGIL | Free Italian General Confederation of Labor (1948-50) |
| NA | Nuclear Unions (1968- ) (UIL designation for plant union) |
| NF | National (category or industry or sector) Union-Federation |
| PU | Provincial Unions (CISL designation for Chambers of Labor) |
| SAS | Factory Section of Union (1968- ) (CISL designation for plant union) |
| SSF | Union Section of Factory (1968- ) (CGIL designation for plant union) |
| UIL | Italian Union of Labor (1950- ) |
| UILM | Metal Workers Union of UIL |

## Economic and Political and Other Labor Activities

| | |
|---|---|
| AC | Catholic Action (1915- ) |
| ACLI | Christian Association of Italian Workers (1944- ) |
| DC | Christian Democratic Party (1945- ) |
| IFAP | Institute of Management Studies |
| INAM | National Health Insurance Institute |

| INAIL | National Institute for Insurance against Industrial Injuries |
| INPS | National Institute of Social Security |
| IRI | Institute of Industrial Reconstruction (1933- ) |
| MSI | Italian Social Movement (1948- ) |
| PCI | Italian Communist Party (1921- ) |
| PDUP | Party for Proletarian Unity for Communism (1974) |
| PPI | Italian Popular Party (1919-26) |
| PSDI | Italian Social Democratic Party (1951- ) |
| PSI | Italian Socialist Party (1895- ) |
| PSIUP | Socialist Party of the United Proletariat (1964-72) |
| PSLI | Socialist Party of Italian Labor (1947- ) |
| PSU | United Socialist Party (1966-69) |

## The Netherlands

### Industrial Relations Institutions

| ANMB | General Union for the Metal Workers (NVV affiliate) |
| AWV | General Employers' Association (1919- ) |
| BBA | Extraordinary Decree on Labor Relations (1945-70) |
| BIW | Bureau of Industrial Employers |
| BRKV | Bureau of Roman Catholic Trade Unions (1909-25) |

| CAO | Collective Bargaining Agreements |
| CNV | Protestant National Trade Union Federation (1909-  ) |
| CvR | Board of Government Mediators (1940-45; 1945-70) |
| CSWV | Central Social Federation of Employers (1945-67) |
| ER | Economic Council (1932-40) |
| EVC | Trade Union Unity Center (1945-64) |
| FCWV | Federation of Catholic and Protestant Employers' Associations (1967-70) |
| FEWO | Independent Trade Union Federation (1964-  ) |
| FME | Employers' Federation for the Metals and Electrotechnical Industries (1961-  ) |
| HRA | High Council of Labor |
| KAB | Catholic Labor Movement (1946-64) |
| NCW | Netherlands Christian Employers' Association (1970-  ) |
| NKV | Netherlands Catholic Trade Union Federation (1964-  ) (successor to KAB) |
| NKWV | Netherlands Catholic Employers' Federation (1915-70) |
| NVV | Netherlands Federation of Trade Unions (1905-  ) |
| OVB | Independent Union of Industrial Organizations (1964-  ) (independent radical unions) |
| PBO | Industrial Organization under Public Law (1933-  ) |

| | |
|---|---|
| RBA | Governing Board of Labor Affairs (1941- ) (employers) |
| RKWV | Catholic Workers' Federation in the Netherlands (1925-46) |
| RNW | Council of Netherlands Employers' Associations |
| RO | Union Consultation Board (1958- ) |
| RVV | Council of Trade Union Federations for Interorganization Cooperation (1943-54) |
| SvdA | Foundation of Labor (1945- ) |
| SER | Social Economic Council (1945- ) |
| VNO | Association of Netherlands Enterprises (1968- ) |
| VNW | Association of Netherlands Employers (1899-1926) |
| VNW | Federation of Netherlands Industries (1926-67) |
| VPCW | Federation of Protestant Employers in the Netherlands (1937-70) |

## Political, Religious, and Other Institutions

| | |
|---|---|
| ARP | Protestant Anti-Revolutionary Party (1878- ) (moderate Calvinist) |
| CHU | Christian Historical Union (1908- ) Dutch Reformed) |
| CNP | Netherlands Communist Party (1918- ) |
| D'66 | Democrats '66 (1966- ) (moderate radicals) |

| | |
|---|---|
| DS '70 | Democratic Socialists '70 (1970- ) (right-wing socialists) |
| GPV | Reformed Political Federation (1948- ) (strict Calvinist) |
| KVP | Catholic People's Party (1946- ) |
| LSP | Liberal States Party (1927-46) |
| PPR | Political Party of Radicals (1968- ) (dissident left-wing Catholics) |
| PSP | Pacifist Socialist Party (1957- ) (radical socialist) |
| PVV | Freedom Party (1946-48) |
| PvdA | Labor Party (1946- ) |
| RKPN | Roman Catholic Party of the Netherlands (1972- ) (dissident right-wing Catholics) |
| RKS | Roman Catholic State Party (1904-46) |
| SDAP | Social Democratic Labor Party (1894-1946) |
| SDB | Social Democratic League (1881-94) |
| VVD | People's Party for Freedom and Democracy, Conservative Party (1948- ) |

## Belgium

## Industrial Relations

| | |
|---|---|
| ACS | Socialist Common Action |
| BPE | Economic Programing Bureau (1959- ) (Planning Bureau since 1970) |
| CCE | Central Economic Council (1948- ) |
| CCI | Central Industrial Committee (1895-1946) |

| | |
|---|---|
| CE | Works Councils (1948- ) |
| CER | Regional Economic Councils (1970- ) |
| CES | Economic and Social Conference (1970- ) |
| CGSCLB | General Confederation of Christian and Free Trade Unions (1912-23) |
| CGSLB | Federation of Liberal Trade Unions of Belgium (1930- ) |
| CGTB | General Confederation of Labor (1937-45) (successor of CS) |
| CNE | National Conference on Employment (1972- ) |
| CNEE | National Committee on Economic Expansion (1960- ) |
| CNIT | National Independent Confederation of Workers (1938- ) (apolitical) |
| CNT (1936-56) | National Labor Conference (1936-56) |
| CNT | National Labor Council (1952- ) |
| CP | Joint Industrial Commissions (1919- ) |
| CPr | Industrial Councils (1948- ) |
| CS | Union Commission of POB (1898-1937) |
| CSC | Confederation of Christian Unions (1923- ) (successor to CGSCLB) |
| CSHELT | Plant Safety and Health and Amenities Committee (1954- ) |
| CSI | Cartel of Independent Trade Unions in the Public Service (1926- ) |
| CSUB | Confederation of Unified Trade Unions of Belgium (1963- ) |

FEB      Federation of Belgian Enterprises (1972-  )
(successor to FIB)

FENIB      Federation of Belgian Nonindustrial Firms
(1946-72)

FGTB      Belgian General Federation of Labor (1945-  )
(successor of CGTB)

FIB      Federation of Belgian Industries (1946-72)
(successor of CCI)

LDB      Belgian Democratic League (1891-  )

MOC      Christian Worker Movement (1945-  )

OBAP      Joint Declaration on Productivity (1954-72)

SDR      Societies for Regional Development (1970-  )

## Political Parties

CP      Catholic Party (1831-1945)

FDF      Democratic Front of French Speakers in
Brussels (1965-  )

PCB      Communist Party of Belgium (1921-  )

PL      Liberal Party (1846-1961)

PLP      Party of Liberty and Progress (1961-  )
(successor to PL)

POB      Belgium Labor Party (1885-1945) (successor
to Belgium Socialist Party)

PSB      Belgium Socialist Party (1945-  ) (successor
to POB)

PSC      Social Christian Party (1945-  ) (successor
to CP)

RW      Walloon Assembly

Volkunie      People's Union in Flanders (1954-  )

## Industrial Relations

| | |
|---|---|
| ABF | Workers' Educational Organization, 1912 |
| AD | Labor Court, 1928 |
| AFA | Labor Market Insurance Company, 1962 |
| AKN | National Joint Committee for Workers' Protection, 1942 |
| ALN | Supervisors' and Foremen's Labor Market Council, 1959 |
| AM, 1938 | Labor Market Council, 1938 |
| AMK, 1936 | Labor Market Committee, 1936 |
| AMK, 1938 | Labor Market Council, 1938 |
| AMK, 1951 | Labor Market Council for Women's Questions, 1951 |
| AMP | Labor Market Insurance, pension, 1971 |
| AMS | National Swedish Labor Market Board, 1947 |
| AMS | Labor Market Insurance, sickness, 1971 |
| AMY | Labor Market Vocational Council, 1944 |
| AS | Time and Motion Study Council, 1961 |
| ATP | Supplementary Pension System, 1959 |
| ITP | Complementary Pensions for Salaried Employees, 1960 |
| KF | Cooperative Union and Wholesale Society, 1899 |
| KFO | Negotiating Board of KF |
| LKAB | Luossavaara-Kiirunavaara AB: state-owned mining company |

| | |
|---|---|
| LO | Swedish Confederation of Trade Unions, 1898 |
| PA-radet | Swedish Council for Personnel Administration, 1952 |
| PTK | Cartel of Private Employee Unions, 1973 |
| RLF | Swedish Farmers' Union, 1929 |
| RTI | Council for Training of Salaried Employees in Industry, 1960 |
| RR | Rationalization Council, 1972 |
| SAC | Swedish Syndicalist Union, 1910 |
| SACO | Swedish Confederation of Professional Associations, 1947 |
| SACO-CF | Swedish Association of Graduate Engineers, 1954 |
| SAF | Swedish Employers' Confederation, 1902 |
| SALF | Swedish Supervisors and Foremen Association, 1905 (TCO) |
| SAV | Swedish National Collective Bargaining Board, 1965 |
| SF | State Employees' Union, 1970 (LO) |
| SFO | Negotiating Organization of National Enterprises, 1970 |
| SIF | Swedish Union of Clerical and Technical Employees in Industry, 1920 |
| SKTF | Swedish Union of Municipal Employees, 1970 (TCO) |
| SR | National Federation of Government Officers, 1917, 1944 |
| TBV | Educational Organization of Salaried Employees, 1935 |

| | |
|---|---|
| TCO | Swedish Central Organization of Salaried Employees, 1944 |
| TCO-K | TCO Municipal Section, 1967 |
| TCO-S | TCO Central Government Section, 1967 |
| TM | Salaried Employees' Labor Market Council, 1957 |
| URAF | Development Council's Working Party for Collaboration Research, 1969 |
| URS | Development Council for Collaboration Questions, 1966 |
| VF | Swedish Engineering Employers' Association, 1900 |

## Political

| | |
|---|---|
| BF | Farmers' Party, 1913 (succeeded by Center Party) |
| C | Center Party, 1957 |
| FP | Liberal Party, 1900 (People's Party) |
| H | Conservative Party, 1904-69 (Party of the Right) |
| KP | Communist Party, 1921-67 |
| M | Moderate Unity Party, 1969 (successor to Conservative Party) |
| SAP or S | Social Democratic Party, 1889 |
| VPK | Communist Party, 1967 (successor to KP) |

## Industrial Relations

| | |
|---|---|
| BAG | Federal Labor Court |
| BDA | Federal Union of German Employers' Associations, 1949 |
| BDI | Federation of German Industry, 1949 |
| BVG | Law on Constitutional Organization of Enterprises, 1952 (Works Council) |
| CGB | Christian Trade Union Federation of Germany, 1955 |
| DAG | German Salaried Employees' Union, 1945 |
| DBB | German Civil Service Union, 1915 |
| DGB | German Trade Union Federation, 1949 |
| IG-Bau, SteineErden | Construction, Stone, and Clay Workers' Union, 1949 |
| IG-Chemie DGB | Chemical Paper and Ceramic Workers' Union, 1949 |
| IG-Metall DGB | Metal Workers' Union, 1949 |

## Political

| | |
|---|---|
| ADF | Action for Democratic Party, 1968-70 (leftist) |
| BRD | Federal Republic of Germany, 1949 |
| CDU | Christian Democratic Union, 1945 |
| CSU | Christian Social Union, 1945 |
| DDR | German Democratic Republic, 1949 |

| | |
|---|---|
| DKP | Communist Party of Germany, 1968 (reconstituted, Moscow-oriented) |
| DP | German Party, 1945 |
| FDP | Free Democratic Party, 1946 |
| GIM | Trotskyite Group of International Marxists, 1969 |
| Jusos | Young Socialists of SDP, 1946 |
| KDP | Communist Party of Germany, 1970 (Maoist) |
| KDP-ML | Communist Party of Germany, 1968 (Marxist-Leninist) |
| NPD | National Democratic Party, 1964 (right wing) |
| SDS | Socialist Students' Federation, 1969-70 |
| SPD | Social Democratic Party, 1945 |

France

Industrial Relations

| | |
|---|---|
| ANDCP | Association of Personnel Directors |
| AFPA | National Association for Adult Vocational Training (1949-  ) (successor to ANIFRMO) |
| ANPE | National Employment Agency (1967-  ) |
| ASSEDIC | Association for the Employment of Workers in Industry and Commerce (1958-  ) |
| CDF | Coal Industry of France |
| CFDT | French Democratic Federation of Labor (1919-64; 1964-  ) (Christian-Socialist) |
| CFT | French Confederation of Labor (1959-  ) |

| | |
|---|---|
| CFTC | French Democratic Federation of Christian Workers (1964- ) (Christian) |
| CGC | General Confederation of Management Employees (1944- ) |
| CGE | General Company of Electricity |
| CGT | General Confederation of Labor (1895- ) (Communist-led) |
| CGT-FO | General Confederation of Labor, Force Ouvriere (1948- ) (Socialist) |
| CNPF | National Council of French Employers (1946- ) (Patronat) |
| EGF | Electricity of France |
| FEN | National Federation of Education (1946- ) |
| FNE | National Employment Fund (1963- ) |
| GDF | Gas of France |
| RATP | Parisian Subway and Bus System |
| SMIC | Minimum Interindustry Growth Wage (1970- ) (successor to SMIG) |
| SMIG | Guaranteed Interindustry Minimum Wage (1950-70) |
| SNCF | French National Railways |

Political

| | |
|---|---|
| CDP | Democratic and Progress Center (1966- ) |
| MRP | Christian Democratic Party (1945-62) (Popular Republican Movement) |
| PCF | Communist Party of France (1920- ) |

| | |
|---|---|
| PS | Socialist Party (1905- ) |
| PSU | Unified Socialist Party (1960- ) |
| RI | National Federation of Independent Republicans (1966- ) |
| SFIO | French Section of Labor International (1905-69) (Socialist) |
| UDR | Union of Democrats for the Fifth Republic (1958- ) (Gaullist) |

# CHAPTER 1

## THE THIRD POSTWAR DECADE (1965-75): PROGRESS, ACTIVISM, AND TENSION

Solomon Barkin

Militant trade union movements emerged in Europe in the third postwar decade out of the cooperative and adaptable ones of the first two decades. During the war and early postwar period, unions on both sides of the Atlantic acquired great prestige and a large following and played a central role in the political and social life of their respective countries. Radicals began charging them with being part of the establishment. Workers and their dependents enjoyed high employment, progressively advancing living levels, security, earnings, and public benefits and services. Feelings of affluence and confidence in progress suffused the society, reaching into the working class. The welfare reforms, it was assumed, reached the unemployed and the needy as they benefited the employed and provided all an underpinning of benefits and services. A political consensus prevailed.

This euphoria receded with the ascendancy of the postwar generation, which demanded the materialization of the expectations on which it was raised. Disturbances spread through many diverse groups as each registered its complaints and supported other protests. Governments and society granted some demands either fully or partially. The swing in European opinion turned the electorate to the left. Division increased within the political system. Further development of the federal European state appeared aborted and a malaise spread on its future course. Further complicating the era were the problems of inflation, shortages, serious imbalances in international payments, and intermittent increases in the volume of unemployment and fears that it may become a serious enduring problem. Political leaders tried hard to find new policies and programs acceptable to the population including labor groups to achieve economic growth, stability, and rising standards and maintain high employment. The anxieties increased.

1

Those developments and the new challenges penetrated the
European trade union movement and produced demands for sweeping
improvements in terms of employment, working conditions, and
worker and trade union rights in the economy and political life.
Some were met; the others continued to be steadfastly and force-
fully pressed. They appear to be of sufficiently sweeping character
to call for fundamental changes in the structure of the capitalistic
system to make it more consistent with the visions of employees
and trade union movements. The depression made their radicalism
even more apparent.

The present chapter offers a broad description of the developments, the nature of the changes and new attitudes in the political,
economic, and social life of Western Europe and the two North American countries, Canada and the United States, in order that we may
understand the presence or absence of the new activism, militancy,
and growing tension within them. Contrasts will be drawn primarily
between Europe and North America and distinctions will be made as
to the trends or occurrences in individual countries to prepare the
reader to follow the developments in the national trade unions and
industrial relations systems described in subsequent chapters.


FROM POLITICAL CONSENSUS TO AN UNEASY NATIONAL
BALANCE: A STALLED REGIONAL UNION

Reconstruction (1945-50)

Largely unfettered capitalism and rampant national competition had catapulted the world into two World Wars. For these President Franklin D. Roosevelt and Prime Minister Winston Churchill in
1941 offered the principles of the Atlantic Charter. It spelled out the
war aims and the fundamentals of the new world order. Men were
to be entitled to four freedoms: freedom from want, freedom to
worship, freedom of speech, and freedom from fear.

A new rational order was later heralded. At the international level, the United Nations would serve as moderator. At the
domestic level, national governments would implement these visions
and promote economic stability. The principles and mechanism for
attaining these ends in the Western advanced countries were broadly
drawn. Socialist governments in the Scandinavian countries in the
1930s had capably administered the new "social capitalism" for
achieving growth, high employment, and greater social equity. Socialist parties in Belgium and the Netherlands had learned before
the war to collaborate with other parties in coalition governments.
And others participated during the war in "national-unity" governments, both at home or, more usually, in exile. John Maynard

Keynes offered the theoretical tenets for converting members of the establishment to the economic programs of this new era. Individual socialists and economists provided the insight and the techniques for coordinated national planning in capitalistic societies. Wartime experience had reinforced the belief in the effectiveness of these ideas and tools. They provided the designs for practical legislation, the administration of postwar reconstruction and subsequently, the welfare state with its stress on economic and social equality and protection. The Organization for European Economic Cooperation (OEEC), administrator of the Marshall Plan, assisted in developing these patterns.

The programs secured the support of groups from many walks of life that had joined together in the war against nazism and fascism. As a result, the early postwar coalition governments embraced most parties from the center to the left, including both Communists and Social Democrats. Some conservatives, untouched by the collaborationist brush, also participated in socially oriented reconstruction. The programs they fostered often shaped by the governments-in-exile, reflected the common visions and unity of purpose to achieve national economic growth along with the wider and more equitable distribution of benefits.


## Political Consensus (1950-65)

But, in 1947, this agreement started to fall apart with the Cold War and with the completion of the period of reconstruction. The communist parties were the first to be eased out of cabinets by the other parties; often they themselves withdrew (Austria, Belgium, Finland, France, and Italy). Management and property interests regained confidence and increasingly secured the restoration of most prior rights and privileges. Market and private economic forces and power groups took over the operation of much of the economy, guided, aided, or, controlled in varying degrees, but usually in a limited manner, by the government.

Centrist political positions were in the ascendancy in more and more European governments. The Christian Democratic parties increasingly dominated nominally Catholic continental countries as well as such pluralistic nations as Germany and the Netherlands. They tended to be coalitions of moderates and some conservatives and in some countries also included differing proportions of leftist or trade-union-oriented groups. For the most part, however, they followed middle-of-the-road domestic policies moderating the impetus to social reform initiated in the immediate postwar period. These parties governed for long periods of time, sometimes with

the help of other centrist and occasionally, conservative parties.
At times, when suffering reverses in elections or in parliaments,
they invited socialist parties to become junior or equal members of
their coalitions. Their foreign policy followed the lead of the United
States on defense and relations with the communist Eastern bloc,
and advocated, eventually with success, the integration of the Six
into the Economic Community. France deviated from this pattern
when Charles de Gaulle in 1958 became president and followed a
conservative domestic policy. In the United Kingdom, Conservatives dominated after 1950 for a decade and a half. A conservative
Republican held the U.S. presidency after 1952 to the end of the
decade.

The influence of socialist parties (Labor or Social Democratic) outside the Scandinavian countries generally dwindled in
these years. They attempted to offset this trend by recasting their
image and platforms from a class to a "people's" party; their support, however, continued to come primarily from blue-collar workers. The German Social Democratic Party played down its attack
on property per se and religion and its emphasis on the nationalization of industry, focusing instead on greater equity and opportunity.
It accepted the dominant Keynesian proposition that government had
a central role in assuring economic growth and stability, and in
realizing other public ends, including the elimination of the ravages
of capitalism and poverty. It would direct the private sector to conform to the tests of the public weal. On parliamentary floors the
parties fought for and secured social reform as well as legislation
to improve the operation of the economy. And many of these social
goals became the common heritage of the age.

While the prewar and wartime generations dominated the national moods and opinions, economic growth and high employment
prevailed, and, as benefits expanded and rose, the masses supported
the design. A feeling of consensus existed on current issues. Intellectuals and writers perceived in this state a marked change from
the prewar pattern. They saw a more homogenized society with
differences based upon personal and local conditions rather than
class or group identifications. Class conflict did indeed diminish
as more groups accommodated their disparate interests through
bargaining and compromise. Political life was substantially democ-
ratized. Moreover, the stark brutalities of the Stalinist regime and
the suppression of the 1956 Hungarian revolt turned some fellow
travelers and Communist Party members toward a more Western
perception of freedom. These perceptions were articulated at the
1955 Milan Conference of the Congress for Cultural Freedom, which
assured the Western world that it was to be free "from the harass-
ments of ideologists and zealots."

This optimism was reinforced in 1951 by the formation of the European Coal and Steel Community and in 1957 by the signing by six states of the Treaty of Rome, creating the European Economic Community (EEC). To be sure, seven other countries constituted their own European Free Trade Association (EFTA). But the Six had found a way to construct a customs union. Moreover, many leaders hoped they had also built a base for a larger political community, which would overcome the loss of hegemony in world affairs. Now the continent could contemplate dealing with the superpowers, the United States and the USSR, on a more equal footing. But this dream was premature. The nation-states remained supreme, jealously guarding their sovereignty. Only begrudgingly after a crisis in 1965 and 1966 did the Council of Ministers, the final legislative organ, allow majority votes to be binding, but unanimous agreements remained necessary on issues where important national interests were at stake, a concept that in practice was most liberally interpreted, forestalling further advances. When France in 1974 showed a disposition to support binding majority decisions other countries rejected this principle.

The EEC completed its customs union in July 1969, some 18 months ahead of schedule, introducing a common external tariff with it. Restraints on intra-Community manpower and capital movements were also removed by 1968. A modest Social Fund provided compensation to countries for employee retraining and relocation programs. A system of value-added taxes became operative in 1973, when Italy applied it some six years after agreeing on the concept. The Investment Bank began extending loans for economic development to member countries and associated members. These positive moves climaxed with the final admittance of Great Britain, Denmark, and Ireland in January 1973, after two prior failures. Nonetheless, aspirations for a federal regional body remained unsatisfied.


Uneasy National Balance: After 1965


The apparent consensus began to unravel in the third postwar decade. As the postwar baby generation matured and entered adult society and the work world, it demanded fulfillment of expectations for a long time publicly voiced. This generation sought not modest improvements on prewar standards but further changes and progressive advances beyond those of their youth. These expectations and demands became a forceful motivation for further change.

Politically, this new generation reinvigorated the move to the left. The lifting of restraints on individual Catholics who wished to join leftist parties that had been initiated in the 1950s received

further sanction from the new freedoms suggested in the statements
of the Second Vatican Council (1962-65). Leftists and political liberals within the Christian Democratic parties demanded greater
recognition and acceptance of their views than in the past, leading
in some countries to a shift in power to the left within the Christian
Democratic parties, to a liberalization of programs, or to the formation of splinter groups as in France and the Netherlands that
joined leftist parties in political coalitions. Consideration of detente
between the Western countries and the USSR removed a significant
prop supporting the Christian Democratic parties. Confessional
politics and trade unions lost much of their appeal, for polarization
now occurred more freely along economic, political, and social
lines. The Christian Democratic and denominational parties remained major but weakened power blocs in most countries.

The eruption of student and later citizen protests in Europe
and North America significantly destabilized the prevailing consensus. Their demonstrations, provocative militant mass action, and
even violent onslaughts awakened some national populations from
complacency, prompting Europeans, particularly, to reexamine
their society. The young in Europe and North America focused on
the disadvantaged, discrimination, overindulgence in the affluent
society, the shambles of urban living, pollution and despoliation of
the environment, the inadequacies of the universities, and the exploitation of as well as the parsimonious assistance to developing
nations. They reflected an awakened social consciousness as well
as a striving for personal self-realization. Perceiving in the Vietnam war a repetition of the old link between capitalism and war,
they demonstrated against it and warned of a possible East-West
conflict. They voiced a yearning for a classless and stateless utopia
of perfect freedom and self-government but not the abolition of the
nation-state.

During its heyday in the later 1960s, the New Left in Europe
infiltrated established leftist parties, created enclaves within them,
formed new parties, and urged more ambitious demands and militant tactics upon trade unionists. Essentially reflecting humanistic
values, despite disruptive tactics, the activities of New Left adherents popularized new concerns in the quality of life for all men and
the protection of the environment and resources. Though their influence in the 1970s declined almost to insignificance in most countries, their legacy of ideas, slogans, and demands was rich and
continued to affect most social movements. In Germany they remained a serious continuing force prodding the Social Democratic
party to more radical measures. In France they staged recurrent
demonstrations, particularly among foreign workers. In Italy, their
influence was restricted to the universities and among the literati.

In the United Kingdom, they conditioned the outlook of some left-wing elements of the Labour Party.

Countering this destabilizing force is the drive of the communist parties for legitimacy within individual countries. Their influence steadily declined to relative insignificance except in Finland, France, Iceland, and Italy where they retained major strongholds. In Denmark and Norway, noncommunist leftist parties in addition to the Socialists exceeded them in size. Two forces favored their accommodation and collaboration with the existing political and social systems. First, they sought a show of independence from control of the Soviet party for internal national party reasons, particularly in Italy, and second, the USSR policy of detente with Western countries, particularly the United States after the Cuban incident, demanded such rapprochement.

The communist parties in time sought a common political front with socialist but not ultraleftist parties. They endorsed labor parties in elections in Austria, the Netherlands, and the United Kingdom or supported socialist governments in parliament, as in Norway and Sweden. But, except in France and Italy, socialists rejected collaboration. Communists, moreover, abandoned violent protests, avoided ultraleftist tactics, and favored the resolution of spontaneous worker or youth protests through negotiations and the consummation of agreements.

In proposing joint action, the French and Italian communist parties announced their commitments to the independence of the individual parties and their readiness to compromise doctrine and tactics in the interest of collaboration. In Italy the party offered tacit support to the center-left governments. In France, it made common cause with the socialists in several presidential and parliamentary elections, helping to bring the leftist front to near victory. And in 1974 the Communist Party delegates entered the European Parliament and gained official recognition as a bloc. This policy of collaboration gained official endorsement at a 1974 conference of 21 Western European communist parties.

Socialist parties became the primary beneficiaries of the swing to the moderate left. They recast their platforms, but principally their positions, in response to the militant reformist pressures and humanistic values generated in the latter half of the 1960s, stressing structural economic as well as social change and social reforms. Issues that received most attention were the eradication of pockets of poverty, increased opportunities for lower-income groups particularly in education and vocational preparation, workers' control, more social services, and civil liberties, in contrast to the situation in the so-called socialist states. The stress on full employment and economic growth was complemented by measures to protect individuals, prevent pollution, preserve the environment, and advance the quality of life with worker and citizen participation in decision-making to counterbalance state power. Economic controls and guidance to business were to be more intimate and direct than previously, based on more extensive reporting by management on its operations and policies and discussions between industrial leaders and the governmental economic authorities. The state would become more of an innovator, risk-taker, and entrepreneur in an economy in which private preferences and interests would be subordinated to public and social interests. The new tax measures were aimed particularly at the very rich, thereby relaxing financial pressures on the lower- and middle-income groups.

Such support and revitalization of platforms resulted in a marked upswing in the number of European nations governed by socialists or socialist-led coalitions or those in which socialists participated. France was an outstanding exception. Of course, the United States had a Republican conservative president since 1969, and Canada had a Liberal Government since 1963.

Significantly, in no country other than Italy is the extreme right truly visible. While the main body of Italian rightism (the Italian Social Movement--MSI) seeks legitimacy and is present in Parliament, a militant extremist group operates on the political fringe through acts of violence. Occasionally such extreme rightist groups appeared in France and in Germany, as well, in response to leftist or to articulate local national issues. But generally they found little or no audience.

In the 1960s, Western countries moved to implement populist objectives. To be sure, there were some reversals in France, the United Kingdom, and the United States, but these proved temporary, and generally governments sought ways to satisfy popular expectations despite limited resources.

Middle-income groups and doctrinaire conservatives showed their disapproval in various forms, including support of nontraditional parties. In the December 1973 Danish election, for example, these blocs supported a new party that proposed the abolition of income taxes, the armed forces, and most of the civil services. Norwegians in September 1973 made a similar but less dramatic move for a new lower-tax party. In Switzerland the diversion from established voting patterns in referenda took the form of a growing nationalism, partly as a result of the protest against the large influx of foreign workers. Sectionalism in Belgium, Scotland, Wales, and Ulster ran strong as issues in February 1974 elections. Canada faces this perennial issue in Quebec. Higher-income groups also expressed their discontent by escaping from the rising tax burdens by utilizing tax loopholes, migration, and capital exports.

But the population at large looked to the state for new solutions, and disparaged the prevailing malaise and uncertainty. Shifts in voter loyalties produced changing regimes, and, consequently, more countries than before are governed by political coalitions that reconcile differences among its members (Belgium, Finland, Germany, Iceland, the Republic of Ireland, Italy, Luxembourg, the Netherlands, Portugal, and Switzerland). When the differences are not resolved, the regimes topple and new governments are constituted, often composed of the same parties but represented by new individuals. Minority governments exist in other nations (Denmark, Norway, and Sweden). In the United States, Republicans hold the executive branch and the Democrats the legislative, with the two constantly disagreeing. Austria, Canada, and the United Kingdom boast majority single parties in power. The French president governs with the aid of a personally selected cabinet.

Current evidence does not suggest the early likelihood of a break in this uneasy state of affairs. Nevertheless, the dynamics of national political life in these countries do promote progressive change, allow for increasing accommodation of views, and dispose governments to negotiate directly with the major interests, be they economic, ethnic, sectarian, or regional, to find acceptable solutions for critical issues. This process facilitates the adaptation of national institutions to new conditions and policies and to bring new appropriate leadership to the fore. It may produce more collectively oriented programs and wider collaboration among the interest groups and between them and the government, and ultimately a more viable state. The British have in the past relied on the "muddling-through" process; now other countries appear to be turning to it. The alternative is outright conflict and sharply opposed philosophies, a course generally rejected in these countries.

## The Malaise at the European Regional Level

At the European regional level, member states are ready to acknowledge the advantages, benefits, and imperatives for maintaining and elaborating the common efforts of the European Economic Community and the urgent need to extend the customs union to an economic, monetary, political, and social union. But the national determination is lacking to yield authority to a regional federal agency. Short-term national interests dominate the thinking of the diplomatic spokesmen. Nor can pro-European lobbies overcome this parochialism and national resistance. Some of those dedicated to federalism such as trade unionists are concentrating their efforts on obtaining power and influence in existing regional agencies. In sum, the transcending need for a regional instrument lacks the necessary priority among political leaders.

The monetary crisis of May 1971 dramatized these difficulties. Plans for an economic and monetary union to be consummated by 1980 made little headway. Instead, the parties are turning to ad hoc decisions on current problems to achieve greater integration, such as the creation of a fund to assist in the recycling of oil revenues and to assist in the conversion of short-term credit into medium-term loans. The 1973-74 oil crisis gave rise to even greater divisions, with individual countries seeking to reach separate agreements with producer nations. Since then, Britain and France agreed on prior consultation on economic pacts restoring the EEC control of trade agreements. Over France's objections, the other EEC countries accepted the U.S. invitation to a February 1974 Washington conference of oil-consuming nations, which produced an agreement for cooperation and for the development of a positive action program for dealing with energy problems. An International Energy Agency resulted, to promote alternative sources of energy in the medium and long term and to share scarce supplies in times of crisis.

Comparable difficulties exist in obtaining pacts on other subjects such as farm prices, industrial, regional, and scientific policies. In the spring of 1974, Italy confronted the Common Market with its own far-reaching restrictions on imports to head off a huge trade deficit threatening the very existence of the customs union. The EEC Commission temporarily accepted this action under Article 109 of the Rome Treaty to meet a "sudden crisis in the balance of payments." But it exacted a condition: the removal of farm imports, with the provision for compensating increases in revenues to the farmers. Denmark followed with its own tax system changes to limit imports. The United Kingdom added the next blow by demanding the revision of membership terms. The outcome of these negotiations will influence the Labour Party's recommendations to the nation on the planned referendum that will decide Britain's continued participation in the EEC.

Similar confusion exists respecting Soviet military might. Allied forces and materiel appear to be shrinking, while Soviet military power is increasing. Some experts contend that the balance of power is slipping in favor of the USSR, with fears being expressed of the "finlandization" of Western Europe--that is, the growing Russian ability to influence domestic and foreign policies of individual countries in support of Soviet growth and hegemony at the expense of support of the United States. But both governments and the people shy away from making appropriate defense expenditures or political commitments. Dependent upon U.S. military

power for ultimate protection they nevertheless are uneasy with its
presence. They resist America's claim to a global range of interests. As former world powers, they are irritated by abrupt U.S.
procedures and conduct or the neglect of established diplomatic pro-
tocol prior to major U.S. decisions. Fear is expressed that U.S.
understandings with the USSR might overlook or subordinate European interests. Key European officials were distressed by 1973 U.S.
actions in the Near East, fearing American preemption in an area of
primary interest to them. Equally threatening to them were U.S.
positions on other issues such as energy, monetary reform, nuclear
strategy, mutual force reduction, and most recently, the $25 billion
recycling facility. The presence of U.S. multinational corporations
within their own borders also provokes concern; they dominate key
industries and, at times, it is alleged, act in conflict with national
practices and policies. But the EEC members find it difficult to
reach agreement on these issues among themselves. European countries are divided among themselves and also fearful that the United
States will pursue policies shaped primarily by its own interests,
using its power and now the oil-financing crisis to exact conformance
by European nations with its views.

A number of steps for improved understanding have been taken.
One is the settlement of disputes on tariff concessions to the United
States to compensate for the entrance of three new members into the
EEC. Arrangements have been made for more direct consultation
between the United States and the European powers, and broader
acknowledgment of and accommodation to European views are to be
made in future dealings with the USSR. The 1974 Ottawa Declaration
represented a formal affirmation of the need for continuing consultation. Closer cooperation has been assured in the discussions and
negotiations at the European Cooperation and Security Conference in
Geneva and at the Vienna talks on mutually balanced force reductions.

These internal and external developments led the chairmen of
the Council of Ministers and the Economic Commission to express,
in a joint statement in April 1974, the prevailing alarm at the state
of disarray and inertness in the Community. They called for action
"to overcome the stagnation which is threatening the Community."
Guidelines, they hoped, would be adopted to "ensure the existence of
the Community, prevent disintegration, and keep it moving in particular in all these fields in which important decisions have to be
made."

Hope has been expressed that the new political leaders in France
and Germany who came into office in June 1974 will strike new bar-
gains to revitalize the Community. After intensive negotiations, the
summit meeting of members of the Community in Paris in December
1974 produced an agreement on a modest number of steps to strengthen

the Community and advance regional policies. There is an awareness that the alternative to a resurgent Community is its further weakening and greater dependence of individual members upon the United States for economic, military, and political support, a possibility viewed with alarm by all nations, including the United States.

The malaise at the European political level inhibits member countries from reaching a firm agreement on the transfer of authority to the EEC and a common political program for the member countries of the NATO. Parallel to this state is an uneasiness at the national levels, reflecting the approximate balance between the forces seeking to satisfy the people's expectations through progressive reforms and more collectivized policies and those confining their solutions to traditional values, making minimal concessions to the new pressures. The contending forces are engaged in intense political bargaining on policies and programs resulting in frequent changes in political regimes and increasing the political tensions in these countries.


ECONOMIC PROSPERITY OVERTAKEN BY INFLATION,
SCARCITIES, AND NEED FOR URGENT
STRUCTURAL CHANGE

Governments Redesign Instruments for Modern
Open-Market Private Economies

Current political tensions originate in part with the new economic problems confronting nations and the persistent demands made on governments by the people. To achieve reconstruction in the immediate postwar period, countries employed many forms of direct economic control. As this end was achieved, they relaxed controls and restrictions, encouraging the reestablishment of the open-market private economies and the use of indirect economic instruments to promote their ends. But the countries in the postwar years also accepted a wider number of economic and social objectives inspired both by internal compulsions and obligations assumed in international commitments. To advance these ends, governments supplemented existing direct and indirect economic instruments with newer ones specifically directed at the expanded series of goals. These were to guide the private actors in the economy and the public agencies and enterprise.

But with the appearance of new problems of intense and prolonged inflation and scarcities, large deficits in the balance of payments and the possibility of economic stagnancy or low rates of economic growth and higher levels of unemployment, the nations slowly realized that they faced strikingly new issues for which existing theories and experience provided no sure guides. Governments scurried around for short-run escape hatches, such as bilateral arrangements and long-term programs to moderate the impact of price rises. Worried leaders are seeking answers that would assure both economic and political survival for their countries and themselves. They are keenly aware that the solutions must be collective, socially equitable, and both national and international in nature. The new flurry of activity and desire for answers contributes to current uncertainty and tension, the unsteady political state, and, as we shall see, the turbulent industrial relations scene.

## National Objectives Defined and Broadened

National objectives are now defined and officially acknowledged. The public commitment to full or very high employment is, after three decades, well-entrenched. If the private economy fails to maintain this level practically, European countries are prepared to initiate measures toward such an end. This priority exists and, except in the United States under a Republican administration, is everywhere stressed. The growth goal was 50 percent for the 1960s and according to an Organization for Economic Cooperation and Development (OECD) ministerial resolution, 65 percent for the 1970s.

Price stability is also sought, but the governments learned that integrated multiinstrument approaches--that is, a combination of complementary measures--are essential but not necessarily sufficient to this end, an alternative that European countries accept more readily than the United States. Such stability predicates a steady level in the balance of payments.

These direct economic goals alone are no longer satisfactory. They were complemented by significant social ones emphasizing rising standards of living, greater equity and opportunity, and the elimination of poverty. Moreover, in the third postwar decade, additional concerns and objectives confront governments. There is, for example, the demand to reduce the human costs of production and pollution and to restrain the despoliation of the environment and to prevent the exhaustion of natural resources. Individual countries and international organizations now pronounce their general dedication to improve the quality of life for all people.

While there is a loudly voiced dedication to help developing countries, actual assistance is modest. The crisis in this field is attributed in part to the prior emphasis on capital-intensive projects in investment plans and the failure to funnel benefits to the masses of the population.

With the appearance of severe restrictions in domestic consumption to meet the high costs of foreign oil, political leaders began to voice support of "disinflation" measures that assure equitable sharing by all groups of the social costs of a low or negative rate of economic growth. A social consensus is essential for effective political action.

## Instruments Extended and Diversified

Indirect economic instruments for attaining national objectives by acting through the market economy in the 1950s replaced direct controls. Nevertheless, direct controls remained for rents, the volume, types, or location of construction, and recurrently over price and wages. Except for the last, these controls supplement rather than constitute the mainstay of the state guidance system. The reluctance to employ them is reflected in the failure of most countries to use rationing during the oil crisis.

For the greater part of the period, fiscal policy instruments served as the major regulatory device. Nations used expenditures, budget deficits and surpluses, and the tax system to overcome slackness and cool overheated economies, assure growth and full employment, develop physical and technical resources, alter the economic structure, and attain social expectations. Public expenditures for 21 OECD countries grew from 1955 through 1969 at a rate of 23 percent faster than the GNP; and at the end of the period they closely clustered around 31 to 37 percent of the GNP. Tax systems relied increasingly upon higher social security contributions and personal income taxes rather than direct corporation taxes as the total volume of revenue expanded from 25.8 percent of the growing GNP in 1955-57 to 30.5 percent in 1967-69.

The 1944 Bretton Woods monetary system with fixed exchange rates for national currencies served well while the United States underwrote the arrangements through grants and expenditures and later when European countries held dollar surpluses and did not convert them. But finally to gain greater freedom from the U.S. dollar and gold the countries agreed in 1971 on a new currency reserve in the form of special drawing rights managed by the International Monetary Fund (IMF). But the dollar surpluses mounted abroad and the dollar became more overvalued and less firm. The United States finally in August 1971 suspended its convertibility. Subsequently, two major devaluations of the dollar occurred; other countries thereafter realigned the exchange relations of their currencies to the dollar. Finally, in 1973, the major currencies entered upon a general float, except for five Common Market and two Scandinavian countries, which continued to operate on a fixed exchange rate with the German mark and a common float against the other currencies.

The old Bretton Woods system is now gone. Negotiations are proceeding with difficulty among the leading advanced countries to devise a new international monetary system. It calls for a new system of reserves and rules for managed flexible exchange rate changes as well as the float. The discussions became ever more complicated with the growth of the enormous deficits in the national balance of payments due to the huge increases in fuel costs. Leaders of oil-consuming nations are increasingly cooperating to induce producer countries to reduce prices, make grants to needy developing countries, engage in domestic expansion entailing vast expenditures in industrial countries, offer low-interest loans, presumably through the IMF, and recycle through long-term investments their huge earnings, estimated to produce a reserve of $65 billion by the end of 1974 and $200 billion by the end of 1976. The oil-consuming countries need time to realign their economies to the higher energy costs, a problem of unprecedented proportions, given the large cost rises and the drain on foreign exchange, a huge tribute from the national economy to foreign powers.

To function satisfactorily, a technically adequate monetary system calls for internal economic stability and international equilibrium. But the present highly disturbed economic state hardly meets these tests. The nations are therefore increasingly turning to a combination of additional measures along with monetary policy to bring about the desired stability and economic growth.

In this new era, countries made even greater use of other instruments. Structural policies sought to improve the nation's competitive positions and spread prosperity more evenly. Agrarian land reform helped in several countries to consolidate holdings into viable farms and improve productivity on the one hand and hasten the exodus of surplus and ineffective labor on the other. To several sick and moribund industries, reconstruction plans brought public funds for modernization, production and market research, improved management, and the orderly liquidation of excess capacity. Many European nations supported internal mergers to create national viable units for international competition. No comparable effort existed to contain monopolistic price setting. Several countries established investment funds to encourage promising industries, to offset likely job losses resulting from the contraction of older industries.

Public funds and special incentives sought to induce industry to locate in depressed and underdeveloped areas. Regional planning and development received attention and substantial funds both to encourage decentralization as the diseconomies of the large megalopolis became obvious and to achieve more geographically balanced economic development.

Manpower issues and techniques graduated from the status of relief measures for individuals or aids to management to procedures for advancing socioeconomic goals. But they failed to gain the prominence urged by the OECD's program for national integrated active manpower policies, though the number of discrete plans and the funds for them increased. Training, counseling, and aids for mobility and relocation multiplied. People needed preparation for the newer jobs and encouragement to relocate in areas in need of manpower. Housing programs in a few countries increasingly were coordinated to meet the needs of people responding to these manpower calls.

Much hope was placed on the planning mechanisms introduced in France, the Netherlands, and Norway immediately after the war. But they were not to be the magic keys to continuing prosperity. In France, "indicative planning" initially promoted essential investments in selected industries and stimulated modernization. But in most countries the government took over the decision-making authority and relegated the agencies to analytical functions. Planning bodies improved their techniques and insights and became more important to both governments and private economic interests in helping them reach their decisions.

## International and Regional Economic Policy Agencies

In Europe the Economic Community represents a significant potential influence for the coordination of economic and social efforts toward national and regional objectives. But as previously noted, the plans for an economic and monetary, political, and social union and regional and industrial policy remain essentially position papers, awaiting implementation. The EEC is also considering new problems such as the regulation of the multinational corporation. The OECD is a less significant vehicle, but it has been useful for evolving new approaches and programs for action disclosing new trends in thinking, and exchanging ideas among nations. Moreover, it enjoys the additional advantage of including all nations in the "Western" world, permitting the EEC countries regularly to discuss policies with other countries.

Governments became in the postwar period the major agents for dealing with economic problems and promoting the nations' varied objectives. These goals increased with popular expectations. Old instruments have been progressively adapted to the new era and new ones introduced. European and Western agencies provided additional channels through which the governments would work toward meeting their responsibilities. But as old problems appeared in new forms and obstacles grew more formidable, new techniques, approaches, and principles of economics and increased collective and international action became imperative and, of course, had to be devised. Private initiatives have been encouraged. Although they remain central to ultimate effectiveness, they are being relied upon less and less for economic development. Mixed public-private or entirely public enterprises and programs are springing up, reflecting the new emphasis on the government's readiness for positive action. While the United States participated in and promoted international action, it has been more reluctant domestically to employ direct interventionist economic instruments, and when it adopted them their administration has tended to be deficient, and support for them has declined with time.

## Economic Growth and Stability Threatened

### Economic Growth and Its
### Structural Consequences

The high rate of economic growth and stability of the postwar decade inspired the expansion in objectives and the broadening of the economic instruments employed by governments. Western European countries met the growth targets of 50 percent per decade set by themselves in the OECD. And after the slack year of 1971, they exceeded this achievement in the subsequent two years, coming in 1973 up to 5.5 percent, the highest annual level attained in 17 years.

Many reasons are assigned for this unprecedented record, such as the stimulation of reconstruction, Marshall Plan aid, unmet demands, and military needs. The high rate is also ascribed to the abundant labor force, formed in no small part in the 1950s of refugees and expellees and then, in the 1960s, by migrants. The net addition to the labor force exceeded 20 million. But one must not understate the positive role played by government in stimulating and supporting expansion, moderating instabilities, and helping to overcome obstacles. Growth problems centered about bottlenecks in capacity and insufficiencies in resources, including manpower, that governments helped overcome. International agreements for freer trade and currency convertibility provided a real stimulus. The U.S. growth rate lagged behind the European level in the 1950s and did not fully equal it in the 1960s.

Certainly, rising productivity of both capital and manpower contributed substantially to the gain in gross national product. New investments made industry more capital-intensive; improved education and training prepared more effective producers and managers. Statistical measures indicate a rise in labor productivity in Western industrial Europe from its annual rate in the 1950s of 3.6 percent to 4.2 percent in the 1960s, with the rate of increase in investment output below these levels; U.S. gains were slightly more than one-half of the above rates. Similar ratios continued in the first three years of the 1970s.

Despite the above developments of the mid-1960s, Europeans perceived an across-the-board "technological gap" in favor of the United States, but after sober study, the claim proved questionable. In the early 1970s, the concern was reversed; Americans protested the ascendancy of foreign competitors. Here again the broad claims didn't hold up and had to be examined on a case-by-case basis, both in the light of short- and long-term tests of the whole enterprise and its components.

With expansion and differences in rates of increase in productivity came major realignments in the sectoral mix in most countries. Agricultural productivity mounted at an even higher rate than industry. It produced an increase in output and an extensive exodus of manpower. Agricultural employment declined between 1958 and 1971 by 29 percent, bringing the proportion of agricultural employment in major countries (Belgium, the Netherlands, and United Kingdom) to the total work force below 5 percent, thereby approximating the U.S. proportion of 4 percent. Manufacturing employment rose slowly in industrial Europe and strongly in Southern Europe but declined as a proportion of the total employed force in the United States.

The most striking development was the replication of the U.S. phenomenon of an increasing service sector in European countries with more than one-half of their work force in the sector. Belgium, Canada, Denmark, the Netherlands, Sweden, and the United Kingdom were in this category in 1971, and others were moving in this direction. The expansion of this sector was partly attributable to the growth in government employment.

Many older and newer industries grew. In the manufacturing sector they included those that served consumer durable needs and were research intensive. Chemicals, electrical machinery, electronics, motor vehicles, and plastics were among those that showed the most striking expansion in employment. But a number of established industries lost out such as textiles, light industries, food processing, and mining. Even where the industry as a whole held firm, some subsectors and geographical clusters experienced reverses. Smaller enterprises fared poorly in all countries. The shipbuilding industry--except for those companies that modernized and which thus shared in the boom demand for tankers and container ships--was in grave difficulties for long periods.

Merger movements further altered the face of the economy. Medium and large enterprises both in Europe and the United States combined into national giants both for financial and entrepreneurial reasons--that is, to compete more effectively on the international market. In the United States and Europe the conglomerate became a dominant factor in the economy. A survey on behalf of the EEC for the period from 1961 through the first half of 1969 reported 15,307 instances of business expansion in 15 subsectors of manufacturing. Forty-five percent represented enterprises of one Common Market country extending operations into another; 25 percent, penetrations into third (non-EEC) countries; and the remainder, third-country corporations entering the Common Market area. Foreign-based companies moved into Europe at an accelerated pace. Fifteen percent of recent investment, it is estimated, was of foreign origin and about one-half of this volume was by U.S. corporations. Foreign corporations came to represent 9 percent of the British manufacturing sales, 10 percent of the French, 14 percent of the Italian, 15 percent of the Dutch, 18 percent of the German, and 33 percent of the Belgian. They employed 4 percent of those employed by the manufacturing sector in France, 7 percent in the United Kingdom, and 18 percent in Belgium. Moreover, these multinational corporations dominate many industries, usually the most expansive ones, such as automobiles, petroleum, computers and business equipment, electrical machinery, steel, chemicals, food processing, and rubber tires. With their new riches, Arab interests are making substantial investments both in U.S. and European companies. Recently, direct corporate foreign investments in the United States also increased substantially, reaching an estimated book value of $38 billion, according to one estimate.

The expansion of non-Common Market corporations in Europe prompted the EEC to seek to facilitate the organization of multinational European corporations. For these would thereby be better able to compete with the outsiders. Moreover, the EEC could then undertake overall control of all multinational corporations and align their practices with the objectives of the entire Community. But each effort in this direction, particularly the preparation of a Community company law, has met with many difficulties.

The changing industrial profile had its effects on the economic destiny of individual regions and communities, forcing millions to consider transferring to new areas of employment. People moved from rural to urban areas, from the central cities to the greater metropolitan districts. The location of steel mills, petroleum refineries, petrochemical plants near the seacoasts attracted workers to these areas. Major centers developed in Southeast England, Northeast Belgium, the Northwest Netherlands, Northeast Denmark, the southern ends of Norway and Sweden, the Rhine Valley of Germany, the Parisian suburbs in France, the northern section of Italy, and the Vienna area in Austria. The result was overcrowding in established areas, producing deficiencies in the infrastructure and resulting in social discontent and protests. Governments began to doubt the wisdom and perceived the diseconomies of such geographical concentration of growth.

The Netherlands, Norway, and the United Kingdom were the first to encourage decentralization and new growth centers. Other countries followed suit. Decentralization and regional development became political issues. Substantial investments followed in the wake of these programs, with considerable likelihood that the trend toward centralization would in time be counteracted.

The customs unions established by the EEC and the EFTA as well as international agreements lowering tariff rates primarily for manufactured goods significantly stimulated the volume of international trade. And these developments also changed trade patterns. As markets broadened, greater specialization occurred among the advanced industrial countries. The multinational corporations reinforced this development by rationalizing their production on a continental basis, necessitating more exchanges among their plants. As a result Europe became the largest single trade grouping, doing about 50 percent of the noncommunist world trade, with almost two-thirds of it among member countries. Thirty percent of U.S. trade was with OECD Europe.

European interdependence grew not only in manufacturing but also in agriculture. The EEC's agricultural policy set up tariff walls against imports and protected national agricultural interests. Until 1974 the European countries were able to offset the trade deficits incurred from the purchase of minerals, petroleum, agricultural products, and some manufactured goods through invisible earnings and foreign investments. As indicated, a substantial part of these investments came from the United States.

The dollar glut that replaced the postwar shortage created the basis for the Eurodollar market. These expatriate dollars, German marks, Swiss francs, and other currencies used by banks to support loans to governments and corporations rose to an estimated volume of $185 billion, creating a huge resource with which to finance world trade.

The extraordinary price increases since 1972 and particularly the phenomenal jumps in oil costs rudely shook the foundations of this system. Most Western European countries through their primary reliance upon intra-European trade had become vulnerable to a drain on their monetary resources, for they were dependent on imported petroleum and had to meet this deficit through trade abroad. Only Germany, with its large export trade with other areas, and Norway, with its own oil supply, were relatively secure from this serious threat to its stability. These new high costs called for the reconstitution of the pattern and the composition of trade for most European

countries, a truly formidable task demanding economic and political
statesmanship of the highest order.

## Moderating Business Instability

However impressive the postwar growth record, it was equaled
by the success of the European countries in moderating cyclical instabilities. An OECD study of semiannual deviations between the actual and potential GNP from 1955 to 1972 showed that, for 13 European countries, 53 percent of them were less than 1 percent and over
64 percent for France, Norway, and Switzerland were below this
level. The percentage of deviations below 1 percent for the United
States was only 28 percent and more than 40 percent of U.S. deviations were 5 percent or more. In postwar Europe the GNP of any
one year rarely fell below that of the previous one. Unlike the experience in the "interwar period," these European economies appeared relatively independent of, and their conjunctural movements
helped stabilize, the U.S. economy. Moreover, European unemployment levels fell well below 2 percent. It was only in the 1970s
that higher rates appeared, exceeding the 3.5 percent level in some
countries for the first time in the postwar period. In the United
States, the 1972 rate reached 5.6 percent with a low of 4.6 percent
(seasonally adjusted) in October 1973, from which it subsequently
rose toward the 10 percent level.

Europe's major economic setback in the 1950s occurred in
1958. But it was short and moderate and was overcome in many
countries by a series of countercyclical policies that quickly restored
high employment. The Netherlands and the United Kingdom were the
first to restore the balance in their international payments, and
France improved price relations and its balance of payments before
these countries promoted growth and full employment. The United
States after considerable delay employed fiscal measures, particularly tax reductions, to reverse the setback, only to suffer another
reversal in 1960.

The above cycle lasted until 1966-67, when the next decline
came, which was also short-lived. For most countries other than
Germany, the rate of growth was only modestly reduced. Fiscal
measures, easy money and credit conditions, expanding exports,
higher fixed investments, spending, and inventory accumulation
brought the countries out of the trough to a new peak in 1969. A
third cycle began in 1971, but a strong boom soon took over, stimulated by expansive government policies in several countries and the
pervasiveness of the growth movements among the countries and rising prices. It was only in 1974, when the impact of the high prices,
particularly of oil, was felt, that a fourth cycle began.

Scarcities, Inflation, and Unemployment
at End of Era

Supplies of Commodities

The confluence of long- and short-term factors produced the
commodity crunch of 1972 and impelled the double-digit rate of inflation of the subsequent years. Prosperity whetted the appetites of
expanding populations with converging patterns of living and economic
structures, stimulating demands for similar commodities. The
shortages were further exacerbated by the concurrent cyclical upswing in most countries after the 1971 slackness. As for the food
area, natural phenomena including droughts and crop failures and
cutbacks in U.S. wheat acreage to force price increases reduced
the world food supply and led to an upward swing in world prices.
The devaluation of the U.S. dollar moreover broadened the buying
of U.S. products. The total demand was so strong that it cleared
existing stockpiles, and the world became dependent on current
crops. Starvation continued in areas like the Saheil, where adverse
climatic conditions prevailed, and malnutrition remained a major
global problem. In addition, nations producing several basic materials, particularly oil and bauxite, for political and economic reasons jumped prices to unprecedentedly high levels, exploiting their
monopolistic position over materials essential for running the industrial system.

The doomsday forecast of a "sudden and uncontrollable decline
in both population and the industrial capacity" in the next century
suddenly seemed at hand though in a different and somewhat more
modest form. A serious crisis was now upon us. Those who had
scoffed at such projections now feared that the time would be too
short to develop the abundant and possibly cheaper alternatives on
which their confidence had been based. The world had to accelerate
the search for new sources of energy and increase the production of
food and other materials.

All countries including the United States felt the impact of
these shortages and high prices, as all had come to rely on imported
raw materials. Not only did the countries that produced fuels and
minerals now seek higher prices, but they increasingly insisted that,
as a condition for obtaining the commodities, processing plants
would have to be built at home and political control would have to be
retained over the rate of production and use of materials. A completely new economic world suddenly appeared. Political and military power could not be used directly to resolve the issues. A new
balance of forces loomed, with control over resources a major bargaining weapon. With the deepening of the depression this control

became less effective in the world market. Diplomacy had to take over to secure a balance, to maintain a stable world economy.

The U.S.-sponsored 1974 conference of oil-consuming countries and its later committees worked on plans for coordinated national and international action in this field. An International Energy Agency was established to channel programs for joint action. At the April 1974 UN special session dealing with natural resources, U.S. Secretary of State Henry Kissinger called for broad programs that covered economic aid and development, assistance, the expansion of the food supply, food banks, and the creation of a growth-oriented "trade monetary and investment system." Support for an "overall and global" approach also came from the secretaries general of the OECD and the United Nations and the German finance minister, who would soon become chancellor.

Regional and international groups are now working on new projects: alternative materials, diversified sources of energy, revitalization of the coal industry, consumer and producer self-discipline in the use of fuels and energy, conservation, higher-priced and relatively inaccessible sources, and higher food production. Exigent need is likely to promote continued efforts on such projects. Underlying them is a recognition that reliance primarily on the price mechanism will produce unacceptable inequities and feed unrest. Direct national, regional, and world efforts and programs are essential to meet the emergencies. The cooperation and the acquiescence of trade unions and their following as well as consumer spokesmen must be maintained in order to achieve positive solutions and hopefully to surmount scarcities. At international levels, politically important needy countries unable to meet local expectations and international obligations are being included in programs to answer their human needs and also promote global stability.

Inflation and country deficits in international accounts now claim the foremost attention of the governments. Fears are expressed of being overtaken by "slumpflation," a phrase offered by the London Economist to describe a possible new phenomenon that could bring with it economic, political, and social disasters.

## Rising Prices

Western countries experienced three major spurts in prices in the late 1940s and 1950s: one following the ending of the war, the second during the Korean War, and the third in 1956-58. In the post-Korean period until the 1958 slack, Europe's consumer prices increased annually by 2.25 to 4 percent, and in the United States, the rate was about 1.2 percent. Similar overall increases were reported in the 1960s, with the major upswing occurring in construction and

service industries, offset by drops in the prices of foods and some
manufactured goods. Governmental restraints moderated inflationary pressures, but European nations, unlike the United States, succeeded in maintaining high rates of growth, high employment, and
rising living standards. In the United States, price stability as a
goal held the top priority over high employment, but efforts at containing prices were no more successful than on the Continent.

The current price upswing had its milder antecedent in 1967-71,
generated in substantial part by military expenditures. U.S. funds
and investments also moved abroad, spreading inflationary pressures.
In 1969-70 and in the first half of 1972, the European rate of price increases soared to the 5 to 6 percent levels. Consumer prices rose
in 1970-71 despite the slackness in demand, a phenomenon dubbed
"stagflation."

The explosive upward price movement began in the second half
of 1972 with the escalation in the prices of internationally traded
commodities. Food shortages and speculative inventory buying
spurred prices to new heights. Oligopolistic price administrators
were not far behind. Continued relatively high levels of unemployment in some countries did not restrain prices in them. In the second half of 1972, European consumer prices rose to a rate of 8 percent and remained at that level until the oil price increases shot them
up even higher. U.S. price increases lagged behind, at the 3.3 percent rate in 1972. In the last three quarters of 1973, they attained
the 9 percent level. The new oil prices brought increases in Europe
to the double-digit level with the rise in the first three-quarters of
1974 being 14.7 percent. Consumer prices in the United States rose
by 12.6 percent. This high level of increases continued through all
of 1974, in part because of the new cycle of wage increases justified
by past increases in consumer prices.

These high prices are threatening the stability of Western
countries. When combined with the drain on foreign exchange to pay
for oil and other essential imports, they present formidable problems to most developing and many developed countries, such as
Italy. Such nations cannot easily meet these problems on their own.
They need assistance to secure domestic approval for the long-term
structural readjustments required by their economies to live in a
world of high-priced essential raw material and fuels. Some relaxation of the strains caused by shortages and high raw material prices
came with the reduction in worldwide industrial activity.

With the security of the entire system at stake, plans have to
be devised for temporary relief and long-term changes, acceptable
to the recipient countries and particularly their social activists,
which include the trade unions. Multipartite negotiated plans on an
international level in which the trade unions participate are more

than ever called for to secure smooth, acceptable, and equitable adjustments. In December 1974 Chancellor Helmut Schmidt called for a European Community summit conference of trade unions to help deal with the new crisis. Several funds were established to finance the deficits, on the assumption that the earnings of the producer countries would be unevenly distributed among the consumer countries.

## RISING LEVELS OF LIVING, NEW ASPIRATIONS, AND MILITANCY

### Humanism and Activism Permeate Society

Prosperity inspired widespread optimism in the postwar societies. The postwar generation converted popular aspirations into actual demands. Under the influence of high employment, manpower treated as a commodity to be bargained over in the open market became scarce, permitting employees to seek recognition of their expectations.

Humanistic thinking, in sum, gained prominence. The Humanist Manifesto pronounced that "the end of man's life is the realization of the human personality in this world." According to Erich Fromm, humanistic goals in their social orientation were the "full development of man's potentialities, his reason, his love, his creativity." Man was to achieve a "humanly rich life," which in part involved greater individual participation in decision-making, be it economic, political, or social.

Such sentiments took hold of those entering into the adult society in the third postwar decade. Their expectations became the motive force for an aggressive search for further institutional changes and their activities catalyzed the new demands among employees and other social groups awakened to the legitimacy of their own aspirations.

Among those solicited by the radical activists were students, workers, trade unionists, and the political left. These European outbreaks accelerated the tempo of social unrest, forcing the traditional political left and trade unionists to take more aggressive positions and respond to these new expectations. In no small part because of their activities, the humanistic emphasis on rights and the need for self-government, employee, user, client, and citizen participation underlay the demands in a variety of social fields. In the United States, radical activists also sought to reach workers and trade unionists, but being rebuffed they withdrew. They could find few bridges to the American trade union movement.

Channels of Response

Established social groups became alarmed by this new wave of
militancy and turbulence. They responded with reforms. In the industrial relations field, employers reacted spontaneously to the
tightness in the labor market and the threat of disturbances. They
endeavored to maintain production, reduce turnover and absenteeism,
and minimize other evidences of discontent by granting increases in
wages and fringe benefits and generally improving working conditions.
Ultimately, trade unions throughout the Western world took up the
new demands and converted many into practical collective bargaining
issues. Later chapters of this book discuss these developments.

Governments accelerated improvements in existing social and
industrial controls and standards and introduced new ones. They
created two new institutional channels for reform. First, there is
the Council of Europe's Social Charter of 1961, which went into operation in February 1965 and which announced 19 social principles
with 72 provisions. Ten countries--Austria, Cyprus, Denmark,
France, Germany, Ireland, Italy, Norway, Sweden, and the United
Kingdom--subscribed to the charter. Each signator had to accept
10 principles, five of which must be chosen from the seven basic
ones, which are as follows: (1) full employment; (2) the right to organize and (3) bargain collectively; (4) social security; (5) social
and medical assistance; (6) protection for the family and (7) for migrant workers and their families. Countries usually accepted all
articles but held back obligations on individual subsections. At the
end of the second biannual review a Committee of Experts found that
"more than sixty of the seventy-two provisions of the Charter had
been complied with by a majority of the Contracting Parties which
accepted them."

A second reform was made by the European Economic Community when it adopted in January 1974 the Program for Social Action for its constituent nine members, looking forward to the creation of a European Social Union. This program seeks positive social goals rather than merely correctives for the "social ill effects
of economic progress." Previously, the EEC had improved its Social Fund. It assisted in the retraining and resettlement of persons
affected by the integration of enterprises, by Community policies,
or by structural unemployment. It also helped integrate handicapped
or elderly workers, women, and youth into the labor market as well
as redevelop coal and steel communities and construct housing for
iron and steel workers. But the new program is more ambitious
and is directed at far-reaching industrial reforms, including establishment of the standard 40-hour week by 1975 and a four-week annual paid vacation by 1976 and improvements of working conditions.

The EEC commission also stressed the importance of "including a strong social content in the design of [EEC] policies to improve the quality and standards of living of our people [and] also pay special attention to the needs of the most vulnerable sections of the population." But the difficulties in implementing the program are many, including lack of wholehearted support from the member countries in the Council of Ministers.

Improved Employee Earnings, Benefits,
and Working Conditions

Employees and workers benefited from the new society. Even during the recent extraordinary inflation, earnings of vast groups of workers are after some lag partially protected from rising costs by escalator provisions in collective agreements or by laws or by regular periodic revisions.

Employee real hourly earnings in EEC countries almost doubled from 1958 to 1972. Italy experienced the highest rate of increase and the United Kingdom the lowest. U.S. real hourly earnings in private nonagricultural employment rose only 29 percent. Similar trends obtained for real per capita annual earnings. Overall national earnings showed higher increases as people shifted from low to higher-paying jobs and from agriculture and self-employment in trade and handicraft. Family incomes rose faster as unemployment declined and as women in increasing numbers joined the labor force. Multi-earner families became more common.

These gains hardly reflect the overall improvement in the employee's position as fringe benefits increased both absolutely and relatively to the total hourly labor cost. In 1969 in the EEC direct wages represented 62 percent and social insurance costs, including those prescribed by collective agreements or by law and granted voluntarily amounted to 20 percent. The remainder of the wage bill included other social benefits, payment for nonworking times, and special premiums and gratuities. Similar trends obtained in the United States.

The rate of improvements in hourly benefits and earnings in EEC countries was highest in the years 1958-72 for Dutch workers (383 percent), followed by the German (337 percent) and Italian (312 percent); the lowest were for the French (214 percent) and the Luxembourger (181 percent). In absolute terms the German worker in 1972 was on top ($3.41) followed by the Benelux worker with 92.5 percent of the former, the Italian with 78, and the French with 70 percent. The Swedish Employers' Confederation ranking of countries showed the highest in average hourly labor costs for men and

women for 1972 (in Swedish ore) was United States (2,280), followed
by Canada (2,030), Sweden (1,950), West Germany (1,640), Norway
(1,630), Denmark (1,580), Netherlands (1971: 1,330), Belgium
(1,490), France (1,400), Switzerland (1,320), Italy (1,260), Great
Britain (1,070), Austria (1,060), and Finland (1,010). These differences may be smaller in 1973.

Major efforts were made in most countries, particularly Swede:
to narrow occupational differentials. Rates were increased by minimum wage laws and collective bargaining agreements. Trade unions
obtained special wage additions for lower-paid workers or flat rather
than percentage general increases. But the skilled and advantageously
placed employees usually secured rewards between contract revisions
through the "wage drift"--that is, gains above the general one from
liberal piece rates or other concessions. Employers used these increases as lures for recruiting or retaining workers. Even the most
determined unions and governments (for example, Sweden) could not
effectively implement this "solidary" policy. While countries accepted the principle of equal pay for men and women and trade unions
urged their governments to enforce laws and international commitments and women occasionally struck to enforce these benefits, progress was slow, reflecting both market and job factors as well as the
effects of long-standing discriminatory patterns. As the depression
deepened, their proportion of the unemployed expanded, rising beyond the 40 percent mark.

The European and North American countries made advances
toward closing the differences in benefits and status of hourly paid
and salaried employees. Wage differences sometimes narrowed and
at other.times widened, depending on labor market factors and bargaining power. But status differences fell away quickly. Wage-
earners in substantial segments of many European countries by
agreement became monthly pay recipients. Distinctions lessened on
matters of notice of lay-off, annual vacations, hours of work,
amounts of overtime payment, and other items.

The work week progressively declined over the postwar period.
The five-day week became very common in the 1960s, after a period
in which the 5.5-day week prevailed. Reductions to the 40-hour week
were made more rapidly, so that in 1975 few industries will have
longer hours of work in the advanced countries, and this level will
prevail as well in some less developed countries. Employers, however, continued to offer wage-earners considerable overtime so that
the actual average hours of work in industry in the six EEC countries
in 1972 was 43.3. It was 45 hours in France, but recent agreements
there brought French labor to the 40-hour week, which was the U.S.
norm since the 1930s.

The length of the work year was further curtailed by longer
vacations with pay and larger numbers of paid holidays. The four-

week vacation is becoming the norm for all employees in Europe, and the four and five weeks are becoming pervasive for very long-service employees in the United States. The number of holidays in Europe usually total 14 to 24 days, whereas it is approaching 9 or 10 in the United States. A distinctive recent trend in Europe is to provide supplementary holiday pay for employees, such as a "13th-month bonus."

Another important benefit, which has few parallels in the United States, is the provision for paid training leaves, including instruction periods for trade union shop officials in collective bargaining and union subjects. Restrictions on mass dismissals, guarantees of employment for older employees, benefits for retraining and relocation of employees affected by dismissal, severance pay, liberal unemployment benefits, and advanced pension benefits are all provided in recently negotiated contracts or by new laws. An equally distinctive European development is the introduction of capital formation schemes and laws to promote individual savings.

Working conditions are getting new attention. Europe's employers and unions are seeking ways to overcome the enervating effects of the assembly line. Unions and shop committees are getting more responsibility and the right to intercede on issues of job safety and health hazards to a degree unknown in the United States. They are also devoting themselves to the study of job redesign to see how old and new jobs may be made more responsive to new expectations now common among workers.

## Welfare Society Superseded the Welfare State

With the end of the war, nations ushered in the new welfare state, in the words of Sir William Beveridge, to overcome the four giant threats to social well-being: "Disease, Ignorance, Squalor, and Idleness." Discrete social insurance as well as relief and reform programs were to be replaced by benefits providing security "from the cradle to the grave." Education through the secondary level was to be made available to the entire population. Community housing programs would provide decent shelter for all. The state would guarantee full employment.

Changes over the next three decades elevated the system from one directed primarily to low-income groups to one embracing the entire community. New goals provided not only aid but also contributed to human development and if necessary to rehabilitation toward the end of creating a reliant, independent, and fully realized people. The welfare state thereby graduated into a welfare society. The coverage of social security systems now reached beyond wage-earners to salaried employees, professionals, and the self-employed.

Farmers eventually joined. Nonproducers like students and house-
wives became participants. The covered risks became more elaborate. Coverage included partial unemployment, risks common to
nonworking women, assistance in emergencies, and for household
needs and homebound dependents. Periodic or systematic adjustments of benefits in most countries compensated for rising costs of
living and in some permitted beneficiaries to share in the increase
in national wealth and to enjoy standards relatively higher than had
originally been contemplated.

Further accenting the concepts of the welfare society, super-
annuation benefits now complement basic pensions, allowing higher-
income groups to maintain earnings-related benefits. Individuals in
more countries may choose retirement earlier or later than the
standard age and the latter are rewarded by added benefits. In addition to education and health, public services in other areas multiplied, offering most groups, particularly those with special problems, diverse forms of consultative, informational, diagnostic,
counseling, rehabilitative and restorative, job training and placement, and relocation aids. Reimbursement systems for medical
care exist in other countries. To help such public services adapt to
the needs of people in individual communities, local governments
are in some countries given funds that would stimulate the extension,
coordination, and integration of agencies and services. The U.S.
revenue-sharing system in theory could perform this function but in
fact does not.

National governments also promote higher participation on the
labor market for all adult segments of the population. Where the
private economy falters, the state provides modest facilities at
sheltered workshops or a limited volume of public employment.
Child-care centers, nurseries, and special home aids in limited
numbers encourage women to seek employment and ease their burdens. Most significantly, public agencies may undertake to "reach
out" to those not in the labor force and interest them in active employment. Services are offered to some for their rehabilitation and
training as well as funds for their (and their dependents') maintenance, thereby encouraging them to join the mainstream.

Most characteristic of the welfare society is the renewed interest in the elimination of poverty and discrimination and a new
dedication to "equal opportunity for all." Countries learned that
social unrest born of discrimination or other disadvantages could be
as serious a cause for social turmoil as industrial and nationalistic
discontent. Political citizenship had to be complemented by social
citizenship for overall satisfaction and the realization of national social policy. But the programs for achieving these goals were modest.

It became common to announce voluntary or official bans on
discrimination by reason of age, citizenship, color, ethnicity,

national origin, and sex. National and international agencies now devote themselves to making a reality of this goal in such diverse fields as education, employment, housing, and social services. Where persuasion, incentives, and pilot operations prove inadequate, state power is used in some countries against recalcitrants and chronic violators of codes and laws.

Better to serve the needs of their members, institutions are adopting the principle of "client participation" in decision-making. Ombudsmen were employed to protect users' rights and correct unapproved practices. Organizations of beneficiaries appeared either under the sponsorship of the law or at their own instance to protect their interests.

A similar effort is being made to meet popular expectations in the educational field. Educational opportunities are being universalized. Communities accept the need for a better educated population to fill new jobs or simply to advance the quality of their society. The minimum age of compulsory education is now set at 15 or 16 years. A growing number of people are voluntarily engaged in post-secondary school studies. The quality of education is also being enhanced. The talents of the entire population are to be tapped. Stipends and other financial aids are given and low tuitions are set to facilitate the entry of lower-income persons into college or higher educational institutions. New schools are being built at each level and their faculties expanded.

In response to the protests in the mid-1960s, reforms are being also instituted, particularly in the secondary and postsecondary school systems. Differentiation for selective educational purposes among students at the ages 11 or 12 is giving way to comprehensive secondary schools and a uniform curriculum for all students for more extended periods. Greater flexibility in the organization of programs permits students to shift courses as orientations change. Postsecondary schools are adapting in a limited manner to the needs of a popular-based education. Continuing educational programs for adults seek to satisfy their needs as citizens, persons, and producers, permitting them to acquire the skills and knowledge to adapt to the rapidly changing economic, physical, and social environment and to enjoy the new opportunities for leisure.

Though housing programs in the prewar and early postwar years started out primarily to shelter the needy and eliminate slums, the determination to overcome wartime destruction, obsolescence, deterioration of existing dwellings, and a lag in prewar and wartime construction led to housing programs for much of the population. In fact, middle- and higher-income groups in many countries became the primary beneficiaries. Governments offered capital funds, created a special housing bank with distinctive privileges, and encouraged personal savings for residents so that they could acquire dwellings. Builders and developers, private, semipublic, nonprofit cooperative and union and municipal organizations received cheap or free loans, grants, subsidies on the principal or interest, reduced land costs, or tax relief. From 42 to 50 percent of all new dwellings in the 1960s in the EEC countries were partially or fully subsidized by the government. In Denmark, Germany, and Great Britain about one-third of all housing is under cooperative, public, or trade union auspices while the percentage in France is 15. Communities often with state support established "land banks" to keep land costs low and install social facilities. Governments promoted research to develop new better and cheaper industrialized construction materials and methods. Building codes became more functional. Modernization of existing houses received government support, preventing premature demolition and raising the quality of existing housing. Nations paid particular attention to the needs of special population groups. The United States lagged considerably behind in the social housing field, catering principally to the middle- and upper-income groups. The ratio of nonprofit housing to total new construction is lower in the United States than in Western Europe.

These efforts in Europe encouraged the integration of activities for the physical development of communities to meet individual needs, prevent pollution and the despoliation of the environment, and build sufficient housing. Such government aid and guidance encouraged planned communities that would be more satisfying to their residents. Balanced community development became a goal. Decentralization of residences strengthened the movement for the dispersion of industry.

The dedication to the welfare society is reflected in the impressive rise in public expenditures for social and welfare services and payments and the substantial investments in new structures and facilities. Public expenditures, as indicated, from 1955-57 to 1967-69, rose 23 percent faster than increases in the gross national product. In 1962 the social accounts (social security and other social measures) ranged from 11.9 percent (Italy) to 14.5 percent (Germany) of the GNP for the six EEC countries; in 1972, the range was between 24.1 percent (Belgium) to 28.9 percent (Germany). Studies of direct health services for five European countries show a comparable relative increase, as did a special study of eight countries on education and an analysis of five countries on housing and community amenities.

These policies and programs extended the range and number of beneficiaries. Becoming so general, they practically were universal in their application in many fields. Government health-care systems in 1970 covered well over 90 percent of the total population in the nine EEC countries, a rise of 16 points from 1958 for the original six countries. The U.S. public system now covers primarily the aged and the "medically indigent." Old age pension systems in all countries tend to be all-embracing. Employee injury schemes extend to three-quarters to the entire civilian labor force in Western countries. Three-fourths or more of wage and salary earners are insured against income losses due to unemployment. In the EEC countries, family allowances are granted to two-thirds of the children (0-19 years). The United States still does not have a universal minimum guarantee of benefits for its needy.

Services in education, health, and employment usually cover all or most of the population. School enrollment in the six EEC countries from 1960 to 1971 rose from 50 to 60 percent of those between 5 to 24 years, while university or other enrollments doubled in a decade, reaching 15 percent of those between 19 and 24. In the United States, comparable 1970 figures are 76 percent and 22 percent for the age group 20-24.

The volume of housing measurably increased. From the prevailing level of 220 to 300 dwellings per 1,000 inhabitants in 1960 in the nine EEC countries, it rose 250 to 375 in 1971. Expenditures for residential construction represented 3 to 7.5 percent of the gross national product. Annual completed housing, which was below 5 per 1,000 inhabitants in the 1950s, jumped to 8.1 in 1972. In the latter year, four of the nine EEC countries exceeded the rate of 10 new dwellings per 1,000 inhabitants, the UN's test of an adequate rate of construction. The Netherlands had the highest, recording 11.5 new dwellings per 1,000.

This high construction rate eliminated overall housing shortages in many European countries, particularly the industrial ones. In the nine EEC countries, the average number of persons per room dropped in the decade by between 0.1 and 0.2 of a person per room, bringing the level below 1 in all countries, with the United Kingdom reporting 0.6 persons per room. Furthermore, considerable advances occurred in the proportion of dwellings with bathrooms.

Consumption levels improved as incomes rose and benefits and services expanded. An indirect index of this increasingly adequate life is the declining share of the family budget spent for food. In 1970, it was 33.5 percent of private consumption for the six EEC countries, a drop of 6.7 percentage points (median) in a decade; it was then about half of what it had been before 1914. Food consumption shifted from cereals, potatoes, and other root crops to eggs, fruits, vegetables, meat, and milk. Caloric and protein intakes rose. In the nine EEC countries the ratio of cars jumped from 62 per 1,000 inhabitants in 1958 to 232 in 1972; for televisions, from 47 to 242; for telephones, from 98 to 235. Clothing quality and styles improved, though relatively less was spent for clothes. Installment buying became more common, facilitating the purchase of

many types of durable household goods. A more homogeneous style
of life developed. Many manual workers gave up their distinctive
class appearance, enjoying middle-class ways.

Improved levels of living and the greater availability of thera-
peutic and rehabilitative facilities as well as health knowledge led to
an increased life expectancy and lower infant mortality rates. General mortality rates remained stable, though the causes of death
shifted to degenerative diseases and traffic accidents.

The third decade accelerated the development of the welfare
society through the highly diversified responsibilities assumed by the
state in its efforts to improve the "quality of life" for all groups,
with special attention to the low-income and disadvantaged groups.
The state also sought to assure everyone the "opportunities" for
realizing their maximum potential so that people would not only join
but also remain in the mainstream.

## Inequalities

Enlargement and improvement of the benefits of the welfare
society stand out among the contributions that implemented postwar
commitments. But, as noted, nations became abruptly aware that
large groups had been bypassed. From this awareness came efforts
to combat both in the "war on poverty" and discrimination. Some of
the new benefits accrued disproportionately to the middle- and even
higher-income groups. Expanding opportunities for higher education, for example, meant larger enrollment ratios for those in higher
socioeconomic categories. Only as saturation was achieved at any
one level of schooling did the enrollment rates by income groups con-
verge; thereafter, efforts had to be made to equalize the quality and
kinds of education for different groups. At this point, funds and efforts often dwindled, denying the promised benefits to lower-income
and minority groups and to rural areas. In the United States, minority groups like the blacks and poor demanded desegregation and better
schooling. In Europe, migrants, minorities, and the working class
insisted on equal quality in education. Programs to facilitate the
entry of the children of these groups into schooling vary considerably
as to their size and adequacy. Moreover, the demand is growing for
vocational, professional, and adult educational facilities.

Even greater disparities prevail in housing. The rate of new
housing construction was impressive, but the housing problems of
low-income groups persist. Social housing increased, but now some
high-rental dwellings are vacant, while other low-cost units are occupied by families with above-standard incomes, who prefer to remain.
Tax privileges such as exemptions for homeowners exist primarily

for higher-income groups. Rent controls and housing and rent allowances in some countries also benefit middle-class groups. These conclusions apply even more strongly to the United States. Similar advantages for middle-income groups exist under some welfare payment systems, particularly as benefits become increasingly income-related; social insurance plans tend to offset these advantages with high minimums for the low-income groups and regulations and weighted-income formulas that aid them.

A study by the UN European Economic Commission found that "factors reducing income inequality seem to have been weakened considerably over the last decade or so," subsequent to the reduction noted "between the prewar and immediate postwar years." It adds that "the income gap between the poorest groups and the middle income ranges has, if anything, increased." As for the effects of the tax system, it concludes that "government expenditures rather than the tax system as a whole is mainly responsible in practice for such redistribution as takes place." Such reduction as occurred in income dispersion "appears to be very modest among the bulk of the households deriving their income from employment, self-employment and property. The redistribution that has occurred is largely in favor of nonactive persons (principally pensioners) and has been largely financed by their own payments in the past, either by social insurance contributions or by general taxes."

Similar conclusions are reported in studies of U.S. experience. The Council of Economic Advisors found that income differences between the affluent and poor have not changed from 1947 to 1972. The upper fifth earned 41.4 percent of the nation's aggregate income and the bottom fifth, 5.4 percent; these had altered little over the quarter-century. Income taxes did not significantly redistribute incomes; the higher-income groups enjoy ways of avoiding taxes, where the lower-income groups carry huge shares of the payroll and sales taxes. The distribution of capital ownership has not been equalized on either side of the Atlantic, except in Norway, and some students find some increases in the degree of concentration.

While levels of living have improved, the class society remained. Improvements narrowed the gaps in life-styles between the upper grades of manual workers and lower middle class; mixed-class families multiplied as women from working-class families became salaried employees. Differences between manual and nonmanual employees diminished as the status rewards disappeared and distinctions in benefit formulas were reduced. But lower-income recipients recognize their inferior positions. The barriers to collective class upward mobility remain as yet insuperable.

A similar feeling of disillusionment overtook the population in the latter part of 1974 as the rates of unemployment began to climb to and beyond prior postwar peaks. Doubts began to be expressed whether the older order had in fact been changed. Unemployment benefits were larger, more regular, and continuous; other services continued to be supplied to the unemployed; and in some cases new public jobs were offered. But it was being asked whether the policies and instruments were adequate to deal with the new economic calamities of high prices, oligopolistic controls, raw material and energy shortages, deficits in the balance of payments, and the weakened international banking and financial structures.

### What Are the Priorities?

Social goals have not been fully realized. Inequalities in benefits and class differences persist; conflict about relative positions of groups in the decision-making processes in institutions continue. Frustration is rife, and the upheavals of the 1970s have aggravated it. Intense inflation and high unemployment have created new disparities and a sense of discrimination. Structural changes with its direct impact on employees and business are sharpening tempers. The problems of equitable sharing of the benefits of rising productivity and prosperity have now been coupled with equitable shouldering of the costs of economic stagnancy or negative growth.

Governments now had to mediate the differences among contending interests. With the shift to the left during the last decade, new measures more responsive to the principles of equity are being sought. The trade union movement is pressing this search and offering its own proposals.

Governments face questions of how much more of the national product they can allocate to social goals. What priority should be assigned to each benefit? Should the uneven developments in various areas be balanced as administrators are now doing by integrating and consolidating systems and simplifying programs? Social programs are being closely watched for their effects on other economic and political policy systems. Do these programs support or countervail them? Which shall be accorded priorities and to what degree? Centralization of systems making them more remote from people is increasingly offset by decentralization in administration and by close participation of employer associations and trade unions in the executive agencies. Cost reductions are being sought by limiting benefits and shifting burdens, but the returns to date have proved minuscule, short-lived, demoralizing, and politically not viable. Multipurpose projects, replacing single-purpose ones, will hopefully make for greater effectiveness and lower cost. New decision-making methods, such as cost-benefit analysis, production-planning and budgeting procedures, social indicators, and the social budget, are being called into play. They are being tested for the contribution they can make to these responsibilities. These issues will become even more pressing in a period of low rates of economic growth, stagnancy, and high unemployment.

## CONCLUSION: BARGAINING FOR GROUP ACCOMMODATION IN A DEMOCRATIC SOCIETY

Differences of interest persist in a democratic society. The middle class and its offspring gained access to education, which helped in their upward mobility. Individual workers by reason of personal achievement often advanced, but not the group as a whole. The upper classes held their own, absorbing, as they had done before, the new elites that shared their views.

The direct threat to the order could come largely, if not solely, from social-democratic, leftist, and trade union leaders. As long as they came to terms with the existing elite by accepting the early postwar agreements avoiding fundamental challenges to power relationships, the establishment accepted them. Toward the end of the 1960s and in the 1970s, they moved to more aggressive positions, demanding substantial alterations.

While it was popular in the 1950s to write of the "withering of the class structure" and of older political alliances, allegiances to class parties in Europe in fact remained intact. The new middle classes, now including many employees, remained loyal to the concepts of individualistic competition and personal achievement and sought to readapt them to their changed status. They, nevertheless, shared many claims of skilled manual workers and demanded better definitions of the terms and conditions of employment. Many supported socialist parties, considering them more responsive to their interests and views, particularly as the latter became "people's" parties. Job frustrations strengthened this tendency.

The upper classes and new elite groups retreated in some areas, often after considerable and sometimes prolonged resistance to sharing or yielding power. But after each concession, they recovered enough to maintain a high relative position and to resist new encroachments.

The class conflicts over power continued, with the state now also the arena for these conflicts. Each group and class including organized labor seeks the freedom to express itself and to bargain for its views, interests, and priorities on all fronts, economic, political, and social. The continuing accommodation of their respective claims through mutual concessions and compromise is vital to national survival.

In a progressive advancing society such as has been enjoyed in the postwar decades, interested parties bargained and worked out accommodations largely over the distribution of the benefits of rising output. The third decade reflected an impatience with the results by a new generation that sought to implement the standards on which they were raised. Their demands propelled new advances; employees and lower-income groups made considerably faster strikes. Unrest persisted, but it remained moderate and reform demands worked for the most part through constitutional channels. The efforts of those who preached and acted violently petered out. But they left a legacy of humanistic ideas that shaped the demands of many protesting groups, including trade unions. At issue now is what political, economic, industrial, and social policies and arrangements will deal adequately with the new problems of intense structural change, shortages, high unemployment, and inflation and will be acceptable to the major socioeconomic interests, including employers and the organized trade union movement. The individual country chapters unfold the nature, contents, and results of this ongoing contest in nine Western countries.

# 2

## GREAT BRITAIN: TOWARD
## THE SOCIAL CONTRACT
### John F. B. Goodman

The term "crisis" has been applied so freely in reports of industrial and economic affairs in postwar Britain that it has lost much of its impact. Its use requires qualification when applied to recent developments in British industrial relations. The recent controversies about that system and the conflict within it have indeed been significant when viewed against the broad span of its history, but it would be wrong to infer that they will soon be a thing of the past. The goals of the parties of the industrial relations system including individuals, collective organizations of employees and employers, and the government are different, often conflicting and continuously changing. The pressures and movements for alterations of institutions, traditions, and practices and the process of adaptation will tend to keep the area in ferment.

The scale and intensity of conflict manifested through the industrial relations system has varied over time. In recent years it has been high and has spilled over into national politics. But sociopolitical values in Britain are such that even at the height of the crisis in union-government relations there was no threat to the established framework of government, the economic system, nor suggestions of violent social changes. Trade unionists relied on established forms of industrial action and added new techniques, such as plant sit-ins and occupation and mass picketing, and political action, such as demonstrations, lobbying, and pressures on Labour Party leadership, to secure immediate gains and changes in law and judicial attitudes.

In this context, two important preliminary points must preface this account. First, Great Britain has a long history as a politically stable parliamentary democracy. It has avoided invasion and has seldom been near to political revolution for over 300 years. There

is a deep-rooted respect for constitutional processes and the liberal
protection of the rights of minorities. Certainly there are pressure
groups--some of the major ones form the subject matter of this dis-
cussion--but they accept the rules of the political system and seek to
work within it. This orderly, and apparently unchanging, feature of
British society acts as a major constraint on those who wish to introduce or to oppose the introduction of changes in the industrial relations system or in the wider society. It constitutes an important element in the fabric of societal attitudes, which seemingly inevitably
set limits to the power of destabilizing forces or groups.

Second, the stability of the political system and the absence of
large-scale social unrest <u>outside</u> the industrial relations system tends
to focus the public's attention on industrial conflict. Periodically
clashes in other areas, such as the unrest among university students
over student rights in university government in the late 1960s and
occasional evidence of racial tension in some cities, cause temporary
concern and displace "news" from the industrial front. These issues,
however, have been spasmodic, limited, and mild, in comparison
with the violence such matters have generated in some other countries. Any survey of the tensions in postwar British society would
find most of its evidence in the industrial relations system.

Public interest with industrial relations in the 1950s and 1960s
stemmed primarily from a concern about the effects on the economy,
on Britain's competitiveness and on relative living standards in the
longer term. Latterly, with greater government involvement and the
attempts to reshape the industrial relations system and to restrain
collective bargaining, the tendency is for the conflicts within the
system to move into the political arena. Confrontations between the
government and unions are occurring both on the industrial and political levels. Public anxiety therefore derives not only from economic
considerations but also from the disorderliness of the industrial relations scene and the perceived threat to stable political processes
possibly flowing from industrial unrest or union or employee militancy

Contemporary pressures center around economic issues, notably inflation, the freedom of collective bargaining and its future
organization. Dispute over the function, content, and extent of legal
regulation of trade unions and industrial relations is a major issue,
especially at the political level. These questions will cause continuing restlessness. Institutional adjustments to improve bargaining
arrangements at all levels are anticipated, indicating the resiliency
of the unions' traditional adversary approach. Despite the socialistic
language and rhetoric employed, union pressure is not directed toward fundamental changes in the economic, political, or social systems. Suggested new forms of shared decision-making at plant,
company, or national levels evoke caution and suspicion, although
wider scope for bargaining and employee influence is being sought.

## THE POSTWAR ECONOMIC AND SOCIAL CONTEXT

Economic Changes

Full Employment

Many of the postwar socioeconomic changes in Britain have also occurred in other countries. The most significant change in Britain has been the unprecedented period of full employment, with unemployment averaging less than 2 percent in each five-year period between 1945 and 1965. This high level of demand for labor contrasts sharply with an annual average unemployment rate of 13 percent between 1920 and 1940 and reflects the use of economic management techniques by postwar governments.

The implications of this change have been profound. Determination of employment levels is now regarded as falling within the discretion of government, and departures from "full" employment are seen at best as evidence of mismanagement and at worst as calculated callousness or insensitivity. Certainly no government has been able to delay for long reflationary measures aimed at reducing its level. On this issue governments have faced pressure from nearly all sections of the community. Moreover all postwar governments pursued policies aimed at reducing unemployment in particular regions where it is above the national average, largely through financial and other incentives to induce industrial investment in these areas. Thus, the "right to work" has become an established expectation nationally, and active microlevel policies have been applied within the overall national-level commitment to promote full employment.

The effects of this sustained period of high labor demand have been manifold. It has given individual workers expectations of continuity of employment, albeit not necessarily in a particular job or with the same employer. It has shifted the balance of bargaining power toward the unions and created conditions favorable for fractional bargaining within plants and companies. It has, when taken in association with generally buoyant product market conditions, reduced employer resistance to union and work-group claims, and stimulated some employers to pursue more generous employment policies. Equally, until the late 1960s, it encouraged labor hoarding and contributed to the high levels of overtime working, which became an important component of manual worker wage packets and of intra-plant bargaining during the postwar decades. Although unions have negotiated reductions in the nominal work week from 48 to 40 hours at intervals over the period, average actual male manual hours of work have fallen only slowly, averaging, for example, more than 45 in 1972, when a nominal 40-hour week had been common for six years

or more. Overtime became customary and, indeed, a way of life in
many industries. Full employment facilitated industrial labor mobility but threw into sharp relief the problems of workers made redundant through secular changes in the economy.

Redundancies became a major element in industrial unrest in
the late 1960s. Between 1967 and 1970, the volume of unemployment
rose slowly but then accelerated to a postwar peak of over 4 percent
early in 1972. Fears of redundancy increased and protests mounted.
Some workers faced with closures took direct action to protect their
jobs, occupying factories, as in the case of Upper Clyde Shipyards
(UCS) organizing a "work-in" whereby workers declared redundant
continued to work. They were paid out of a fund subscribed by fellow
workers and others throughout the country. Despite statutory redundancy payments (introduced in 1965) and better unemployment benefits, widespread fears of unemployment lent wide support to displaced
workers. Pressure on the government for reflationary measures was
successful; it took measures, which brought unemployment down
rapidly in 1973.

Absolute Improvement in
Living Standards

Associated with the period of full employment has been the improvement in living standards, which although occasionally broken
and of varying rates, has proceeded fairly continuously, creating
expectations that living standards will continue to rise. The living
standards of working people in Britain are higher than ever before.
Ownership of consumer durables is high, and consumption and use of
such former prerogatives of the rich as cars, foreign holidays, and
central heating systems is now broadly based. Britain may have
lost its early postwar leading position and has indeed fallen behind
in the European materialist race, but things are very much better
than they were during the boyhood and early manhood of many of
Britain's workers.

Despite the wide publicity given to Britain's relative decline--
for example, in terms of per capita income, growth rates, and so on--
the reality of this relative decline appears as yet not to have got home
to few ordinary workers. For most of them, the perennial warnings
of economic doom and perpetual talk of crisis have made little impact
on their day-to-day lives. Their union leaders have, on occasion,
cooperated with government attempts to reduce the inflationary spiral
through wage restraint, thus offering a "breathing space to get the
economy right," but successive rounds of this have not been effective.
The threatened consequences of repeated failures in economic management appear to many workers to be perpetually postponed.

## Price Inflation Endemic

The consequence over the postwar period is continuous price inflation. People have become accustomed to rising prices and seek to adjust incomes as best they can but continue to complain. The adjustment process has not been automatic; little use was made, for example, of cost-of-living escalator clauses in collective bargaining. Each group sought sectional compensation and found little advantage in unilateral restraint. They were not deterred by exhortations that higher rates of inflation than those of Britain's trading rivals would adversely affect employment; these warnings were not obvious to the workers and, moreover, were obscured by monetary policies dictated by the commitment to full employment. To the individual or organized group, the risk of loss through unemployment due to high wage increases was less than the risk of loss through lower-than-average money wage settlements. They wanted compensation for past price inflation and advance protection against anticipated prices. The dramatic acceleration of price inflation in the 1968-74 period (when it reached an annual rate of 17 percent) increased the anxiety about falling behind and served as the motor behind many wage disputes. They had lost confidence that governmental wage and price restraints would be effective and in the government's overall economic competence. Moderate union leaders (or groups standing to gain more from incomes policies than from "free" collective bargaining) could not confidently support new moves in this field. Moreover, they were offered no new areas of union influence over economic and social policy to compensate for the inevitable inroads that incomes policies make into the traditional bargaining functions of the unions.

## Increases in Larger Establishments
## and Multiplant Companies

Both the size of employment establishments and the output and employment share of the largest employers have increased rapidly. An increasing proportion of employment in manufacturing is in large establishments, which in turn form part of large multiplant companies or groups, whose operations are often multinational in scope. Foreign-owned companies provide an increasing proportion of total employment.

This trend toward largeness and the consequent remoteness of decision-making has a number of important industrial relations implications. Direct contact between corporate decision-makers and shop-floor employees is now impossible, while union leaders also face difficulties in attaining access to the leaders of huge conglomerate firms. The management and control of industrial enterprise has shifted further away from proprietor-entrepreneurs in favor of professional managers--a factor that lies behind the shift away from benevolent paternalism in employment policies. On the wider front, the increased divorce of ownership from control has begun to raise concern about the accountability of those in positions of power within an increasingly concentrated industrial structure, and there are demands for changes in Britain's 19th-century-based company law.

### Social Changes

Socially, the postwar period also brought fundamental changes. Early postwar legislation setting up a National Health Service and improved provisions for state benefits covering unemployment, sickness, social security, and pensions created the "welfare state." Rising real wage levels were reflected in the boom in consumer durables, the growth of hire purchase, and an escalating demand for home ownership. Educational provision increased rapidly, and there has been a massive increase in higher education and the number of full-time students, particularly in the 1960s.

Associated with this last development, although not necessarily caused by it, is a more skeptical, questioning approach to established norms, institutions, and authority. The value systems of the older generation face a considerable challenge. Significant legislative changes in a liberal direction occurred in such fields as capital punishment, the age of majority and voting, race relations, and sexual questions. The development of mass media, particularly television, exposed the "Establishment" in general and national political leaders in particular more directly to the population as a whole, and their attitudes, styles, and values have been satirized irreverently. Moreover, the rapid communication of political issues and events sharpened the contrast with communication systems in the employment context.

Well-researched evidence, as opposed to intuitive comment or that based on casual observation, of the impact of rising living standards on traditional British working class attitudes and lifestyles is somewhat limited. Some writers suggest that the increased level of home ownership among younger manual workers, often located away from the older working-class districts, led to a loss of cohesion and a reduction in working-class community identification. Secondly, slum clearance programs dispersed working-class communities to large council estates on the outskirts, and these estates developed the community spirit of the old urban areas.

Perhaps the most authoritative study of worker response to affluence, conducted in the early 1960s among groups of relatively high-earning, younger (21-46) married male manual workers in a prosperous town in the Southeast, [1] revealed a predominantly instrumental attitude to work among these "affluent workers," and a private life that was increasingly family-oriented rather than community- or work-centered. Work was a means of gaining resources for the pursuit of extrinsic--largely familial--ends.

This instrumental attitude extended to trade union activity also, with worker involvement being focused not on the branch or wider union organization but on the particular and largely economic issues of their own shop and factory. As affluence became widespread and as manual workers' central life interest moved more toward the cultivation and enjoyment of their private domestic lives, their commitment to trade unionism as a movement or expression of class or occupational solidarity was restricted. However, the emphasis on material rewards from work would intensify their involvement in union activity concerned with matters of wages and conditions of immediate interest. Finally, the authors suggested that while militancy directed, for example, toward worker control would become more difficult to sustain, greater aggressiveness in the field of cash-based bargaining was a very probable development.

## Changes in Labor Force Composition

Certainly many of the above trends continue to operate in the 1970s, and the demand for wider ownership of homes and consumer durables remains high. One consequence of the drive to raise family incomes and living standards is the increased participation of women, particularly married women, who now comprise more than half of the females in the active labor force. After long being shelved, legislation on equal pay was finally passed in 1970 and was immediately followed by pressure for legislation to outlaw discrimination against women, particularly in employment opportunities. Females constituted 38 percent of total employees in 1971.

The occupational and industrial mix of the labor force has also changed. Most dramatic is the increase in white-collar workers, who formed 38 percent of the total working population of 24.6 million in 1966. Their number rose from 6.9 million in 1951 to 9.4 million in 1966. Over the same period, the manual worker proportion of the occupied population fell from 64 percent to 58 percent. Employment in several older industries, notably coal, cotton, railways, and shipbuilding, declined rapidly, and a marked shift in favor of the service sector occurred. Immigration of colored workers was substantial, many moving into low-level unskilled jobs. Despite antidiscrimination legislation, many immigrants (and their children) face difficulties

in securing promotion or upgrading. This has precipitated several
bitter industrial disputes.


### The Shifting Emphasis in Governmental Economic Policy

Economic problems have been the major domestic preoccupation
of postwar governments and can be seen as the precipitating factors
in the crisis in industrial relations in the late 1960s and early 1970s.
Governments sought to achieve and reconcile four broad policy objec-
tives--those of full employment, price stability, sustained economic
growth, and a balance-of-payments surplus. They varied the priorities accorded to these interrelated if mutually contradictory aims,
and the policy measures. Price stability has been the most expend-
able of the objectives, and the balance of payments the most pressing
in most short-run periods. Prior to the late 1960s unemployment
was kept to very low levels (discounting periodic short and mild recessions), but the balance-of-payments constraint frequently led to
the premature curtailment of attempts to raise the growth rate.
    The connection between domestic demand levels, price inflation,
export price competitiveness, and wage bargaining led to fairly continuous exhortation for restraint, and periodically to firmer but essentially nonstatutory restraint measures in the field of pay determination. The frustrations associated with "stop-go" policy phases in
the 1950s produced a shift toward national economic planning of an
indicative type in the early 1960s, but this was abandoned following
the currency crisis and deflationary measures of 1966. The conversion to indicative economic planning in the early 1960s, and the election of a Labour Government in 1964--after 13 years of Conservative
rule--saw the introduction of Britain's longest period of prices and
incomes policy, introduced in 1964 on the basis of a voluntary Trade
Union Congress (TUC) and Confederation of British Industry (CBI)
agreement. Trade union support did not last long. It lapsed after
the imposition of a statutory freeze and nil norms for income increase
in 1966 and 1967.


### Industrial Relations and Trade Union Control
### by Government: A Revolutionary Change

The tendency of wage increases to outdistance productivity
growth over the postwar period was one of two issues that drew government intervention more substantially into the industrial relations
system and led to deeper and deeper limitations being set on the freedom of collective bargaining. The second element was the increase

in strike activity, [2] particularly unofficial and unconstitutional stoppages, which, together with work-group opposition to technological changes and innovations, became increasingly identified as a crucial element in the failure to solve postwar economic problems. Rightwing pressure for antistrike legislation began to build up from the early 1960s. Doubts about the compatibility of Britain's old established voluntary industrial relations system with the achievement of economic policy goals became widespread, and there were demands for legislative changes in this system.

The Labour Government, intent on securing trade union support for its prices and incomes policy, resisted these proposals and passed them over to a Royal Commission (Donovan) for thorough and lengthy inquiry, which effectively preempted action for the three years 1965-68. Thus the industrial relations system, which had formerly been regarded only as at most a peripheral problem area in the 1950s--and was indeed the object of some satisfaction and pride--moved to a position as a primary national preoccupation in the late 1960s and early 1970s. Union opposition led to the withdrawal of Labour government proposals to curb strikes in 1969. The year 1970 saw the election of a Conservative government committed to comprehensive legal regulation of strike activity, union organization, recognition, bargaining rights, the closed shop, and many other aspects of collective bargaining. This program was implemented in the Industrial Relations Act of 1971.

Clearly the late 1960s and early 1970s may be described as a period of crisis for the industrial relations system, a period in which criticism and consequent attempts to reform reached crescendo pitch. The 1971-74 period witnessed the most direct confrontation between the unions and the government since the General Strike of 1926.

## THE TRADITIONAL SYSTEM OF
## INDUSTRIAL RELATIONS

The traditional system is based on voluntary collective bargaining--that is, without legal compulsion on either side--implemented through unenforceable agreements negotiated by a large number of joint multiunion and multiemployer industry-wide negotiating committees. [3]

Following the removal of legal obstacles to trade union organization in the 1870s and the grant of specific legal immunities in 1906, the law relating to trade unions and collective bargaining in peacetime remained substantially unchanged until the Industrial Relations Act of 1971. In the present century, the system has evolved in a

predominantly laissez-faire atmosphere, largely free of legal constraints on the behavior of the parties. Successive governments
supported the principle of voluntary collective bargaining and, since
1917-18 in particular, encouraged its development.

Self-determination through collective bargaining has been the
preferred method of regulating industrial relationships, and in peacetime third parties played only a minor role, their use being regarded
by both unions and employers as inferior to "industrial self-government." Apart from support for collective bargaining, the involvement of the government in peacetime has been minimal, limited essentially to the establishment of "temporary" statutory wage-fixing
bodies for those residual sectors where manual worker trade union
organization was weak and wages were low and the provision of supplementary services for voluntary methods of dispute settlement in
the form of conciliation, arbitration, and ad hoc inquiries.

## Forms of Collective Bargaining: Private Sector

The organization of collective bargaining in Britain is complicated and has evolved through a number of stages. Most early collective agreements were negotiated on a multiemployer basis at local
district level. However, by the early years of this century national
industrywide negotiating committees and agreements existed in a
number of industries. These industrywide negotiating bodies, of
which there are approximately 500, rest on a fairly liberal definition
of "industries." At one end of the scale, the largest such bargaining
unit is the engineering industry, which covers a multiplicity of manufactured metal products ranging from bridges to motor vehicles and
aircraft. At the other are limited industries like cement, paint, and
pottery. Some product groups are subdivided--for instance, bus
transport has three separate negotiating bodies, covering the private
company sector, the public (municipal) sector, and London Transport,
respectively. Parallel but separate negotiating bodies are often
found in Scotland.

The "industrywide" negotiating bodies for the employers in the
industry (as defined) are the employers' associations, and for the
workers a number of trade unions recognized as representing workers in the industry. The proportion of employers in the private sector belonging to the association is high, though it varies among industries. Small employers may not belong but often follow the terms
of the agreements. But it is becoming increasingly common for
large firms to negotiate directly with the unions. British subsidiaries of U.S. companies particularly follow this practice. Recent
estimates (1966) placed the workers covered by company agreements

at 1 million.[4] The unions for this purpose join together to form an
ad hoc negotiating committee constituting the "trade union side" or
in rare cases are linked in a federation, as in engineering and shipbuilding.

The final agreements between the two sides usually establish
the composition and constitution of the negotiating body itself, a procedure for handling disputes and settling grievances in the industry,
and agreements on certain substantive conditions of employment,
such as wage rates, the length of the work week, overtime and shift
working conditions and rates, holiday provisions, and the basis for
wage incentive schemes. The nature of the wage rates varies among
agreements. Traditionally many employers and their associations
regarded the rates as standard rates, representing both the maxi-
mums and minimums for the specified occupations or grade of worker.
Although this continues in a small minority of cases, they are now
more usually regarded as minimums. Provisions covering the work
week, overtime and shift premiums, and holidays, are normally
treated as standard, and few companies belonging to employers'
associations deviate from them.

A residual form of wage-fixing in the private sector is conducted by the Wages Councils, which number just over 50, and cover
approximately 3 million, predominantly female, workers. They are
statutory bodies established by the government to set minimum wage
rates, hours of work, and so on in industries where voluntary collective bargaining cannot be sustained. They are found in such areas
as retail distribution, agriculture, and catering, being composed of
an equal number of employer and trade union representatives, plus
three independent members. The minimum wage rates, hours, and
holidays that they establish are enforced by statutory orders and a
wages inspectorate.


Forms of Collective Bargaining: Nationalized Sector

The nationalized industries, including coal, gas, electricity,
railways, and the airline corporations--and recently steel--are
formally independent of government in questions of day-to-day management and in collective bargaining. They are statutorily required
to consult and negotiate with the unions concerned. Since some of
these industries, notably the railways, have frequently incurred financial deficits, the boards concerned have often been directly influenced in wage bargaining by successive governments. They are
generally less free to depart from stated government policies on
incomes than the major private employers.

Collective bargaining in these industries is conducted through
a series of bargaining units at industry (single-employer) level, with,

typically, separate units for manual, clerical, technical, and administrative and managerial staffs. They also tend to have more highly
developed systems of formalized joint consultation with their employees, especially at the establishment level, than is the case in private
manufacturing, but the bargaining relationship between the unions
and the boards is scarcely distinguishable from that found in private
manufacturing. Perhaps the most distinctive features of collective
bargaining in the nationalized industries are the greater relative importance of the industrywide agreements in determining actual earnings and conditions (which may be largely due to the involvement of a
single employer) and the extension of collective bargaining to include
senior levels of management.

### Forms of Collective Bargaining: Government Employees

The above characteristics also apply to collective bargaining
for the employees of national and local government. Unionization has
long been high in the civil service, constituting about 5 million of the
TUC membership, and collective bargaining is well established through
a series of Whitley Committees up to senior levels. The pervading
principle in wage negotiations is that of comparability with equivalent
work in the private sector, with biennial surveys being conducted by
the Civil Service Pay Research Unit. Its studies normally command
the support of government and civil service unions, although on occasion the government's long-term obligation to be a "good employer"
is sacrificed to short-term exigencies and attempts to deescalate
private-sector settlements by public-sector example. It is extremely
rare for civil servants to take industrial action, but the early 1970s
saw overtime bans, demonstration meetings, and selective strikes
invoked to protest the delay in wage and salary reviews consequent
on Pay Research Unit surveys. Separate committees at the national
level exist for the National Health Service, teachers, social workers,
and so on, and similar national negotiations are conducted for local
authority manual and white-collar workers. Finally, a series of
independent review bodies, with interlocking membership, report
periodically on recommended salary levels and other conditions for
groups of public employees for whom collective bargaining is inappropriate or has not developed, for example, doctors and dentists,
the judiciary, the higher civil service, the Armed Forces, MPs,
and ministers. It is much more usual for agreements in the public
sector--those covering teachers, civil servants, and hospital staffs
--to include provision for ultimate arbitration on disputes, including
wage disputes, although in recent years unions in many parts of the
public sector refused to pursue this course in wage disputes due to

the alleged influence of government pay policies on "independent" arbitrators. Provision for arbitration is exceptional in the procedure agreements covering manual workers outside the public sector (although there are some exceptions--for example, cotton and footwear), and the final stage of most private-sector agreements is the joint negotiating body at industry level.

### White-Collar Unionization and Forms of Collective Bargaining

The major gap in the coverage of collective bargaining remains that of white-collar workers in the private sector, although in recent years there have been rapid developments in this area. Despite the absolute growth of white-collar unions in the postwar period, the proportion of white-collar workers in unions remained fairly stable at around 29 percent, just keeping pace with the growth of white-collar employment over the postwar period. However, the late 1960s witnessed some reduction in the growth of white-collar employment and a "membership explosion," which raised the proportion of unionization to 39 percent of those eligible in 1970.[5] This level seems likely to be maintained given the stimulus to white-collar union recognition provided by industrial relations legislation.

White-collar employee bargaining in the private sector has rarely adopted the multiemployer, industrywide form of organization prevalent for manual workers. There are exceptions, as in the banks, but the usual practice is for employers to negotiate directly with the white-collar unions on a company or (less likely) a plant basis.

### Coverage and Content of Formal System Agreements

Such are the bones of the "formal" collective bargaining system. The coverage of collective bargaining is extensive, having been officially estimated in 1965 to cover 18 million of the then 23 million employees in Britain.[6] Industrywide bargaining is usually narrow in its subject matter and far from exhaustive in its coverage of the items it seeks to regulate, but it includes an open-ended grievance/dispute procedure under which it is possible for the smallest work place grievance to be progressed up to the industrywide negotiating committee. The agreements are customarily made for an unspecified time period. In the mid-1960s, fixed-term agreements enjoyed a certain vogue in such important industries as engineering, building, and printing, but their acceptability to the unions declined with the acceleration of inflation. Moreover, the parties have traditionally preferred to rely on the spirit rather than the letter of their agreements, which are sparsely drafted in nonlegalistic language. Consequently, the distinction between disputes of "right" and disputes of "interest" is not customary, nor could it be quickly adopted given the wide gap between the light framework of rules contained in written agreements and actual behavior and practice.

## FILLING THE GAP IN THE COLLECTIVE BARGAINING STRUCTURE: WORK-PLACE BARGAINING

The light framework of substantive rules determined at industry level through negotiations remote from the work place may have filled the needs of an earlier age, but its inadequacy is now manifest in many sectors. Radical changes have occurred in the economic climate, the size of plants, and the types of employment. Workers' ambitions, and ability, to influence directly their wage levels and work conditions have risen markedly. Technological changes produced more highly differentiated labor forces working in larger plants, organized in separate departments with more diverse job interests and attachments. Larger factories and the advancing division of labor produced new occupational groups and subgroups, each seeking to advance its sectional interests. The labor force lacks the historically clear distinction between the skilled and the unskilled and includes an increasingly large body of semiskilled workers whose skills are often specific to the plant in which they were acquired. There is extensive subdivision of job skills and interests, making the labor force less homogeneous than in the past in both outlook and needs. Unions also extended recruitment across widening ranges of skills, including white-collar employees, and are larger.

Groups and subgroups of workers' seek to advance their sectional interests with increasing independence. Grievances are pursued actively at shop level, and improvements sought directly over issues such as pay, labor utilization, job rights, work standards and practices, discipline, overtime, and many others. Local situations are exploited, and advances made are quickly consolidated into "custom and practice." Direct industrial action is applied to secure advances or to preserve gains. The pursuit of self-interest allied with a sense of sectional independence has its roots in the failure of the traditional, external bargaining system to deal with the realities as they appear at the shop-floor level.

The industrywide agreements do not generally provide guidance for the solution of specific work-place problems. Management's exercise of unilateral decision-making in these matters is challenged as irritations arise and militancy grows in the work force. Employees want these questions regulated jointly, and preferably resolved in their favor. They have turned increasingly to direct discussions with local management, developing the bargaining roles of their agents, the shop stewards. This development was not planned; it grew. Moreover, the unions made little effort to exercise close supervision over these operations, interceding primarily when their sanction was needed for written agreements, or belatedly and often ineffectively when strikes occurred.

Managements often favored the internalization of negotiations. The reasons were diverse. Some were impatient with the difficulties caused by multiunionism and favored dealing quickly with shop problems through direct negotiation with representatives of the immediate groups involved. Some hoped that such direct dealings would make for greater distance between employees and the union and weaken the latter. Wartime experience had oriented local managers to factory consultation bodies, and the government continued to promote such agencies. Managements lacked an overall strategy on the specific practical issues and a clear conception of the relationship between local practice and national agreements. As work-place negotiations proceeded, internal bargaining gained an increasing and autonomous importance. Local consultation machinery stagnated as the welfarist outlook declined. By contrast, work-place bargaining grew rapidly, to become an important complement to national bargaining but tended to move in independent directions. It filled the wide gap left by the industrywide system.

The work-place bargaining system stimulated local action and militancy. Unionized workers converted the shop steward and the factory union organizations into active instruments for change. Individuals and groups used these channels to deal with workshop issues, obtain redress for their complaints, and secure gains. Established constitutional procedures were short-circuited, bypassed, or ignored.

Varied forms of industrial action are used, including unconstitutional strikes (which are often short and many of which are later legitimized by the union), overtime bans, incentive work bans, work by the rule, and so on. No measure of the impact of these actions on the national economy is available. Official statistics include only strikes, and have only recently distinguished those that are unofficial and unconstitutional. However, the Department of Employment estimated for the not untypical years 1964–66 that 95 percent of strikes, accounting for 69 percent of days lost, were unofficial.

The work-place agreements produced a profusion of uncodified informal understandings and concessions of a largely pragmatic form. The consequence was at times a profusion of internal anomalies, a tendency for bargaining to become continuous as groups press to generalize gains of one section or to restore their former position,

and an increasing drift of earnings above the levels or rates of increase scheduled in the national agreements.

The Donovan report (1968) centered its attention on these developments. It considered they had created a fragmented, disorderly
structure not clearly integrated into the industry system of negotiations and without adequate institutions and formal arrangements at the
plant or company levels. It favored the incorporation of work-place
bargaining into the wider system, the introduction of comprehensive
formal agreements at plant or company level, for example, shop
steward functions and facilities, discipline and redundancy procedures
and clearly defined bargaining bodies on a plant-wide or company-
wide basis. Decentralization of bargaining was preferred, so long
as there was a clear articulation of the topics to be settled at the
different levels. The Donovan report emphasized procedural and
structural reforms and was confident that changes in the institutional
framework would provide more stable and orderly methods for resolving differences and preventing disputes.

The tidier, more formal system advocated by the Donovan commission may relieve problems arising from vagueness, uncertainty,
and the inequities their inquiries revealed, but there will still remain the pressures from employees for opportunities for direct influence over their work-place conditions and the redress of grievances. This demand underlies the current discontents and sets
limits to the adequacy of purely mechanistic reforms.

Interest in institutional and procedural reform and the discussion of the many questions involved in creating this complementary
and articulated system of bargaining has been subordinated, since the
report's publication, to the discussions and strife over legislative
proposals and action respecting industrial relations and the passage
and resistance to the late Industrial Relations Act.


THE TRADE UNIONS


Union membership in Britain during the postwar period grew
only slowly in absolute terms, with the decline of some highly unionized industries (mining, railways, shipbuilding), and the growth of
white-collar and female employment reducing membership to about
42 percent of employees in the mid-1960s. The end of the decade
saw a large increase in union membership to 11 million in 1970, and
a simultaneous fall in employment raised the proportion of members
to almost 47 percent. The number of unions declined continuously
from the 1920s, falling to a total of 466 in 1972, as a result of mergers, thus raising the average size of unions. Membership, however,
is concentrated in a few large unions, with the 11 largest unions

accounting for 61 percent of union members. More than 75 percent of
all union members belong to the 23 unions, which have over 100,000
members. Of the 469 unions, 250 have less than 1,000 members.

### Types of Unions and Multi-Unionism

Description of British trade unions is made difficult by the
variety of their organizational bases. The taxonomy of craft, industrial, general, and white-collar has become less applicable in the
past decade, although examples of each type remain. The major
manual worker unions have all acquired or developed white-collar
sections; some former craft unions have pursued increasingly "open"
recruitment policies; and some have merged with others to form
multicraft unions.

Although the spate of union mergers has produced greater sim-
plicity of organization in some industries, it has not markedly reduced the extent of multiunionism. In many sectors, different unions
represent the same grade of worker in one company or industry and
are, at least in a residual sense, in competition with each other.
But open displays of predatory recruiting between manual worker
unions are few, due in part to interunion agreements over spheres of
influence and to the general observance by affiliated unions of TUC's
Bridlington rules.

As would be expected, given the lower level of union membership among white-collar workers, the presence of non-TUC-affiliated
unions and staff associations, interunion competition has emerged in
the recent scramble for white-collar members, provoking some work
stoppages.

Despite some membership concentration in certain sectors--
for example, the Transport and General Workers Union (TGWU) in
road transport, docks, vehicles, and chemicals--many larger unions
are parties to agreements in many different industries. Consequently,
the unions are aware of developments and deals made in various industries, and the effects of changes in the central policy or direction
of leadership of the largest unions are not limited to a particular sector. While the manual worker unions, over the years, established
fairly stable interunion relationships on industrywide negotiating
bodies, joint union supervision of work-place bargaining in multiunion plants scarcely developed at all.

### Low Membership Participation

Historically, membership participation in the affairs of British
unions is based on attendance at branch meetings, with the branch

usually being associated with a geographical area rather than a single place of employment. There are exceptions to the latter rule in the case of some industrial unions and the general unions in large establishments. Attendance at branch meetings is low, typically between 5 and 10 percent, with shop stewards playing an active part. Union subscriptions are relatively low and have not kept pace with either earnings or price increases.

## Full-Time Officers and Shop Stewards

Unions generally have not managed to improve the ratio of full-time officers to members, which is approximately 1:3,800. But the number of shop stewards increased over the postwar period, reflecting the spread and intensity of work-place bargaining, with the number of these unpaid lay officials approaching 300,000--as against a total of between 3,000 and 4,000 full-time union officers. Unions rely heavily on the activities of the stewards, for organization and recruitment purposes, for collecting dues (despite the recent spread of check-off agreements), for protecting members' interests in the work place, and for communications between the union and its rank-and-file members.[7]

Shop stewards are elected by members of their union at the work place, usually by an informal show of hands in the section of department concerned, and are then recognized by management following the issue of credentials by the trade union. In large establishments the stewards then elect senior stewards, works committees, and conveners from among their number and establish internal hierarchies (which often spread across multiplant companies through combine committees) cutting across union lines, creating multiunion committees of shop stewards to coordinate their approaches and policies. Although individual stewards are authorized by their union, they generally feel themselves primarily accountable to their electorate--that is, their work mates in the work groups within their constituencies. They are representatives not only of their trade union but also of groups of trade union members and may find themselves with divided loyalties in situations where the wishes, policies, and tactics of these two groups differ.

The bargaining activities of shop stewards vary in extent and nature depending on a variety of factors such as labor and product markets, payment systems, technology, the degree of centralization of management decision-making, the content of formal agreements, and the degree of dissatisfaction among the employees, but they are extensive, having developed pragmatically. Stewards' bargaining activities have largely been free of detailed or formal regulation by the unions.

Throughout the postwar period, there has been a marked tendency for the mass media to link the increase in unofficial strikes with the emergence of shop stewards and to cast stewards in the role of provocateurs or troublemakers. The somewhat independent but powerful position of shop stewards did attract the attention of the Communist Party and other left-wing groups, and there have been some cases (at Ford's, on the docks, and in the building and exhibition industries), where leftist political philosophy and organization became prominent. These cases necessarily attract publicity, but the evidence suggests that political motivation has been insignificant in all but a very few cases. Indeed, the massive survey evidence of the Royal Commission led it to conclude that although changes were required to draw stewards more fully and formally into the system, they were "more often than not a moderating influence," a "lubricant rather than an irritant," seeking to bring order into situations and conditions that promoted disorder. Over the postwar period most unions adopted a pragmatic approach toward the growing bargaining powers of shop stewards, neither encouraging nor discouraging this in principle, but constantly reminding stewards that their role was complementary to that of the union externally. Again the survey evidence suggests that full-time union officers were generally satisfied with their influence over the stewards.[8]

The succession of left-wing leadership in the two largest unions (the TGWU and the Amalgamated Union of Engineering Workers, the AUEW) in the late 1960s brought more explicit policies of promoting stewards' bargaining activities, in the interest of greater rank-and-file participation and "grass-roots democracy." This view contrasted sharply with demands from the political right that union leaders and hierarchies should exercise greater control over shop stewards, a view endorsed by early judicial decisions under the late Industrial Relations Act making unions legally responsible for the (unauthorized) activities of stewards.

## Trades Union Congress: Composition and Role

The decentralization of power within the unions is, comparatively, a recent development; by contrast, the autonomy of unions within the TUC has long been acknowledged. The TUC is the single trade union center in Britain, to which unions representing over 90 percent of all trade union members are affiliated. Its formal authority over affiliated unions is negligible, resting on the threat of expulsion only. The TUC has rarely sought to impose policies on member unions, leaving them free to adopt their own policies, bargaining objectives, and tactics. However, in recent years the annual Congress has set targets for minimum earnings. The TUC has established collective bargaining committees composed of member unions in certain sectors to promote longer-term coordinated discussion of bargaining trends, objectives, and methods.

Further evidence of this trend toward greater TUC influence over bargaining can be found in the operation of the TUC's own vetting machinery, which ran alongside the Labour Government's incomes policy in the late 1960s, although on an advisory and voluntary basis. Affiliated unions adopted an extremely firm line over opposition to the 1971 Industrial Relations Act, when the TUC's General Council was authorized to instruct member unions not to register, and the TUC subsequently suspended and expelled about 20 mostly small unions for failing to observe this instruction. Such mandatory measures are wholly exceptional, as is illustrated by the postwar record of only three expulsions and no resignations prior to 1972. Indeed the customary criticism of the TUC is that as a central body it is too weak, rather than too firm, and its ability to commit member unions to follow particular policies (for example, incomes policy prescriptions) has been shown to be very limited. The TUC relies on advocacy and persuasion to influence union policies and practice.

Apart from acting as a forum for discussion among unions, the TUC's principal function has always been that of spokesman and pressure group for worker interests, particularly in relation to governments. Increased government intervention in the economy has involved the TUC's executives, primarily the general secretary acting on the instructions of the 37-member General Council, in representing the views of organized labor to government on a broadening range of issues. Indeed its position as the major spokesman listened to by government was a key factor in bringing several large, politically nonpartisan white-collar unions (including those for teachers and local government officials) into membership in the 1960s.

The TUC itself is not formally affiliated to the Labour Party, but about half its constituent unions are, and they provide the bulk of Labour Party funds. The relationship between the major manual worker unions and the Labour Party is close, about one-third of Labour MPs are sponsored by the unions, and several prominent unionists have seats on the National Executive of the Labour Party. Personal contacts between union leaders and leading Labour politicians are close. The leaders of the major unions have considerable formal influence over Labour Party policy when the party is in opposition, for they can wield huge bloc votes at the policy-making annual conference, as in 1971 over the Common Market issue. The stresses between the two wings of the labor movement--the parliamentary Labour Party and the unions--become much more apparent when Labour is in power, a fact illustrated most prominently by union opposition to Labour's statutory incomes policy and proposed strike legislation in 1966-69. Despite close historical and ideological ties the unions and the Labour Party moved further apart over methods as Labour's period in power lengthened. The Conservative industrial relations legislation brought them closer together, with the TUC seeking and gaining a Labour commitment to repeal it and the labor leaders seeking a credible concordat with the unions over incomes policy and a joint agreement over the main lines of economic policy to persuade the electorate that a future Labour government would be able to contain inflation and industrial disputes.

TUC policy is determined by the annual congress, which also elects the 37 members of the General Council. Voting is, where necessary, by card votes, with delegates casting votes equal to the total membership of their union. This means that the largest unions carry the largest voting power, with the Transport and General Workers Union (1.7 million) and the Amalgamated Union of Engineering Workers (1.3 million) having almost a third of the votes at the congress. When they agree, as they have done in recent years on generally leftist motions and policies, these two unions can exert substantial influence over TUC policies. Card votes have also been used at increasingly frequent conferences of union executives, which in recent years have been held between annual congresses to determine policy to be pursued by the General Council on crucial issues, such as incomes policy and legislation.

The General Council is made up of leading officers of around 25 unions, elected from 18 trade groups to ensure a spread of union representation. Its composition is a key element in union politics and the interpretation of TUC policy. The power of the largest unions is restricted by the electoral conventions, but they generally gain seats on such key subcommittees as the General Purposes and Economic Committees. In recent years the composition of the General Council has shifted to the left, a shift aided by perceived attacks on trade union "rights," and in 1972 a sitting right-wing member failed to gain reelection to the council--a somewhat rare event and one that led to accusations of personal animosity against the leftist leaders of the two largest unions.

## EMPLOYERS' ASSOCIATIONS

Representative organizations of employers at industry level have long existed in most British industries. Recent estimates suggest that there are over 1,300 employers' associations in Britain, though many are local associations themselves federated to industry-wide bodies. The Confederation of British Industry (CBI) has

estimated that in most major industries the companies federated to
employers' associations employ at least 80 percent of the industry's
labor force, and in few industries is the proportion below 50 percent.
Many organizations combine their functions as an employers' association with those of a trade association.

## Industrywide Agreements as a Reference or
## Minimum for Individual Employers

Despite their coverage and high membership ratios, most employers' associations find it increasingly difficult to maintain uniform
wage and other employment conditions across member firms, except
for a small range of manual worker conditions such as the length of
the work week, holidays, and so on. As the size of firms increased
and as work-place pressures grew, companies built up their own expertise in the personnel and labor fields. Many companies developed
their own wage structures and labor policies to meet their own circumstances, and their reliance on employers' associations diminishe

Industrywide agreements negotiated by employers' associations
with a few exceptions, serve primarily as a base, a point of departur
The scope of the subjects regulated in them remained fairly static,
whereas the subject matter of work-place bargaining broadened significantly.

Despite these trends, few companies have opted out of the
industry-level agreements to which their membership in the employers' association makes them a party. The reasons are tradition,
fear of the unknown, and fears of being "picked off" by the unions.
Moreover, use of industrywide disputes procedure agreements remains available only to federated employers. Though many of these
agreements are severely criticized as inappropriate for many domestic topics, their availability seems to reassure employers that
they will not be isolated in case of disputes.

Employers' associations have rarely been innovators in postwar industrial relations. Companies that left them have often done
so to gain greater freedom to innovate and to depart further from
association policy than the association was prepared to allow. The
rapid spread of plant- or company-based productivity agreements in
the 1960s brought these issues to a head. Wage rates above the industry basic rates are often established in such agreements in exchange for changes in work practices. The explicit negotiation of
above-minimum wage rates--rather than the more common practice
of using supplementary payments of various titles--led a number of
employers' associations to review the role of industry-level bargaining. Employers' associations thereafter softened their line, and

several negotiated agreements at the industry level expressly catering
to lower-level productivity deals. The industry-wide wage rates became more explicitly minimums, which could be exceeded without
violating the spirit of association membership. Some associations
concluded agreements setting minimum earnings levels that override
minimum wage rates.

### New Role for Associations: Service and Adviser

The 1960s saw employers' associations changing their roles
somewhat toward that of centers to which member firms might turn
for advice and other services, rather than that of a central coordi-
nator determining a common line to be followed by all member firms.
This tendency was not uniformly felt in all industries. Most associations continue to hold a common line among members during industrywide negotiations on those wage minimums and other issues governed
by agreement at that level. The effectiveness of this strategy was
demonstrated in the 1972 negotiations in engineering. Employers
effectively resisted union efforts to decentralize negotiations to secure higher local benefits. Employers' associations proved again to
be useful defensive organizations--their major role and stance in
collective bargaining over the postwar period as a whole. The same
association counseled its members to avoid use of the Industrial Relations Act and court actions, which was duly observed.
The other functions of employers' associations vary widely.[9]
Most act as spokesmen for employer interests and disseminate advice to members on the interpretation and application of legislation.
They differ in size, staffing, finance, and consequently the quality
and extent of their service to members.

### Confederation of British Industry: Industry Spokesman
### on National Policy

Although individual employers' associations may press their
views on issues specific to their industry on the government and its
agencies, the employer view of economic and industrial policy and
on legislative changes generally is expressed by the Confederation
of British Industry. The CBI, an amalgamation of the three main
central employers' organizations formed in 1965, admits into membership employers' associations, trade associations, public corporations responsible for the nationalized industries, and individual companies. Most major industrial companies affiliate directly to the
CBI. The CBI does not intervene in wage negotiations or industrial

disputes in individual industries or firms and has little or no formal
authority over member organizations. It is widely consulted by government on industrial and economic questions, and its director general is a key figure in government-industry relations.

The leadership he exercises, together with the president (an
office that changes biannually), is an important variable in the macro-
political relationships between the CBI, the TUC, and the government.
However, the internal proceedings and conferences of both individual
employers' associations and the CBI rarely receive the publicity given
to union and TUC proceedings, and internal differences are largely
obscured from view.


## MANAGEMENT


Over the postwar period managements have been predominantly
on the defensive. Changed labor and product market conditions added
substantially to the bargaining power of work groups. Both workers
and managements perceived this shift only slowly. Managements in
particular treated it for a long period merely as a temporary aberra-
tion. Little serious consideration was given to managerial objectives,
strategies, and policies in the industrial relations field beyond the
mere maintenance of peace and support for established arrangements.
Not until well into the 1960s did management take initiatives to introduce change in bargaining systems, procedures, payment systems,
and employment policies.

Indeed, the quality of labor management and the resources devoted to it as an element of corporate administration was, broadly
speaking, low. With a few notable exceptions, particularly in the
process industries, labor management was not regarded as a central
function of management that merited even approximate "parity of
esteem" with other functions. This attitude began to change with the
spate of labor legislation after 1964, the prominence given to labor
problems nationally, the requirements of income policies, and the
adoption of government's Code of Industrial Relations Practice.


### Acceptance of Unionism as Part
### of Industrial Organization


Management philosophies and ideologies in the postwar years
have gone through a number of phases. Each period saw the rise of
a number of managerial techniques in the labor field. Over the
period as a whole, managements (in larger companies at least)
tended to move from a welfarist orientation toward one that accepts

the pluralism of large-scale industrial organization. Managerial perceptions of the role of the unions changed from that of essentially external organizations, periodically reaching agreements with employers' associations in remote negotiating committees on a narrow range of contentious distributive topics, to an (often reluctant) acceptance of union activity within the work place. In some cases managements fostered the growth of internal employee representation systems, though in the early postwar period, this was associated more with welfarist, unitary view of employer-employee relations and an attempt to isolate trade union activity than with a desire to conclude agreements.

### Human Relations, Personnel Management Systems, and Joint Consultation Committees: A Passing Stage

Management initiatives in labor relations in the first prewar decade were heavily influenced by a welfare tradition and the teachings of the Human Relations School. The maintenance of "good industrial relations" depended, for example, on the quality of managerial "leadership" and "effective" communications with employees. To achieve this end, many leading companies developed formalized systems of joint consultation with internal employee representatives, house journals, sports and social club activities, and, less frequently, profit-sharing schemes and modest, noncontributory, nonnegotiated sickness and pension schemes. Despite early managerial enthusiasm and some successes in individual companies and some nationalized industries, most joint committees (which were precluded from discussing "trade union topics" and from making decisions as opposed to allegedly influencing them) failed to sustain a central position in management-employee relations. By the beginning of the 1960s, disillusion with them was widespread. Despite this, employers continue to use joint consultative bodies, although expectations of their impact on internal industrial relations are more modest. Some firms found the distinction between negotiable and consultative topics progressively more difficult to sustain as work-place bargaining developed.

### Wage Payment Systems

The use of incentive payment systems for manual workers increased in the early postwar period and continues to play an important part in many industries. A survey in 1961 showed that 42 percent of wage-earners in manufacturing had some element of payment

by results in their earnings, and that 73 percent of all wage-earners
in manufacturing worked in establishments where some workers were
paid by results. Trends since that time are obscure. Movements
away from piecework systems in favor of time rates or more stabilized performance-related systems such as measured day work, are
well publicized because they involve prolonged bargaining with the
unions. Managements continue to press for these changes even though
they involve some immediate financial cost because they found the
older systems encouraged wage drift and frequent localized disputes
and changing production techniques called for changes in the systems.

Payment system and internal wage structure reform was a major
feature of many productivity agreements in the mid- and late 1960s,
and was latterly supported by the 1965-70 incomes policy. But as
late as 1968 the Donovan commission roundly criticized the "chaotic
nature" of many factory wage structures and pay systems and the
widespread lack of control in this area.

## Productivity Agreements: A Major Innovation

The leading example of managerial initiative in collective bargaining was productivity bargaining. This technique brought topics
such as manning, occupational demarcation lines, working arrangements, and labor mobility out of the hazy world of ill-defined "custom
and practice" to the bargaining table and favored formal agreements.
With the official support of the government under the 1965-70 incomes
policy, under which productivity agreements were almost continuously
allowed as exceptions to the wage increase norms and ceilings, this
practice grew apace. But some argue that its growth was so forced
by the incomes policy that much of the spirit and character of the
early deals in the process industries was lost and that many "phony"
deals were made simply to evade the incomes policy norms. Certainly its decline was rapid and was associated with the collapse of
the incomes policy in 1969.[10]

## Work-Place Bargaining: A Developing Institution

Less imaginative and constructive was the managements' response to work-place pressures for additional benefits and protection.
They yielded to sectional demands and made informal and often un-
recorded concessions at shop-floor levels, often unknown to top executives or because they could be passed on in higher prices. Only
with the introduction of productivity bargaining did many managements
begin to think in terms of long-term strategy for incorporating work-

place bargaining within a reformed collective bargaining structure. Subsequently, the Commission on Industrial Relations, the Industrial Relations Act, its associated Code of Practice, and the escalation of industrial disputes in their different ways maintained the pressure on managements to follow through on this program. But it remains part of the agenda of unfinished work.

### Industrial Democracy: An Undefined Goal

British managements are both suspicious of and skeptical about institutionalized approaches to "industrial democracy," whether as "worker directors," works councils, or in some other form. The attempts at joint consultation fell far short of even the loosest definition of democracy. Equally, most British trade unions have until 1973 neither sought nor pressed for direct participation in managerial decision-making, fearing some confusion of role and an insidious weakening of their independence in such arrangements.[11] Unions and employers have, by default, preferred the adversary relationship, with the unions basing their view of industrial democracy largely on their power to influence and to veto decisions by independent industrial strength and sanctions.

Such limited experiments in employee participation in management decision-making as have occurred have been of a partial nature in some nationalized industries and isolated companies such as the retail chain of the John Lewis Partnership. A few managements have applied recent concepts of "job enrichment" to the design of jobs and production processes, though to date this has been on a very small scale. But the technique does not get them to the heart of the democracy issue. Britain's entry into the EEC and the draft statutes on European company law have given increased prominence to the more traditional methods of "democratizing the government" of companies. Another straw in the wind is the provision in the late Industrial Relations Act that (registered) unions have statutory rights to certain company information for collective bargaining purposes.

### THE GOVERNMENT

For much of the present century, British governments of different political complexions played a somewhat neutral, nonpartisan, and generally fairly minimal part in the industrial relations system. The major objectives that guided successive governments have been to maintain industrial peace while promoting industrial self-determination through supporting voluntary collective bargaining. This objective and these methods have a long history and help account for the conciliatory and generally unassertive image of the Ministry of Labour (now the Department of Employment) until very recent times.

The 1960s saw a series of departures away from this philosophy of minimal intervention. Governmental dissatisfaction with the achievements of collective bargaining prompted legislation on such substantive issues as dismissal notice periods, employment contracts, redundancy, industrial training, and equal pay for females. Concern with the short-run inflationary effects of collective bargaining and free market operations led to a variety of incomes policies and the statutory limitation of pay and price increases. The dispute about the failings of the essentially voluntary collective bargaining system produced the major legal changes of the 1971 Industrial Relations Act. New institutions, like the Commission on Industrial Relations (CIR), the regional Industrial Tribunals, the Industrial Training Boards, various agencies to operate incomes policies, the National Industrial Relations Court, and the Manpower Services Commission, all reflect a burgeoning of governmental activity on the labor scene. If the objectives of policy, namely the maintenance of industrial peace, the avoidance of inflationary pay settlements, the promotion of greater equity and fostering economic growth remained the same, the detailed methods have changed radically. From a position of supportive umpire between the two parties, government policy has now become a major factor in the situation. Labor policy--which for long periods was primarily bipartisan as between the major political parties--is now at the center of political divisions between them.

## TRADE UNION CONFRONTATION WITH GOVERNMENT AND EMPLOYERS

The essence of the confrontation was the determination of governments to define the boundaries between the sectional freedom of action and autonomy of the unions (and employers) and the area of legal regulation and administrative (state) control. There were two primary constituent elements as viewed from the aspect of government initiatives. The first was the extent of the role of the law--and its content--in structural questions such as the status of collective agreements, legal definition of the right to strike, the specification of bargaining units and agents, union recognition, internal union rules and government, and union security issues such as protection of bargaining rights and the closed shop. The second element concerns the freedom of the parties to determine privately substantive issues such as pay, hours, holidays, and other conditions to their mutual satisfaction, free from overriding state control. The former question was the immediate precipitant of the confrontation between the unions and the 1970-74 Conservative government. The changes proposed represented a major break with the voluntarist tradition, to which the unions were very firmly committed. Also, unlike price-wage policies, which have usually been explicitly temporary measures, action in this area had the implication of greater longevity.

The circumstances of 1970 had all the elements of an imminent showdown between the unions and the newly elected Conservative government. Few major changes had been made in the industrial relations system to adjust to and to accommodate new pressures. Criticism of the system and pressure for reform reached a crescendo.

### Conservative Government's Policy
### Precipitates Showdown

The new government implemented laissez-faire, market-oriented economic and social policies. These the unions considered inequitable and divisive. The Conservatives' abrasive style contrasted sharply with that of the outgoing Labour administration, over which the unions had exerted substantial influence and, on some issues, a virtual power of veto. The intensity of employee dissatisfactions and fears underpinned a shift to greater militancy in the unions. Most specifically, the unions were fundamentally opposed to the Conservative's program for industrial relations legislation. Social unrest and frustration were focused firmly on the industrial relations system.

The Conservatives' attempt to impose controls in industrial relations through the introduction of extensive legal regulation was met by strident opposition from the unions. Although the electorate did not understand the technicalities, there appeared to be wide support for the view that something had to be done to "curb the unions." The Labour Party's failure to carry through its 1969 proposals had undermined its credibility and contributed to its electoral defeat in 1970. The new government refused to consult with the unions about the principles or pillars of the legislation. Union leaders regarded the government as hostile and repressive. Their response was both emotional and militant. The legislative attack provided conditions favorable for left-wing union leaders to sway the center and assume leadership within the TUC.

### TUC's Countermoves

The TUC's hostility crystallized into total noncooperation with the 1971 Industrial Relations Act or with institutions established by it and a coordinated attempt to make it inoperable. TUC unions were instructed not to register as unions within the meaning of the act nor to initiate legal actions to secure advantages under its provisions. This strong line was accepted by all but a few unions, despite its high costs. Government-union relations were ruptured totally, with the TUC demanding repeal of the act as a sine qua non.

Implementation of the act led quickly to a series of disputes that blurred the previously clear distinction between industrial action over conventional industrial objectives and the use of industrial power for political purposes. This major departure raised disturbing constitutional issues.

The government's wage policy also blurred this distinction and transformed public-sector wage disputes into politico-industrial confrontations between the unions and government. The government was explicitly opposed to statutory price-wage restraints, while the alienation of the unions precluded any voluntary concordat on wages. The government's strategy was to deescalate pay settlements by stiffening employer resistance, a policy that it could pursue most vigorously in the public sector. This outraged the public-sector employees and unions, which took vigorous action against this discrimination. Four times between 1970 and 1972, the government declared a state of emergency due to industrial action over wage disputes. The number of days lost through stoppages rose to postwar record levels as large and long stoppages occurred in support of pay claims from workers in electricity, coal, the postal service, local authorities, engineering, building, and the docks.

Industrial action also took on new forms. The miners made their six-week national strike effective by large-scale picketing of power stations, sending mobile groups of pickets to areas remote from the coal fields. The dockers and building workers copied this tactic in 1972, causing occasional violent clashes with the police and other workers. Sit-ins and factory occupations occurred in the engineering disputes, and resistance to plant closures developed in many industries. Left-wing groups were active, notably in the docks dispute over job security and the effects of containerization, which led in July 1972 to the imprisonment of five rank-and-file dockers' leaders under the Industrial Relations Act.

As the costs of industrial strife rose to threaten political stability, public attitudes became much more ambivalent. There was widespread public sympathy for the miners' 20 percent claim, despite the power cuts and layoffs their strike caused. The Industrial Relations Act seemed to be having the opposite effects to those intended. A compulsory ballot on the railways failed. Employers were extremely reluctant to use its provisions, and the imprisonment of the dockers brought widespread sympathy action and the threat of a national strike by TUC unions.

The antagonism between the unions and the government in the 1970-72 period was greater than at any time in postwar history. Political strikes against the Industrial Relations Act were organized by militant unions and the communist-led Liaison Committee for the Defence of Trade Unions. Fines against the unions imposed by the National Industrial Relations Court (NIRC) were similarly protested. The act appeared to be promoting industrial ferment rather than restraining it at a time when exceptionally high levels of price inflation and unemployment were further undermining the government's authority.

## CONFRONTATION TEMPORARILY SUBSIDES; CONTINUED SPARRING AND NEGOTIATIONS

The subsequent reduction in tension between government and unions owed more to changes in the government's position than in that of the unions. The economic and political costs of its early, somewhat doctrinaire, stance had proved to be high. It failed in its attempt to pursue a laissez-faire economic policy (with union restraints) in the face of union and widespread working-class opposition.

### Changes in Government Attitude and Policy

The government's change of approach followed the defeat of its wage increase deescalation policy by the miners and the momentous events of July 1972 surrounding the dockers' imprisonment. It was midterm in the government's period of office, and by-election results showed considerable swings against it. Inflation was not being contained and was accelerating, despite the relatively high unemployment level. The balance of payments was moving strongly into deficit and the parity of the pound was again threatened. The Industrial Relations Act could show few successes, and union resistance to it gave no sign of weakening.

The government moved toward greater flexibility and sought the participation of the CBI and TUC in discussing the country's economic problems and policies. Indeed the prime minister offered the union and employers the opportunity "to share with the Government the benefits and obligations involved in running the national economy" but yielded no rights to make the final determination. Measures were taken to reduce unemployment and to accelerate economic growth, policies long sought by the TUC and welcome to the CBI. The upgrading of these objectives, and early evidence that the measures were taking effect, allowed some tensions to recede between the

government and the unions. They were followed by further conciliatory measures, indicating the government's desire to move away
from confrontation and its willingness to modify its policies. A review of the operation of the Industrial Relations Act was promised,
implying amendments in line with union opinion. Controversial proposals on industrial training were shelved, and it announced a Manpower Services Commission with TUC and CBI membership with
overall supervision of some areas of manpower policy.

## The Union Response

The unions did not react enthusiastically to the government's
overtures. They were skeptical about whether they really indicated
a fundamental or permanent change. Gradually the view of union
moderates that some advances could be made through discussions
with the government gained ground. The employers were conciliatory
and prepared to participate. The imminence of the next election influenced both unions and the government to assume positions more
likely to appeal to center opinion.

In autumn 1972 TUC and CBI leaders attended open-agenda
talks about the economy initiated by the government. These tripartite discussions proceeded intensively, with the government seeking
agreement to voluntary price-wage restraints in the context of its
commitment to double the growth rate. The TUC entered these discussions as a bargainer, with a wide-ranging but specific list of demands including nonoperation of the Industrial Relations Act, tax
changes, increased pensions, suspension of rent increases, food
subsidies, and statutory price controls. Its posture as a direct
negotiator seeking gains outside the area usually covered by price-
wage policies contrasted sharply with its historic lobbyist or pressure group position. In any event the talks proved abortive. Their
failure was followed immediately by the government's imposition of
a 140-day statutory pay and price freeze from November 1972. A
second phase of restrictive statutory controls over pay, price, and
dividend increases for the six months to November 1973 was followed
by a third slightly more flexible but still statutorily enforced stage
that continued past the Conservatives' election defeat in February
1974, lasting into July.

This unilateral government action on wages stimulated a further
surge of union militancy. The TUC invited affiliated unions to join
in a national day of protest and stoppage on May Day 1973 against the
pay legislation. There were strikes against its application in several
industries and services, including gas, the civil service, and the
hospitals. These lengthy stoppages failed to break the policy, and

workers elsewhere acquiesced in settlements that fell within the permitted ceiling. Union opposition to the restrictions on wage bargaining was temporarily disarmed by the lack of active rank-and-file support. However, this lull in 1973 was only temporary and was resoundingly broken, again by the miners. Their four-week strike over a pay claim led to power restrictions and a government-imposed three-day work week in much of industry and precipitated a general election in February 1974, at which the Conservatives were defeated.

## THE 1974 LABOUR GOVERNMENT:
## A CHANGE OF APPROACH

A major plank in the platform of the Labour Party, which took office as a minority government after the February election, was its so-called social contract with the unions. Labour pointed to the Conservatives' inability to work with the unions and the devastating results of Conservatives' unilaterally imposed policies and proposed a new alliance with the unions, in which the new government's introduction of measures sought by the unions would be reciprocated by voluntary union restraint in wage-bargaining. The new Labour government rapidly set about fulfilling its side of the "social contract." This is not a written agreement but, rather, according to the prime minister, "a living and developing relationship covering the whole range of social and economic policies--a voluntary relationship, a constructive concensus between the Government and the unions." Labour's early measures included settling the miners' strike outside the pay limits, repealing the 1971 Industrial Relations Act (and later abolishing the NIRC and the CIR), abolishing the Pay Board and removing the statutory limitations on pay bargaining but not on prices, profits, and dividends, introducing food subsidies and a rent freeze, raising pensions, making the income tax more steeply progressive and announcing a wealth tax. These measures were to be followed by the creation of a Conciliation and Arbitration Service independent of government, a Royal Commission on Income Distribution and Wealth, an Employment Protection Bill offering new minimum standards, and legislation on worker participation in the management and control of companies in an Industrial Democracy Bill. In view of the new government's minority position the TUC and the unions were under pressure to give the "contract" some credibility by being seen to respond in wage bargaining. The TUC, for its part, announced that negotiated wage increases in 1974/75 should aim to do no more than maintain real wages. However, individual unions found it difficult to contain rank-and-file pressure to exceed this as the statutory controls were lifted. White-collar groups that had suffered under the

1972-74 restraints were particularly prominent, and many union leaders were unable to commit their unions to the "contract" due to skeptical or hostile votes at annual conferences. Others, most notably
the AUEW and the miners, remained insistent on the retention of traditional wage bargaining freedoms, despite the political pressures to
act in ways that would not reduce Labour's electoral chances if it
sought a working parliamentary majority through an early election.

## PROSPECTS FOR REFORM

The sharp confrontation between the unions and the Conservative
government is best seen as a diversionary interlude in the development of industrial relations in Britain. The resounding failure of the
attempt to impose new legal constraints on the unions and union hostility toward rightist policies in other areas demonstrated the patent
inability of the government to implement successfully policies that
were cohesively and actively opposed by the unions. Indeed, this
realization led the Conservative government to modify its policies
and adopt a more consultative posture in its last two years in office.
This interlude demonstrated, whatever the truth of the accusations
of leftist infiltration of the unions may be, that militancy and the
rhetoric of union leaders are related to the degree to which the basic
economic and social problems are, or are not, being solved. Most
significantly, it gave the unions a new realization of their potential
power and has ensured that a future Conservative government will
pursue more moderate, "national-unity" policies on industrial relations.
Consideration of the prospects for reform must be prefaced by
an indication of Britain's weak economic situation. Its rate of economic growth and the level of investment remain low. Some temporary success on the balance of payments in 1970-71 gave way to
record deficits in 1973-74 (only partially due to oil). Despite 18
months of statutory wage and price restrictions, inflation accelerated
to 17 percent per year. Britain's commitment to the Common Market
was weakening further. The prospect of North Sea oil cutting oil
imports in the later 1970s was the only optimistic feature of an
otherwise depressing outlook. The 1974 minority Labour Government's ability to pursue antiinflationary policies was constrained by
its insecurity and the likelihood of a further general election. Indeed in 1974 it took measures to reflate, anticipating an upward shift
in unemployment, and initiated a wide range of policies sought by the
unions in return for somewhat nebulous assurances from the TUC on
wage-bargaining goals.
The complexion of the government has a determining influence
on the future direction of British society. In postwar years, Britain

has had a succession of single-party governments, but the 1974 election was indecisive, with a center party (the Liberals) making significant advances in its share of the vote.

The overriding current problem is rapid inflation, which has sharpened social divisions and militancy and threatens social stability, although paradoxically in the short term it has acted as a release valve by appearing to allow the incompatible demands of different groups to be reconciled.

## The TUC

The Labour Government's pursuit of a TUC-endorsed legislative program has facilitated a more wholehearted dialogue with the unions, a sharp contrast with the Conservative period when leftist union leaders opposed even talking with government. This is likely to bolster the moderates in the TUC, although the leftists will continue to provide the stimulus and to coin the battle cries.

However, the TUC can only deliver if it persuades constituent unions to accept any agreement that might be reached. There will inevitably be dissidents, whose influence will depend on the extent of worker restlessness and their assessment of the fairness or otherwise of the "social contract." The trade unions are unlikely to be won over by mere places on consultative bodies. Nor are they satisfied by talk fests. Their participation in the 1972 tripartite discussions rested on their hopes of securing firm advances through bargaining, and this will continue. The pragmatism and down-to-earth quality of trade union leaders and members make for realism and eliminate the possibility of "phony" deals.

During the 1960s, the unions became increasingly unwilling to accept government decisions that might be handed down. The TUC began to spell out detailed political programs. Its annual economic reports specified objectives on broader issues such as employment, growth, housing, taxation, and pensions, thus illustrating its new determination to lead opinion in the Labour Party and providing an explicit bargaining counter with the government. Trade unionists in Britain want social changes toward greater equality. Union leaders do not want to rule the country nor to challenge the government, but they do want to bargain. They are willing to accept incremental changes if they are offered in a cooperative spirit but will resist a government that fosters inequality.

Cooperation between unions and government is much more probable when the Labour Party is in power, although this brings its own tensions. The unions tend to be more responsive to leftist approaches than the Parliamentary party and are critical of its past pragmatism and the concessions made to economic orthodoxy. The unions and the Labour Party are necessary partners, but both avoid identification with the other.

Although the TUC expects and seeks more active and effective consultation and influence at the national level, it has been unable to define clearly for itself what this means. The failure of agreed price-income policies and economic planning agencies to secure labor gains created disillusion. The unions are knowledgeable on how to discharge adversary relationships; they have not experienced successful tripartism.

## Employer Organizations and Management

The CBI, after early support for antiunion measures, became more conciliatory. It tried to help the Conservative government's antiinflation policy by voluntary price restraint, and had far fewer reservations about tripartism than the unions. Bilateral cooperation between the TUC and CBI has been, and is likely to remain, limited. Their still-born bipartite conciliation service launched in 1972 was one of the few serious attempts at ongoing cooperation. The TUC and the CBI place different interpretations on government noninterference. Both are inclined to mean noninterference in their spheres, but restrictions on the other. For example, in 1974 the TUC pressed successfully for free collective bargaining alongside statutory price restraint. The CBI's stance on major issues other than extended nationalization and some proposed forms of worker participation is likely to remain low-key and moderate.

Corporate management has been largely defensive and uninventive. Managements were slow to recognize the permanence of the shift in power to shop-floor work groups. However company-level personnel and industrial relations management is developing quickly, especially in the larger firms. Employers' associations failed to redefine their role in a shifting social context and to promote a clearly articulated bargaining structure. The indications are that they are now coming to terms with this and developing a new advisory role.

## Government

Although the conflicts between the unions and the previous government arose out of major differences of philosophy, and the closer relationships with the new Labour government rest on a wider area of shared objectives, any government must recognize that trade union opposition or cooperation is somewhat apolitical. It is an ongoing challenge; it rests not on political expediencies but on real restlessness among union members. If a compromise is reached that disappoints followers, it is later rescinded. Constant incremental change to meet issues is necessary. Attempts to muzzle and straitjacket trade unionism, or to force it to acquiesce, will enjoy little success. The challenge facing governments is to combine successful economic policies that will provide the basic satisfactions sought by the labor force with durable institutional arrangements at the macrolevel for the determination of policies and priorities. The search for an articulated consensus is in its early stages but is being pursued by the government through the "social contract."

There is little indication of any long-term answer to the problem of combining free collective bargaining and full employment with the achievement of other economic policy goals. Recent experience suggests continuation of the wide oscillations in government incomes policy between crisis-precipitated periods of tight control, followed by "free" and uncoordinated collective bargaining once the immediate crisis has receded. A longer-term agreed policy for incomes would require a sustained period of freedom from currency and other economic crises, and virtually complete acceptance of a comprehensive compact between government and unions over economic and social policy. It would also require institutional changes giving the unions greater opportunities to participate in the formulation of agreed policies than those currently available through the aging National Economic Development Council (NEDC). The TUC would need much greater influence over the wage-bargaining of individual unions, including some commitment from them not to press for any sectional advantage they might achieve under autonomous collective bargaining. None of these prerequisites are likely to be fulfilled in the short term. The alternatives are statutory restriction or higher unemployment and slower growth, which would alienate the TUC.

## Worker Participation

Most British unions are skeptical of becoming involved in management. They rely on collective bargaining to influence management decisions and policies from the outside and preserve an adversary position. Flexibility and voluntarism are preferred to legal enactment. Entry into the EEC and its proposed statutes on company law have created a fresh interest in worker participation. Government, unions, and employer organizations are currently formulating their ideas on this question. The TUC has indicated tentative support for worker participation on supervisory boards under the two-tier board system

suggested by the EEC Commission. Its support, however, is subject
to conditions, such as 50 percent of the seats going to union-designated
employee representatives. The major employers' organizations have
opposed the EEC Commission's more limited proposals. Their preference is for works councils at lower levels.

Traditional management concepts of management's rights,
prerogatives, and responsibilities are likely to be modified by a reform of company law. During the next decade, managements are
likely to face a statutory commitment to take account of employee
interests as a general obligation and/or through supervisory boards
with some employee representation as well as works councils with
statutory powers over a wide range of issues.

Both unions and managements have serious reservations about
worker participation. The unions fear some loss of independence is
inevitable. They will continue to press for an expansion of the scope
and subject matter of formally concluded collective agreements. The
employers are apprehensive of loss of control, slower decision-
making, and reduced efficiency. Significantly, current interest in
this subject was not generated internally in Britain.

## Collective Bargaining and Other Issues

Present institutional arrangements and attitudes do not portend
well for an integrated bargaining system. The industrial bargaining
system is fragmented. The central union and employer federations
are weak. Constituent members have considerable autonomy. The
unions have little control over work-place leaders.

Since the 1968 Donovan report, official agencies have pressed
for work-place bargaining arrangements and procedures to be more
clearly defined and formalized. But tidy bargaining arrangements
and concise agreements will not by themselves ensure more orderly
work-place relations. Employee pressure on substantive issues such
as job security and equitable pay structures remain and cannot be
repressed by procedural devices. More explicit company agreements
on domestic issues will allow a more orderly accommodation of shop-
floor demands for direct influence over work conditions. The areas
of jurisdiction of individual company managements and those of the
employers' associations are being more clearly defined, leaving
managements free to take initiatives and pursue positive industrial
relations policies. The formalization of work-place bargaining offers
better prospects of achieving equitable internal pay structures, effective grievance procedures, and periodic rather than continuous
bargaining.

Movement toward a more formally decentralized and clearly
articulated bargaining system is proceeding slowly. Employer fears

of isolation, difficulties arising from multiunionism, and other tactical questions have induced caution. The unions find industry-level agreements effective in spreading the gains made across an industry. Industry-level agreements are not being abandoned; their role is to set up a platform on which more detailed work-place agreements can be built. Industry agreements will remain prevalent although their scope and function will be more clearly defined and limited. The priority given by the unions to longer-term reformist goals is reduced by their annual preoccupation with securing wage increases that at least keep pace with double-digit inflation. The growth of white-collar unionism both in manufacturing and the service sector is likely to continue with increasing company size and policy provisions favorable to recognition. Higher grades of technical and administrative employees are becoming unionized. Competitive recruiting is causing some interunion conflicts. In some areas, notably banking and insurance, unions have met resistance, unions have met resistance from company-based staff associations and internally organized staff consultative systems. New organizations of professional and technical employees are emerging.

The TUC unions remain determined to maintain the voluntary system of collective bargaining. Their general disposition is toward incremental change within the established system.

The major internal problem facing the unions is to clarify the position of shop stewards and to accommodate grass-roots initiative. The unions are disinclined to take direct action against stewards, fearing rank-and-file revolts. The approach of major unions is to delegate more authority to the stewards, emphasizing their position as front-line negotiators. Reformed and more clearly articulated bargaining arrangements are considered important ways to build up steward-union relationships. Informal influence rather than authoritarian measures are preferred. Few if any unions have the resources in full-time officers to reduce the bargaining activities of the stewards.

Britain's entry into the EEC has already increased the attention paid to nonwage benefits. Holidays, sickness, and pension arrangements are much more favorable in other EEC countries. Movements toward staff status for manual workers have begun in electricity supply, oil, and chemicals. National concern about the relative position of the low paid has grown, and further policy attempts to reduce wage and salary differentials are likely. The 1970 Equal Pay Act, which prohibits discrimination against women in pay and other terms of employment, will go into effect at the end of 1975. Legislation against discrimination in employment opportunities may follow.

Protection of real wages through "threshold agreements" geared to the retail price index was allowed and introduced under the 1973 incomes policy and may spread due to the high inflation rate, despite reservations in some union and employer groups. Union wage demands are being more fully researched. Leading companies have faced claims based on movements in real disposable incomes and on their profitability as disclosed by profit and cost data. Union entitlement to such information is likely to be strengthened.

The rapid growth of multinational companies has so far brought only a limited response from the unions. In the short term, internationally coordinated union action against the multinationals is unlikely to develop, beyond opposition to closures and transfers of production, particularly during single-country disputes.

## CONCLUSIONS

The replacement of confrontation by cooperation, which followed the change of government in 1974, is likely to be only a passing phase. The situation is kept in flux by economic and social instability. Many general and specific economic and employment problems remain unresolved. The rising expectations of workers for security, better material standards, and greater influence maintain the momentum. The unions seek to preserve the long-established voluntary system and free bargaining, while demanding joint decision-making power on the broad economic and social issues at the macro-level. Their commitment to an independent adversary position is strong and is likely to limit their involvement in tripartism. Further evolution of the emergent's "social contract" is dependent on Labour's continuance in power. It will secure union gains, but the payback from the unions remains problematic.

## EDITOR'S NOTE

The minority Labour government organized in March 1974 secured the repeal of the Industrial Relations Act of 1971. The National Industrial Relations Court, the Commission on Industrial Relations, and the Registry of Trade Unions and Employers Association went out of existence. Subsequently, the majority Labour government sought to repeal and modify the restrictions on trade unions added by parliament to the Trade Union and Labor Relations Act, 1974. A later short bill cancels restrictions on closed shops and the Registrar's powers to drop the listing of unions or employers' associations that do not meet standards. The government also offered proposals in a consultative document for a proposed Employment Protection Bill for the extension of the rights of workers and strengthening of collective bargaining including also statutory provisions for a Conciliation and

Arbitration Service, set up provisionally, new authorities for trade unions, reforms of wages councils, negotiated procedures respecting redundancies, and a series of additional innovations. An industry bill submitted in February 1975 offered new opportunities for trade unions to participate in company planning agreements on strategic business decisions negotiated with the government and for them to receive vital company data.

In the wage control area, the social contract entered into between the Labour Party and the TUC became the operative document, after the expiration of the wage controls. The TUC Congress endorsed it in September 1974. The Labour Party election manifesto declared it to be "at the heart of this manifesto and our programme to save the nation!" After the election of October 1974, which provided the Labour Government with a slim majority, Prime Minister Harold Wilson described it as "a contract under which the Government has pledged itself as no other Government in British history, to the promotion of social and economic justice." The alternative, he added, was deflation and more unemployment. The secretary for Employment subsequently publicly urged the trade unions to abide by the TUC wage guidelines and gave official recognition to the social contract in Department of Employment publications. The TUC General Council reaffirmed that the government was carrying out its part of the bargain and that its measures represented a "courageous endeavor to protect employment, stimulate investment and promote social justice." The General Council called on its constituent unions "to continue to operate within the guidelines of the social contract."

While the parties to the social contract exhorted their following to observe its terms, outside observers found "that the majority of wage deals being struck bust the compact."[12] The economics correspondent of the London _Financial Times_ reported that the data on wages for October 1974 permitted the TUC and members of the government "to claim that the statistics are in line with the TUC guidelines and the social contract, in that they appear to indicate that wage movements are broadly keeping up with the cost of living."[13] But a 28.5 percent wage increase negotiated in February 1975 by the Miners threatened the program, particularly as other large public sector unions (railroads and electric supply) made similar demands. Government spokesmen including the Prime Minister and the Chancellor of the Exchequer warned of the likely damage resulting from this proposal including large scale unemployment. The TUC in its 1975 annual economic review avoided making demands for the stringent observance of the terms of the social contract. Both the TUC and individual union leaders requested higher public expenditures to mop up the rising volume of unemployment, which stood at 3.4 percent of the work force. A direct confrontation between the Labour Government and the TUC appeared in the making.

As for the trade union movement's influence upon the Labour
Party, it was evident at the annual Party Conference held after the
election, both in the selection of the members of the National Executive Committee and its resolutions. While it is traditionally believed
that the parliamentary Labour Party may act independently of Party
sentiment, the Labour government's dependence on the continued
practical support from the rank and file for the implementation of its
economic and political programs rules out the disregard of these
views, necessitating continuing interchange and negotiations between
the two centers of power within the labor movement to reach an accommodation of views.


NOTES


1. See J. H. Goldthorpe, D. Lockwood, et al., The Affluent
Worker: Industrial Attitudes and Behavior (Cambridge: Cambridge
University Press, 1968).
2. There is an extensive literature on strike activity in Britain.
For the most recent contributions see H. A. Turner, Is Britain Really
Strike Prone? (Cambridge: Cambridge University Press, 1969);
W. E. J. McCarthy, "The Nature of Britain's Strike Problem,"
British Journal of Industrial Relations, July 1970; R. Hyman, Strikes
(London: Heinemann, 1972); and M. Silver, "Recent British Strike
Trends," British Journal of Industrial Relations, March 1973.
3. The outline given in this section is necessarily brief. The
best full-length descriptive account is H. A. Clegg, The System of
Industrial Relations in Great Britain (Oxford: Blackwell, 1972).
4. Trades Union Congress, Trade Unionism, 1966, para. 224.
5. G. S. Bain and R. Price, "Union Growth and Employment
Trends in the U.K. 1964-70," British Journal of Industrial Relations,
November 1972.
6. Ministry of Labour, Evidence to the Royal Commission on
Trade Unions and Employers' Associations, 1965, para. 48.
7. See Royal Commission Research Papers No. 1, The Role
of Shop Stewards in British Industrial Relations by W. E. J.
McCarthy (London: Her Majesty's Stationery Office, 1966); Research
Paper No. 10, Shop Stewards and Workplace Relations by W. E. J.
McCarthy and S. R. Parker; and J. F. B. Goodman and T. G.
Whittingham, Shop Stewards (Pan Books, 1973).
8. Workplace Industrial Relations (London: Her Majesty's
Stationery Office, 1968).
9. See Royal Commission Research Paper, No. 7, Employers
Associations (London: Her Majesty's Stationery Office, 1967); and
Commission on Industrial Relations, Study No. 1, Employers'

Organizations and Industrial Relations (London: Her Majesty's Stationery Office, 1972).

10. For accounts of productivity bargaining see A. Flanders, The Fawley Productivity Agreements (London: Faber, 1964); National Board for Prices and Incomes, Reports Nos. 36 and 123, Productivity Agreements (London: Her Majesty's Stationery Office, 1967 and 1969); R. B. McKersie and L. C. Hunter, Pay, Productivity and Collective Bargaining (London: Macmillan, 1973).

11. For a full account see R. O. Clarke, D. J. Fatchett, and B. C. Roberts, Workers' Participation in Management in Britain (London: Heinemann, 1972).

12. London Economist, November 23, 1973, p. 88.

13. London Financial Times, November 21, 1973.

## ITALY: CREATING A
## NEW INDUSTRIAL
## RELATIONS SYSTEM
## FROM THE BOTTOM
Pietro Merli Brandini

Postwar economic, cultural, intellectual, and social forces converted Italy into a modern industrial nation, while still maintaining a dual economy and society and a country divided into a North and South, but also intimately, if not inexorably, integrated both with the European Economic Community and the world of leading advanced nations. Most phases of Italian life are being affected, if not transformed, by these forces. But the past lingers on visibly, standing as contrast to the present and as vestiges of a shrinking, receding civilization or as laggard sectors. The latter are ill-adapted and remain sources of resistance and irritation and provoke conflict as its beneficiaries, and often even the victims defend their present state.

The industrial relations field is not exempt from these developments. It is both the product, and a major mechanism, of change. The institutions inherited in this area from the prefascist and fascist eras, were blended together into a system at the conclusion of Italy's alignment with the Nazi forces. Now they are being reshaped into a new system of attitudes, beliefs, institutions, and relationships built around active plant factory councils and national industrial federations working together. The employee–employer plant relations and procedures of representation and negotiations are being basically altered. The process of change is accompanied by disturbances and at times violence.

Unions not only increased in membership but also in bargaining power and national influence. Slowly, though with some backsliding, the confederations are severing their intimate ties with the political parties from which they sprung. They are struggling to create an autonomous movement expressing its special roles as spokesman and leader for the mass of employees in the plant and in their relations with employers and representative of the interests of the low-income and forgotten common man in the community and nation. They are inspired by the militancy and needs of the rank and file and the desire to weaken and eliminate the appeal of the more extremist leftist groups. But their associated parties are reluctant to lose this captive following and obstruct the moves for the merger of the trade union centers. The role of the national government is being activated as a mediator, extender of standards developed through collective bargaining, an agent for providing, though generally tardily and ineffectively, services and funds, and a facilitator of negotiations through the responsive use of fiscal policy.

The history of industrial relations of the postwar years may be divided into the immediate postwar period, which lasted until the end of the era of the "economic miracle" (1959-62) and the subsequent years into the present. The latter period may be separated into two: 1962-68 and 1968 to date. In the latter, innovations are being made at an accelerated pace with far-reaching effects on the system.

Recent Italian industrial relations developments display many unique characteristics. The process of change was stimulated and, in fact, propelled in 1968 by the spontaneous eruption of protest among and industrial action of the rank-and-file worker and employee throughout the entire country. The protest was a byproduct of employee frustration in the private and public sectors. The direction it took and the rhetoric it employed were greatly influenced by concurrent political and radical militant movements, which propagated anticapitalistic slogans for decentralized democratic participation in decision-making in industry. But the trade union leadership proved alert and adept enough to assert itself and take command of the protest and channel it into the institutionalized trade union movement and into a new industrial relations system. The ties with the radical movement waned with time, although they have not disappeared. The latter groups recurrently magnify their presence by criticism of the main leftist parties and by organizing protests or participating in resistance to housing evictions or other local action by authorities.

Since the base of the new movement is in the plant, the factory organization of worker delegates has become an increasingly more important unit in the decision-making and administrative processes of the union and collective bargaining. Disapproval of the national political inertia that inhibits the government from adopting needed social reform or implementing it effectively or quickly enough to satisfy the working population catapulted the trade unions and their membership into an active role in the political scene. They have fought actively both to get change approved and to make a reality out of newly accepted policy. But resistance to these changes from vested interests and the governmental bureaucracy continues strong, frustrating efforts at substantial progress, as have also, more recently, the restraints placed on the government by its austerity programs to fight inflation.

We shall not be able to speak of having arrived at a new mature system; changes are taking place; innovations are constantly being introduced; wholesale adjustments may be made. Projections must be made cautiously. An observer should be both intrigued by the creativity of the process of confrontation in industrial relations and speculate on the likely new developments and the speed of their introduction in a society in the course of general change, burdened by an inadequate political system and an economy in need of further structural changes. The fundamental impulses generated by the dissatisfaction and aspirations of employees, given specificity by the concurrent radical debate and tempered by the growing realism and sense of responsibility of the trade union leadership, are creating a truly new system of industrial relations.

## THE EARLY POSTWAR INDUSTRIAL RELATIONS SYSTEM

### Trade Unions

The changes recently and currently being effected are transforming the industrial relations system developed at the end of the war. The latter was an amalgam of elements devised in prefascist and fascist days. Employees were organized into local industrial unions affiliated at the local level in chambers of labor or their equivalent (Provincial Unions, PU, of the CISL) and at the national industrial level into federations. These are aggregated into one of three major national confederations organized on an ideological-political basis: the Italian General Confederation of Labor (CGIL), the Italian Confederation of Labor Unions (CISL), and the Italian Union of Labor (UIL). Generally speaking, workers of a Marxist orientation tend to gravitate to the CGIL; of a Catholic outlook, to the CISL; of a Social Democratic and Republican persuasion, to the UIL. Each confederation has been associated with specific political groupings. The Communists and (Nenni) Socialists are likely to favor the CGIL; the Christian Democrats, the CISL; and the Social Democrats, right-wing Socialists, and Republicans, the UIL. There is also a small rightist labor organization called the Italian Confederation of National Unions of Workers (CISNAL), which claims members among the rightist party members. There are several autonomous national unions, particularly among the civil service, management employees, and teachers. The inflated membership claims of the unions in 1958 were 8 million persons: CGIL, 3.7 million; CISL, 2.3 million; and

UIL, 1.1 million. However, many members did not pay dues or contributed only intermittently. Dues were collected through volunteers.

From the earliest days of the Italian trade union movement, the territorial organizations of unions, chambers of labor, or their equivalent have competed with the national category federations for influence on policy within the national confederations. Usually the former represented the more significant force because of their local ideological cohesiveness and identity with specific leadership. It was not unusual for local splinter groups to transfer from one confederation to another. Unions after the war were also substantially financed by political parties or other outside organizations. CGIL leaders were often assigned to the trade union movement by the political parties, with individuals shifting from political to trade union operations or the reverse as the party decisions dictated. Close ties made the unions responsive to political influences although their own financial resources also supported some of their activity.

There was a considerable disposition and frequent use of trade union mass power for individual party purposes either to support the policies of their favored political parties or governments or to embarrass their opponents. Economic and union issues were invariably subordinated to political goals. When revolutionary anticapitalist leftist groups and philosophies gained the upper hand over moderates and reformists in the union leadership, the number and scope of industrial stoppages increased.

## Employers and Associations

Small, medium, and large employers tended to follow paternalistic-autocratic personnel policies because of the traditional nepotistic rural life, the desire to repel or isolate efforts at unionizing the work force, and the unfamiliarity with modern personnel attitudes, procedures, and techniques. Relatively low wages and labor costs, an abundant supply of labor, and in the 1950s, profitable operations favored these approaches. Not only did employers resist unions and collective bargaining but when possible they employed vigorous repressive measures to eliminate people carrying on the organizing work and providing worker leadership. FIAT's antiunion activities were particularly notorious.

Industry employer associations and later, particularly beginning with the fascist period, a national all-industry association, Confindustria (General Confederation of Italian Industry) far removed from the work place, negotiated occasional agreements. The resulting contracts remained skeletal in character relating primarily to wages and hours, setting minimum standards attuned to economic capacities of the smaller firms. Larger and more efficient firms could then grant more generous terms of employment in accordance with their own paternalistic formulas. Moreover, they created a veritable array of fringe benefits to be disbursed regularly or capriciously and in a discriminating manner, favoring preferred groups. In the postwar years, the all-industry Interconfederal (three trade union confederations) agreements with Confindustria broadened the issues covered by agreements to include the organization of the internal commissions (CI: Internal Commissions, Works Councils), regional wage differentials, mass layoffs, dismissals, equal pay for equal work, and cost-of-living escalators. These provisions applied to all Italian employees and industries.

## Collective Bargaining

Employers resisted plant-level collective bargaining, and the unions only began in 1953 to press for plant agreements at the initiation of the CISI and only later to be followed by the CGIL. Plant contracts during this period constituted supplements to the national category agreements and could deal with specifically designated issues (wages, incentive schemes, and job evaluation). Regional union federations negotiated these agreements without active participation of the local membership.

The CIs (Internal Commissions), which originated in 1919 in response to the then current move for greater worker participation in plant operation, were reconstituted in the postwar years. The CISL and UIL, however, looked suspiciously upon the CI because of its domination by the CGIL. Employers limited the CIs' consultative powers; or at best, the CIs became grievance agents or administrators of social services in the plant with limited powers and rights. While the rights of employees to organize and bargain were granted in the 1948 Constitution, no special administrative process existed to pass on complaints of discrimination or repression, and so both flourished. Union staffs rarely visited the plants to deal with internal worker problems and had little contact with management respecting shop-level issues.

The national agreements in the 1950s provided for minimal wage increases and economic improvements. Union economic power was low despite the unions' high membership claims. Division among the unions, high unemployment, and the influx of large numbers of rural workers securing their first opportunities in industrial employment with little knowledge about unions or grievance-handling limited organizational growth. Employers took advantage of the situation to foster further interunion division and competition and to divert the bargaining procedure away from their own plants.

## STIMULI FOR NEW SOCIAL UNREST
## AND EMPLOYEE MILITANCY

The "Economic Miracle" and Subsequent Economic
Changes and Problems (The Dual Economy)

Italy responded to the new opportunities provided by European
economic reconstruction with an export-led expansion. The Italian
"economic miracle" (1959-62) emerged with an annual increase in
GNP of approximately 7 percent, and unemployment fell in 1963 to
the 504,000 level, or 2.5 percent of the labor force. Then followed
a decade of growth in some sectors accompanied by setbacks in
others. Dislocations became common, changes more disturbing, and
international competition keener. Finally, price increases ran very
high, stimulating economic and social disturbances.

The relatively overall stable rate of growth in the 1950s was
followed during the 1960s and 1970s by a decided cyclical pattern of
economic development, bringing a real recession in 1964-65, and
slowdowns in 1968 and 1971-72 and the first half of 1973, when the
rate of economic growth dropped to a postwar low. Unemployment
rose and dropped as these economic gyrations produced successive
displacements and later rehiring programs. The government followed stop-and-go economic policies to effect stability, manipulating
both fiscal (including economic development) and monetary policies.

With local and total employment opportunities still inadequate
during the entire period to absorb the hundreds of thousands lured from
rural areas, Italians continued their high rate of mobility with about
one-third of the migrants becoming emigrants, particularly to the
Northern European countries. The numbers rose as employment opportunities increased in these immigration countries. The average net
loss to the country from emigration in 1967-68 was 127,500 and for the
1960s was 1.2 million, consisting largely of young adults of working age
and predominantly male. In periods of peak domestic demand Northern Italian employers advertised for these people to return despite
the supply of rural manpower because of the disadvantages of employing and inducing them to move, particularly to the large northern
industrial communities. (The level of unemployment is presumably
higher than officially reported as participation rates among adults
of working age, 15-60, continue to decline and underemployment is
widespread.)

Economic development is not uniform throughout Italy. The
rate of economic growth in the South (Mezzogiorno) remains considerably below that of the North. The net population growth during the
1960s in the South was only 1.2 percent because of outmigration in
comparison to a national rate of 6.7 percent. The national govern-

ment continues to make large-scale investments in the region, through public corporations and incentives offered to the private sector, but the region has not reached a level of activity that would produce spontaneous growth.

Italy is particularly plagued by economic dualism. There are declining sectors such as agriculture, which witnessed a shrinkage of its share of the labor force from 48 percent in 1950 to 17 percent in 1971. Nonetheless, farm units remain small, making real modernization difficult. About one-third of the work force consists of family workers and the self-employed. The average plant according to the 1971 census consisted of eight employees. In some industrial divisions, very small and medium-sized owner-operated units predominate. In the same "backward" categories, one could place many public services that are underfinanced and the inadequate managerial leadership for achieving the desired level of efficiency and technical competency. Employees in these areas resist change while they are agitating and striking for reform and modernization.

On the other hand, there are many large advanced capital-intensive industries led by both private interests and publicly financed and controlled corporations, such as the Institute for Industrial Reconstruction (IRI) and the state-owned Oil and Energy Corporations (ENI). These tend to be concentrated in the newer growth industries, though some such subsectors recently suffered striking reverses. In 1971, public enterprises employed 1 million persons with six companies among them having over 20,000 employees and 56 percent of the total employment. An increasing number of companies are now owned by foreign interests, particularly American, British, and West German. The government watches over mergers and foreign takeover moves to avoid departures from national economic growth plans, particularly in the chemical industry, and prevent excessive foreign control of significant industries where outside know-how is not essential. The domestic economic and financial giants, usually assuming the form of conglomerates, have grown strikingly, extending themselves to diverse interests including ownership of newspapers and generally have holdings in foreign countries. The greatest of these giants, the FIAT and Angelli interests, employ 200,000 persons in the Italian automobile industry.

These major structural differences became particularly aggravating in recent years as the bloom has fallen off the growth process. International competition has become keen, and the economic toll has been heavy for an export-oriented country like Italy. Small and medium-sized as well as some large plants and companies began to feel the cost pinch and rationalized their use of equipment and manpower and initiated new product designs. In this move, the educated professional management came into its own, often replacing older types of operators. But even where these steps were taken, they were often not sufficient. Plants began operating on a part-time basis and closing; some went bankrupt. Foreign interests and a new government corporation, Industrial Participation and Management Company (GEPI), took over some. The fatalities and contraction in personnel sent, and are continuing to send, tremors through the work population.

For many years, the surplus accrued from exports, the large emigrant remittances, and tourism helped build a healthy surplus in foreign exchange, but recently these have proved insufficient. Italy had to resort to costly large-scale foreign loans to boost the country's foreign exchange reserves, even before the oil price crunch. Also, some Italians have moved their capital to Switzerland and other foreign countries, forcing a shift in attention among the government's economic policy-makers and experts to monetary and balance-of-payment problems and restrictive policies. With the rising deficit from oil imports the imbalances in international payment have grown. Italy was the first industrialized country to borrow from the IMF oil facility fund to help cover the oil deficit. But it continued to rely for its major loans on other EEC countries. These countries have exacted government promises to restrain expenditures and increase public revenues.

### The Dual Social Organization

Economic dualism is matched by social dualism. Economic growth brought many improvements in the standard of life and prosperity to many Italians, but large numbers were left behind, with millions keenly sensing the great gap between themselves and the sharers of the new wealth. The luxurious living of the elite and recurrent stories of scandals and tax-dodging aggravate the feelings of injustice.

Per capita aggregate income rose during the decade but the poor continue to represent a substantial proportion of the population. Evidences of the prosperity abound. In 1971 there were 171 telephones, 187 passenger cars, 181 television sets per 1,000 inhabitants, and average protein consumption per inhabitant per day was 43 grams, placing Italy closer to northern European standards than ever before. The weekend is a pleasure now enjoyed by millions of city dwellers. But unemployment and underemployment are common both in urban and rural regions. In the second quarter of 1973 the official count of unemployment again reached 818,000 persons (seasonally adjusted); it declined thereafter in 1973 but moved up in 1974.

The contrasts are sharply projected, particularly in the large industrial cities experiencing phenomenal growth. In the last decade, the population of Rome expanded by 65 percent, Turin by 63 percent, and Milan by 18 percent. But the expansion of services has not matched this population increase. People came from the South and rural areas to find jobs; while many got them, they found little else. Housing is deficient or unavailable; schools are overcrowded as they seek to meet the demands of the growing child population; the appetite for secondary and university education grew, but the number of schools and teachers did not; transportation is limited and cannot adequately serve the commuter, necessitating long, exhausting rides; health-care facilities and personnel are insufficient and overburdened. The migrants, finding that the established population had easier access to these services, regard the differences as personal affronts, evoking angry protests, which are at times converted into violence.

Migrants and residents without jobs or those that had lost them during the last few years had an additional source of disgruntlement. Declining economic areas have become concentrations of disillusionment. The public employment services (a monopoly) are numerous (7,500 offices), but they are small and inefficient. They serve political clients rather than the total labor market. Part-time and temporary labor markets remain unserved. Funds for and access to training and retraining agencies to help people adapt to change are too limited to make a dent upon the scene. To all of these frustrations must be added the current annual rise in the cost of living, over 20 percent, which exceeds the rate of most European countries.

### Political and Administrative Strangulation of Change

The "opening to the left" in 1962 with the Socialists' (PSI) acceptance of a Christian Democratic cabinet committed to social reform and then its participation in the four-party center-left cabinet (1963) was to initiate an era of great social reform. The left-wing groups of the Christian Democratic Party (DC), the reigning party in postwar political life with which the CIS leaders tended to be associated, hoped this addition would override opposition to reform in parliament and initiate the needed bureaucratic reforms to energize the government structures. These changes were to shift the former concern for economic growth to the modernization of the social infrastructure and services. This center-left coalition in different combinations has prevailed for the whole decade except for short periods in 1968 and 1972-73, when center and center-right cabinets took over. Stop-gap cabinets ("beach governments") are organized to govern while interparty negotiations seek to produce agreements on programs

But this coalition has not met the people's and the parties' expectations. Reforms of the scope and the volume desired were not forthcoming. The opposing economic, political, and social interests strangled these efforts and buried the projects. Communist opposition added to the difficulties of the center-left coalitions, but it was not strong enough to overwhelm the coalition. The Christian Democratic Party leadership could not discipline its parliamentary following. Feuds, scandals, and personal vendettas complicated the course. The "fragile state" was the result.

The major social reforms of the entire 10-year period included legislation on elimination of share-cropping (1965), school construction (1967), improvements in social security (1968), regional decentralization (1968), divorce (1970), the workers' charter (1970), and housing (1971).

Political frustration and disappointment and decreasing faith in the political process became evident. Individual employers who offered some services found their benefits grudgingly accepted as carrying the stamp of paternalism. People continued to expect the government to serve them, as many political parties preached.

Where the parliament did act, there was no assurance that the plans would be implemented. Billions of dollars (11,000 billion lire) of appropriations remained frozen, for the bureaucracy failed to push the projects into reality. The minilaws passed by parliament to regulate the operation of the system also complicated the administrative process. Some 50,000 public agencies with officials and employees earning distinctly better than prevailing pay rates cause overlaps of functions, increase cost, and complicate the maze. The system is rigid and unresponsive. Inertia, bureaucratic resistance to change, the lack of a government will to tackle the civil service and agencies and the resistance of vested interests hold back the effective operation of the governmental machinery.


## Work Place: Focus of Unrest

Both external and job discontents have combined in Italy to use trade unions as the instrument and collective bargaining as the process for effecting improvements and changes both in the work place and the community.

Few studies are available that probe the industrial relations scene in depth. Observations of meetings, strikes, and demonstrations and conversations with workers in other connections provide clues to the issues to which they respond and the areas in which they seek remedies. These the author and associates have examined.[1] Two themes of recent labor dissatisfaction are egalitarianism and the degree of satisfaction with the work place, organization, and job demands. Among the prominent issues are excessive demands

of work, often described in the rhetoric of controversy as dehumaniz-
ing, "sweatshops," undue speed of the assembly line, hazardous and
unhealthy conditions or surroundings, rigid work schedules, frac-
tionation of work duties, unusual skill requirements, undue compulsory overtime, or inappropriate work schedules. Demands are made
for workers' control and participation in decision-making on these
matters and for union time-study specialists to protect the employees
against abuse by these systems, and, in some cases, outright abolition of incentive systems is demanded.

Employees are aware that, within the shop, absolute fatigue or
work-load schedules cannot be precisely measured. When economic
conditions are unfavorable, they are likely to yield on standards to
preserve employment; on the other hand, when labor demand is high,
they may exact a better bargain.

Again, as regards technical change, an employee is likely to
be alert to progressive minute changes in job designs and demands as
well as major technical innovations that alter the nature of the job.
He fears for his security, earnings, status, opportunities, and work
assignment and load. Where jobs raise the skill and training requirements, he is keen to know whether he can meet them and fulfill
the requirements of the training program, for his limited schooling
will usually make such new learning difficult.

The employee is aware that paternalistic personnel relations
make him dependent upon the management, with few avenues of redress. Moreover, management has employed benefits and its power
to discourage, if not repress, unionization. The CIs were tolerated,
but unions were discouraged and fought. Discrimination and caprice
were widespread, and wide differences in benefits existed.

Employees experience a whole host of conditions causing frustration, uncertainty, and fears within the work place. Behind these
lurked the unending realization of the insufficiencies of income and
suspicions about the inequity of the divisions of the enterprise's
income.


## New Intellectual Influences and Employee Aspirations

The above complaints and the resulting unrest provoked considerable frustration among the mass of employees in industrial centers
as well as in the rural population. The disgruntlement obtained direction and the new aspirations gained specific meaning from the
prevailing public debates, the goals popularized by the media, the
assurances of rights pronounced by the regular political debates, and
the rhetoric and philosophical outlook promoted by the radical leftist
and trade union movements.

Leftist political groups were particularly influential in penetrating workers' ranks and establishing footholds in joint shop committees. They started from a position to the left of the Italian Communist Party (PCI), which they characterized as a reformist party. They called authority into question, protested repression, and supported the workers' claims to decide their own fate. They preached a new anticapitalism and a humanistic socialism. The work place and society had to be humanized. Affluence was not enough; anticapitalistic action was essential. Mere higher global production was not enough if the output didn't satisfy the criteria of distributive justice. The Mezzogiorno had to be developed, and the "new model of economic development" had to replace the old one. The new truly desirable society was to be built on the essential goodness of man and his basic disposition to voluntary cooperation.

Change was to be achieved through mass action. The institutions of the new society would arise from the ongoing struggles of shop delegate (steward) councils for egalitarianism through the elimination of all occupational status, wage, salary, and benefit differentials and through workers' control of shop conditions. In the community, neighborhood councils would support the forceful occupation of vacant housing by the homeless and make demands for more schooling and medical care and other services. Youth would gain its rightful equal place and be assured the educational benefits it had been promised. Resistance from vested interests would be met by demonstrations and strikes and even violence, with some groups urging worker operation of plants. Collective bargaining agreements would not have clauses providing for the maintenance of industrial peace but would be open-ended and call for continuous bargaining, permitting workers at all times to ask for changes and call strikes to achieve them.

The more important groups of the new left were the Manifesto (splinter groups of the PCI), Potere Operaio (Workers' Power), Lotta Continua (Continuous Struggle), and the Moviemento Studentesco, which concentrated on organizing university and high school students. They succeeded in winning some support among workers. But their major role was to assert themselves in places where unrest existed and to offer some direction to the protests.

This need for change was supported by the new spirit of inquiry ushered in by the Second Vatican Council of the Catholic Church (1962). It altered existing concepts of authority and allowed for greater decentralization of church power by endowing the national churches with new rights of self-government and assigning greater participatory privileges to the laity. The new emphasis was on basic spiritual values rather than the ecclesiastical structure. Following these innovations, there began a general reassessment of doctrine and dogma as well as of organizations, which brought all phases of the church into question. Catholics in many walks of life, including trade unionists, reexamined the existing value system and their relations with the church and church-sponsored organizations. The views of the Frankfurt School of Critical Theory respecting both capitalism and socialism provided points of departure for the thinking of many groups in the CISL.[2]

## UNREST, PROTEST, AND INDUSTRIAL CONFLICT

The above irritations, the frustrations impelled by the new aspirations, and the confidence in rights generated by the ongoing discussions became the foundation for 1967's intense industrial unrest and conflicts. Wildcats, "hiccough," and general strikes were part of the underlying scene of the 1950s, but their volume and intensity were moderate in comparison with later developments.

The strike peak occurred during the "hot autumn" of 1969 in connection with the negotiations of the metal agreement. The volume of economic and political strikes thereafter declined due to the slowing of the economy, the disposition toward greater realism on the part of the leaders of the trade union movement, and their deliberate decisions to employ strikes primarily to support demands in connection with contract renegotiations, which usually now occur at three-year intervals. This restraint is in part also explained by the provisions in the agreements for recurrent automatic wage adjustments to cost-of-living changes. As a consequence, strikes in 1970-71 even at the plant level were primarily associated with contract negotiations. The peaks in stoppages occurred in 1962-63, 1964-65, 1969-72, and 1973, when contracts expired.

Strikes continue to be employed to force settlements of complaints, grievances, and demands within a plant. Other forms of industrial action are also applied, including work according to rules, slowing-up of output, reduction or prohibition of overtime, boycotts, and stoppages of truck movements and ingress into the plants of executive and clerical staff. But greater use has been made since 1971 of less disruptive collective bargaining techniques to resolve differences without stoppages or to cut them short. Work stoppages for job-related complaints increased from 21 million man-hours lost in 1968 to 35 million in 1971 and 23 million man-hours in 1972. The proportion of job-related complaints to all stoppages varied as follows: 29 percent in 1968; 7 percent in 1969; 21 percent in 1970; 34 percent in 1971; and 17 percent in 1972.

Much of the strike action of 1968-69 was "spontaneous." It spread rapidly throughout industry. But in subsequent years, the trade unions increasingly sought to avoid all-out strikes. Instead, they staggered them to produce the maximum economic impact on employers with the least adverse economic effects on workers and the least cost to their union treasuries. Strikes became shorter and were spread over a period of time (for example, 20 hours over a three-week period) or were restricted to selected companies or individual plants. The local plant committees scheduled and conducted the strikes within their own operations. Trade unions sought to conduct orderly and disciplined stoppages. And, after 1969, they organized themselves effectively to exclude student and external political groups from participation in strikes and at a minimum to prevent them from taking over the leadership. Among the new strike techniques was the coordination of industrial action directed against multiplant companies including multinational ones, such as the Dunlop-Pirelli chain, including the British plants and Montedison, particularly in the case of plant closings.

The political strike or demonstration became a generally accepted procedure in the era of coordinated action of the three confederations. But unlike previous political protests called for doctrinaire causes, the recent ones are directed specifically at legislative goals seeking to persuade the government to secure parliamentary action on needed or promised social reforms or to implement programs where policies had been approved by either parliament or the government or both or to express disapproval of government policies, as in the case of the 1974 deflationary program. This program dates back to the joint action in 1968 to promote reforms of the pension system. These political strikes as well as some industrial ones frequently are accompanied by demonstrations and huge processions in the centers of the communities to dramatize the protests. The gatherings at the central points often attract hundreds of thousands of people and provide a means of rallying public support to the union cause.

During the last few years, extreme rightists employed or provoked violence and street fights and used bombs in order to intensify the unrest or confusion. But the established trade union organizations rejected violence and at times countered these groups. The more violent outbreaks found a ready following among the youthful male migrant workers living in the overcrowded northern cities, often unemployed or disgruntled with the treatment they received and disposed by their rural background to participate in such brawls.

The high absentee rates experienced in Italian industrial plants reflect this same unrest. A study for the years 1967-71 indicates that absentee rates in northern plants run about 4 percent over the year and may rise to 20 percent at the beginning and end of the week. They tend to be a larger source of lost time than strikes, as indicated by the fact that the latter represent the following percentages of the total absences: 1967: 3.8; 1968: 4.9; 1969: 22.7; 1970: 8.4; and 1971: 4.4.

Migration is at times called "strikes by the feet"; its magnitude provides another measure of unrest. Since the end of the war the number moving from the South is set at 6 million and during the 1960s at 2.5 million, with a considerable proportion transferring either temporarily or permanently to foreign parts, particularly Northern Europe.

Employers during recent years also constantly refer to a decline in man-hour productivity. Unlike previous years, when the increase in the Italian rate of man-hour output exceeded that of other European countries, it has been on the low side from 1969 onward. Widespread student, intellectual, and journalist support for radical anticapitalistic movements is another index of fundamental unrest.

The country has been teeming with people seeking change and those who look for improvements and redemption of their expectations. Countering them are the vested interests with their great economic and political power, the conservatives, some right-wing church groups, and others who resist change. Open clashes are common between and among these groups. Collisions such as occur in the church between the conservatives and reformers and in political and intellectual life are everywhere in evidence in this country. But industrial action remains among the dramatic central forms of protest and is regularly reported by the media.


## CHANGES IN THE EMPLOYEE AND EMPLOYER INSTITUTIONS, PHILOSOPHIES, AND COLLECTIVE BARGAINING

### Trade Unions: Revitalized Spokesmen for Employees as Producers and Citizens

#### Older Trade Union System Dysfunctional

These external changes and the new worker outlook have called for major alterations in the structure, functions, and philosophy of the trade union. Workers demanded an institution responsive to their expectations for achieving gains and rights within the plant and in their community. Therefore, the old system, which stressed national, centralized, all-industry, or category agreements on minimum terms of employment and allowed only for supplementary plant contracts negotiated by the trade union official had to be supplanted. Workers had come to expect to be intimately involved in every phase of the union's operations and their representation. The belief took hold that employee organizations should not be subverted for partisan political purposes and competition, as had been true in the past; leaders had to separate themselves from their political parties and give up elected public office and acquire real expertise in bargaining respecting matters directly affecting the worker. Internecine political conflict had to give way to unified political action to advance worker interests. Fundamentally, unions had to be close to and directly relate with the people.

These new attitudes demanded fundamental changes. Some were to come from the adaptation of the trade union leadership to the new spontaneous developments; others were to follow from the new doctrines promulgated by workers and radical leftist groups through the "delegate movement"; and still others were to spring from the trade union's desire to maintain its preeminent position as spokesmen for employees as producers and citizens, and much progress has occurred in these areas.

Structure

The trade union membership under the impetus of the new militancy generated since 1968 grew considerably. In 1968, conservative estimates placed the numbers at 4.5 millions. By 1973, the figure stood at 6 million. These included about 40 percent of all employees in industry and about 36 percent of all employees, including those in agriculture, services, public administration, and others.

Among the factors that favored this growth of union membership was the new protection provided, in the national and enterprise collective agreements, (1) of the employee's right to join unions and (2) of the facilities assured unions to collect union dues, particularly through the check-off. Both rights were not confirmed until the parliament in 1970 adopted the "workers' charter." The sums collected in the shops are divided among the respective National Industrial Unions or Federations (NF) in accordance with agreements reached among the local plant union leaders. The total income is estimated at about $60 million per year (on an average), on the assumption of annual per capita dues of $10 to $12. With these increased financial resources, unions have become relatively independent of outside funding sources and now conduct aggressive recruitment programs and actively proselytize the cause of unionism.

Despite very optimistic membership claims, there are probably only slightly more than 5 million dues-paying members. The ranking of the confederations remains practically the same as before, with the CGIL heading the list. But the number and size of the autonomous unions has declined.

Workers responded to the new call for enlistment because of
the new confidence in the organizations as their representatives and
spokesmen.  Moreover, the willingness of the three confederations
to cooperate and coordinate their programs and engage in joint action removed a former deterrent to joining unions.  Employees who
participated actively in official and unofficial strikes or other industrial and political activities or saw their colleagues do so were more
easily persuaded to join.  Moreover, the new benefits were impressive.  Continual consultation of workers through plant assemblies or
meetings in the formulation of demands and in negotiations and ratification proceedings also heightened interest.  Unions acquired the
image among employees of a constructive aggressive force in society
promoting their interests.  Unions in multiplant and multinational
companies sought to coordinate their efforts even across national
lines, thereby creating a new structural level.

One result of this shop-level activity was the growing ascendancy
of the NFs in national confederation deliberations as compared with
the prior preeminence of the regional confederations, Chambers of
Labor (CL) or Provincial Unions (PU).  This ascendancy is in no
small part due to the pace-setting roles the metal and chemical
unions developed through their agreements with such critical companies as FIAT, Montedison, Olivetti, Zanussii, Pirelli, Alfa Romeo,
and the public corporations, the provisions of which became the yard-
sticks for collective agreements for other Italian private and public
enterprises.  Nevertheless, a moderate shift in influence back to the
chambers of labor is now in evidence in areas where militant attitudes prevail.

## Local Shop Leadership:  The Key Group

The most significant change in local union structure has been
the appearance of the shop delegate as a critical force in the union.
Hitherto, shop-level union representatives served as a conveyor
belt, communicating orders from the top and collecting dues and
servicing the members.  Their influence was usually limited.  The
important people at the plant level were members of the Internal
Commission elected by all blue- and white-collar employees.  The
trade unions developed their slates and fought hard for their respective members.  Trends in the proportion of members elected by each
confederation provided an index of its individual rising or declining
influence among employees.  But the CI served primarily as an information, advisory, or administrative agency for social services
and social security benefits; and it was usually not too effective.  (In
1969 CI elections, the vote results were as follows: CGIL: 54 percent; CISL: 36 percent; UIL:  8 percent; and others: 2 percent.)

Since 1968, the shop delegate gained power and displaced the
CI members in importance. The delegate now participates in the
negotiations, representing the rank and file in deciding and then implementing policy and strategy. The outside trade union leadership
keeps in closer touch with and depends on him to protect the confederation's interests within the work place. Because of his critical
role and the easy access the activist leftist political groups have to
him, the shop delegate has become a particular object of attention of
both the trade union leadership and the external radical leaders.

Though the shop delegate became more central in the union
structure, the regional and national trade union leaders assumed an
increasingly more important role as they became more responsive
to workers' needs and aspirations. The external radical groups soon
recognized the real seats of power and increasingly addressed themselves to the leaders to win them over to their views, thereby maintaining the pressure for more militant and aggressive trade union
leadership.

New Types of Demands

The shift of emphasis to specific worker-shop problems and
social reform and away from broad quasilegislative national minimums radically altered the issues of negotiations. They now center
on worker interests in controlling working conditions, overtime,
health hazards, special job problems like the speed of the assembly
line, rest periods, job design, work loads, promotional patterns,
subcontracting of work, job categories, work schedules, hourly
schedules, training, number of holidays and length of vacations,
size of pension benefits, wage incentive, wage and job classifications and bonus plans, time study controls, and uniform benefits for
all classes of employees and internal enterprise issues. Monthly
salary guarantees are now a common goal. Collective agreements
at all levels and the law regulate displacements, severance pay and
unemployment benefits to be paid to the affected, the rights of individuals, and the order of layoffs and rehiring. Concurrently, unions
are seeking to deter changes that spell the elimination of jobs in both
the private and public sectors. A Joint-Labor Management Committee for the metal industries established under the agreement of 1966
was set up to study ways in which to reconcile the conflicting interests of the competitive employer and the worker so as to encourage
investment and minimize the injury done to the worker.

As governmental efforts to promote the economic development
in the South faltered, unions took to the collective bargaining mechanism for making practical gains in this field. In 1974, the demand for
new jobs in the South was strongly pressed in contract negotiations,

producing a guarantee by managements of the leading corporations to
provide more than 80,000 new jobs, most of which are to be located
in southern communities. Unions also developed other new approaches
to job development. They insisted on in some contracts and obtained
guarantees in others for a minimum level of expenditures on research
and development to promote future job opportunities. Assurances
were obtained from some companies not to reduce the number of job
posts. In the same way, unions turned to managements to make investments and finance improvements in local transportation and nursery schools. They also negotiated for a minimum number of paid
hours' educational leave for employees to further their education.
With rising costs of food, many 1974 contracts provide for subsidies
to plant meals to reduce their costs to employees. The Italian trade
union movement is increasingly recognizing the opportunities afforded
by direct bargaining for achieving gains for which in the past they
turned to the government.

(In September 1974, the Turin unions undertook to combat
higher costs and prices and taxes by organizing a campaign to refuse
to pay increased commuter bus fares and electricity bills. In a number of instances, they organized fare collections on buses and paid
only the equivalent of the old fare in a lump sum to the bus companies.
They called on their following to pay only 50 percent of the electricity
bill as a partial payment, with the remainder to be paid when the
unions negotiated a new bus rate schedule.)

The 1974 negotiations produced another significant innovation,
besides opening up the range of union demands and concerns. Trade
union negotiators had carefully formulated their proposals both in
terms of areas for advance and the size of the gain and steadfastly
pressed for them. The final terms closely approximated the federations' demands and reflected their new realism and heightened responsibility.

Not only have the confederations not given up on their expectations of broadening and making more effective the central government's role in improving the social infrastructure and benefits but
they have also assumed the responsibility for more vigorously pressing it to get legislation on social reforms adopted by parliament and
to implement these approved programs. Trade unions have grown
impatient with the center-left governments and their procrastination.
Their members suffered from these failures and therefore the unions
responded often by calling national or regional staggered strikes
(first in 1969 and then in subsequent years) or conducted demonstrations in local areas or in Rome itself to dramatize this attitude.
Joint confederal protests have become a significant form of political
action congenial to the confederations' new view of their functions.

These negotiations and protests relating to reform gained wide public support for the unions even though some conservative groups became alarmed at this interference with the regular legislative process. Much debate developed on whether unions negotiate or merely lobby with the government during these meetings. In any event, most people agreed that the step represented a positive contribution to progress in these fields and helped make democratic institutions work. Much of the advance in housing legislation, particularly for low-income groups, and construction resulted from these interventions. Other areas in which they effectively pressured the government are the taxation of capital gains on land, a national health system with consumer participation, a shift to direct, and away from indirect, taxes and greater reliance on government financial contributions to the social security system rather than levies on employers, improved education, transportation, and development of the South, with the latter becoming a truly central issue. In 1974, they helped persuade the coalitions to relax the credit restraints in the deflationary programs, so as not to be so harsh on smaller enterprises. The trade unions have carefully limited themselves to specifically defined concrete issues involving the social conditions of their following, thereby avoiding sectarian issues and internal divisions.

Unions' Political Autonomy

One consequence of the rising pressure toward plant and worker interests and away from a political ideological orientation is the growing demand for unions to establish complete autonomy from their associated political parties. This is not a new issue. The debate may be traced back to the beginning of the century when trade unions in a number of European countries extracted commitments from their respective national socialist parties to respect their independence and not to interfere with trade union decisions or call political strikes involving trade union membership without consultation. But, in practice, revolutionary Socialists, Syndicalists, Anarchists, and Communists over the years used, whenever possible, the trade unions for the promotion of their political policies and objectives. This was also the case in Italy.

In 1969, the three major confederations reaffirmed the incompatibility of concurrent political and trade union activism. A trade union leader is not to be a member of parliament or communal council or similar body or the executive organs of the parties. The CGIL asked its secretary general to resign his post with the Communist Politburo and his seat in parliament but he resigned his CGIL post, retaining the latter positions. Trade union leaders did resign their parliamentary seats, but it was more difficult to get them to break

with their parties. When the 1972 election was called, the three confederations suspended discussions on unity because of their desire to
help their own respective parties. The Communist leaders of the
CGIL did not withdraw from the deliberative bodies of the PCI (Central Committee); while confederal leaderships are unwilling to take
this final plunge by severing this relationship with their political
partner, organic unity is unlikely. The Spoleto CISL 1972 Convention witnessed a battle on this issue, but the issue remained unresolved.

Trade unions gained special prominence as spokesmen for their
members and low-income groups through their participation in and
testimony before special parliamentary commissions on various subjects of interest to them and their presentations to various social
security and other government agencies on behalf of their members
and their direct meetings with the prime minister and individual ministers in the center-left coalitions in which economic and social policies were reviewed.

A number of trade unionists are at the head or are among the
principal officers of social security or other public agencies, with
the expectation that they will be particularly knowledgeable about,
and responsive to, worker interests. A trade unionist is the head of
INPS, and he had been selected after an agreement by the three confederations.

## Trade Union Unity

The pressures for the unification of the confederations of the
trade union movement are continuing and strong. There is a common awareness that organic integration would provide greater power.
But there lingers the suspicions among the confederations engendered
by the experience immediately after the war, when the CPI took control of the integrated movement that created the CGIL. The result
was the severance of its parts. Since 1969, common programs and
action on the practical workaday level produced great cohesion among
the confederations. But there is no such strong feeling for unity
among workers in the smaller factories, in agriculture, in the social
service sectors, and in the South. The new humanistic philosophy
pervading all ideological groups has cemented the confederations and
federations in their practical work. But progress toward national
unity, as witness the high degree of cooperation in the metal industry,
is inhibited both by the reluctance of confederations to adhere closely
to the pledge of political autonomy and the insistence of some national
unions like the metal workers upon organic integration of the diverse
local unions at the shop level through the councils of delegates as an
initial step to the consolidation of the national confederations.

In July 1972, the confederations agreed on a federation of the
three confederations, but steps to this end continue to be most halt-
ing. Both the CISL and UIL fear that a merger would spell CGIL
control and dominance by the communists. Nevertheless, cooperation among the competing confederations has markedly increased,
and they have acted together on the major issues and programs. The
leadership of each group has respected the others' sensitivities.
Compromises have been reached to maintain agreements and unified
action. One illustration of the new relationship is provided by the
support by the CISL and UIL for the CGIL's candidacy for membership in the European Trade Union Confederation (ETUC), which was
confirmed over the opposition of a number of other national federations particularly the French Force Ouvrière (FO).

## Attitudes to the Peace Pledge
and Worker Militancy

The confusion in values produced by recent developments is
exhibited in the attitudes toward the pledge for labor peace and existing contracts and the attitudes toward wildcats, violence, and disturbances within the plants and public employee strikes on behalf of
parliamentary policy and administrative reform. On the one hand,
the trade union movement adopted the position implied by plant action that there is no peace pledge inherent in the agreements at any
level. Nor is there a restriction on areas of bargaining implicit in
national agreements. The collective bargain must remain open, and
"continuous bargaining" must be the practice. Workers with complaints or new aspirations should be able to raise them at all times
and take industrial action to achieve their remedies or gains. The
CGIL moved considerably away from its prior position in which it
rejected contractual relations at all levels toward one in which it
pragmatically accepted these relations. The CISL advanced from
its collaborative position to a more anticapitalistic or adversary relationship with management and is ready to accept the bargaining
process as a continuing ongoing relationship. In neither organization is there a crystal-clear definition of attitudes, but pragmatically on a day-to-day basis they behave alike.

The Italian confederations do not now look to legislation for
initiating social advance. Particularly since 1964, they stress the
critical position of the collective agreement. Using the model of
the process of the adoption of the 1970 Workers' Charter, they prefer
to achieve their gains through industrial action and then have the
benefits blanketed by legislation on all parts of the economy.

But all trade unions are apprehensive of the disruptive effects
of sporadic and wildcat strikes or violence and have disowned these.

They not only disturb the ongoing productive process but also constitute a threat to the organization. The secretary general of the CGIL
has said that "a factory which has closed down is not a socialist factory; it is a closed factory." More effort is now being made to intercede in plant disputes to get them resolved to minimize the possibilities of wildcats and promote more rational solutions. The trade
union spokesmen disapproved of the strikes by the autonomous civil
service unions for failing to clear their action with the big confederations. Violence provoked by the extremists on the left and right are
both being increasingly condemned. Nevertheless, all such statements are cautiously phrased. What is difficult to appraise is the
degree of opportunism inherent in these positions and the likelihood
of the competitive confederations resorting to these tactics if they
consider them essential.

The same pragmatic attitude is also visible respecting governmental mediation in negotiations and strikes. Italy has no formal
system of governmental conciliation. But the minister of labor is
the guardian of the industrial relations situation and frequently, particularly in 1969 and subsequently, interceded in negotiations to facilitate the reaching of an agreement. His sympathy for union positions
has been so marked that employers charge him with dictating the
agreement's terms and employing his pressure on the Public Corporations Collective Bargaining Association (Intersind) to reach agreements that set the pace for the private sector.

But unions remain ambivalent on the government's presence.
They are quite appreciative on the one hand of its good offices in effecting the positive gains and are aware that such services are essential to collective bargaining. On the other hand, they prefer to
stress the critical importance of industrial action in effecting changes
and securing gains and concede only begrudgingly the relevance of a
conciliation process.

## Evolving Policies

The trade unions are evolving new programs and tactics for
older and new problems. As for southern development, some federations have sought in their negotiations to limit the amount of overtime and number of shifts to encourage development and prove their
concern for this region, partly to thwart neofascist progress there.
As for technological change, they are aware of the paradox between
protection for workers and the need for technical innovation and
change and have accepted operative arrangements. All unions have
been opposed to incomes policy. The CISL in the period from 1953-65
advocated the adjustment of wages to the productivity of the individual
firm rather than the total economy to secure special gains from the

more productive companies. The CGIL was even against the latter, and the UIL never adopted any policy. Since 1968, no confederation has espoused a formal incomes policy. But the 1974 agreement provided for small general increases and stressed fringe benefits and the financing of services and various schemes for promoting job expansion. At the shop level, the pressure continues for wage and other direct benefits.

Trade unions are seeking methods of dealing with multinational corporations, which until recently had occupied no significant position in the Italian economy but now are growing in number and importance. The trade unions are therefore keenly following and participating in the European trade union discussions on methods of dealing with these business units.

General Notes

The Italian confederations in the light of the new bargaining are evolving new policies, seeking pragmatically to shape a new flexible industrial relations system and create the force that will not only win direct economic gains but also force social reforms and greater democratization. Their strength is built on an awakened aggressive militant shop leadership, but they are concurrently leaning toward an integrated stable collective bargaining system that maintains local worker participation, stable contractual relations, and quasi-legislative powers to deal with the many practical, broad, and political problems of a changing economy and society. All of these moves are being made in an environment favorable to the ultimate merger of the confederations, but suspicion is strong and the basic political affiliates are squeamish about accepting the severance.

Employers and Employer Associations

The Modern Firm and Management
Gaining Broader Hold in the Economy

The economic and political developments that impacted upon workers and trade unions are also being felt within management circles. And the latter, as indicated, are in themselves generating new forces for change. The older, small or large, paternalistically operated family business enterprise permeated with secrecy and nepotism is giving way to a modern organization guided by professionally trained persons.

The transition has been slow because a new generation of middle and senior management had to be trained, and resistance to

its entrance is strong.  Both business successes and failures accelerated this process.  The public holding corporations are supporting
extensive management education either within their own organizations
or within special organizations such as the Institute of Management
Studies (IFAP).  The introduction of personnel management and the
events of recent years also impressed the top management with the
need for specialized personnel and industrial relations policies and
for dealing professionally with the individual employees and the
trade unions in collective bargaining.

One indication of the new trends is that companies are initiating
experiments with methods of humanizing their work processes.  FIAT
reconstructed one assembly line to overcome the deadening effect of
the routine, and plans for its extension have been announced.  A flexible work schedule is being tried out with a group of white-collar employees.  Finsider and Olivetti have done similarly and are trying
out job-enrichment programs.  Job training is being conducted by
companies to facilitate promotion and to increase their supply of
skilled workers.

## New Employer Bargaining Mechanisms

At the collective bargaining level employers are also changing
their institutions.  The Confindustria reorganized itself in 1970 with
the appointment of a new general manager and new policies.  The
power and conservative attitudes of the small and medium-sized
plants were replaced by more progressive groups and approaches.
In 1974, following considerable internal debate, the chairman of
FIAT, Giovanni Agnelli, was elected president, in order to provide
a prestigious leader and to press more strongly the position of the
private sector before the government and the trade unions.  Besides
becoming more receptive to reforms of company law and favoring a
law for the introduction of mutual funds, Confindustria now supported
the organization of category associations to take over the bargaining
for its respective national and regional agreements with the trade
unions.

The organization is not opposed to decentralized bargaining but
has argued strongly for articulated bargaining among the separate
levels, with their jurisdictions appropriately defined and terms of
reference prescribed for each level.  It has been quite insistent upon
the establishing of and obtaining compliance with a "peace obligation"
to eliminate wildcats and funnel disputes through the prescribed
channels.  The present state of competition among the confederations
and the high tensions it produces (resulting in great power being concentrated in the hands of delegates, turnover of representatives, and
avoidance of agreement procedures) are considered unfavorable for

the development of Italian enterprise. Confindustria hopes for more coordination among the unions, particularly at the enterprise level.

The public corporations in 1960 established Intersind as their collective bargaining spokesman since the law of 1956 forbade them to join associations of private employers. Intersind consists principally of large companies employing more than a half million employees, which are generally run by trained professional personnel who favor modern management techniques. Intersind, being the spokesman of governmentally controlled corporations, is most responsive to political pressures. Its agreements with the confederations have set the norm for such important innovations in collective bargaining as the supplemental plant agreement in 1962, the formulation of the new pattern of agreements, and the national minimum wage in 1968, which were later followed by private industry.

## Collective Bargaining

The nature, process, and scope of collective bargaining are undergoing radical changes. The most significant one has been the decentralization of the negotiations and consummation of local company agreements. The articulated system of contracts worked out in 1962-63 remains in many industries in form but not in effect. Local company agreements are quite independent and not restricted by prior national or regional contracts. Terms of agreement therefore vary widely. Local union shop committees at times deal spontaneously and independently with their own problems and demands, though this freedom is being narrowed. But there is a tendency for the national category agreements to regain importance for specific purposes. They are recognized as being particularly important as setting norms for less well organized employees and weaker units. Innovations in the specific plant are universalized through these instruments.

The local union plant committee, comprising the shop representatives of the three major unions through which the employees are able to conduct their union affairs, has become the crucial unit in negotiations and contract administration. It helps define demands and determine strategy and tactics, keeps in touch both with local and national negotiations, and provides the mechanism for the ultimate review and ratification of the agreement by the people. The creation of this vital group and its practical relations to the work floor has forced the broadening of bargaining issues. The spirit in which the agreements are administered is that of continuous bargaining. Local unions feel free to raise issues and negotiate changes and introduce innovations to meet new problems. The presence of these

committees and the growing sense of responsibility for plant operations particularly during the last several years of slackness produced
a keener interest in finding immediate local solutions for complaints
to reduce the volume of unrest and the disturbances in the plants.
The CI shrank in importance and became subordinate to these committees and restricted in other cases to the administration of social
services and facilities.

Topping the present system of bargaining is the process of
political negotiations with the government respecting actual social
reforms, which often impinge on the terms of the collective agreements as in the case of the understanding that employers be relieved
of substantial social security costs and that they be public costs.


## Government

The government has played an aloof role in the nation's industrial relations system and in the decisions on terms of employment.
The 1948 constitution spells out the right to form unions and to strike.
Except for the "workers' charter" adopted in 1970, little significant
industrial relations legislation exists to implement this protection.
And this act reflects the gains obtained during the 1969 flurry of
strikes. The courts do play a role in the adjudication of problems
arising respecting dismissals for just cause. But the trade unions
continue to resist efforts for more detailed legislation, for they foresee it as being restrictive in effect rather than extending their power,
which had grown in recent years. Trade unions acknowledge the usefulness of occasional intervention of public conciliators but don't want
this step to diminish the importance of their own economic action.

The role of the government in the economy is openly acknowledged by all groups including the Confindustria. Economic planning
as a concept is accepted, but specific applications do lead to conflicts, as in the case of the recent battle over control of Montedison
Corporation, resulting in part from the determination of the public
economic policy agency to restructure the nation's chemical industry.
The public sector and publicly controlled holding companies represent an unusually high portion of the total economy including--as they
did in 1971--12.5 percent of the nation's employment concentrated
substantially in the manufacturing, transport, communication, electric, gas and water, and metallurgical industries.

The nation is burdened by an outmoded, inefficient, and paro-
chial public administration system and is almost paralyzed by its
political system. Hitherto, it could not look hopefully to government
as the channel for significant leadership in reconstruction and stimulus. The parties to the collective bargaining process--except for

tactical purposes such as the employers' desire for legislative action on the forms and procedures of collective bargaining and enforcing a code of rights and obligations upon trade unions and the unions' demands for social reforms--look to themselves to find solutions to the problems in their relations.

## ADVANCES IN WORKERS' WAGES, BENEFITS, AND WORKING CONDITIONS

The increased worker organization and militancy and the aggressive pursuit of specific improvements in wages, working conditions, and participatory rights in decision-making on matters directly affecting workers brought vast changes in the position of the Italian worker. Wages, rates, and earnings rose decidedly. A comparison between the rate of increase in median gross hourly earnings for industrial workers between 1958 and 1972 among the Common Market countries shows that, in current prices, the rise was 273 percent, exceeded only slightly by the Netherlands and in real terms, 121 percent, far in excess of that of other countries in the EEC. During the same period the labor cost per hour worked in Italy soared by 312 percent and from 1960 to 1972 by 69 percent, reflecting the expansion of public and private benefits, in addition to direct wage increases. Another measure of the improvement is that the labor costs per hour worked in Italy in 1958 were 58 percent of the average of the EEC country with the highest average. The same ratio for 1969 was 75 percent and 78 percent in 1972. By 1974, collective agreements prescribe a standard work week of 40 hours, 18 public holidays, and 20 days of paid vacation.

The collective agreements brought many other benefits including joint decision-making on wages, work assignments, working conditions and incentive plans, the reduction in the number of wage grades and the greater equalization of wages for white- and blue-collar employees and men and women, more automatic advancement in the lower steps, control of working time and night work, rest periods, regulation of subcontracting, elimination of many hazardous and unhealthful conditions, and more flexible work schedules. Of course wage levels and benefits in the small and medium-sized plants tended to lag behind those in large ones. In the field of social reform, improvements were also being affected in many areas though the rate of advance was far below the level urged by the trade union movement.

## REACHING A CONSENSUS ON CHANGE

The future goals and role of trade unions and the structure and rules for the industrial relations system will be determined profoundly by the nation's course and success in dealing with its administrative, economic, political, and social problems. Employees are restless and expectant. They seek improvements in their lives and living standards. The political system had made promises of benefits but had not delivered on many of them. As a result, workers increasingly looked to the trade union movement as their primary leverage for pressuring for social change. They also sought benefits, improvements, and relief on the job. Demonstrations, wildcat strikes, and disruptive tactics developed to pressure both the industrial relations and political systems to provide both smooth and functioning channels for recording complaints and grievances and effective remedies for handling them.

Some national political leaders realized the complexity and urgency of their work. But past governments undertook few tasks and made little real progress toward these ends. A left-center coalition ruled for eight years but enacted only a handful of major reforms. A later right-center coalition enacted none. The present left-center coalition knows that the future stability of the democracy is dependent upon its undertaking and pushing positive, constructive, and forward-looking programs, moving toward an equitable expanding full-employment economy and progressive society while it respects people's expectations. It secured a temporary truce and achieved the acquiescence and cooperation of many groups, but its accomplishments in the economic and social fields at the time of this writing were minor. So long as the present malaise exists in the political field, it will be difficult to develop a stable well-articulated industrial relations system.

The economy had been suffering for some three years and began to recover at the end of 1972 and through most of 1973 and the first half of 1974, only to be overtaken by deflationary policies. The gross national product grew at a 1 percent rate in 1971; 3.5 percent in 1972; and 5 percent in 1973; but in 1974 it may be close to zero. Investments were at a standstill for a period up to 1973, companies generally recorded only small profits, with small and medium-sized companies suffering losses and some closing their plants. Capital moved abroad in great volume, estimated at $5 billion. Unemployment was high, reaching in the second half of 1973 the 3.7 level, though it dropped to 2.6 percent in the first half of 1974. The rate of inflation was high; the national deficit was large; and the lira was floated. Strikes were numerous.

Many pressing issues exist. First, the nation's capital equipment is underemployed. In part, labor resistance interferes with its fuller utilization. Public and parapublic organizations and agriculture call for higher investment and innovation. The lower resulting costs could possibly open up markets and increase demand and compensate for lower labor input per unit of output. Industry must become more competitive in the international markets and meet the challenge of imports. The higher productivity per employee in the economy should provide the means with which to finance higher living standards and benefits, better working conditions, and greater public expenditures.

Second, the social infrastructure is in need of urgent modernization and expansion. Much current social dissatisfaction stems from deficiencies in this area.

Third, the economic development of the South continues to claim the highest priority. Its expansion could reduce the volume of out-migration and thereby lower the pressures on northern communities, enabling them to deal with the backlog of social needs in their communities.

Fourth, public administration needs to become more efficient; its current sluggish, costly, and inefficient performance makes governing difficult and enrages the population. Economic, political, and social progress is dependent upon the correction of this condition.


## Political Resolution

It is quite apparent that the ineffectiveness of the political system is a major obstacle to progress. The present left-center government formed in July 1973 gave some promise of introducing a new era. On its formation it acted quickly and deliberately to impose price controls, freeze rents, and enforce these regulations. Its performance in these areas originally won popular support. As part of these understandings, the government agreed with the trade unions on further substantial improvements in pensions and unemployment and subsistence benefits. The union confederations for their part accepted a position of "benevolent understanding." They agreed to a system of price control and offered in return restraint wage demands. They promised to hold down their purely monetary demands and concentrate in their negotiations on improved working conditions, more holidays, and cheaper foods. They showed a readiness to look to newer productivity arrangements and facilitate higher rates of plant utilization. A period of "social truce" followed in which wildcat strikes and production interruptions declined. The trade unions agreed to move in quickly on disruptions at the local level to secure their settlement. The government was to gain time to develop the new system.

The PCI also joined in creating this new era of collaboration by adopting a "new form of opposition." It offered its indirect support of the government's program. Moreover, the party proposed a "historic compromise" whereby it would join the coalition. Its increased willingness to come to terms with the Vatican on issues such as abortion and its offer to accept existing obligations under the Western alliances also suggests a readiness to become more acceptable to the general body politic. It seeks formal membership in the ruling establishment. But older doctrinaire groups within the PCI and the militant young resist this idea, and the parties in the coalition fear the adverse political consequences of the acceptance of the PCI for their own parties and the likely realignment of the internal balance within the DC. Moreover, the anticapitalistic left, reorganized in 1974 as the Party for Proletarian Unity for Communism (PDUP), is ready to attack such moves. The issue gained new relevance in the summer of 1974 as the issue was revived by some Communist leaders, after the DC suffered defeats in the May referendum on the divorce issue and in the subsequent Sardinian elections. But political commentators are divided on the seriousness with which to consider this proposal for PCI participation in the government. Some suggest that it is really an insincere political maneuver. In the meantime contacts are being continued with the PCI, which has the second largest following in the country, by other political groups that are sympathetic to the arrangement to bring the PCI into the government in a responsible position.

But irrespective of the views on the above issue, there is agreement among groups sympathetic to the center-left coalition that it must find a way to pursue a reform program and stabilize the economy. Continued trade union support depends upon its carrying out an effective broader distribution of income, with the rich paying an equitable share of the taxes and the lower-income groups being given some measure of protection from the impacts of rising prices. There is considerable fear that the coalition is not likely to follow this course and that the restrictive economic measures on which it has embarked spell higher unemployment. The result would force the union movement to respond more sympathetically to the more militant groups within its ranks and weaken the influence of the counsels of moderation.

In this state of affairs, the central government controlled by the center-left is unlikely to initiate major reforms in the field of industrial relations. It is dependent upon the cooperation of the trade union movement for the adoption and effectuation of stabilization, structural changes, and growth programs. Even if it had a clear view of the types of systems and legislation it desires, it cannot be diverted from its primary political tasks and responsibilities. Only if it is relatively effective on the broad governmental front and its innovations and leadership continue to be accepted will a setting evolve on which to develop a stable industrial relations system designed with the central government's assistance. In the meantime managements and trade unions will pragmatically shape the industrial relations system.


### Trade Unions and Industrial Relations

Both trade unions and big business leaders recognize these weaknesses and the limitations of the governmental structure (however much they would like it to be different) as well as the serious problems facing the economy. But each is also confronted with developing a course in the face of the diversity of positions held by important segments of their constituencies. In the trade union movement there is on the one hand a leftist orientation, strongly represented by the key industrial federations and especially the metal workers federation (FLM), which insist on active shop struggle and reject enduring compromises, binding constraints, and the "social truce" found in the "peace obligation" of the agreement. They are opposed to compromises and emphasize fighting aggressively for union remedies and solutions of complaints and grievances and direct achievements through plant and community pressures. The councils of shop delegates are their motor force since they assemble these demands and provide the industrial support to push them. A conference organized by the three confederations in April 1974 of these councils was to further their development.

The national union leaders attempt to see the nation as a total macrocosm. They assign the highest priority to general social reform and prefer its realization to concentration on individual industry or group demands. They want more homes, schools, communal facilities, and urban and suburban transportation as well as national social reforms. The development of the southern economy is on the top of their agenda. They are willing to offer concessions or moderate their direct demands on employers in exchange for more attention to working conditions and new corporate investments in the South. They see the trade union movement as the primary voice for the total working class. The amelioration of the communal conditions would do much to satisfy the people's longing for improvements, as well as moderate the discontent in the councils of delegates. The movement not only must press for reforms but also must see that they are realized. Reforms in the social areas would provide the foundation for a stable industrial relations system.

At the July 1973 Congresses of the CGIL and CISL, both views were represented. At the former, the accent was on the priority of

general social reform, while at the latter the stress was on the leftist position. The differences persist and the predominance of one or
the other approach is dependent upon the success with which the government deals with the basic social problems. The confederation
leaders follow events closely, seeking to strike a balance between
those favoring noncompromising positions and the emphasis on industrial action and collective bargaining and those who support more
moderate procedures and the pursuit of the course of reforms through
governmental action. In handling these pressures the three confederations agreed in February and July 1974 to conduct what has been
called "gentleman's" strikes, which expressed disapproval of the
government's restrictive deflationary policies. Instead of a paralyzing strike, they approved a series of staggered ones of short duration
to allow for the forceful expression of employee attitudes without
foreclosing continued efforts at working out agreements with the
coalition governments. Ultimately, the government's practical
achievements or lack of them will determine the course the movement will take.

A new trade union movement is in the making that is based on
a strong mass base and organization at the local levels with factory
delegate councils as the major liaison between the membership and
the leader. The latter is constrained to keep in close touch with the
attitudes and expectations among the people. He cannot follow merely doctrinaire positions prescribed by party programs, as had been
true in earlier eras. The NFs are the key organizations for the new
industrial relations system. Their central activity is bargaining
with management on company and plant contracts with the stress on
concrete issues in which the individual employee has a direct and
personal interest. A new pragmatic spirit pervades the activities
and negotiations for agreements, to provide practical answers to
present issues that include procedures for promoting the ongoing
resolution of differences.

The membership at the local level tends to be led by militant
individuals dedicated to unions who seek these improvements in the
life of the individual employee. Protests and strikes are tools in
the bargaining process rather than mechanisms for paralyzing the
society. The confederations continue to work together and join in
common programs and activities, though they maintain their institutional separateness and continue to respect each other's approaches.
In their tactics, they have maintained a highly flexible attitude, turning to political reform on matters where this course has been traditional but also employing the bargaining procedure with employers
to obtain improvements in communal services and benefits where the
government appears to be laggard. They seek to balance militancy
and responsibility in the conduct of their aggressive programs,

hoping that the center-left government will provide the constructive policies and reforms on which they could further build.

As for the employers' community, big business, unlike the smaller businesses, recognizes that the understandings between the trade union confederations and the left-center government could provide a basis for the constructive redesign of the economy's future. They are yielding to trade union demands to establish a new relationship with labor. Evidence is found in the new management attitudes and their acquiescence after prolonged disputes in the latter half of 1973 to discuss jointly problems of working conditions, general company policies, and investments. Michelin accepted the union's rights to review matters affecting the future of specific plants and the size and timing of investment and not to close out jobs. Pirelli in its new contract agreed to review general plans for expansion to increase investments in the South and to introduce improvements in health and safety conditions within the plants. Giovanni Agnelli headed the 1973 negotiating team for the FIAT organization and affirmed that it was ready to discuss all issues presented by the union including shift arrangements, extension of plant operating hours, and shortening of personal weekly hours, on the condition that the unions recognize that FIAT must remain a viable and profitable economic group.

In 1974 further practical steps were taken. Under the pressure of union strike threats and after intervention by the minister of labor, managements of the leading corporations, although voicing their protest against the duress being applied, signed contracts that included precedent-making concessions. The wage increases were modest, but the managements undertook to guarantee investments in new productive capacity particularly in the South and in research looking to new job opportunities. They agreed to spend money on antipollution controls and improved working conditions, extend the experiments in new forms of work arrangement particularly on the assembly lines, establish funds for improved local transportation and nursery schools for children, grant free hours for employees for further study, reduce the number of job grades, and remove more distinctions in benefits between blue- and white-collar employees. Monthly wage guarantees are to protect wage-earners from loss of pay due to layoffs, shortages of materials, and production slowdowns. It is suggested that, in entering these agreements, employers gained a self-interest in supporting and promoting a more adequate governmentally financed social infrastructure, so that their own direct obligations and commitments will be moderated.

A new era may be in the making as leaders of the large business organizations guide Confindustria, replacing the leadership of the small and medium-sized business groups who in the past tended

to be resistant to innovation and change. They often sided with the
petit bourgeoisie in their opposition to reform. A number financed
the rightist groups both inside and outside of parliament.

Indicative of the new lines taken by the Confindustria are statements by its new president supporting the PSI in its criticism of restrictive credit policies. He also publicly rejected the idea of including the PCI in the governing coalition. The new overall approach
suggests that there is now a basis for cooperation between progressive industrial capitalism and the trade union movement in fighting
"parasitic" elements in the society and the bureaucratic and political wastes that abound in the government. These leaders are ready
to revamp prior thinking, favoring a positive attitude to investment
and expansion of employment.

The changing attitudes of both the trade union movement and
industrial capitalism provide a positive base for future developments.
An effective, activist center-left governmental coalition would do
much to reinforce these trends, for it would continue to hold the support of the trade union movement, a key factor in the maintenance of
political, social, and economic stability, and reinforce the continuing
efforts of management and trade unions to shape the new industrial
relations system, built on strong participation by local employee
groups and individual managements.


EDITOR'S NOTE


The sharp drop in production and employment in the second
half of 1974 spelt layoffs and short work weeks for employees. Workers reacted against the cutbacks with protests and stoppages. After
extended negotiations, the union in the metal industry and the FIAT
management concluded a landmark agreement concentrating the reduced operations in the Christmas and Easter holidays, providing
concurrently for job guarantees for the year 1975. Management
undertook to supplement the unemployment insurance benefits virtually to assure full earnings during the period. Coresponsibility of
the unions and management for handling the problems of the period
became the guiding rule, thereby extending the collaborative relationship, which had been growing in big business establishments. A
national agreement between the confederations and Confindustria in
January 1975 liberalized, updated, and unified on a national basis
the wage escalator clause to better protect employee earnings from
inflation.

Despite the above progress at the industrial front, the three
confederations were unable to advance their program for organic
integration. Meetings to discuss unity were further postponed,

particularly at the initiative of the UIL, whose position is allegedly inspired by its political party associates, the Social Democrats and the Republicans.

Economic policy became the central issue of division within the governments. Toward the end of the year, a third center-left coalition with a stronger leftward stance was formed with two parties participating in the cabinet and the other two assuring external parliamentary support. The trade unions in concert called three separate short staggered regional demonstrations in support of their political programs for alleviating conditions, stimulating the economy, and moderating the rate of inflation, which had attained a level of 25 percent. The third such demonstration in December brought out 14 million workers, it is reported. Further demonstrations took place in January 1975. The new Moro government is considered receptive to the so-called neocapitalistic ideas developed by Giovanni Agnelli both as president of Confindustria and spokesman for FIAT. Moreover, it is also expected to be accommodating to the trade union demands for price and business subsidies on basic commodities and aid to low-income groups and to try to conclude a social contract providing specific social reforms, including liberalized credit, for key sectors in exchange for wage moderation and greater flexibility in negotiations.

In the meantime, local labor and union militants throughout most of the country and particularly in the North are increasing civil disobedience by illegally occupying new housing projects, refusing to pay higher electricity bills and public transportation fees, and blocking railway lines.


NOTES


1. The following studies by the Industrial and Labor Relations Research Institute (Isril) are informative: G. Bianchi, F. Frigo, P. Merli Brandini, A. Merolla, M. Musazzi Cella, Grande impresa e conflitto industriale (Big business and industrial conflict) (Rome: Coines Edition, 1970); R. Aglieta, G. Bianchi, P. Merli Brandini, Delegati operai (Worker representatives) (Rome: Coines Edition, 1970); G. Bianchi, F. Frigo, P. Merli Brandini, A. Merolla, I CUB: comitati unitari di base (The CUB: basic unit assemblies) (Rome: Coines Edition, 1970).

2. For a description of the Frankfurt School, see Martin Jay, The Dialectical Imagination: A History of the Frankfurt School and the Institute of Social Research, 1923-50 (Boston: Little Brown and Company, 1973). For discussions by Italian Catholic intellectuals and trade unionists, see the magazines Dibattito Sindacale, no. 1 (1965) and no. 5 (1968) and ACIL, Collana Ricerche, no. 9 (1969).

CHAPTER

# 4

## THE NETHERLANDS: FROM AN ORDERED HARMONIC TO A BARGAINING RELATIONSHIP
Bram Peper

The prevailing impression[1] about the state of industrial relations in the Netherlands--that it is ordered and harmonious and that
there is a rational, easily reconcilable dialogue between management
associations and enterprises and trade unions that calls for few labor
conflicts--no longer holds true. The new state of affairs is not broadl
understood at home or abroad because the changes are recent and
because of the transitional nature of the current period. The elements
of the future system of relations are only vaguely perceptible.

An early pattern of industrial relations was set immediately
after the war and lasted almost completely intact until the end of the
1950s. It was characterized by the absence of overt conflict. A
Dutch scholar in 1960 in addressing an international audience described its outstanding characteristic as the "low number of strikes."
John Windmuller in his excellent and authoritative book on industrial
relations in the Netherlands identified the same attribute.[3]

Since 1969 the ordered harmonious system has been crumbling.
Strikes, some large and long ones, have occurred. Relations between management and grade unions and employees have hardened.
Managements, like the trade unions, are aggressive, and industrial
strife has gained ascendancy and displaced the previous rational,
national-centralized deliberations and formulas. The agencies that
served as the vehicle for these orderly, careful, and studied reviews
by the interested parties, the Foundation of Labor and the Social and
Economic Council, are losing their significance, and some have begun to doubt the former's relevance.

The concurrent outbreaks of industrial conflicts and the erosion
of the established procedures and relations confuse many people in
the Netherlands. There is no general agreement on the cause of the
conflicts, the direction of the changes, or the manner in which to

reconstruct the industrial relations system better to serve the aspirations and needs of all parties and the nation. There is nevertheless a prevalent feeling, which is conducive to debate and search, that an organized, well-articulated system should be evolved. Deliberate efforts should be made to define it, and developments in this direction should be assisted.[4]

The following discussion will consider the changes in the cultural, economic, political, and social setting within the country that favor broad and fundamental changes in the industrial relations and will enumerate those that can already be observed. The analysts will end with an effort to identify the more durable characteristics of the current design and the likely future directions that the industrial relations system may take.

## THE CHANGING CULTURAL, ECONOMIC, POLITICAL, AND SOCIAL FRAMEWORK

### A Stable Society Dominated by the "Pillar" Elite (1945-65)

An understanding of the Dutch industrial relations system demands a knowledge of the distinctive social cultural characteristics of its society. Much has appeared in English-language literature on this subject, but it would be best to identify briefly some distinctive attributes.

Dutch society is organized into ideological blocs. According to the sociologist Cornelis S. Kruijt, pillars are "blocs of social organizations and societal forms, based on ideological convictions and enjoying the same status in law and situated within a greater democratic society (nation), which is ideologically mixed, but predominantly racially and ethnically homogeneous."[5] If one belongs to an ideological bloc in the Netherlands--the Catholics (40 percent), Protestants (35 percent), and Socialists/humanists (25 percent)-- then one lives for the most part within the associations of that pillar. A Catholic is educated in Catholic institutions, is a member of a Catholic trade union, votes for a Catholic party, and spends his free time for the most part with fellow Catholics. Living in areas in which members of his pillar predominate, he is likely to work in an establishment with members of his pillar. Loyalties tend to be primarily vertical and only secondarily related to one's socioeconomic position (class). An individual joins an organization because he is a Catholic, a Protestant, or a Socialist. This arrangement is sometimes called "vertical pluralism."[6]

The system owes its existence to the harsh struggle that raged among the groups over the organization and control of the society.

Moreover, at the beginning of the century, Catholics and Protestants concurrently and at times jointly carried on a common struggle to dam the tides of social unrest and fight the rise of socialism. As recently as 1954, Catholic bishops issued a pastoral letter that decreed that it is

> not permissible for a Catholic to be a member of the Socialist unions (such as the NVV and unions affiliated with it), regularly to attend Socialist meetings or read Socialist newspapers or to listen regularly to the VARA [Socialist radio]. Holy Sacraments must be refused to those Catholics known to be members of a Socialist union or, if they, without being members, still regularly read Socialist literature or papers or attend Socialist meetings.[7]

To hold their members within these confines, a wide range of service organizations exist to cater to these people. The system was reinforced by laws that granted individuals the right to control their own education. Moreover, many publicly financed agencies are administered by the separate pillars, as in education, health, and social work. Ideological group solidarity--even as regards the relationship between employees and management--is more preeminent than solidarity based on economic interest.

This pillarized structure paradoxically had a stabilizing influence on Dutch society. Though the individual pillars are competitive and at times antagonistic they have had to cooperate. No single one is large or strong enough to govern by itself. The guarantees for their separate existence offer the leaders the freedom to deal with one another on issues of national significance. But this cooperation is limited to the members of the cultural, economic, and political elite in the individual pillars who determine the direction of developments. Little collaboration exists at the lower levels in the fields of education, trade unions, leisure activities, and so on.

The population is docile, conforming, modest, and serious in its loyalty. It accepts and trusts authority.[8] The hierarchical orientation, found in Christian ideology, is also applied to economic life. Everybody, even the elite of the individual pillar institutions, including political, social, and trade union leaders, accept direction from above. Initiative from below, the "grass roots," is not fostered and not considered relevant or necessary. The stress is on conformance and the maintenance of the closed front against the other pillars. The relationship between leaders and members is paternalistic; leadership is exercised by a combination of legal and charismatic powers. Even an opposition group, when it appears, tends to conform to the same pattern, provides a wide range of services, and demands similar allegiance from its members.

In political matters, the leaders of the pillars saw it to be in their interest to cooperate with one another at the national level, a system appropriately described by Lijphart as the "politics of accommodation."[9] Cooperation meant the maintenance of the balance of power among the blocs.[10] But the Socialist group was least enthusiastic about this division. The Socialists who entered the government shortly before World War II instituted soon after the war a program aimed at breaking up these religious-political ties. They invited both Catholics and Protestants to join their party. But the leaders of the established religious pillars were not immediately disturbed. They had confidence in their hold on their followings and the effectiveness of their affiliated institutions in implanting and maintaining the desired solidarity of members of the pillar. The postwar coalition enjoyed the trust of employees, unions, management, employer associations, and the pillars.

Similar cooperation prevailed in postwar economic life. The groups had grown dependent upon one another during the war, and postwar needs demanded cooperation in the program of reconstruction to overcome the physical destruction and the loss of the empire. Labor and management and other groups agreed to collaborate for a common end. They set their self-interest aside. The sharp memory of the crisis of the 1930s and of large-scale unemployment restrained trade union leaders from making large wage demands, though the rank and file at times broke ranks to protest their suffering, shortages, and economic and social disorganization. The leadership recognized that the population was accustomed to a low standard of living and sober life, was exhausted by the war, sought stability, and worked primarily in small and medium-sized enterprises. Large multinational corporations like Philips, Royal Dutch Shell, and Unilever were the exceptions. The people were ready to accept the restrictive economic policies of 1951 and 1957 with the accompanying rise in unemployment in 1951-52 and 1958-59 and actual reductions in real wages in the interest of the national economy.

### A Changing Society: Depillarization
### (1965 to the Present)

During the mid-1960s many changes occurred, drastically altering Dutch society. The process of depillarization began and continues up to the present. The Catholics, formerly considered the most deeply dedicated to the traditional society, now became the leaders of change. Youth challenged the rules set by the pillar elite. There

was a need for reorientation. People began looking for new faiths and
orientations. A number turned to secular beliefs, thereby cutting
their ties with the past. One popular alternative was to urge renewed
cooperation among the pillarized institutions (ecumenical programs).
But no consensus exists on how to respond to the new forces. Some
major developments in several fields will be set forth below.

Sociopolitical Setting:  Ascendancy
of Progressive Parties

The first sign of the breakup of the old arrangement was the
collapse in 1958 of the four-party governmental coalition when the
Labor Party (PvdA) withdrew from it. The Christian parties (ARP:
Protestant Antirevolutionary Party; CHU: Christian Historical Union;
and KVP: Catholic People's Party), which turned more conservative,
plus the VVD (People's Party for Freedom and Democracy; the Conservatives) governed after 1958, except for a short period in 1965-66
when the Socialists returned, until 1973, when a Socialist-headed
progressive coalition took over. The study of the parliamentary
elections from 1959 through 1972, five in all, projects three major
developments: the decline of the KVP, the recovery of the PvdA, and
the appearance of new small political parties, most of which arise as
splinters of old ones. It would be well to discover what is at the
bottom and the nature of these trends, beginning with the Catholics.

The Dutch Catholics until the 1960s had been among the most
loyal followers of Rome. But vast changes took place after the
Second Vatican Council (1962). The Catholic community took an independent course on many matters of church dogma, sharing progressive opinions on marriage and the family, the question of celi-
bacy for the priesthood, and other issues. Priests resigned in considerable number from their offices, and the number of new recruits
declined. Laymen sought a stronger voice in church matters. The
hierarchical structure was called into question. The result was a
quick loosening of ties. Division appeared among Catholics. Rome
sought to reestablish the traditional power structure by appointing
two loyal bishops. A conservative Catholic party made its appearance
(Roman Catholic Party of the Netherlands--RKPN) and gained one
seat in the 1972 parliament. But the more radical groups formed
their own party (Political Party of Radicals--PPR) and gained seven
seats in the 1972 election, a rise from the 1971 elections. Catholic
trade union leaders began heading on a more radical course, following the pattern of the French Catholic trade union movement. A
number of Catholic organizations--trade unions, social work institutions, and newspaper and other mass media--dropped the adjective
"Catholic" from their names. Individual Catholics left the church,

their Catholic party, or their trade union. They began to doubt the utility of a pillarized series of organizations for politics, society, and trade unions.

The Socialists early shed their pillarized cast and by the middle 1960s instituted, under the influence of the new left, a movement for political polarization. They sought a regrouping of people on the basis of class membership and political leanings. The PvdA, which after the war became reformist in its orientation, was converted into a more or less anticapitalist party. In the process the right wing withdrew and created its own party (DS'70: Democratic Socialists, 1970). As a result of this reorientation, cooperation developed among the progressive parties including the PvdA, the PPR, a splinter of the KVP, and the Democrats '66 (D'66), a progressive middle-class party. The members of the group in 1971 combined their resources to support progressive policies. They gained 52 seats in parliament in 1971 and increased their number to 56 in the 1972 election, with the PvdA delegation rising to 43 seats.

The prevailing restlessness produced a number of smaller parties both on the right and left, a system favored by the nation's proportional representation system. The result was further polarization of all parties along the conservative-progressive range and a diminution in the power of the Christian center parties. The process is still in progress. The result is increasing difficulties to form new governments. It took almost half a year to constitute a new government after the November 1972 election. A coalition was formed between the Progressive and Christian parties with a Socialist heading the cabinet. One of the three Christian parties, the CHU, remained aloof. The two participating Christian parties (ARP and KVP) joined, it is alleged, out of fear for the further polarization of the Progressive parties. The trade union movement supported the Progressive parties during the process of cabinet formation, hoping for policies more to its liking. Both the trade union movement and the progressive government maintain both formal and informal contacts and constructive relations.

## Cultural Life: Weakening of Taboos and Stress on Participation

The traditional spirit and sober life-style, hemmed in between taboos regarding marriage and family, deviant behavior, and various types of spontaneous forms of expression made way for a more varied pattern. The Provo (hippies) movement through its activities in the years 1964-67 played a significant part in this change. Its behavior aroused the authorities, and the confrontations resulted in collisions that inspired further doubts in the population about the authorities. A number of new organizations appeared, demanding more citizen participation in policy-making in all institutions. The 1969 student uprisings, which began at the Catholic universities, led to granting students by law a substantial voice in the decision-making organizations of the university. The upsurge of youthful activity also played a leading role in breaking down the prevailing taboos with respect to sexuality, including homosexuality, free expression of opinion, and so on. The new attitudes are reflected in a 1970 survey by the Netherlands Stichting voor Statistiek (Netherlands Foundation for Statistics) for the Dutch magazine Elsevier. People were found to want more career opportunities for all and equal pay for men and women doing the same work and a greater voice in the decision-making process in economic and political affairs. They foresaw by 1980 more protest movements and demonstrations, more working-class students in the university, a rise in the school-leaving age to 18, and a reduction in class and social differences in the country.

Economic Life: The Netherlands--
A Modern Industrialized Nation
Confronted by Stagflation

The Netherlands was converted in the last two decades into a modern industrial state. Its per capita real gross domestic product rose from 1960 to 1971 by 54 percent, at an annual rate of 4.4 percent. Industrial output increased sevenfold between 1946 and 1972, with the chemical and natural gas industries showing the largest rate increase. Industrial employment expanded most rapidly in the metal chemical, construction, trade, and service industries. Economic development brought with it a rapid rise in the people's standard of living both because of higher private purchasing power and the expansion of the collective services including a highly expanded and improved system of provisions for both temporary and permanent social disabilities. Very high employment prevailed through most years. When recessions overtook the country and unemployment increased in 1952, 1958, and 1971-72, the government provided supplementary work and increased public expenditures in high-unemployment areas. Similar public-employment programs continued in the following years. Subsidies were also paid to employers to encourage them to employ the long-term unemployed. Regional economic development policies not only encouraged the creation of new jobs in less developed areas but also restricted further investment in the built-up areas.

The central governments maintained these programs in periods of general prosperity. Unemployment, until the years 1972-73, receded as an active concern. Labor, and especially young working people, no longer feared unemployment though new problems of adjustment arose for people displaced from contracting industries, such as mining and textiles. The repeated increases in earnings also raised expectations for continuing improvement in living conditions.

Among the secular developments with a very substantial impact on industrial relations was the merger movement (the concentration of economic activities), which gained particular momentum after 1968 and appeared to attain its current peak in 1970, averaging about 300 mergers per annum from 1968 through 1971, which gave added importance to the large corporation in the economy. About one-quarter of the mergers involved acquisitions by foreign enterprises. Significantly, some mergers resulted in plant closings. Other plant shutdowns occurred because management was unable to compete in the current market. Collective dismissals caused 12,500 to lose their jobs in 1968; 14,000 in 1969; 10,000 in 1970; 24,000 in 1971; and 23,000 in 1972. These wholesale layoffs reinforced a prevailing feeling of insecurity and inspired much protest and were a stimulant for the militancy visible in 1972-73. Administrative, technical, and professional personnel expanded and, in some sectors, exceeded the number of manual workers.

Stagflation also added to the uneasiness in the working population. This nation like others was experiencing a high rate of inflation during the years 1971-72 along with a very low rate of economic growth and high rates of unemployment. The rate of price increases in the Netherlands exceeded that of other Western countries.

Aggravating this inflationary force was the new system of value-added taxes (VAT), which became effective in January 1969. Changing rates in the VAT as well as increases in public service charges further stimulated prices upward and sent trade unionists searching for ways to protect themselves. The consensus was that steps had to be taken to bring these inflationary pressures under control to protect the nation's competitive position, maintain real living standards, and assure meaningful collective goods and services. But there was no unanimity on the measures needed.


STABILITY, DISINTEGRATION, AND CRISIS
IN LABOR RELATIONS


Period of Stability (1945-59)


The close cooperation of management, trade unions, the government-in-exile, and the underground during the last years of the German occupation provided the base for the cooperative effort

during the early postwar years. The groups accepted a planned and
centralized organization as necessary to overcome the great scarcity
of goods and reconstruct the economy. During the war, agreements
had been reached among the three trade union centers for the coordination of their policies and programs through a Council of Trade Union
Federations for Interorganization Cooperation (RVV), which lasted
until 1954. Management and unions came to an agreement on arrangements for the industrial relations system. The goals were agreed
upon, and the elimination of unemployment was foremost among these
ends. Economic growth, rising living standards, and stability also
enjoyed high priorities. All interests were recognized as highly
interdependent if reconstruction of the economy was to be achieved.

Building upon this agreement, the parties in 1945 organized a
privately constituted bipartite council of employers' associations and
trade union federations, the SvdA, to ensure good and permanent relations based on organizational cooperation between management and
trade unions. Though only an advisory agency on labor and social
policy issues to the government, it became closely involved through
its wage committee with the evolution of national wage policy.

All parties further agreed on a total system of labor relations
modeled in part on the acceptance of the prewar system of pluralistic
organization of workers and employers and a series of national consultative relations between the parties, industries, and the government. It took immediate shape in the Extraordinary Decree on Labor
Relations (BBA) (1945), which provided for three basic elements:
(1) voluntary quits from jobs by workers and discharges or layoffs
by management were to be unlawful except for good reason, which
would be subject to review by the government employment agencies
and their bipartite advisory boards; (2) a 48-hour week was to be
instituted to ensure workers a minimum income, based on calculations of what it would cost to supply the bare necessities of life; and
(3) a national wage control system operated by an Independent Board
of Mediators (CvR) was to go into effect under the supervision of the
minister of Social Affairs to establish rules for and concerning wages
and other conditions of employment, approve or reject terms of collective bargaining agreements (CAO) and extend them to industry
after consultation with the SvdA on guidelines and decisions.

The resulting system of "guided wage policies" lasted until
1959. Under its procedure, all CAOs, both those of industry-wide
scope and those that only involved individual branches, had to be
submitted to the CvR for review according to prescribed tests set by
the government, developed after consultation with the SvdA, thereby
reflecting its influence. The close understanding between the national management organizations, trade union centers, and the government permitted a quick agreement on the goals of economic-social

policies so that the parties could feel that the terms represented a consensus of their views.

Under this system, seven general wage rounds occurred. In fact, they were in the nature of freezes of real wages since they compensated primarily for cost-of-living increases, higher premium payments for social insurance and rents, and the removal or cuts in price subsidies. Beginning in 1954 and until 1959, wage increases actually effected improvements in real income, including the elimination of zonal rates and special increases for skilled workers. The general wage regulations were so precise and far-reaching that industry agreements required little negotiation, and the national trade unions were relegated to the role of applying and enforcing the overall formulas.

The close cooperation of management and trade unions and at the government level of the Christian parties and the PvdA provided the base for two additional basic institutions of the Dutch industrial relations system. Even before the war, the governments had established joint labor-management Industrial Boards for consultation on a broad range of economic and social issues (1933), and by the end of the 1930s, 21 of them existed. But they never engaged in significant activities. In 1950 these bipartite industry regulatory boards (PBOs) were authorized by law to allow the parties to determine the organization of their own industrial branches. Coupled with the PBO in the same legislation was the SER, constituted as a tripartite independent advisory body on economic and social policy, supplanting the SvdA in this area and entrusted with the responsibility of supervising the PBOs. Its antecedent was the High Council of Labor of 1919 (HRA). The law required the government to seek the advice of the SER on all social and economic measures before the government took final action. The SER consisted of an equal number of representatives of management, trade unionists, and the public. While the PBOs acquired some importance in a restricted number of highly decentralized industries such as agriculture, trade, and handcraft, the law was never put into practice. The SER achieved a central position in the development of social economic policies, for while its reports reflecting the discussions of the members have not necessarily been followed, they exercised considerable long-term, and even sometimes an immediate, influence.

The third innovation was the legislation for works councils for each enterprise. They replaced employee representation systems, where these existed, and consisted of representatives of all employees, including the white-collar personnel. The expenses of these works councils were to be paid by management, and the employer chaired them. They had advisory functions with respect to enterprise policies and were instructed "to contribute according to its

ability to the effective operation of the enterprise." These works
councils exist in less than 50 percent of the affected enterprises,
those with more than 25 employees, though they are quite common in
plants with 101 employees or more. Dissatisfaction with their operation and limited rights periodically surfaced and was reflected in the
recurrent studies and reports on methods of expanding their responsibilities and rights.

Trade unions accepted these very constricting, formal, and
centralized policies because they believed that they served best to advance worker and national interests, and they were in no position to
counter the works council. The latter's weaknesses at the plant level
also inhibited direct industrial action. Overall national and industrial
rather than enterprise action and coordination of all groups in advancing economic reconstruction and in the industrialization of the nation
were believed by the trade union movement to be the ways for achieving its goals.

Trade unions accepted the system, for it endowed them with
new importance. The leaders at the union centers enjoyed a heady
feeling of power. They had fought for the right to participate in the
decision-making process, and now they were enjoying this opportunity.
They were members of advisory boards. Their views were listened
to. The government included PvdA members who consulted them,
and they enjoyed easy access to some ministers who had been former
colleagues. PBOs and the SvdA allowed for intimate discussions with
management associations of industry problems and industrial relations issues. The SER opened the way for participation in consultation
on an ever wider range of issues. The unions accepted the discipline
of the guided wage policy though the Christian unions were more reluctant to endorse it than was the NVV.

In the pillarized society, the trade union movement was split
into Catholic (NKV: Netherlands Catholic Trade Union Federation),
Protestant (CNV: Protestant National Trade Union Federation), and
Socialist trade union centers (NVV: Netherlands Federation of Trade
Unions). Cooperative action among them could best be effected at
the central level. They were weak and had no firm organizational
structure within the individual enterprise. Cooperation among unions
at the industry or enterprise level was most difficult, as the separate
Christian unions sought to prevent intermingling of rank and file and
local groups. Finally, each division saw in these labor-management
agencies a fulfillment of its outlook. The Catholic and Protestant
trade unions favored it because the structure underscored and emphasized the community of interests. The Socialists perceived in
these structures the antecedents to the further nationalization of the
industry branches.

Employers cooperated because they came out of the war with
a strong feeling of disarray. They were dependent upon workers and

the government to reconstruct, reorganize, and reorient their enterprises. They accepted guidance from the employer associations, loose organizations that looked after their interests with the government and offered protection from extremist labor groups and from intervention into their enterprises. The individual entrepreneur was left free to operate his business except for price regulations. The looseness of the labor market made it unnecessary for him, except for some special types of labor and markets, to engage in black payments. He could continue his paternalistic, even patriarchal, personnel practices without strong pressure from competitors. Works councils either were controlled by him or were weak.

Differences between management, employees, and unions were resolved through rational deliberations and agreements reached by the elite and passed on to the members. Interunion disparities were reconciled at the central interunion consultation boards or continued unchanged as each proceeded quite independently of the other. United aggressive action was absent or if present not urgent. Initiative at the membership level was essentially irrelevant.

## Period of Disintegration (1959-68)

This accommodation of interests at the national level began to disintegrate as the economy was industrialized and the country enjoyed greater prosperity. Management and the Christian trade union centers sought more freedom from centralized wage control, and the NVV later joined them in this position.

The first evidence of the disintegration of the consensus in the industrial relations field appeared in the wage policy field. The principle of common interest was replaced in 1959 by a differentiated wage policy. Managements sought greater freedom in shaping their wage and working conditions. In response, the government introduced the productivity criteria for defining levels of wage increases by enterprises or branches of industry. But this system satisfied neither the parties nor the government. Data for calculations of productivity were unavailable or inadequate, and measures could not be made precisely. Moreover, workers accustomed to uniform increases in wages could not accept the practice of differentiated wages by industry depending on productivity, for it savored of discrimination. The wage increases were higher than the government desired. Black wages spread and were tacitly condoned because of the failure to prosecute violators.

Unwilling to abandon the principle of guided wage policies, the government substituted in 1963 the SvdA for the CvR as the agency for contract review, retaining the right for intervention. This

marked the end of the rigid wage system, for the new one was pre-
ventive in nature and the SvdA was not bound by the rules set by the
government. But the CvR could still approve or disapprove collective
agreements and the government had still the right to intervene. The
new arrangement also proved unsatisfactory to all, particularly the
government. Increasingly the employers and the trade union centers
demanded the termination of central negotiations and the recognition
of free collective bargaining with the right of the minister of Social
Affairs to intervene in exceptional crisis situations. Wage guidelines
would only be indicative in character. In 1966 the government transferred the power of review back to the CvR, restoring conditions to
the pre-1963 arrangement. SvdA again became an advisory body. A
two-month wage freeze in 1966 reflected this governmental effort to
maintain the older system of control.

The concept of free wage negotiations, as reflected also in SvdA
and SER recommendations, complemented a parallel demand in industrial circles for the removal of price restraints. The older system
had disintegrated and could no longer hold. The government wage
system had to give way to a new freer structure of wage negotiations.

The new economic forces had in effect made the system of tight
control no longer feasible. Moreover, the economy prospered. The
average annual real increase in gross national output reached a level
of 5.3 percent (1959-68) and the per capita real gross national product,
3.8 percent. The Netherlands shared in the growing world acticity
particularly because of its favorable location in relation to many
highly productive Common Market countries, which increased its
importance as an entrepot and made it attractive for the location of
petroleum refineries, petroleum products, and chemical industries.
The new industrial base expanded and included the above industries
and electronic and metal enterprises, and a large service sector
developed.

For the first time in Dutch economic history, manpower became a relatively scarce commodity and shared this distinction with
land. Workers' aspirations began to expand, particularly as some
could, with ease, seek employment in the neighboring countries of
Belgium and Germany. Emigration to foreign countries dropped as
employment opportunities expanded within the country. Workers
began to seek comparable conditions to those in the neighboring
lands. Single women joined the labor market in increasing numbers,
and pressures increased for married women to do likewise.

But it took some time before the new restlessness exhibited
itself in overt action. Black wages and "labor contractors" became
more common, particularly for the building industry, since that industry offered labor at higher wages. Wildcat strikes broke out in
1963, and union members participated in them. The resulting wage

explosion in hourly earnings of 15 percent can be compared with the average annual rise from 1950-59 of 11 percent. The average percent of wages increased for 1964-68 to 8.1 percent, when the consumer prices rose annually on the average by 4.6 percent and the unemployment rate averaged 1.2 percent, reaching the 2 percent level in 1967. The economy absorbed these differential increases in real wages, which corrected the previous relatively unfavorable earning positions of the Dutch worker.

The 1963 wage explosion and the subsequent rejection of central wage controls until they were finally completely dismantled were the turning points in the industrial relations history of the postwar years. The trade union centers recognized that their close adherence to these policies or centralized negotiations and rigid enforcement had estranged their following. Unions were blamed for conspiring with management to repress wages by agreeing to rigid wage controls. Independent unions arose, and wildcat strikes became more frequent. Their own membership remained stagnant and in some years even decreased. Members became more critical. In 1966 the Amsterdam building workers, through independent action committees, successfully resisted a discriminatory wage reduction for nonmembers of the union to finance a vacation fund. Union members liked the special rebate but resented the treatment of the nonmembers. They forced the withdrawal of the procedure. Union-sponsored studies of members' opinions and investigations confirmed the growing gap between the leadership and members. Moreover, PvdA left the government in 1958, so that the NVV no longer had any ties with the ruling coalitions. National governmental policy became more conservative. The social-political climate was more charged as splinter movements multiplied and radical and progressive groups gained more influence within the trade union and Socialist movements.

Finally, little was left of the spirit of cooperation among the various interest groups that developed during and immediately after the war. The PBO existed only in the weak economic sectors. The new growing modern industries operated independently and according to their direct self-interest. Of all agencies, only the SER continued to function according to original plan--as an agency bringing together diverse interests and experts to consider and work out a consensus or offer divided counsel to the government on national social and economic problems. The older order was disintegrating, and this process was particularly visible in the industrial relations field. The course of change was apparent in three areas: (1) the relation of the heads of the trade unions and their constituency; (2) the relation between the government and the leaders of the national institutions (trade unions, employers, SER, and SvdA); and (3) the relation between the three pillarized trade unions. The depillarization process,

or the weakening of vertical pluralism, ushered in a need to integrate
or coordinate the trade unions on a horizontal basis.


Transitional Era: Evidence of Disorder
(1968 to the Present)


The disintegration of the rigid wage system and the substitution
of the free wage policies, accompanied as this development was by
economic, cultural, and political alterations in the total Dutch society, ushered in a transitional period of industrial relations during
which unusual disorders were in evidence and new relationships between and within management, trade unions, and government began
to evolve.

## Important Crisis Events

**The Struggle over the Law of Wage Formation (1968-71).** The first
general crisis focused on the statutory basis of the prevailing system
of labor relations (BBA). With the pressure for greater freedom, a
new industrial relations law had to be developed. It was submitted in
1968 by the government to the parliament. It was directive in spirit
in that it provided for governmental intervention in the collective-
bargaining process permitting the minister of Social Affairs to inval-
idate individual contracts in whole or in part if he considered them
detrimental to the national economy.

The trade union movement opposed this right to intervention
into individual contracts, though it agreed that the government should
retain the power to extend all collective agreements for a period up
to six months in case of an economic emergency, a right similar to
what the government already had with respect to prices. All three
national trade union centers were united in opposition to this law and
demonstrated jointly against the government's effort to block wage
increases. But the trade unionists' efforts were to no avail, as the
government made the issue a matter of a confidence vote by threatening to resign. The issue passed the lower house in the face of much
opposition (82 in favor and 59 against), and the more conservative
senate voted 44 in favor and 24 against in February 1970. The adoption of the Wage Law terminated the life of the CvR, which had begun
losing its central importance in the early 1960s. Wage discussions
were to be conducted by the government with the SvdA.

The new law increased the tension between the government and
the trade union movement. The NVV and the NKV withdrew from all
discussions on wages before the SvdA and in the preparation of the
semiannual economic reports in the SER, an act of key significance,

an open show of noncooperation, which ruptured the established system of industrial relations. The CNV did not follow the above union centers but disapproved of the government's act.

The government, in the meantime, had approved a two-year agreement for the metal industry, which precipitated the resignation of the minister of Economic Affairs. But this show of conciliation did not last long, as negotiations between the government and management and trade unions at the end of 1970 could not effect a consensus on wage policy for the following year. The government, therefore, issued its Wage Moderation Decree, which ordered a freeze on wages for six months, except for a 3 percent rise in January and 1 percent in April to compensate for the estimated cost-of-living increases, with a provision for the reconsideration of all wages in July 1971. The trade union centers reacted furiously and ordered a one-hour strike in December 1970 just before parliament approved the measure. This demonstration was the most widespread exhibition of industrial and political action witnessed in postwar Netherlands and occurred despite the abstention of the CNV. This event further embittered the relations between the trade union movement and the center-conservative government.

When the new cabinet took over in the summer of 1971 after the April parliamentary elections, during which the Christian parties suffered setbacks, and included members of the right-wing Socialists (DS'70), it immediately sought to reestablish amiable relations with the trade union movement. The Wage Moderation Decree was nullified retroactively to January 1971, and the cabinet agreed not to implement Article 8 of the Wage Law, which permitted reviews of individual agreements. All price decrees were repealed. The result was the further confirmation of a system of free wage negotiations. The central structure of wage negotiations under government auspices had been removed, marking the end of the old order and inviting consideration of the shape of the new order. The trade union centers had definitely repudiated the old system of wage negotiations.

The Rotterdam Harbor Strike of September 1970. A second event, the Rotterdam harbor strike of September 1970, seriously impaired the central system of wage setting and concurrently made it evident that the trade unions had lost their hold on their members and needed to revitalize their internal relations with their rank and file.

The strike among 10,000 shipyard workers was precipitated by the differentially higher wages paid to "contract" labor hired through recruiters, even though they had less training. A union settlement for 400 guilder was at first rejected by the workers but later accepted and the workers returned. But the 15,000 dock workers who went out spontaneously on a sympathy strike and to secure the abolition of "contract labor" on their jobs would not accept a similar increase

and continued their strike without union sanction. The tension grew
and the contest became grimmer, particularly as new proposals were
submitted by the strikers. It was finally settled by the acceptance of
the 400 guilder plus a number of other improvements in working conditions including the abolition of "contract labor" in the port.

These strikes had started without union approval and had continued after rejection of the union agreements, thereby illustrating
the great gap between union officialdom and workers. Moreover, the
newly formed workers' committees wanted to participate directly in
the negotiations and would not accept the authority of and the settlements made by the trade union officials. They were neither responsive to the workers not equipped to handle the new types of demands
nor capable of leading mass industrial action.

The immediate practical effect was that employers could not
limit the granting of the 400-guilder increase. Trade unions throughout the country demanded similar compensation for their members.
The building trade unions even took strike action in face of the peace
obligation clause in the collective agreements. Employers tried to
secure injunctions against the strikes, but the courts would not issue
the injunctions. The 400-guilder increase became universal and in
the next year was included in the base for the calculation of future
increases. This step in defiance of the centralized wage system re-
dounded in favor of the trade unions.

The Building Strike (1971). The 1971 building strike marked a significant shift in the role of trade unions from being passive respondents to worker discontent to active leaders of worker action. Negotiations for the 1971 wage contracts had been stopped by the passage
of the Wage Moderation Decree and were resumed only in early spring
of 1971. The union not only made demands for wage increases but
also for an escalator clause linking wages with the cost of living and
facilities for trade union activities within the enterprises. Negotiations lagged, so the unions initiated a carefully planned system of
selective and organized strikes, ruling out wildcat eruptions. Close
coordination among the regional negotiating teams and the careful
scheduling of strikes made the strikes most effective. They did not
place an excessive burden on the union strike fund. Employers responded in kind with a tightly disciplined organization and careful
preparation and a fund to aid companies adversely affected by the
strike. The strikes lasted for the entire month of May 1971, an unusually long period for the Netherlands. Settlement was finally
achieved through ad hoc mediation, since the established institutions
for negotiations and intervention are not designed to deal with these
types of industrial conflicts.

The strikes further undermined the wage freeze. Moreover,
the Catholic construction union took a strong position in opposition to

the center-conservative government and its policies and asked its
members to vote for the progressive opposition parties, an unprecedented step in Dutch political history.

The Metal Strike (1972). The differences among the divisions of the
trade union movement became visible in the metal strike of 1972.
Management and trade unions in central national negotiations failed
to reach a conclusion on a wage policy for 1972. The trade unions
sought a modest real wage increase and other improvements such as
facilities for union activities in the shop, the right of union delegations to negotiate with the enterprise management and differentiated
percentage increases for different grades of employees to favor the
lower-income groups. In the face of this deadlock, the chairman of
the Catholic metal union and the chairman of the employer's side
negotiated a compromise acceptable to the Protestant metal union but
not to the NVV metal group. This union was furious that the chairman
of the Catholic union had informally negotiated without the consent of
the NVV group. Until this event, the unions had coordinated their
actions.

The NVV metal union then advised its following to seek contracts for each enterprise since an industry contract was not possible.
The employers resisted and secured an injunction against strikes
against individual enterprises. While the trade union and its leadership were thus debarred from taking action, the workers initiated unofficial strikes, particularly in the Rotterdam area, where 20,000
workers left their jobs. In many instances, Christian unionists
joined. Because of the confusion resulting from the division among
the unions and the absence of strike benefits prohibited by the injunction, there was a great readiness to find a solution both to effect
a better understanding among the unions and to secure a further compromise. An arbitrator was agreed upon and his binding award was
granted. The unions obtained a higher wage than the Christian unions
had agreed upon, and trade unions were granted privileges and facilities for their activities on the shop floor. The employers also
agreed to pay for the lost time of the members of the Christian
unions involuntarily forced to stop working and for the NVV union to
pay strike benefits to its members without contesting it in court.
But some worker resistance to the arbitration award occurred in
several units. The NVV was most unhappy about the result, and its
president declared that the unrealized demands would be presented
again in the 1973 negotiations. Division in labor's ranks and the
prevailing recession had limited trade union achievements.

The Occupation of the Breda-Enka Plant (1972). Another landmark
in trade union relations and tactics was recorded in the occupation

of the super-modern Breda plant of the Enka Company, a subsidiary
of the AKZO multinational concern. Somewhat comparable plant occupational tactics had been adopted in a Rotterdam dockyard in 1965
and an Utrecht metal plant in 1969. An additional unique feature of
this case was that the trade unions of Belgium, Germany, and the
Netherlands closely coordinated their action against this company in
their respective countries.

The company had decided in the spring of 1972 to shut down
several plants including two in the Netherlands (Breda--1,700 employees and Emmercompascuum--500), a German plant (3,000 employees), and smaller ones in Belgium and Switzerland; total workers
to be fired: 6,000. Negotiations with the unions at Breda brought no
resolution. The trade unions in Belgium, Germany, and the Netherlands after joint discussions in August rejected the plan and adopted
an action program to resist the closings. The Dutch trade unions
then began the occupation of the Breda plant on September 18 and did
not withdraw until the management under public and government pressure canceled the shutdowns.

The 1973 Metal Strike. The most dramatic rupture in the established
industrial relations system occurred with the 1973 metal strike, for
it involved the wage-setting procedure, internal trade union relations,
and the attitudes of employers, trade unions, government, and the
employees. An agreement had been reached at the central level to
consummate a social contract among the government, management,
and trade unions to define a precise wage-price program for the following year. But in the summer of 1972, the DS'70 members of the
cabinet demanded strict wage and price controls rather than free
bargaining. When their proposal was rejected, they resigned. A
government crisis ensued, resulting in a decision for early general
elections in November 1972. The minority government in its September budget message offered its own economic and social program,
which the trade unions considered unsatisfactory. In later negotiations, the government agreed to some additional union demands. As
a result, the parties abandoned the concept of a tripartite social contract and entered into a bipartite central agreement between the
central employers' organizations and trade unions, including a statement of the government's commitments as part of this document.

In the meantime, differences developed within the NVV, particularly because of the dissent of the metal union, which objected to
the failure of the government to agree fully to the union's fiscal demands and resisted the center's desire to sign the document. It
argued that there was no need of a "central agreement" and feared
it marked a return to the former "guided wage policy" system in
which the trade union centers exercised complete control over

industrial wage negotiations. After a week of continuing discussions, the metal union said it would sign the agreement on the understanding that the Union Consultation Board (RO) would urge the new government to grant the remaining union demands and would cancel the central agreement if the government and employers did not observe it. These conditions were accepted by all, and the agreement was signed in December 1972.

The document represents a departure in the development and method of formulating policies. The dispute had brought to the surface the internal differences within the NVV. There were those, led by the president of the organization, who favored continued progressive incremental improvements in the material conditions of the employees. The spokesman for the metal union advocated greater social reform. Also involved in the differences was the question of the relative authority of the central federation and the individual trade unions in a system of free collective bargaining.

The central agreement combined declarations of intent and a contract. The government's commitments were indicated, though it had not signed the document. The contract contained a government obligation to extend the agreement to its employees, institute work programs for the unemployed, enforce the program on the self-employed and nonmembers of the employers' associations, and grant a second release day for the education of 15-year-olds.

The substantive wage provisions included an improvement factor of 3.5 percent and a cost-of-living adjustment factor without a maximum, in which wage increases would represent 0.75 percent of the increase in the price index. Price increases, it was expected, would not rise beyond 5.75 percent. Comparable restraints would be effective for all other types of income, and the government instituted a deflationary policy with more severe limitations on price increases. The agreement looked to the gradual introduction of the 40-hour week by 1975.

With these developments as a background, the negotiations for the metal industry assumed critical importance. It was to be the significant test of the role of the central agreement. The metal unions determined to maintain a joint front and not to be torn apart, as they had been in 1972. They sought to level incomes by substituting a range of flat increases throughout the scale in place of the percentage raises and in addition hoped to extend the agreement's coverage to categories not formally included, particularly the higher grades of the work forces, a demand that came to be known as an "integrated collective bargaining agreement." It sought approval for trade union activities within the enterprise and for the employer to contribute a percentage of the wage and salary bill to trade union activities.

The trade unions again followed the selective-target approach to strikes. The first confrontation occurred at the Hoogovens steel works. The higher levels of the personnel of this organization were opposed to the "integrated collective bargaining agreement," as they had their own arrangements with the management and were generally not union members. Management filed for an injunction by the court, and the latter directed a two-month cooling-off period, during which negotiations were to be carried on, but they failed.

In the meantime, starting in February, there began a series of regional and short strikes, usually for one day, but in several instances reaching several days and weeks. At the peak, there were 40,000 workers out on one day. It exceeded in scope and duration previous strikes, with the total working days lost greater than those for the year 1946. The strikes cost the metal unions a total of 16 to 17 million guilder. Moreover, during the strike the leaders of the NVV and NKV sharply reprimanded the chairmen of the central employers' associations for intervening in the metal industry dispute. To dramatize their disapproval, the central union withdrew for the second time (the first was in 1969) from discussions in the SvdA and SER. Finally, the chairman of the SER, after confidential discussions with the parties, pleaded with the trade unions and employers to end the strike and complete their negotiations. An agreement was thereafter reached, though some strikers resented the abrupt ending of the strike without close consultation of the membership.

The agreement provided for general increases of 1.25 percent plus 20 guilder a month, plus a cost-of-living adjustment factor that granted a 1 percent increase in wages, with a minimum of 156 guilder for each 1 percent rise in the cost-of-living index, for those with earnings up to 28,000 guilder, 0.5 percent and 0.25 percent rise for each 1 percent increase in the index for those between 28,000 and 34,000 guilder and 34,000 guilder and higher, respectively. Provision was made for an independent scientific study of the course of the price index for different income groups for the period 1971-73 to determine whether any group was overcompensated or undercompensated. Other provisions prescribed a 41.5-hour week for 1974 and a 40-hour week in 1975, a four-week vacation period with an annual bonus of 8 percent, with a minimum of 1,296 guilder, again reflecting the concern for the lower-salary groups. At the conclusion of the agreement, the NVV and NKV returned to the SvdA and SER.

But this 1973 settlement constituted no pattern for the future. Tripartite negotiations on November 1973 produced no "central accord" as employers rejected a draft agreement providing for the division of the 2.5 percent general increase in real disposable income as of January 1, 1974 into half to be applied on a percentage basis and the other half as a flat sum, with adjustments for cost-of-living increases to be on a one-for-one basis for those earning up to 35,000 guilder per year and a declining rate of compensation for those earning above that sum. The government stepped in under the 1973 Special Powers Act to prescribe a uniform rise of 15 guilder per month for January 1,1974 and a like sum for April or earlier back to January 1, where the contracts expired earlier than April 1. These provisions were coupled with income tax concessions for low-income groups and tax incentives for investment.

An Appraisal of the Selected Strikes. The above strikes reflected the growing disapproval of the established system of wage controls and industrial relations. They projected a demand by both management and trade unions and particularly of workers for the replacement of the central national control and negotiations of wage agreements by free wage negotiations. Workers no longer were happy to leave the decision-making powers in the hands of the trade union officials and sought direct intervention even to the point of participating in wildcat strikes and rejecting agreements that didn't satisfy them. They were prepared under union guidance to engage in disciplined, short, well-orchestrated strikes to impress their determination upon management and engage in concerted action with unions in other countries and occupy plants to further their position. The trade unions, particularly in the building and metal industries, increasingly responded to the renewed member militancy by adopting a more determined aggressive position within their own industries even where it meant challenging other unions in other union federations or even precipitating internal dissension within their own federation. The established systems of mediation no longer were satisfactory, and new forms of ad hoc intervention by public figures became increasingly more common. The courts were found to hold different views on employees' rights to strike, and the need for clarification of the law on this subject became more apparent.

The Rising Volume of Strikes. The above recital of the hardening of attitudes and the intensification of conflict by employees, management, and trade unions is amply illustrated by the rising volume and intensity of strikes and the difficulties encountered in reaching settlements. Strikes have become more frequent and affect larger numbers of workers and cause an unusually high loss of working days. The present level of working days lost far exceeds the levels in the 1950s and 1960s, except for such intermittent outbreaks as the building strike of 1960. Each strike appears to be directed toward breaking an established procedure or assumption in the industrial relations system. New structures and relations and benefits are being sought.

The high level of industrial conflict was visible in 1970, 1972, and particularly 1973. The outbreaks in the first years of this current period were often spontaneous. But later they became organized and were directed by the trade union leadership and individual trade unions. The older traditions of the separate trade union centers persist, but at the rank-and-file level there is a considerable respect for the efforts of the more militant groups and the inclination to support them no matter how restrained the national leadership may be.

Negotiations have become more difficult, and management has become determined to hold its own. Trade unions are better prepared to use strike action, both short and long, depending on the individual circumstances and resources and even turn to plant occupation. New skills in the organized use of seemingly unofficial strikes are matched by careful strike management. Use is made of sizable strike funds, which had previously gone unused.

Gains in Agreements. Major gains have been recorded in the terms of the union contracts, which increased worker protection and granted unions greater rights within the establishment, especially for union representation at the plant level. Also the number of plant agreements is increasing--for example, from 471 in 1969 to 543 in 1971.

The central agreement of 1972 provides a guide to the new benefit levels. Most significant, it spelt out the acceptance of the principle of the escalator provision, which automatically compensates workers for increases in the consumer price index. While this concept of compensation dates back to the wage policies followed since 1945, incorporation into contracts had to await the disintegration of the central wage policy system and the awareness of the importance of the enterprise and industry agreements. The 1965 Philips contract set the pace in this and several other areas. By 1970 these escalator clauses were already in many contracts and have since spread. Under the 1973 metal industry contract, the leveling factor offers special benefits to the low-wage workers. In the wage field, workers gained the elimination of zonal, regional, and sex differentials in the Philips contracts. The goal to integrate the white-collar and blue-collar wage structures and benefits was first realized in the 1966 Hoogovens contract and has been successfully incorporated in others, leading to the common practice of the payment of manual workers on a monthly basis. The 40-hour week is a target set in the central and metal agreements for 1975 and progressive reductions to that level are specified in most contracts. The basic number of paid vacations is now 20 days, or four weeks, with the compensation specified as 8 percent.

The problems of dismissals or dislocations resulting from technological change and mergers has attracted more union concern.

With respect to the latter, general principles have been laid down by various public bodies. As for mergers, the Social Economic Council provided guidelines for handling of dismissals resulting from mergers and plant closings, which provide for prior discussions with the union and careful provisions for retraining and dismissal compensation and aids in relocation. The so-called merger code allows the SER to cancel mergers in conflict with the guidelines.

The movement for employer-financed funds for union activities got its start in the 1965 contract for the paper industry and has since been adopted in a number of agreements, including the one for the metal industry. Trade unions also sought recognition for their representatives to enter the plants and deal with management and for their plant representatives to enjoy the same protection as work council members. The latter principle is included in the 1972 central agreement. They also negotiated acceptance of union bulletin boards and meetings in the plants. These significantly reflect the persistent union efforts both to reduce the monetary incentive for people not to join the union and to develop closer contacts with people in the establishments. The number of members of the NVV moved ahead, whereas that of the other large centers declined.

### Decentralization of Authority, Increased Coordination, and New Ideology in the Trade Union Movement

Decentralization. A number of coordinate developments within the trade union movement reflect the pressures for structural reorganization. Decentralization of authority is being realized in several different ways. The national trade unions are growing in size and importance within the individual three federations. Mergers are increasing, particularly in the metal, building, and food industries. Three big metal industrial unions now exist. The frequently voiced goal is to reduce the total number of trade unions to about six or seven in each federation. Some speak of the ultimate goal as being three per federation. The reasons are several. The larger unions can be more efficient, can provide more services to their members, and are better able to reach them within the individual plants. Some fear is expressed, particularly within the NVV, that this merger movement would counteract the move to greater internal freedom. It would make all union members direct members of the central federation, but this possibility is now considered too remote for serious consideration.

The removal of the central system of wage control and the shift in emphasis toward industry bargaining placed the industrial trade unions in a strategic position for determining the course of

wage and bargaining developments. They now have to define their
own bargain, sometimes aided as in 1973 by a central agreement, but
often independently or without such guides. They have to negotiate
the new understandings and implement the central agreement. In this
new position, they must rely on their own strength and skills, which
has endowed a number of them, particularly the building and metal
unions, with a new vision of purpose and aggressiveness of spirit.

More thought is being given by the unions to building up more
direct contacts with the rank and file, determining their needs and
complaints, improving the mechanisms for representation, and, finally, gaining their confidence for the support needed in direct industrial action. Even before the recent wage of wildcat strikes and aggressive rank-and-file action, there were recurrent spontaneous
outbreaks, such as the strikes that produced the wage explosion in
1963. Trade union leaders have long been disturbed by the rising
number of categorical unions for specific groups of workers, especially clerical and professionals, who would not join the federations.
They now constitute some 20 percent of the organized work force.
The NVV metal union early in the 1960s initiated efforts to bridge the
gap between its leaders and membership. It concluded that the way
to do so would be to establish a system of union representation
within the plant.

The above proposal is truly radical for this country. The Dutch
trade unions are highly centralized and governed by an elite that emphasizes guidance from above. Ideological unity within each center
assures cohesion. Local representatives receive their instructions
from above, from the national organization. These persons being
coopted by the latter, their future and promotion dependent upon their
superiors, their loyalty to the national leadership is generally firm.
Moreover, members are organized according to their place of residence rather than their work. Even in a small country like the
Netherlands, this arrangement often creates a disparity of goals.
Local union leaders may not be oriented to local factory needs as
they may have no contacts with the work sites in which their members
are employed. A network of union and pillar activities, services,
and insurance strengthened the ideological solidarity and knit the
members closely together. Dissent is therefore rare. People accepted the centralized national global system of bargaining, which
offered them little opportunity for intimate review or control of the
leader's action.

The efforts of the NVV metal union to introduce a system of
plant representatives met resistance from both its full-time staff of
administrators and employers. With the increased emphasis on industrial representation, the metal union, particularly since the 1970
agreement, has made more and more progress in getting management

to accept the principle and provide facilities for union activities. The other two metal unions then followed suit and adopted a similar system of organization. By 1971 about one-half of the workers in this branch of industry were covered by these arrangements. The building industry unions adopted this approach and secured recognition of this principle in the 1973 agreement. But progress in other industries has been much slower. Both employers and trade unions in other fields resisted this procedure. Trade union leaders and members and management are not prepared to undertake the vast responsibilities that such representation and activities require. Moreover, the entire collective bargaining system would have to be adapted to this degree of decentralization and increasingly allow local organizations greater latitude in negotiations and reaching agreements and for the new high degree of member participation that will be required. Ahead lies also the problem of defining the arrangements for articulating this system of negotiations with the general industry and central agreements that will probably coexist.

Coordination within the Trade Union Movement. Coincident with these tendencies toward decentralization of authority and the rising importance of the local plant union representation and negotiations is the movement for greater coordination among the three federations. The basis for this action was laid during the war and in the immediate postwar period with the formation of the Council of Trade Union Federations in 1943 (RVV). After the issuance of the Catholic bishops' ban against their communicants belonging to or associating with the NVV or Socialist organizations or reading their literature, the NVV resigned from this body.

In 1958, a new Union Consultation Board (RO) was organized. It has made considerable progress toward effecting a joint position on many issues. Beginning in 1963, the NVV and KAB, and its successor the NKV, regularly issued joint action programs concerning public issues addressed to the government and on their joint position to its budget message with the CNV joining them in 1967 and later adhering to statements, as in 1971 for a program for 1971-75. In 1967, the groups engaged a full-time administrative officer, and in the following year the three centers demonstrated jointly against the government's efforts to block wage increases. In 1969, they agreed on a joint working youth council to promote the interests of this group both through legislation and collective bargaining. A break in this rising understanding occurred with the failure of the CNV to join the other two federations in the boycott of the SvdA and SER in 1969 and 1972.

Nevertheless, cooperation continued at the central levels and efforts at more intimate cooperation increased, particularly between

the NVV and NKV. In 1971, they agreed on the organization of select
advisory committees with representation of the individual national
trade unions and the integration of the social insurance programs. In
the following year, they determined on the consolidation of policy
preparation and decision-making agencies and the principles for representation in the governing body of a projected new unified body for
the movement. The pressure for increased integration is so strong
that though the CNV has been reluctant to go as far as the other two,
it recently agreed to the organization of a joint body so long as the
individual federations could maintain their separate identities. The
degree of understanding at the trade level is epitomized by the intimate cooperation of the three unions in the metal industry in 1973 in
the face of the tension in 1972. Moreover, two of the three building
unions, NVV and NKV, have determined to be located in one new
building.

        Nevertheless, the merger of the three centers remains a dis-
tant goal. The strikes of 1973, centering as they did around the issue
of narrowing the wage differentials, further intensified the differences,
particularly between the CNV on the one hand and the NVV and NKV on
the other. Plans for the consummation of a merged federation of the
NVV and NKV in June 1974 had to be postponed. The more aggressive
and radical positions of the strong unions in the building and metal
industries tended to polarize support for the more moderate unions
particularly among the organizations of higher-paid personnel in
banks and trades and among management groups. Unions for the
higher-paid personnel are growing markedly, and several unions for
these groups have seceded from the NKV.

        Moreover, the special union for these employees is represented
along with the CNV, NVV, and NKV in top-level public negotiations,
thereby constituting an independent force and multiplying the difficulties for shaping a united position on the part of the entire trade union
movement on social-economic issues.

        During recent years, the trade union federations, particularly
the NVV and NKV, increasingly relaxed their ties with their associated political parties. As noted, the Catholic building workers
urged their members during the 1972 election to vote for progressive
candidates because they were so distraught at the position taken by
the KVP. In their joint policy statements, the trade union federations
have been very careful to observe their political detachment and
speak in terms of specific measures rather than individual parties
or governments. They have become politically more independent.

New Ideology within the Trade Union Movement. The above trends
toward decentralization of authority and coordination among the three
centers looking possibly to complete integration within the trade union

movement are matched by parallel national movements in the sphere of ideology. Traditional loyalties and ideologies are weakening, and new ones are claiming support. A more pragmatic view is penetrating all groups. They are questioning whether general political and economic philosophies and outlooks should not supersede the older religious orientations.

The NVV is departing from its older socialistic orientation in favor of a Universal Declaration of the Rights of Mankind. In 1971 it took a major step in nullifying the 1956 and 1960 decrees barring members of the Dutch Communist Party (CNP) from joining the NVV. As a result of a similar impulse, Catholic trade unions are considering dropping the word "Catholic" from their name and following the French Catholics in yielding their confessional identification. But the CNV clings to the established outlook.

Coupled with these developments is the increased influence of radical thinking involving the adoption of a more critical stance respecting society and capitalism. In 1970 a Task Force for a Socially Critical Trade Union Movement (MKV) appeared, composed of some 400 trade union officials, members of executive boards, staff, and some "outsiders." It supported worker self-management of industry, which has become identified as the demand for "workers' control," and urged a more democratic trade union structure. The NVV metal union, at its 1971 congress, endorsed a similar view, urging the replacement of capitalism by socialism based on workers' control. Several groups in the Catholic trade union movement are oriented in the same direction. Both the Catholic unions for transportation personnel and building workers endorsed the need for social reconstruction. The Catholic agricultural and food industries unions advocated withdrawal from the SvdA and the SER as representing acceptance of cooperation with the existing social order. As regards internal reform and trade union tactics, the MKV in 1973 urged the election, instead of the appointment, of trade union officials, a demand being widely reechoed within the movement. Even within the Protestant trade union movement, new attitudes are being espoused; for example, the CNV has finally yielded some of its hesitation to use the strike weapon.

These trends are strongest in the NVV and NKV and weakest in the CNV. The office personnel and civil servants tend to be more conservative than the building trades and metal workers. During the 1973 struggle in the metal industry designed to level the cost-of-living adjustment in favor of the lower-wage and salaried workers, some industrial trade unions such as the union of functionaries of the NKV took strong exception to this position and threatened to resign. These developments led some leaders in the CNV to urge close cooperation with the other trade union centers in the formation of a

united federation in order to dampen this radical trend, but they were
not persuasive enough to win the organization over to take the final
step of joining the other two major centers in a merged organization.

## Employers Organize for
## Industrial Combat

Developments within the employers' ranks exhibit trends toward
better organization and greater cohesion to meet the trade unions.
Already in 1967, two of the general employers' organizations united
to form the Association of Netherlands Enterprises (VNO), and in
1970 the Federation of Catholic and Protestant Employers' Associations (FCWV) was formed as a cooperative organization for confessional organizations. These bodies maintain close contacts with the
Council of Netherlands Employers' Associations (RNW). But these
were not considered adequate for direct combative purposes, so that
the metal employers established in 1973 a special agency, the Bureau
of Industrial Employers (BIW), to meet the trade unions head on.
The bureau used newspaper advertising to present the metal employers' position. While it was originally conceived as a special temporary agency, considerable thought is currently being given to making it permanent.

Two other developments merit note in the organization of employers for industrial relations that stand out in sharp contrast to
past behavior. First, the personnel of the associations is being professionalized to gain full-time people with expertise to be made
available to employers. The older practice of relying on prominent
men of industry is giving way to the new type of leader. Second,
funds are being built up for supporting or reimbursing employers in
serious combat with unions (mutual employers guarantee arrange-
ment--OWG), and payments are being made to individual employers.

The prior system of informal and cooperative relations with
trade unions is yielding to a more professionalized, disciplined, and
centralized employer organizational system ready to resist trade
union demands in open social combat, a striking innovation in the
Dutch industrial relations system.

## New Laws for Improved Employee
## Participation in the Enterprise

Three new industrial relations laws reflect the political determination to dissipate the unrest through actual reform. By far the
most important innovation was the new law on works councils (1971),
which replaced the 1950 one. The original law conceived of works
councils as cooperative endeavors for the furtherance of production

and consultation of employees by management. Dissatisfaction with its operation led to repeated proposals for changes to satisfy the criticism. The new law does not fundamentally alter the institutions since they remain advisory in nature and have the same cooperative orientation, but it provides employee members greater rights for initiative and independence. They may hold meetings prior to the formal ones at which they can develop their common positions. Moreover, the management is now required to secure the council's advice before making any transfer of control to another interest group, before closing any plants or other operations, and before undertaking programs for curtailment or expansion or changes in production or relocation of plants or entering or changing agreements with other enterprises. Exceptions to this compulsory consultation requirement may be made only when "important interests or those who have a direct interest in the enterprise oppose same. "* The areas of joint review and agreement have been extended to include issues respecting working hours, holidays, safety, training, health, and hygiene as well as welfare funds. The Plant Commission of the SER is to supervise the operation of these councils. It has yet to be proven that these councils in their new form will be any more satisfactory than the 1950 councils.

A significant segment of the trade union movement looks to direct trade union activities within the establishment as the most effective way to achieve worker representation and direct bargaining. Some of the latter would substitute the trade union for all plant employee institutions. Others are suggesting the formation of independent personnel councils, with "members chosen by the personnel and [which] would be empowered to negotiate agreements with the management on important decisions regarding changes in production, mergers, shutdowns, the selection of directors, important investments and legal structure of the enterprise and personnel policies." It is still not clear which direction the trade unions will ultimately choose. In the meantime the new progressive government has asked the SER for advice about the work councils and representation of the trade unions at the plant level to strengthen the workers' position.

A second important change involves the passage of the new company laws that require companies with 100 or more employees and works councils to establish a supervisory board to which the works

---

*The unions and staff approved the merger of Commercial Union and Delta-Lloyd (insurance companies) after reaching an agreement safeguarding employee interests. Negotiations for the merger of two chemical companies failed because of hostility from unions and staff councils.

councils could nominate members and that would have the right to veto nominees offered by the stockholders. This supervisory board would then choose the board of management.

A third change requires larger closed corporations to publish complete balance sheets. These are to provide all interests, including the government, with the requisite information to enable them to anticipate, and possibly call into question, developments in the enterprise. In general, one can say that the traditional Dutch industrial relations system follows the course laid down by law. But, especially in periods of rapid change, lawmaking is not an adequate answer and law enforcement is difficult and sometimes impossible.

### The Position of the Government and
### Industrial Relations Institutions

The period of consensus and stability during the first 13 years after the war implanted principles of government and created institutions that now need redefinition.

Underlying the entire system is the principle that the government has a responsibility for involving itself in the state of industrial relations. Because there was a widespread consensus on purpose and priorities, government, management, and unions could, in the 1950s, reach understandings and accommodations on specific practical programs. Moreover, management and trade unions were brought directly into the process of deliberations on policy through the SvdA and SER, which were responsible for effecting, first, an agreement between management and trade unions and, second, an understanding between the two and public experts on broad economic and social policy. Their counsel was offered on the broadest range of issues, often involving direct public questions only remotely related to the operational industrial relations.

But with the disintegration of the system of guided wage policies and the acceptance of a free wage system and the increasingly conservative cast of the cabinet, the governments sought a new system to replace the previously orderly arrangement. The 1970 Law on Wage Formation was one such effort, but it didn't prove viable. The law has not been repealed, but it has become inoperative.

The blueprints for the new relationship have not been developed. The parties and the public recognize that there must be efforts at accommodation. Two distinctive developments may be observed. First, the trade unions seek directly to influence the direction of broad public economic and social policy by offering their action programs, such as the one they proposed for the years 1971-75 and the more limited one they have drawn up for individual years, as in 1973 and 1974. In this way, they pronounce their own views on the action needed in the matter

of taxes, public expenditures, and collective services and provide
guidance to the political parties. There is still much discussion
about this procedure because some people object to what they see as
an infringement by the trade unions on the prerogative of the parliament. Second, management and trade unions were able in 1972 to
negotiate the elements of a social contract that prescribed both industrial and political practices as an integrated social program. In
the course of the changing political scene, this "social contract"
became a central agreement. It became a measure of agreement
between management and trade unions on public policy and a gauge
for evaluating the nation's achievements. It also served as a guide
for collective bargaining in the individual industries. But this procedure was not duplicated in 1974. Similarly, there is considerable
support among both governmental and private groups including the
trade union centers to repeal the 1973 Special Powers Act, or let it
expire.

In these new instruments one may begin to perceive the way
government policy and administration are to be related to the total
system of collective bargaining. First, there is the CvR. It disappeared in 1970 with the adoption of the revised BBA, the Law of
Wage Formation, but no formal arrangements have been substituted
for actual mediation in the disputes arising at the plant or industry
level. To date, only ad hoc arrangements exist, and the courts have
further confused the scene with markedly varied decisions on the
employees' right to strike. Legislation respecting the latter has not
yet been formally presented by the respective governments, because
there is no consensus on the subject.

The SvdA continues to exist, but its functions depend upon the
degree of consensus between management and trade unions, and it
has been relatively inactive except for the understandings in the 1972
central agreement. The SER continues to serve as a public forum
for discussion on a broad range of economic and social issues and
offers statements pointing to areas of agreement and disagreement
among the participating persons and groups. Both institutions have
lost their former sure footing and carefully defined positions, but
they continue to perform the functions of bringing the parties and
opinions together and help them effect recurrent accommodations.
The purpose and operations of the SER are under attack. A special
commission was recently formed, consisting of six employers, six
employees, and six so-called independent members, to study the
position and function of the SER (such as the relation to parliament)
in the changing Dutch industrial relations system. The question is
whether in a free collective-bargaining system these institutions can
serve any more positive function than merely that of helping the three
groups, labor, management, and government, to participate in face-
to-face discussions and deliberations and often negotiations.

## SUMMARY AND OUTLOOK

The direct effects of the disintegration of the established system
may be summarized as follows:

1. The central guided system has been increasingly replaced
by industry and even company negotiations and contracts.
2. Wage and other terms of employment are more freely determined in these bargaining negotiations.
3. Employees and unions are disposed to resort to wildcat and
orchestrated strikes and other forms of militant action interfering
with production.
4. Trade union leaders are assuming a more active role in
aggressive mass leadership, anticipating rather than responding to
their membership.
5. The area of collective bargaining is broadening, encompass-
ing new issues affecting direct working conditions and employee rights.
Major gains were made, and new ones were being sought. The 40-
hour week will be realized in 1975; the same holds true for the four-
week vacation; differences between wage and salary workers are being
eliminated; protection against cost-of-living increases was confirmed,
and assurances of gains in real wages were provided.
6. The trade union structures are being decentralized as the
industry unions become more strategic. Services to the members in
the plant and organizational relations are increasing.
7. Trade union penetration of the plant for bargaining is also
increasing so that unions probably will transcend the works councils
in importance.
8. More radical anticapitalistic rhetoric and views surfaced
in debates and became more significant in shaping attitudes and views
both of leaders and members. The stress is on major social change
and worker participation in decision-making at the local level. But
there is recognition of the reality that the ends will only be slowly
realized.
9. Membership in unions began to rise, particularly among
the young and newer categories of employees in the lower technical
and white-collar groups. Some categorical unions are individually
joining the mainstream.
10. Union centers are coordinating and, in some instances,
merging their policies and activities and offering a united front. The
NKV and NVV are negotiating an intimate merger, while the CNV is
more modest, insisting on maintaining its separate identity. The
movements for such integration among all three centers are strongest
in the building and metal industries.

11.  Union strength and resources are also being improved by the wide adoption of employer contributions to union activity funds and dues check-offs.

12.  Employers, to counter these developments, centralized and disciplined their own organizations to improve their effectiveness in bargaining and in winning the public or influencing the government. Aid to individual companies is now systematically provided to assure resistance to unions and constrain worker militancy.  Unions will have to take into account that management is likely to meet them head on in these negotiations.

13.  Employees and unions may now be more deeply involved in the operation of works councils and company management and can be better acquainted with the operations of their employers and may be required to take specific positions on plant policies to assure more sympathetic managements and favorable policies.

14.  Unions learned that they have an intimate interest in political developments not as partisans in support of particular parties but as advocates and protagonists of specific policies.

15.  The national political leadership is sensitive to these developments and new aspirations in the working population and has responded by adopting new legislation and promoting the evolution of a new approach to collective bargaining, but the major outlines of the new system are not clear.

These developments have not yet created a new institutional framework for stable relationships and established methods of reaching accommodation.  The industrial relations system is in a state of transition.  It is unlikely to turn backward and reestablish the older ordered harmonious model.  The choices appear to be the evolution of either bargaining or conflict relationships.

A number of different indicators suggest that, in the absence of highly disruptive unforeseen events, the future course lies in the direction of the bargaining model in that there is rather vague consensus on goals and a high degree of independence of the political parties.

1.  Major social changes will have to be effected both through the political process and collective bargaining, and the rate and scope are likely to be constrained by the minority position of the progressive parties.

2.  Both the government and employers' associations are inclined to make concessions in negotiations to achieve greater accommodation and increased stability.  But the possibilities are limited.

3.  While the goals of the trade union movement may be more or less anticapitalistic, its stress is upon immediate and practical proposals.

4. Trade union leaders in many sectors adapted themselves to
the new mood and assumed the responsibilities of guidance, and their
positions are endorsed by their followings, so that their agreements
are accepted, though isolated disgruntlement is at times expressed.

5. The national trade union leadership is aware of the need of
national economic and political discipline and for the formulation of
national benchmarks for decentralized negotiations. The leadership
will favor central agreements, if the government is willing to legislate in favor of some of the political goals of the unions. In the future, this will raise problems in the relationship and responsibilities
of the parliament, government, and pressure groups like the trade
unions. Some new institutional accommodations will probably be
evolved to resolve the different views.


EDITOR'S NOTE

The May 1974 metal industry agreement covers both manual
and white-collar employees, recommends that employers allow employees individually to choose their holidays, increases employer
contributions to the fund for organized workers, and specifies that the
cost-of-living adjustments at the end of year be based on the rise
from April to October 1974. Unions agreed not to strike when employers determine to merge, close, or reorganize enterprises.

Another attempt by the central employers' organizations and
trade union centers to reach a central accord for guiding negotiations
in 1975 failed, necessitating the reversion of bargaining to the sector
level between the individual trade unions and employer groups. The
causes for the disagreement were primarily differences over trade
union demands for making the accord applicable to the higher-paid
white-collar employees, the broadening of the unions' rights to review management decisions on new investment, the contraction or
abandonment of facilities, a real wage increase of 2 percent, and the
publication of all wages and salaries.

Unofficial strikes continue to be called, such as that of the
truck drivers who returned to work only when the government assured
them that it would flexibly administer the new laws requiring tacho-
graphs to monitor truck speeds.

As the levels of unemployment rose to and beyond 3.5 percent,
the government increased its 1974 expenditures and provided for even
higher budgets for 1975, allowing for special benefits to the building
industry, farmers, and retailers, reductions in income taxes for
low-income groups, and social premiums. Both employers and
trade unions disapproved of the program, with the former seeking
broader investment incentives and cuts in corporation taxes and the

latter more extensive programs for reemploying the unemployed. The government in February 1975 increased the support for the building industry, provided subsidies to companies willing to hire the unemployed, and raised the school-leaving age by one year. The three main trade union centers subsequently organized large demonstrations seeking in addition higher unemployment benefits. Financial aid to troubled companies has also been expanded. The country's foreign exchange earnings from the export of natural gas saved it from balance-of-payment problems.

## NOTES

1. Much of the factual information in this chapter is derived from the weekly Informatie en Documentatiebulletin issued by the SER. I wish to express my gratitude to R. Weemhoff, head of the Information Department of the SER, for his excellent help and my friend Joop Ramondt, of the Free University, Amsterdam, for the advice he gave me on earlier drafts. I also want to thank Professor Solomon Barkin, the editor, for his stimulating cooperation. His impressive knowledge of the Dutch situation and his editorial guidance helped me to find the final form of this contribution.

2. W. F. de Gaay Fortman, "Industrial Relations in the Netherlands," Delta (Autumn 1960): 30.

3. John Windmuller, in his preface to the translation of his book Labor Relations in the Netherlands (Ithaca, N.Y.: Cornell University Press, 1969). The Dutch version is called Arbeidsverhoudingen in Nederland (Utrecht/Antwerp: Het Spectrum, 1970), p. 28.

4. For a discussion by some experts, see Bram Peper, ed., De Nederlandse arbeidsverhoudingen: continuiteit en verandering (Rotterdam: Universitaire Pers Rotterdam, 1973).

5. A. Lijphart, The Politics of Accommodation: Pluralism and Democracy in the Netherlands (Berkeley: University of California Press, 1968).

6. D. O. Moberg, "Social Differentiation in the Netherlands," Social Forces 4 (May 1961): 335ff.

7. P. J. A. ter Hoeven, ed., Breukvlakken in het arbeidsbestel (Alphen aan den Rijn: Samsom, 1972), p. 63.

8. H. Daalder, Leiding en lijdelijkheid in de Nederlandse politiek (Assen: Van Gorcum, 1964).

9. Lijphart, op. cit., pp. 100ff.

10. For a historical background of the Dutch political situation, see Hans Daalder, "The Netherlands: Opposition in a Segmented Society," in Robert Dahl, ed., Political Oppositions in Western Democracies (New Haven, Conn.: Yale University Press, 1966), pp. 188-236.

# 5

## BELGIUM: COLLECTIVE
## BARGAINING AND
## CONCERTATION MOLD
## A NEW SYSTEM

Marc-Henri Janne
Guy Spitaels

The cornerstone of the Belgian postwar industrial relations system was laid during the last year of the war. The leaders of the government-in-exile, management, and the unions were in constant contact with one another in the National Union, in their common fight against the occupying forces. During the discussions and planning for the postwar society, they concluded a Pact of Social Solidarity. Its provisions were progressively implemented after the liberation by the establishment of a social security system, an autonomous parity bargaining system in industrial relations including at each stage representatives of employers and trade unions meeting in negotiating sessions chaired by public representatives who at times act as conciliators and at the national level, in tripartite meetings including the government itself, and the creation of a series of multipartite institutions for the collaborative development of economic and social policy and programs.

Throughout the early postwar years, a fundamental of political and social life was the clear understanding among the parties of the need for social peace to achieve the desired economic growth and improvements in social conditions. This attitude was so strong that it has not been broken either by the violent strikes during the 1950 dispute over the continued reign of Leopold III, the 1961 conflict over economic policy, or the unceasing differences between the Walloons, the French-speaking part of the population, and the Flemish.

The dominance of this cooperative outlook in the common cause is epitomized by the 1954 Joint Declaration on Productivity. The spokesmen for the trade unions and employers undertook to "collaborate faithfully" and examine the ways and means of advancing the competitive capacity of national enterprises:

The representatives of employers declare that
increases in productivity should not be made at
the expense of the physical and moral integrity
of the workers nor by infringing on their human
dignity.

The representatives of workers declare
that, for their part, the common effort at increasing productivity will not be employed to
modify the status of the private enterprise in the
economy or call into question the authority of
their heads [Point 4].

Nevertheless, the 1960 strikes, dubbed the "strike of the century," led by the single Socialist trade union center, profoundly affected political and trade union attitudes. But the emphasis on national common interests remained deeply embedded in the national
consciousness, as witness the appearance in the same year of the
procedure for "interprofessional social programing."

The years since 1960 also witnessed a far-reaching technical
revolution. New industries derived from modern sophisticated scientific research and advanced managerial competences assumed increasing importance while the traditional industries such as the extractive
and textiles suffered major losses. Foreign investments, particularly American, increased markedly in the form of subsidiaries of multinational corporations. Also economic policy for promoting private
investment became increasingly more significant for coordinating,
and promoting a balanced system of, economic development to
achieve the desired growth and regional balance.

This chapter presents and analyzes the evolution of the industrial relations system and the manner in which the changing expectations of the people and its composition as well as the economic structure interacted to create a wholly new relationship and new agencies.
The major question with which we shall be concerned is whether
these innovations have produced a system of relationships adequate
to deal with a dynamic society and the growing needs and aspirations
of the nation's employees and to channel the conflicts into efforts at
reaching positive constructive agreements and solutions.

## EMPLOYEE, EMPLOYER, AND OTHER REPRESENTATIVE
## ORGANIZATIONS: THEIR STRUCTURE AND INTERNAL PROBLEMS

### Organization of the Unionized Employees

#### Belgian General Federation of Labor

Unions began to be organized in Wallonia despite repressive
measures in the second half of the nineteenth century. Belgian

Socialists provided the impulse and leadership for the movement.
Toward the end of the century, they coordinated the local and regional
organizations into a national trade union commission (CS), which in
1937 became the independent General Confederation of Labor (CGTB)
but continued intimately associated with the Belgian Labor Party
(POB), and after 1945 the latter was renamed the Belgian Socialist
Party (PSB). National trade unions developed to pursue workers' demands, and they affiliated directly with the CGTB. The latter was reorganized in 1945 into the Belgian General Federation of Labor (FGTF

The union center (FGTB) consists of 12 separate trade unions
bound by the decisions of its statutory national bodies. There are 24
regional federations, which coordinate activities within their areas.
The top body is the congress, which is composed of delegates both of
trades and regional organizations, which respectively designate two-
thirds and one-third of them. The latter elect their delegates from
the local trade unions.

The close ties between the trade unions and the party originated
therefore in their earliest days. This intimate relation is further
fostered by the fact that union leaders are or were members of parliament and have held ministerial posts. Following the tradition established by the CS, the practice is that issues affecting employees
are discussed jointly by the two organizations gathered in one assembly. But the Declaration of Principles of 1945 proclaimed that "the
trade union movement will meet with the parties where they can undertake joint action for the realization of their objectives without
considering themselves obligated in this regard or interfering in the
conduct of trade union affairs." Similarly, the structural independence of the trade union organization is visible in the Socialist Common Action (ACS) in which the four divisions of the socialist movement (PSB, FGTB, mutual benefit societies, and cooperatives) discuss matters of common interest. This formal but loose agency for
coordination facilitates the adoption of common policies and program
and assists the FTGB in securing the PSB's assistance for changes
through the parliamentary and governmental routes.

The choice of the preferred channel for action, be it industrial
or political action, depends on the views of the individual union. The
senior author of this chapter has observed that,

> for some, it is obvious that as soon as the Par-
> liament takes up or determines an issue, the
> trade union movement should yield to political
> action. It can protest and organize orderly
> demonstrations, but it should not oppose the
> parliamentary process by "direct action," the
> strike. Others believe that since current

> parliamentary democracy is undermined by the
> power and influence of the dominant economic
> class, it is proper for the working class to use
> the best weapon that the system allows it; name-
> ly, the strike.[1]

These views clashed during the strike of 1960-61. The movement began among the Walloon (FGTB) membership and organization,
but the Flemish sections of the FGTB (except the Antwerp dockers)
followed with much less enthusiasm and generally withdrew earlier.
The Confederation of Christian Unions (CSC) members abstained
throughout the country. A compromise was finally reached with the
government through the board of the PSB, which was more moderate
than the FGTB, and particularly, the charismatic Walloon leader
Andre Renard. Demo-Christian leaders, fearing further irreparable
damage to trade unions as such, intervened discreetly but firmly at
the governmental level, which was then led by a coalition headed by
Social Christians. The history of the 1960s is replete with similar
differences on the choice of approach to gain socialist, union, or regional ends.

A militant anticapitalist outlook integrating both the Marxist
and Proudhonian views remains a basic tradition of the Belgian socialist movement. However much it has in practice followed a pragmatic policy, the rhetoric still reflects these historic philosophies.
FGTB's basic documents still speak of the day when there will be a
"society without classes and the disappearance of the employee class
through the total transformation of society."

The above ideological position still distinguishes the FGTB
from other unions. It seeks structural reforms to change the capitalist society; wage demands are not to be controlled by the enterprise's financial condition. The movement rejects proposals for
limiting its demands or otherwise subordinating its aspirations to
prescriptions set by other agencies. Left-wing philosophies are
regularly proclaimed by its congresses. The 1971 congress voted
out a resolution for "workers' control of the individual enterprise."

## Confederation of Christian Unions

Unlike the FGTB, the CSC did not originate as an extension of
a central political party. Rather, it was organized in 1912 as the
General Confederation of Christian and Free Trade Unions (CGSCLB)
and then reorganized in 1923 as the Confederation of Christian Unions,
joining other independent national and regional federations and trade
unions, themselves federations of local groups. It has 34 regional
federations, in contrast to 24 in the FGTB. The CSC is oriented

more to regional trade union action, whereas the FGTB emphasizes large trade organizations enjoying considerable autonomy. Similarly, both have national unions or sections as affiliates, with the CSC with 19 and the FGTB with 12. The services offered by the CSC are largely administered in the local offices, whereas the FGTB stresses the industrial offices as the point of contact.

Unlike the FGTB, in which each trade union maintains its own strike fund, there is a central one in the CSC administered by its national executive. While there are few cases where this agency refused such aid, the need for local groups to appear before it limits the ease of calling strikes.

The CSC rests upon the philosophy enunciated in the Encyclical Rerum Novarum by Pope Leo XIII. The Catholic population later stimulated the organization of workers to limit the growth of Socialist unions. The latter looked upon these organizations as "yellow unions" or "company unions," a label that stuck until the groups began actively to emphasize the protection of employee working conditions.

The union is closely linked with the Social Christian Party (PSC) which has governed or been part of all but six cabinets in the postwar years. The Catholic trade unions exercised considerable influence on the party, particularly through its agenda commission. But the membership, particularly in Wallonia, is moving toward greater independence from the party, and the Christian Democratic left is increasing its demands for the CSC to take more radical positions.

This convergence of the movements has been strengthened by the cooperation among the major union centers and the common union front developed on many issues. But there is an ideological gap between the two that is hard to bridge. Progress toward a merger is not impressive. The CSC accents the principles of Social Christianity, which underscores the "community of labor" and the necessity of an "open and sincere dialogue" between the social partners. The CSC speaks of the need of "preserving the freedom of enterprise" and rejects the concept of a class struggle and questions the demands for the socialization of the means of production, both ideas dear to the Socialists. Nevertheless, the CSC through its affiliation with the World Labor Confederation (WCL) at the international level, joined in the issuance of more radical statements than had been common on the national level, expressing opposition to capitalism and approving more activist methods.[2]

Comparative Strength of Union Organizations

In addition to the above two major unions, there are three small ones. They are the Federation of Liberal Trade Unions of

Belgium (CGSLB), the Confederation of the Unified Trade Unions of
Belgium (CSUB), and the Cartel of Independent Trade Unions in the
Public Service (CSI). The first is associated with the Liberal Party
(PL). The two major union centers and the liberal union movement
enjoy a monopoly of representational functions at the national level.

The majority of the members of both major organizations are
in Flanders, with the Walloons constituting only 18 percent of the
CSC and 40 percent of the FGTB. While the FGTB was the larger
of the two in prewar years and in the early postwar period, the CSC
grew to equal its size by 1959 and subsequently outdistanced it. In
1972-73, the FGTB had 937,430 members, the CSC had 1,046,360,
and the CGSLB had 145,580. (Neither the CSUB nor the CSI provided
membership information.)

The FGTB reports a majority of union members in cities like
Antwerp, Charleroi, and Liege, whereas the CSC holds the majority
in Roeselare, Hasselt, Turnhout, and Ghent. The FGTB is particularly strong in large plants and in the metallurgy, energy, and transportation sectors, which enable it to exert great economic power on
key industries. Both unions usually have members in the same
plants. The election results for membership in the works councils
(CEs) and the Safety and Health Committees show that the FGTB has
a strong following (see Table 1). It appears to appeal particularly
to manual workers, while the CSC seems stronger among the nonmanual employees and young workers. *

Changing Relations of Unions and Members

The growth of union organization has been most pronounced.
The ratio of organized workers has risen from 1957 to the present,
from 60 to 70 percent of the work force, which is impressively high.
With such a substantial following, both government and management
are impelled to recognize the importance of securing trade union
sanctions for, or negotiate with them respecting, their policies.
Therefore, the former seeks to associate the trade union centers
closely with its political policies. The trade union leaders also find

---

*Members are affiliated with the union either through the en-
terprise union delegation, if the plant is large enough, or the local
trade union office. In both major trade union centers, employees
are in principle affiliated with the specialized trade organizations
for white-collar employees (FGTB: Syndicat des Employees, Tech-
niciens et Cadres de Belgique [SETCA], CSC: Centrale Nationale
des Employees [CNE]). There is no special trade organization for
youth, but both the FGTB and CSC provide special activities and
training programs for them.

it useful to underscore the importance of their relationship with the government, particularly in the face of the attacks by militant union and political groups.

TABLE 1

Votes Cast in Elections for Belgian Works Councils,
by Class of Employee and Union, 1967 and 1971

| | Votes Cast | | | |
| | Total | Workers | Employees | Youth |
|---|---|---|---|---|
| Number (1971) | 620,738 | 403,412 | 171,880 | 45,446 |
| Percentage participation | -- | 86.74 | 76.25 | 75.99 |
| FGTB | | | | |
| 1967 | -- | 54.08 | 44.53 | 46.12 |
| 1971 | -- | 51.01 | 44.16 | 44.86 |
| CSC | | | | |
| 1967 | -- | 40.32 | 47.53 | 50.42 |
| 1971 | -- | 43.10 | 49.55 | 50.84 |
| Other | | | | |
| 1967 | -- | 4.60 | 7.94 | 3.86 |
| 1971 | -- | 5.98 | 6.29 | 4.30 |

Source: Jean Neuville, Les Elections Syndicales de 1971, CRISP, no. 597 (March 23, 1973), pp. 16, 17.

It is not surprising that--being involved in the development of overall national policies and the administration of national institutions and growing in size and performing many diverse administrative services, such as the payment of unemployment benefits, and devoting more time to national rather than local negotiations--union leadership faces problems of communication with its local members. The latter call for more direct access to officialdom both to answer their personal needs and to be more responsive to their views and aspirations. The union has to convey its view to its members that it is their support that creates union power and that the union is committed to their interests and to the aggregation and use of power solely for their advancement. This truly challenging task has become more difficult to discharge satisfactorily with the growth in the size of the unions, the lengthening of the distance between the leaders and the rank-and-file members, the smallness of the unions' full-time staff serving the members at the local level, the complexity of the subjects, and the ultimate reality of job displacements and plant and mine liquidations. Nevertheless, the unions cannot escape the need for perfecting their performance. Education and increased service and larger staff are solutions being tried, particularly to reach special groups.

To provide the funds, dues-paying union members are essential. Unions have negotiated sufficiently significant improvements in working conditions, incomes and benefits, and rights of participation in decision-making to gain support among members. But to help overcome the usual inertia among people to pay dues, the unions in recent years have secured contractual employer-financed special benefits solely for union members. Presently, almost 80 percent of the workers enjoy such benefits. These appear in various forms such as annual bonuses and complementary social security and other special benefits particularly interesting in periods of full employment. Quasiunion shops are being established in some plants or sectors of industry. Public authorities are also contributing to the financing of union training of leaders and lesser officials to enable them to understand and handle the technical problems arising in current contract negotiations and administration.

The continued administration of the unemployment insurance systems by trade unions also encourages union affiliation even though these activities are administered by autonomous specialized organizations associated with each particular ideological trade union center.

Organization of Employers: Belgian
Federation of Enterprises

The earliest central employer agency was the Central Industrial Committee (CCI), which dated back to 1895. It was replaced in 1946 by the Federation of Belgian Industries (FIB) and the Federation of Belgian Nonindustrial Enterprises (FENIB). Some 35 industrial and commercial employers' associations for different industries belong to the former. Other federations nevertheless maintain close relations with them, since the former's agreements with trade unions and government are norms and are frequently binding on all employers.

The above two organizations recently decided to merge into a Federation of Belgian Enterprises (FEB) better to represent management. It will maintain close relations with the government to press its position in favor of "free enterprise" and its opposition to the principle of price control and higher public expenditures and social costs that compromise the competitiveness of Belgian industries.

The FEB philosophy is to accept the existence of unions and their value in the face of the potential disturbances likely to be

generated by the small militant and violent groups dispersed throughout Belgian industry. One study based on interviews with trade union
and management officials concluded that employers are persuaded
that where "the rate of unionization is high, human relations . . .
are better . . . and the businesses in which human relations are the
best are also the ones in which the rate of unionization is highest."[3]

Insofar as industrial relations are concerned, the central employers' organization prefers national to local or plant agreements to
depersonalize the process of negotiations, minimize the pressure on
marginal firms, reduce the likely number of local and sectoral demands, and limit wage grants to the rise in productivity. The FEB
hopes ultimately to obtain legal sanctions for collective agreements,
which inferentially would impose a "legal" personality and, therefore,
responsibilities on trade unions. The latter strongly oppose this move.

The inclusion of the financial groups and holding companies in
the discussion of the 1972 National Conference of Employment (CNE)
considerably expanded the economic interests formally participating
in collective negotiations and economic collaboration. The inclusion
of the new groups followed on the demands of the trade unions and
particularly the FGTB.

At the industry level, bargaining is carried on with the employers' associations included in the FEB as well as with independent
ones. Of course, as regards individual company agreements, these
are consummated directly with the individual employer.


## Middle Classes

One unique feature of the Belgian scene is the organization of
a substantial part of the independent workers, entrepreneurs, and
professionals in organizations representing their interests. There
is currently an effort to unite them into a common front for negotiations on their own behalf rather than through management delegations
in joint or tripartite bodies. The development of a system of direct
negotiations with the medical profession on fees and conditions epito-
mizes the new trend.


## THE THREE LEVELS OF INDUSTRIAL RELATIONS

### Overall National Level

#### Collective Bargaining

A hierarchy of collective agreements exists depending on the
level at which they are concluded. The law affirms the practice of

according precedence to agreements reached at a higher level over those concluded at the lower ones where the terms are more favorable to the employees.

The signing of the interprofessional Social Programming Accord in May 1960 signaled an outstanding event in the history of Belgian industrial relations. It initiated the interindustry national agreement whose provisions are blanketed over the entire nation. A number of factors converged to favor the completion of the existing industry and plant system of negotiations by the addition of a national negotiating body: the widespread adoption of uniform demands by trade unions and the increased uniformity of terms of employment, the existence of a general social security system, and the growing volume of social legislation. The system was particularly attractive to unions as employees in economically weak industries could thereby obtain benefits they would otherwise not secure. It established, moreover, the principle and precedent for the social partners to meet at fixed dates to negotiate a package of general benefits applicable for a given period to all employees. The terms usually allow for their progressive application over a period of two or three years. In return trade unions agreed not to instigate disputes and strikes and to maintain industrial peace at the national and interprofessional levels, a commitment that called for no specific series of acts. Salary and wage demands other than those negotiated at this level are referred to the joint industrial commissions (CPs) of the individual industrial sectors. This new accord was concluded independently of the Central Economic Council (CCE) and the National Labor Council (CNT). Though they carry with them no legal status or administrative provisions for their enforcement, the individual national industrial agreements are applied generally and set the subsequent climate and direction for industrial relations in the country. The government, which is not a partner to the agreement, is expected to implement designated provisions when necessary either through law or administrative procedures. The effectuation of the provisions respecting such general responsibilities as the extension of "economic democracy" within the enterprise is most difficult. Small firms tend to delay and otherwise impede the realization of the goal.

The first social programing accord prescribed the payment of double pay for the second week of vacation and an increase in family allowance. The second one in 1963 awarded employees a third week of vacation. In 1966 the third granted double pay for this third week. The fourth in 1969 programed a progressive implementation of a reduction in weekly hours of work. Major advances were made in 1971 that included improvements in pensions and social security, allowances for traveling, and company support of trade union education of union delegates. It was decided that the 40-hour week should be

realized in 1975, with the maximum for 1972 being set at 42 hours.
Two more paid holidays were granted for 1972 and provision was
made for a fourth vacation week in 1975. In 1973 the agreement provided for a project to improve the education of those active in trade
unions and an increase in transport allowances for workers, increased
pension allowances, and guaranteed salaries in case of illnesses or
work injuries and longer periods of advance notification to workers
losing their jobs, so that the period approached that for clerical workers. No agreement was reached on a minimum guaranteed salary for
full-time adult (21 years or older) workers; this issue was remanded
for further discussion to each joint industrial commission. Particularly noteworthy is the 1969 agreement, which provided for a study
of employment and unemployment trends, especially as they relate to
the young, and to consider measures for ensuring full employment.
The study commission was attached to the National Labor Council,
a body jointly administered by labor and management.

Tripartite Negotiations and Collaboration
on Broad Economic and Social Policy

Precedents for such national interprofessional negotiations may
be traced as far back as 1936, when the state intervened as a mediator to help settle the general strike of that year. It called a National
Labor Conference (CNT, 1936-56) of representatives of the government, employers, and trade unions, with the prime minister presid-
ing over the proceedings. The settlement of the dispute led the way
to further sessions of the body immediately before the war and regularly from 1944 to 1948. One result was the agreement reached in
1947 on the manner of the selection and responsibilities of union delegates in the individual shops. Its role diminished thereafter as the
Central Economic Council and the National Labor Council gained in
prominence. After the failure in negotiations in 1956, it ceased to
exist.

Rising industrial tension in 1970 and the outbreak of strikes
prompted the unions to demand the restoration of the former interprofessional negotiating procedures. The unions preferred this
course to the use of the National Committee on Economic Expansion
(CNEE) for tripartite discussions of general economic policy, feeling that the occasion required a superior body. But the ministers
devised a completely new organization, an Economic and Social Conference (CES). Employers agreed because they desired to strengthen
union control in the face of the spread of wildcat strikes and to reinforce the established industrial relations system. The results were
particularly significant as the recommendations prescribed far-
reaching principles to guide future negotiations. They included the

following: (1) a commitment to economic planning and decentralization of the economic structure; (2) a guarantee to blue-collar workers
of 80 percent of the regular take-home pay during the first month of
absence from work due to illness or accident; (3) a hike in the wage
ceiling used in calculating social security, invalid, and illness benefits, with increases in contributions to be absorbed entirely by employers; (4) liberalized eligibility criteria in the payment of indemni-
ties to workers made unemployed through plant closings; (5) broadening of the rights of works councils and trade union delegates; (6) increases in social security pensions; (7) provisions for renegotiation
of wages in collective agreements; and (8) the establishment of a
single works council for all Limbourg mines, where the January
strikes began. The parties agreed on a time schedule for implementing the program and for the essential laws to be passed and governmental measures to be invoked and the consultations involving the
CCE, the National Labor Council, and the CNEE. Significantly, it
illustrated the close tie between the private collective bargaining system and government policy, with the latter adopting agreements
reached in the negotiations between the private parties. Belgium
follows this course more extensively than any other European country.

To complete its initiatives and deal more specifically with the
problems of employment, the government also convened in 1972 a
National Conference on Employment (CNE) to review investment
policies particularly directed to increasing the volume of employment. Again, a completely new organization was preferred to the
CNEE in part because the unions stressed the need to include the
financial groups, particularly the large holding companies not represented in older agencies. A new opportunity appeared for the
trade unions to negotiate with the government, management, and
financial groups on economic policy. The unions took the occasion
of this conference to urge the further extension of economic planning,
the need for more economic and financial information from individual
enterprises to the works councils, and better control of public aid to
enterprises. A new law followed these deliberations to further general economic expansion and aid to special distressed areas.

## Consultative Activities

The trade union centers also influence the development of
broad economic and social policy through their participation in a
number of national consultative bodies that are highly significant
and critical in the development of law and administration in these
fields. The CCE, instituted by a law of September 20, 1948, consists of an equal number of members of labor, including the consumer cooperatives, and management and entreprenurial interests,

who are assisted by outstanding technical and scientific experts. The council provides the ministers and parliament, either on its own initiative or at the request of the authorities, with opinions and reports or proposals on questions of the national economy, including a statement on the diverse views expressed by its own members. Its semi-annual reports on economic developments are widely reported in the mass media. On the whole, its influence has been most positive in the formation of public and government opinion and political measures, particularly as all governments were constituted of one or more parties responsive to trade union positions.

While the above consultative body deals with economic matters, the National Labor Council, also composed of an equal number of people from trade union and management organizations with an independent chairman created by the law of May 29, 1952, advises in a similar manner on social issues. Ministers and parliament must obtain their counsel on proposed legislation in these areas. Its opinions and proposals are in the form of reports that also record the different points of view within the council. During the course of the first 21 years of its operation, it submitted 427 opinions and proposals to the latter, or about 20 per year. The council also advises on conflicts over jurisdiction arising between national Joint Industrial Commissions. It may also serve as a conciliation body in cases of industrial conflict involving disputes of an industrial national scale. But this role has remained a theoretical one. Conciliation is usually initiated by the staff of the minister of Employment and Labor. In important cases the minister himself will intervene, as for example, in the instance of the dispute at the Caterpillar and Westinghouse plants, or in exceptional cases, the prime minister will take up the mediation functions, as occurred in the strikes involving internal shipping. Since 1968, it is authorized to sponsor the consummation of overall national collective agreements and accords for industries where there are no joint commissions. Fourteen such agreements have been concluded. This function has grown in importance. Finally, it administers the enforcement of a number of laws pertaining to terms of employment, such as hours of work, holidays, Sunday work, and the employment of children and women.

A third consultative body, the CNEE, is tripartite in its structure and is presided over by the minister of Economic Affairs. It was instituted by royal decree in 1960. The chairman of the Central Economic Council and the National Labor Council and the secretary general of the Economic Planning Bureau attend meetings in an advisory capacity. Its function is to recommend the general objectives of economic policy, especially with reference to investments, employment, and wages. Being most organically tied into the government, the committee promotes close coordination of the attitudes

and decisions of the economic and social groups in the nation with
the government's activities.

The above three organizations gained additional importance
with the adoption of the law of 1970 in response to the recommenda-
tion of the Economic and Social Conference for the further development of planning and economic decentralization. The Economic Programing Bureau (BPE) was given clearer directives respecting not
only general but also sectoral and regional policy. The planning process is compulsory for the public sector, contractual for enterprises
receiving state assistance, and indicative for the remainder of the
private sector. The incorporation of these new guides for economic
planning into law assured more formal consultation among these
bodies and particularly with the economic and social groupings represented on them. A superior Council on Hygiene and Amenities in
the Work Place was created for the purpose of studying modifications
needed in existing legislation in this area.

## Comanagement and Trade Union Participation
## in Public Management

Following the law of April 25, 1963, the comanagement of social security and welfare agencies is the rule. The purpose is to
give the insured themselves a substantial role in the administration
of these bodies and to ensure the agency's autonomy without compro-
mising overall the national government's rights. Actually, the trade
unions nominate the "insured's" spokesmen who are generally appointed by the minister. Among the bodies now governed by comanagement boards are the National Office of Social Security, the National Office of Employment, the National Fund for Sickness and Dis-
ability Insurance, and the National Office of Family Allowances.

Representatives of the trade union and employer organizations
are also on important public bodies such as the National Bank of
Belgium, National Society for Industrial Credit, National Society of
Investment, the Banking Commission, Office of Industrial Promo-
tion, National Society of Belgian Railways, National Housing Society,
Belgian Office of Foreign Commerce, and the Consultative Council
on Cooperation and Development. The above organizations are also
represented on bodies with specific responsiblities such as the High
Council of Finance, the Committee of Price Regulation, the Coun-
cil of Consumers, the National Council of Cooperation, the National
Council of Scientific Policy, and the Superior Council on Population
Education. The total list would probably number 37, of which 14
are financial, 12 economic, and 11 social bodies.

Industry and Regional Levels

Collective Bargaining

Joint industrial commissions originated in 1919 but did not multiply until the strikes of 1936, following which a veritable network of
CPs appeared. They gained legal status with the decree of June 9,
1945, and their standing was improved by the law of December 5,
1968. There are now about 85 such commissions, of which 77 are
national and 8 are regional.

These commissions are composed of equal numbers of representatives of management and trade unions designated by the minister on the nomination of the representative organizations. The chairmen and secretary are independent experts. Their functions are to
promote collective agreements, offer advice to the government, National Labor Council, Central Economic Council, and Industrial
Councils (CPr) on social and economic matters and to forestall or
conciliate disputes between employers and workers. In 1973 they
successfully participated in 65 cases of such conciliation. To discharge the last function, the commissions may establish a conciliation body or secure the inclusion of a procedure for conciliation
within the collective agreements, which the parties agree to follow
before calling strikes; the parties also agree to observe defined wait-
ing periods. The minister of Labor has a permanent group of conciliators at his disposal to aid in such tasks.

The agreements, of which there were more than 400 concluded
in 1973, made before the CPs, must be in writing and published in
Moniteur Belge. These agreements may be made binding at the request of one or more of the signatory parties upon all employers and
workers within the jurisdiction of the commission. Some groups
recognize no benefit in securing such legal status for their agreements, since compliance is general in their industries.

The parties to the agreement gained in recent years increasing
appreciation of the need of maintaining its flexibility in view of the
changes in economic and social conditions, requiring frequent adjustments in the terms of the agreement. The Economic and Social Conference of 1970 recommended inclusion of reopening clauses in the
agreements to achieve this end. Other industries merely shortened
the period of validity of some provisions in the agreement, causing
more frequent review.

Some industry agreements are negotiated outside of the framework of these Joint Industrial Commissions. These are concluded
principally for large plants in several industries. But they are not
numerous. Their negotiating procedures tend to be less formal.

Consultative Activities

Industrial Councils, created by a law of September 20, 1948, deal with the economic problems of the specific industry. Unions are represented there on an equal basis with management. They advise the ministries, on request or their own initiative, or the Central Economic Council on problems affecting their respective industries. Particularly important is their review of sectoral conditions in conjunction with the semiannual national economic review and their assistance to the BPE on its programs for the sector. The CPrs have only been slowly and progressively established beginning with councils in 1951 for the construction, fishing, and textile industries, 1952 for metals, 1956 for the chemical industry, 1957 for the food industry, 1961 for the leather industry, and 1972 for the paper industry. There are eight in all.

The 1970 Economic and Social Conference gave greater impetus to the spread of these councils by urging the improvement of their operations, particularly stressing the need of more intensive study of industrial structural and economic problems, and their establishment in new industrial sectors, particularly in the tertiary sector. During the same year, the CCE endorsed the proposals for extending the number of such consultative bodies, particularly emphasizing the need for supplementing sectoral councils with those dealing with horizontal issues cutting across industry lines.

A further advance in this field was the organization under the law of July 15, 1970, of Regional Economic Councils (CERs) for Wallonia, Flanders, and Brabant. These councils include representatives of local political organizations in addition to the social parners. They advise the national government on the allocation of funds for regional economic expansion, such as for infrastructure and social services, and general laws for regional growth and for the determination of zones of development.

Finally, trade unions and management organizations are also represented on the Boards of the Societies of Regional Development (SDR) provided under the "cadre" law of July 15, 1970, to promote economic development in specific areas. Seven such societies were organized; five for Flanders, one for Wallonia, and one for Brussels. The societies not only furnish data to the regional Economic Councils but may themselves also ensure the implementation of industrial projects. Recently, the minister of Employment and Labor created 18 Regional Employment Committees, with nine for Flanders, eight for Wallonia, and one for Brussels recommended by the 1972 CNE. Their function is to design programs for an active employment policy.

Joint Control and Management

The FGTB at its 1954 congress proposed the nationalization of basic industries, particularly electricity. Management in the latter industry responded immediately, since the proposal was publicly acclaimed and it feared industrial unrest. A convention agreed upon by the representatives of the national labor and management leaders of the sector resulted in 1955 in a revised industrial structure. The signing of the instrument was witnessed by the minister for Economic Affairs.

It provided for a double management structure, one consisting of the business interests and the other of a committee of control on which trade unions were equally represented with management. The latter may raise questions, obtain the desired information, propose recommendations, which may or may not be accepted or reconciled, and supervise retail prices. The general purpose was to reduce prices in the public interest. This convention was extended in 1964 for another 10 years to include the public sector in the electricity industry (particularly distribution) and the gas sector (both private and public).

A comparable convention for the iron and steel industry was signed in 1967 providing for tripartite representation to modernize and improve conditions within the industry and provide for the reemployment of persons displaced by rationalization and reorganization of the industry. In connection with the "oil crisis" the trade union common front asked for similar joint control machinery for this sector of the energy industry.

Level of the Enterprise

Collective Bargaining

While the above national and industrial agreements set the pattern for the country or the regions, enterprise agreements continue to be negotiated, and, in a few industries such as chemicals, they are the dominant instruments. But aside from such full agreements, many supplements to national agreements are consummated at the plant level. While some national conventions limit the range of issues to be dealt with, others do not. On the whole, local contracts tend to reflect local bargaining strength, labor market conditions, and management policy, making for considerable disparities in actual earnings and terms of employment.

It is in the conclusion of these agreements that the local membership participates directly both in formulating the claims and in approving the results, with rejections occurring from time to time, requiring the negotiators to go back to the bargaining table. Where there are plural union organizations in an enterprise, they are likely to develop joint strategies for negotiations, though union competition is not unknown. There have been dramatic cases of conflict among the unions.

The key figures in such negotiations are the union delegations and the regional trade union full-time officers of the major centers. The National Labor Conference of 1947 produced an overall agreement recognizing the delegations and defining their functions. A further agreement on May 24, 1971, flowing from the 1970 CES, improved their status. They are composed of employees of a plant either elected by their shop constituency or designated by the trade union officers. The delegates deal with grievances and the observance of the contract and are the continuing contact of the employees with the union officials. Since the latter agreement, they are entitled to receive prior warning of changes in contractual or established working conditions or rates of pay. They have a place in the plant where they can meet and the time off from the job to discharge their union responsibilities. The delegates are protected from dismissal because of the work they perform as delegates, and they are also paid by the firm for lost time. Employers are now required to receive the delegation for discussion of disputes or grievances or litigation. Provision is made for the delegation to inform the personnel at the work site, and during working hours, of agreements reached between the management and the union delegation. Moreover, the 1971 Social Programing accord provided for the payment of lost time by delegations for their training on methods of dealing with their problems.

## Consultative and Management Activities

A second agency for plant employer–employee relations is the works councils required under a law of September 20, 1948 in enterprises employing 50 or more employees (1963 law lowered the level to 50 employees). The works councils are composed of employer and employee representatives with equal voting power, with the latter elected by the personnel and the former including the chief manager of the enterprise and one or several of his delegates, usually members of his staff. They range in size from 8 to 36 persons and call for specific representation for youth and white-collar employees. The candidates are usually sponsored by the unions and may include foreigners. The chairman is an employer and the secretary, an employee. Employees are paid for their time and protected against discrimination. In smaller plants, union delegations in the enterprise or the local trade union represent the employees in all industrial relations matters.

Although the CEs were conceived originally as a vehicle for cooperative relations between management and trade unions, the latter have sought to increase the councils' powers to complement their direct collective bargaining and supervisory functions in the enforcement of the contracts. Regional trade union officials and delegations often intervene directly within the plant when plant agencies prove unresponsive to employees or weak in their bargaining.

As an advisory or consultative body it is entitled to information, the scope of which has been periodically broadened by law and agreement. It should receive information on the economic and financial experience of the enterprise and the results of business operations. According to an agreement of December 4, 1970 made obligatory by a royal decree in 1971, it should receive data on business developments and prospects and the likely outlook for employment. The agreement spelled out the frequency with which the employment data are to be furnished, annually or trimonthly, and in case of unforeseen additions and dismissals, reports must be promptly offered. A further royal decree on October 7, 1972, calls for reports to the works councils at its request respecting the reasons and measure of control for state aid as well as the copies of periodic audits by the minister granting the subsidies. Directives issued by the CCE on the accounting methods and reports and on the qualifications and responsibilities of the auditors will also be helpful to the CEs in discharging their responsibilities.

A second recent innovation following on the agreements of the 1970 CES assured the works councils of information on the likely effects on employment of mergers, concentrations, and the reopening, closing, or serious modifications of plants or structures or operations.

Besides rights to information, the works council must be consulted on decisions affecting the employment situation. It may offer advice on its own decision on working conditions, the expansion or reduction of the work force, the organization of work, and productivity. It is responsible for the management of welfare facilities provided by the enterprise for its personnel.

The royal decree of November 1973 specifies in greater detail the economic and financial information to be furnished to the CEs. These include data on the competitive position of the firm in the market including developments on sales volume, costs of production, production and productivity for a five-year period, financial information, including a five-year comparison of annual accounts, the budget and calculations of production costs, costs of personnel, prospects and programs for the future, research and development plans, public aids and subsidies to the enterprise, and the organizational structure of the enterprise. But the firms may apply for and secure exemptions from the need of furnishing this information and seek to persuade the Ministry of Economic Affairs that the release of data would be injurious to the establishment.

The works councils direct bargaining functions cover the authority to develop jointly the works rules and the definition of a holiday schedule. The unions discharge these functions on other matters.

The final plant employee agency is the Safety and Health and Amenities Committee (CSHELT), prescribed by the law of June 10, 1952, for enterprises with at least 50 employees. The committees are constituted like the works councils; their powers for obtaining information are broad, but supervision is limited to consultation. Employers retain the final power for decision-making. Dissatisfaction with these agencies is sufficiently general that after the 1970 CES, a new model set of instructions for this committee extended its responsibility for the adaptation of work to man, for the development of annual prevention plans, and for CSHELT's management of the safety and health program. CSHELT is empowered to require management to implement its findings and conclusions. Trade unions have suggested that broad district safety and health committees be established to cover plants with less than 50 employees.

## NEW TENDENCIES, FORCES, PROBLEMS, AND PROSPECTS IN THE NATIONAL SYSTEM OF INDUSTRIAL RELATIONS

The preceding review highlighted the structure and the tensions pervading the partners as well as the institutions of industrial relations. This section will deal with the unrest and attitudes among the total and special groups in the work force, the institutional pressures, policy issues and aspirations within the trade union movement, the differences within the industrial relations scene and political life respecting claims and workers' degree of participation in decision-making, and the influence of the European economic integration movement and multinational firms.

### New Factors in Worker Unrest

#### Rising Activism among Employees

The employee group is definitely expanding both in relative and absolute terms. According to social security records, this group, as a proportion of the total, rose from 1950 to 1968 from

21.2 to 30.6 percent, primarily through the growth of the tertiary sector. But the rate of unionization is weak among them as 73 percent of the workers, 33 percent of the employees, and 65 percent of the public service employees are unionized. The distribution of union membership is 70 percent workers; 22 percent employees; and the remaining 9 percent public service employees.

Three major issues evolved from this upsurge in the size of this membership: (1) employees have expressed a concern that their wages since 1950 only moved in unison with those of workers; (2) employees are increasingly being distinguished from the staff and are being exposed to employment risks and conditions similar to those faced by workers; and (3) workers are seeking to eliminate the disparities between the two groups. But it would appear that employee unions are not troubled by the loss of their distinctiveness. They are seeking to improve their position without insisting on privileges. The higher echelons among employees, the "staff," are increasingly debating the question of their need for union organization and the special advantages they may gain therefrom.

Working conditions are becoming increasingly similar for the workers and employee groups as work units expand in size and the business firms become larger and more complex. Work is more specialized and the anonymity of the hierarchical relationship is more apparent; workers are concurrently given more responsibilities and required to have greater schooling and training for their jobs. They have come to occupy strategic positions in the production system. The privileged position enjoyed by employees in former days is now restricted to the "staff." At the same time more employees are being laid off as a result of the reduction of administrative staffs following business mergers, which result in a relatively high rate of unemployment, particularly among older employees.

Employee organization is therefore spreading and reaching beyond the traditional tertiary sectors such as department stores, banks, and insurance companies. A new militancy has appeared among them as they seek to improve their protection. They collaborate more freely with workers. These developments are illustrated by two recent strikes.

The first arose in 1971 out of a merger of two Walloon metal companies (Esperance-Longdoz and Cockerill-Ougree Providence). The small plant was most modern with a high rate of union organization and paid among the best wages in the area so that it served as a reference point on wage comparisons by others. The workers' unions took the disputes arising out of the negotiations to harmonize the wage scales of the two plants to the CP, which satisfactorily resolved their issues. But the employees encountered greater difficulties and the negotiations were prolonged. The resulting strike of

5,000 employees including foremen, technicians, and draftsmen and administrators prevented the operation of the plant and caused the unemployment of all workers. The latter's unions morally supported the employees in their strike, who in turn were highly appreciative of this cooperation, recognizing that this solidarity was crucial to their success.

A strike in 1972 among the employees of the petroleum sector further illustrates the expanding cooperation between the unions of workers and employees. The dispute resulted from a disagreement on the duration of the collective agreement; management demanded a two-year, and the union a one-year, agreement. The workers actively aided the employee strikers by refusing to drive the tank trucks out of the refineries and depots. This cooperation developed, though employees had on the occasion of a workers' strike some seven years earlier replaced the workers in the operation of the automated installations. The strike was settled with an agreement for one year that permitted the agreements for both employees and workers to expire at the end of the year. The expectation was that the workers would in the future reinforce the bargaining power of the employees with their greater strength and would also be able to demand the further narrowing of the differences in benefits between the two groups.

The workers' unions are demanding in Belgium as in other European countries the adoption of the practice of guaranteed monthly salaries and the extension of benefits previously limited to employees. These practices incidentally present the unions with internal problems of redefining the distinction between workers and employees for the purpose of assigning them to the appropriate trade union.

## Women's Activism

Women are a second group demanding the elimination of prior discriminatory practices. This movement is particularly significant because their absolute numbers and proportions in the work force are rising, from 28.8 percent in 1950 to 32.3 percent in 1970. In the latter year 42 percent of the women of working age held jobs, as compared with 34 percent in 1950. About two-thirds are in the tertiary sector, and more than three-quarters are salaried.

The principle of equality of remuneration is inscribed in Article 119 of the Treaty of Rome (1957). The movement for the elimination of the differences in pay has gained strength, but the differences have since 1960 only been slowly reduced, declining from a ratio of men-to-women earnings in 1960 of 1.7 to 1.61 in 1968. The differences are greater among employees (1.88) than among workers. But it must be noted that female workers are younger, work for shorter terms, have less training, and occupy less advanced positions. Collective agreements, other than for a substantial proportion of the food industries, usually contain nondiscrimination clauses and some call for the merger of the men and women wage schedules into one. But the demand for equality continues to trouble the industrial scene.

The strike of the female workers at the National Armament Factory dramatized this issue. The 1962 national agreement in the metal industry for the promotion of equal pay for men and women brought to light the nature of the disparities, and when it expired at the end of 1965 the unions made large demands and the negotiations were prolonged. Enraged by the delay, 3,000 women without warning joined in a strike, causing the further unemployment of some 5,000 workers. The union formally recognized the strike, which lasted for 11 weeks without the use of picketing or other tactics to keep the plant closed. All workers supported the strike. It was finally settled with an increase in female wages, which stimulated the process of equalization of wages throughout the country. The law of 1971 implemented prior international agreements for parity in wages between men and women.

Both major union centers are devoting considerably more attention to the organization of women, the promotion of their active participation, and their specific demands, thereby significantly stimulating the level of union activity.

Foreign Workers' Activism

Immediately after the war, the Belgian state adopted a liberal attitude toward immigration to fill the manpower needs of the economy. With the economic setback in 1966 and the rise in unemployment, a more restrictive policy was applied. Immigrants are limited to occupations where there are shortages of nationals. The total proportion of foreigners rose from 4.3 percent of the population in 1947 to 7.4 percent in 1970. In 1967 they numbered 181,155. The largest group entered in the middle 1950s. In later years, a larger proportion of the immigrants came from the Mediterranean countries. While they are employed in most sectors of the economy, they concentrate primarily in jobs calling for "hard and unhealthy work," which have no special status in society.

The social position of foreigners improved considerably with the application of the equal rights rules of the European Economic Community to the citizens of its member countries and the adoption of more severe requirements in 1970 for the issuance of work permits for other foreigners. It is hoped that the latter will induce management to be more cautious in its recruitment and more careful in remedying unfavorable conditions.

Foreign workers have played an active role in wildcat strikes in protest against their conditions and insecurity. During the 1970 strike of Limbourg miners, which started off the entire cycle, investigators concluded that foreigners tend to align themselves with the militants, in part because they followed the Belgian workers and in part because they were not sufficiently posted on the alternatives for securing redress for their conditions. On the occasion of the wildcat strike at the Michelin plant among foreign workers protesting their working conditions, one issue that came to the fore was the discrimination created by the minimum service requirements for candidates for seats on the works councils and plant safety and health committees. Though the CNT had urged its repeal in 1962, the provision was nullified only in 1971, placing all workers without distinction as to nationality on an equal legal footing for running for these posts.

## Activism among Young Workers

Younger workers have joined the militants to secure satisfaction for their particular grievances. Their numbers, moreover, make them significant parts of the work force, as those between 15 and 24 years of age constitute 20.6 percent of the salaried employees, 18.5 percent of the service workers, and 22.5 percent of those employed in industry. They are seeking first to eliminate traditional age wage differentials for similar tasks. Second, they are resentful of the failure of the trade unions to take up their cause and secure solutions of their problems and the authoritarian attitudes of the union leaders. They now enjoy the right to one or two seats in the CEs and plant committees on safety and health, depending on whether the enterprise has less or more than 200 employees. On the whole, the trade unions have not yet grappled with the particular problems of younger workers in a forceful manner.

## New Pressures and Policy Issues and Aspirations in the Trade Union Movement

The above description of the frustrations, dissatisfactions, and demands of the general body of the work force and specific groups provides the background for understanding the new demands for changes in policies, demands, and structure within and by the trade union movement.

## The Spontaneous Strikes and Social Protests
## of 1970 and Subsequently

A great body of the workers had become impatient with the traditional orderly process of dealing with issues and grievances. Their dissatisfaction burst out in a rash of strikes in 1970, including 10 cases in which workers occupied factory buildings.

The Limbourg miners started the cycle, dramatizing their protest both by violence and open opposition to the established unions, shown by the workers' committee. The tension in this area, of course, is longstanding, for the mines are relatively noncompetitive and have been kept in operation by governmental subsidies. Threats of, and actual, mine closings are constant concerns in the area. The situation was aggravated by the decline in coal consumption in Western Europe. Moreover, the miners had not fully understood or accepted the fact that the newer industries brought in to redevelop Limbourg would pay lower wages for some occupations. The recession, moreover, sharpened the frustration. The strike lasted for eight weeks, bringing some improvements. When the miners found the agreed-upon wage investigation was not forthcoming, they again came out and gained further advances in wages. The strike rash spread throughout the country and did not subside until the end of the year with the conclusion of many new agreements, the convocations of the CES and CNE, and promises of new legislation.

Discussions on the causes of the outbreaks stress many different factors, including the activity of leftist and nationalist Flemish groups, the defects in the system of union communications, the limitations of the powers and facilities granted to union delegates, and the highly biased nature of the news accounts. But it would appear that a central cause is the growing gap between the leadership and the national agreements and the membership and the local issues. In addition, the modesty of the settlements in 1968 in the face of the boom of 1969-70 incited the demands of workers for a greater share of the new prosperity. The German wildcat strikes of autumn 1969 and the strike wave in other countries provided a pattern for Belgian workers.

The trade unions recognized thereafter the need for more educational activities and improvements in their relations with the local situations and a staff adequate in number and quality to achieve these goals. The unions look to the assistance they will get under the new 1973 law to permit them to organize more extended training for their local leaders.

Another wave of strikes in 1973 increased industrial tension. Workers sought "cost-of-living bonuses" over and above the compensation received under the escalator clauses in contracts. Unions and workers charged that the cost-of-living index did not adequately reflect the real rise in prices, for it made no provision for the rise in the price of fuel.

## Ideological Evolution

The new militancy stimulated a swing to the left in political orientation, particularly in the FGTB but also among many elements in the CSC. The pressure increased the move from a policy of pragmatism and the use of negotiations and compromise to a more "political attitude," accenting structural reforms in society and the economy. An indication of this shift is the substitution in both Christian and Socialist union circles of the phrase "social interlocutors" for the older expression for the participants in collective bargaining—namely, "social partners," a phrase born in the early postwar period when the management and unions cooperated in the reconstruction of the economy and society. Further reflecting this trend in attitude was the adoption of the Workers' Control Resolution at the 1971 Extraordinary Congress of the FGTB. The resolution was formulated in highly "political" terms, looking to the replacement of capitalism by a society oriented to socialist values. The solution to the problems of employment, "future incomes, of careers, and of the destiny of towns and regions" demands that "the union movement open up a new stage in the fight for limitation of management authority, to multiply the centers of democratic decisions." The document calls for self-management of the enterprise and "workers' control . . . as an obligatory stage . . . to training workers in the tasks and responsibilities which they have to assume in the world of the future."

Its conception of workers' control, which includes workers, employees, staff, and agents of the state, is based on the following views: (1) the agency for workers' control is the trade union; (2) information is to be furnished by management prior to actual decisions being made; (3) there should be accessibility and distribution of the pertinent economic and financial data; (4) the union has the right to offer its own proposals and to use economic weapons for their acceptance; and (5) there should be active participation of workers in these controls through meetings during working hours at the work site. (In 1972, the PSB presented itself as party of moderation, promoting a socially minded management of society. But, under the pressures of the trade unions, the party is preparing a "policy Congress." The reports prepared for this meeting and the debates reflect a definite radicalization in thinking. In the election of 1974, the PSB took a decidedly anticapitalistic stance.)

The Christian unions recently adopted a similar approach though they quote frequently from the encyclical Mater et Magistra.

They hold that the "present holders of economic power (high finance, management, large capitalists, both Belgian and foreign managers) should accept the right of workers' participation not only in the administration but in the totality of the common task." The document argues for the need for workers' controls and, calling it "a step towards self-management of the enterprise and the economy by workers," makes a favorable reference to the Yugoslav system. (The emphasis on the "common task" distinguishes its attitude from that proclaimed by the FGTB, which emphasizes the "right to strike.")

There is no doubt that these and other leftist conceptions currently have a strong hold on the trade union leadership. One indication of the effect of these ideological developments is the decline in the support of the Joint Declaration on Productivity (OBAP), leading in 1972 to its final abandonment.

A special CSC congress in 1974 proposed to transform the CEs into workers' councils, to be composed of elected employee members to meet monthly to discuss all issues of interest to them and to meet at least once every three months with management. The consent of the workers' council would be required on matters such as the partial or total closing of the plant, changes in works regulations, and mass dismissals. The new emphasis on social conflict is further reflected in the discussions at the April 1974 Walloon Christian Workers' Movement (MOC) on alienation, which produced recommendations for workers' self-government on working conditions within the plant. Also, the CSC followed the other European members of the World Confederation of Labor (WCL) and joined the European Trade Union Confederation (ETUC), thereby providing a further link at the European level with the FGTB.

## Union Common Front

The two major trade union centers are on a pragmatic basis drawing closer together, while preserving their ideological differences. Trade unionists are keenly aware that the abstention of the CSC from the strikes of 1960-61 considerably weakened the trade union position. As soon as the passions cooled, the idea of rapprochement between the CSC and FGTB became increasingly more acceptable, particularly as the workers' demands were generally identical. Young members of the organizations are especially receptive to the need for unity. In the preparation of demands for the negotiations in individual industries and with the public services, the unions deliberately reconciled their differences to offer a single set of proposals. In October 1965, the organizations, for the first time, presented a common program at the interprofessional level to management and government. Their respective memoranda to new governments express similar concerns though they each formulate them according to their distinctive ideological outlook.

The concept of organic unity is not acceptable to the Christian unionists who plead for pluralism. Such division, it is urged, permits workers, in matters of immediate issues, to choose between the unions on the basis of their relative effectiveness in serving them and forces the two organizations to conform to the workers' preferences. As for long-term issues, where the worker is less able to make a studied decision on effectiveness, he suffers from a division.

The FGTB is generally in favor of extending the areas of common action beyond the trade interests and bread-and-butter issues. In 1971 it suggested a continuing discussion between the organizations to try to agree on long-term objectives for the reform of social structures. But the CSC at about the same time discharged the secretary of its Trade Union of Employees at Liege because he had conducted discussions on the subject of such a merger. The matter is therefore a subject of discussion but not practical negotiations. In both national centers, many are actively promoting this ultimate union. Nevertheless, political ties of two major centers with the PSB and the PSC respectively continue to be strong. Witness of this fact is the joint declaration of February 13, 1974 by the FGTB and the PSB in the electoral campaign in favor of institutionalized regionalization as contrasted with federalism.

## Regionalization of Organization and Society

One major source of further tension in the country is the differences in attitudes between the Flemish and Walloon communities. The conflict is further aggravated by the marked change in economic trends in the two areas. The 1960-61 strike protested the economic decline in Wallonia. Many strikes had their origin in the marginal and shrinking coal industry both in the north and south of the country.

This factor, moreover, obtrudes in industrial relations because of the differences in wage levels in the two regions. It was the serious cause of the metal strikes of 1964. The 1967 disputes in the gas and electric industry and the German-Anglo enterprises, it has been suggested, can be best understood in the light of the shrinkage of employment in the areas in which these plants operate. The most troublesome strike was in Hainaut, the province most sharply hit by the economic recession. It may be persuasively argued that the reason local populations often keenly support the unionists is that they too are troubled by the economic decline of their areas.

Another operative influence within the trade union movement is the consequent demand for the abandonment of national collective

bargaining in favor of regional ones. It is argued that the former
tends to overlook local concerns.

The sharply contrasting rates of unemployment by regions
further accentuates this sensitivity. At the end of September 1972,
the rate of unemployment in the Walloon region was 5.2 percent, in
the Flemish region 3.2, and in the Brussels region 2.3. And these
differences are, in the near future, to be aggravated by the higher
rates of growth likely to be experienced in the latter two regions.

The trade unions have become sensitive to these regional or
community realities. The FGTB in response created separate Walloon
and Flemish interregional agencies, which with the Brussels group
meet with the organization's national economic commission. In 1968
the CSC at its congress took a step in the same direction by considering the possibility of requiring separate regional positions on some
issues.

While the national centrifugal forces are growing stronger,
the centripetal influences continue very dominant, both in union and
management organizations.

## Economic Policies and Trade Unionism

Besides problems relating to the internal structure of the
unions and their relations to one another, their broad philosophies
and the upsurge of unrest within their own ranks, they must face up
to many new challenges in the economic area. One demanding issue
is continuing inflation, for which few if any groups in Western society
have a ready answer.

The working population in Belgium has since the early 1950s
been protected from the loss of purchasing power from inflation because its earnings and social allowances are linked with the consumer
price index. The latter is itself often open to attack for its alleged
unrepresentativeness of the actual pattern of consumption, as services
have become an increasing proportion of the budget.

The trade union representatives participate as members of
consultative bodies on economic policy but have not directly tied themselves to their dicta. They prefer to issue independent statements.
Moreover, they don't consider the union demands or agreements to
be the cause for the waves of inflation. They have resisted the proposals for an income policy and rejected management's demand on
government for a "social pause." They argue strongly that their following would necessarily suffer from such a program since wages and
salaries are more easily controlled than the incomes of other groups
in society. They prefer that controls be initiated on prices without
recourse to similar regulations on wages and salaries.

Nevertheless, pragmatically agreements have been tied into
a rounded system of direct controls, subsidies, and regulations and

taxes to effect a largely regulated income system. The trade unions recently persuaded the government to link the lower levels of taxable income to changes in the price index so as not adversely to affect their real income and its growth.

## European Policy

Unions in this and other European countries are wrestling with the multinational corporations, a substantial number of which are U.S. in origin, which control an impressive amount of the employment and output of the country. A number of different international trade union approaches are being tried to coordinate national unions' efforts and increase their effectiveness in negotiations. The ultimate answer is only vaguely perceptible. In 1971, the success of the unions in Belgium, Germany, and the Netherlands in securing an agreement on employment with the AKZO group encouraged additional steps in this direction of trade union cooperation. The Belgian trade union centers are diligently searching with other national centers for effective programs for reaching and possibly controlling the multinational corporations.

The Belgian trade unions supported the overall European economic integration movement and are urging strong common economic and social policies together with community collective bargaining systems.

## Workers' Participation in Decision-Making

As we have seen, trade unions have considerable influence at every level on the process of decision-making in the social field and substantially affect the results. But their impact on economic decisions, though they participate in the discussions, is most limited. They sought to become a countervailing force in the economic field, but they have not realized this objective, in part because they still lack the facilities, manpower, and expertise to implement this aspiration over the wide range of issues they seek to cover.

## The Dilemma of Democratic Participation in Economic and Social Decision-Making

The present situation produces many frustrations for trade union leaders. They have entered into many agreements with management and governments and are represented in many agencies. But they lack the necessary skilled manpower and time to discharge these obligations. They would like to check on the application of

their agreements and the operation of its provisions. But they are
unable adequately to do so. As their responsibilities broadened and
union activities increased, they expanded the size of their bureaucracy.
But their staffs are still too limited, and this recourse produces new
problems in a democratic organization dependent on close contact with
its members. The consequence is a constant tendency for the distance
to broaden between the union representatives and negotiators and the
membership. Even as respects the representatives, they have to deal
with such a variety of subjects and at such great speed that their own
competences are diluted and their time to prepare for each meeting
is too short. Their effectiveness in negotiations with management or
government is consequently reduced. The results of their efforts are
less satisfactory, and frustration ensues. In the social area, their
special area of competence, they generally are able to proceed com-
fortably, but in the economic field their limitations and inadequacies
become increasingly more serious.

One consequence is the trend for an increasing number of
problems and issues to be handled and reviewed within the individual
plants by the local union membership, a procedure that is proceeding spontaneously. This recourse permits the members to participate directly and promotes democratic control. It is assumed that
they will be able to deal with the concrete limited local problems.
But here again, the individual union spokesmen recruited directly
from the work floor are themselves handicapped in dealing as an
equal on complicated issues--particularly as respects economic,
financial, or juridical matters--with sophisticated and trained managements. They need union experts to assist them, and these are
not available in the necessary numbers.

Furthermore, the members themselves are now participating
to a lesser degree than in the past in union administration. Their attendance at union meetings is low. There is a disposition to leave
issues to the "bureaucracy." Modern life and its opportunities for
satisfactory leisure-time activities in the home, such as television,
dampen interest in attending meetings and devoting oneself to union
responsibilities. The active participants are few in numbers, and
they are called upon to assume much of the onus for decision-making
and negotiations. The consequence is that worker control even at
the local shop and union level becomes weaker and weaker in regard
to review of union policy and administration and even in the selection
of union officers.

Works Councils: Still Unproven Instrument
for Workers' Participation

The CE enjoys a long history but is still unable to operate
effectively and satisfactorily as an instrument for creating a

fundamentally new relationship between employees, unions, and management of the enterprise.

The "most representative trade unions" enjoy by law the monopoly of presenting candidates for election for members of the works councils. And these persons when elected enjoy special legal protection against management's rights to discharge employees. Because members of these councils are persons nominated by the trade unions, they provide a major stream of personal contacts between the union and workers. Moreover, the councils themselves had considerable powers for decision-making relative to all social issues and activities so that they severely limit management's paternalistic powers.

However welcome these gains may be, there are many unfulfilled aspirations. To date, the promises of legislation for worker participation in the management of the enterprise are still to be achieved. The causes for this deficiency are many. First, there are diverse views of the purpose of the institution. Employers, who accept the works councils, see them as a means of obtaining worker collaboration in the realization of enterprise goals. Unions see it as another channel for bargaining with management and control of conditions in the plant. To the legislator who supported the legislation, it is a vehicle for promoting understanding and worker participation in management to increase his interest in his work. With such diversity of purposes, the parties are necessarily viewing the institution from different angles, and it is difficult to satisfy all of them.

Second, employers who view the works councils as an encroachment on their managerial rights, tend to sabotage the proceedings, and provide minimum cooperation. They have no interest in making participation in its deliberations vital and substantial or encouraging active support. On the contrary, they tend to limit their information and issue instructions that antagonize the participants. Third, radical unionists and activists and leftist minorities view the council as an instrument for the social integration of workers into the enterprise. The councils are for them a conservative alternative to more intense forms of class struggle.

Fourth, trade unions also view the works council as a potential competitor and threat to their existence. The plant union delegation and the works councils are both representatives of the workers in the plant. Their respective functions are not clearly distinguished. In fact, the works councils in some places become "antichambers" from which unresolved issues are referred to the union delegation for negotiations and settlement. Of course, in some instances the union delegation has also used the works council as a channel for pressing issues it has not been able to resolve in direct negotiations. Unions have been critical of the independence shown by works councils, which do not maintain a continuing contact and discussion with the union.

On the whole, the works councils are conceived rather differently by groups, thereby reducing the possibilities for the concerted
promotion of a single set of goals. They are marginal institutions
among the legal organs of the commercial enterprise. Sociological
surveys repeatedly find that neither workers nor union delegates are
clear about their function or approve of the operations of the councils.

One major deficiency has been the inadequacy and inappropri-
ateness of the information furnished them in the "primary matter" of
their concern. The data have been either insufficient or deliberately
voluminous and technical so that the delegates who are insufficiently
trained for such analysis are overwhelmed by the task of dealing com-
petently and incisively with the material from their points of view.

Right from the start, there have been wide differences among
the parties as to the content and methods of presentation and implementation of the requirements for information by the enterprise. A
significant new advance is contained in the royal decree of November
27, 1973, which spells out in more detail the nature and contents of
such information to be provided to the works councils. A complementary innovation in the royal decree of December 28, 1973 doubled the
allowed paid time for study by employees to 10 or 12 days to permit
CE members and union delegates to receive instruction in the areas
with which they are concerned in their representative functions.
Whether the new provisions will substantially and positively promote
the operation of these councils or whether they will produce new
sources of friction and disillusionment is yet to be seen. But a substantial effort is now being undertaken to correct the formal shortcomings. But, concurrently, employers are developing new ways of
avoiding the obligations. The law permits them to substitute "sufficient information" for detailed data. There are many loopholes to
permit companies to get by with providing only generalized information.

## Increasing the Effectiveness of
## the Safety Committee

Another area in which past efforts to promote worker participation have not met the original more ambitious hopes is in the field
of the safety and healthfulness of working conditions. We have noted
that there are plant employee committees such as the CSHELT for
this purpose. But it has been found that the employee delegates'
skills are insufficient to deal with the engineering and medical problems. One response was to set up a state corps of inspectors consisting of doctors and engineers with permanent tenure to be responsible for inspecting the observance of these laws and regulations.
But the staff is small, the establishments are numerous, and the

problems are complex. They cannot easily cover the country. It
was proposed by a recent minister of Labor and Employment that a
corps of workers be trained to be permanent intermediaries between
the plant committees and the inspectors. They are to be nominated
by the trade unions and trained over a four-year period by the state
in the skills and knowledge needed for this function. This worker inspector was an extension of a practice initiated in 1897 in the coal-
mining industry and in 1963 in the quarries. Here again we find an
example of direct worker participation in the supervision of the enterprise.

## Trade Unions' Influence in Shaping
## National Policy

Trade unions' influence at the national level varies considerably by area and institution. A thorough appraisal of their real power
is difficult to make. It is rather mixed. No clear image of the results is available. As for participation in national consultative bodies
such as the CCE or the National Labor Council, unions usually present their specific views, and these are incorporated into the final
reports along with those of other groups. On the other hand, they
participate in the negotiations of the conclusions with the federations
of employers and government and more recently independent workers,
in bodies such as the CNEE on matters of general economic policy.
In any event the unions constitute strong pressure groups in
Belgian society constantly expressing and advancing their views on
varied issues. At governmental ad hoc conferences convened to resolve all types of economic and social matters such as monetary and
financial issues and social tension, active and articulate trade union
spokesmen do influence the final decisions. In the 1971 election 12
professional unionists plus an additional 12 who are identified with
related institutions such as mutual aid societies and social organizations were elected as members of the 212 member Chamber of Deputies. In the Senate there were nine unionists and five persons from
related organizations out of a total of 176 members. These persons
are not direct representatives of their unions, as they are elected by
the general population, but they are actual spokesmen of the underlying philosophies of their trade union centers and are open proponents
of trade union interests. But, in addition, the Socialist, Catholic,
and Liberal unions have close ties with the political parties with
which they are associated and have direct access to their leaders
both in the chamber, government, and party committees.

GENERAL CONCLUSIONS

Segmented Pluralism and Its Influence

Before any overall evaluation of the industrial relations systems and trade unions system for Belgium is made, we must famil-
iarize the reader with the national sociological setting. It has been
characterized in the literature as "segmented pluralism," which has
its Dutch counterpart in the word verzuiling. There is no French
equivalent, but it is related to the concept of familles spirituelles,
kindredly oriented institutions affecting all aspects of life.

Belgian society is divided into ideological subsocieties, which
permeate all phases of life of the people. Each ideological group
has its own educational, youth, women, trade, and trade union groups,
mutual aid societies, and cultural movements. There are few organizations in these fields that are nonideological. The major exception
is the employer organization, which from the earliest days were
interest-oriented rather than ideological groups (FEB). But even in
this area there is a Catholic body.

As in the Netherlands, the origin of this ideological division
may be found in the nineteenth-century struggle between the anticlerical liberal bourgeoisie, which sought to free the political state
and the educational system from the control of the church, and the
pro-Catholic forces including the church. It was not a contest on religious issues but centered on matters of control of the society. Society was divided along Catholic and Liberal lines, each with its own
system of organizations and school systems. The appearance of the
Socialist Party reinforced the anticlerical tendencies and produced a
class-oriented grouping. The POB joined with the left wing of the
Liberal Party to fight the battle for universal suffrage. Before World
War II, one found three "traditional" parties. Aspects of life where
religion was central such as education, had a distinctive Catholic and
secular system precipitating the "school wars." All cultural and social institutions were segmented along three ideological lines.

Subsequently the Socialist Party appealed for support among
the middle classes and the farm population. But its following among
these groups is still not considerable. Similarly the Liberal Party
and its successor (PLP) had little success in securing a foothold
among workers. But the Catholic parties continue as they did originally to embrace all levels of society, including the workers, as
witness the existence of its own trade union movement, the CSC.

These efforts at breaking through the traditional lines of segmentation became stronger after World War II. Political parties
reached out more significantly to other classes. As witness of this
we may note that the POB became the PSB, the CP became the PSC,

the PL became PLP, and the latter now includes Catholics on its
lists of candidates and its central committees. A number of social
areas are also being secularized, as witness the 1959 School Pact
and the recent suggestion that pluralistic schools be established.
The CSC and the FCTB are creating a common front, as are also the
independent workers.

But as these sources of segmentation are being allayed, a new
division has been exacerbated: the linguistic one. It has divided the
country into three communities, Flemish, Walloon, and Brussels.
New parties representing in all about one-third of the deputies in
parliament were formed by these groups to represent and defend the
linguistic communities. (The 1974 election results suggest that
these linguistic political divisions may have reached their peak.)
The origin of this movement was the resistance of the Flemish to the
dominance of the country by the French language. The movement
spawned its own segmented social organizations. Now that Wallonia
represents a minority and its economic development is less vigorous
than that in Flanders and Brussels, its inhabitants have taken to de-
fending their own identity and rights. They created their own segmented organization. The issue of "regionalization" produced a division within the PSC and the PLP, each constituting itself into an autonomous wing linked only by collaborative bodies.

The PSB has remained united, but it met this new challenge by
creating a system of double presidency, with one Walloon and the
other Flemish. Its ability to remain united is based on its class
orientation despite its efforts to transcend this restriction. The
secularization of the other major parties has accelerated their divisions along linguistic and regional lines. While the major two trade
union centers remain united, the regional issues are constantly de-
bated. Within the CSC, on the other hand, the Walloon wing has not
been able to maintain its position in the face of the much larger representation of the Flemish population. The "federal" origin and
orientation of the FGTB has prepared it for the acceptance of the
"new regionalism." But fundamentally the trade union centers remain united despite the divisive forces produced by regionalism.
We should, however, add that the recent constitutional reforms
recognize regionalism.


## The Unique Belgian Model of Industrial
## and Labor Relations

The convening of the Economic and Social Conference of 1970
and the subsequent detailed implementation of its recommendations
represent a significant reinforcement of the singular characteristics

of the Belgian industrial and labor relations system. Similarly, one
can point to the action taken at the behest of the trade unions to revise the consumer price index employed for wage adjustments to include the cost of heating oil, as further evidence of this same trend.
The trade union centers in a common front appear to be able by mobi-
lizing their resources to achieve their ends, even where these are
rather sweeping in scope.

The sources for this significant influence are both the high level
of union organization and an ability established over the years actively to mobilize their supporters for public demonstrations as well as
to focus their pressures at the industrial and enterprise levels. The
two major trade union centers are able to approach their associated
political parties for support. As either one or both parties have been
members in the governing coalitions, their influence is considerable.
The common front of the two organizations enables them to utilize the
advantages of the system of segmented pluralism and unity of action
to a degree not matched in any other country with a similar variety
of parties.

This effective use of the segmented pluralist system has hardened the resistance to a merger of the two trade union centers, such
as is occurring in the Netherlands. Of course, resistance to this
move also flows from the union militants because of their attachment
to the Christian or Socialist ideology and from the two bureaucracies,
which fear the consequences for themselves. But any significant
change in the political scene that would favor regional orientations or
the polarization of forces around centrist, modern, and progressive
groupings rather than the traditional ones, may make for a change in
the possibilities of merger. But to make a projection about the political scene and its consequence for trade union mergers would be im-
prudent.

Moreover, the conditions of living for the active population have
significantly improved over the period 1953-71. "Wages tripled while
prices increased slightly more than 55 percent. For the longer perioc
from 1948-71 wages almost quadrupled while retail prices rose by almost two thirds."[4] These gains in real earnings exceeded those in
other European countries.

The "Belgian model" of industrial relations is rather unique.
Its outstanding characteristics may be summarized, but many of the
subtleties must also be defined. The system recognizes the adversary relations among the interests but calls for the institutionalization of conflicts. Conflicts and differences in interests have not been
eliminated or necessarily reduced. The parties engaged in negotiations, to be followed by the submission of differences to conciliation
and possibly arbitration without the parties necessarily forgoing the
right to use the ultimate recourse, the strike. Alongside this

negotiating system, there exists a concerted or collaborative system for study, discussion, accommodation, guiding the economy that has evolved in an empirical manner at all levels of economic and social life.

Continuing conflict or adversary relations and "tough, profound reformism" are contained within economically acceptable limits by a complete and effective system of concertation, consultation, cooperation, collaboration, negotiations, and freely-arrived-at agreements in these fields. This model does not spell perfect peace for one can point to major ruptures and strikes on the industrial and political scenes as exemplified by the "strike of the century" in 1960-61. It may even be surmised that if the Belgian system had worked more peacefully, it would probably have ultimately produced more revolutionary eruptions and more intense doctrinaire conflicts.

To date, the system has produced satisfactory results by adapting to the developments flowing from these recurrent and harsh conflicts and incorporating them into the permanent system of industrial labor and social relations. An extreme degree of collaboration between trade unions and management might have at these times fostered greater revolutionary activities, of which we have had much recent evidence. Excessive cooperation might have produced less healthy results than pragmatism.

Within this system three perspectives coexist and seek continuing accommodation. Management wants "social peace" and to limit trade union demands. It wants to integrate workers into the system and maintain management's prerogatives as much as possible. Its underlying belief is in a free-enterprise system in which the state plays a secondary role. Management's accent is on growth of production of goods and services for the "market." All action at the plant and national level should contribute to these ends.

The trade unions, on the other hand, want to improve social conditions and the rewards for workers and to participate in the decision-making processes respecting social and economic issues, while preserving the maximum freedom of action. They have not yielded on their desire to achieve the formation of a new society through successive reforms and to gain for workers the right of participation and "control" of the enterprise. Their immediate emphasis is on gaining more social justice and economic democracy and an improved quality of life rather than quantitative growth as such. They realize that decisions on investment are central because they affect the volume of employment and the course of the society and seek to influence them.

As for government circles, they prefer to continue their present policies of meeting with the representatives of the various interests and seek through and with them to achieve a state of social and economic equilibrium with few disruptions and for the continued increase and appropriate distribution of the new income. Some fear, however, that the interest groups may overextend their use of the organized system of industrial relations to compromise the authority of the state in their own interest.


## PROJECTIONS FOR THE NEAR FUTURE

No matter what the developments within Belgium itself may be, future conditions will be substantially affected by what happens in the European Economic Community. The general conviction is that no matter what difficulties the movement for European economic integration will later encounter, it is an irreversible phenomenon and will become even stronger. Within this setting the Belgian model may be of special interest to other countries and the European federal organization, for they may also accept the principles prevailing in this country--namely, the creation of a system of concertation or collaboration that accepts the inevitability of the adversary relations and provides appropriate agencies for resolving the differences of interest arising from the short- and long-run conceptions held by the parties. This viable approach may be of special relevance to the European scene as multinational corporations grow in importance and the European trade union system seeks to deal with these corporations.

Within Belgium itself, there is a strong indication reinforced by the new problems of inflation and shortages that these trade union doctrines, programs, and political activities will become more radical in character. The menace of recurrent wildcat strikes and the appearance of antiunion strike committees fostered by activist groups during each period of militancy, despite union leaders' efforts in the light of recent experience to improve their contacts with their following and to educate their responsible militants, continue to reflect the dissatisfaction of members with the union bureaucracies. Moreover, this tension is also growing in part because the managements of a number of enterprises are taking severe steps against union delegates and employees elected as representatives to committees and councils, thereby providing more occasions for conflict at the local level. A further reason for this tension is the growing worker and employee fears of displacement resulting from recent steps toward rationalizing (reorganizing) production processes, mergers, and the closing of plants and enterprises. To these factors must be added the disturbing rise in the cost of living and of unemployment.

All of these developments may tend to polarize groups and intensify feelings among them. However, in the past, the Belgian model of industrial and labor relations was able to absorb similar disruptive experiences and build a more progressive and mature system of relations. It may also be able again to absorb them and adapt itself to the wave of disturbances.

## EDITOR'S NOTE

The economic downturn in the second half of 1974 continued through the early months of 1975. Unemployment rose so that the wholly unemployed reached 6 percent of the active population. To their numbers must also be added the partially unemployed. In February 1975 the major trade union centers staged mass demonstrations against the growing volume of unemployment. Workers occupied plants to prevent their closure, and appealed to the government to keep them in operation. The trade unions demanded that the government also undertake programs for the rehabilitation of the declining industries. The country was also affected by rising prices, for it had experienced a 15 percent increase over the year.

The seventh interprofessional social programming accord for 1975-76 introduced new provisions of great significance. It established a guaranteed minimum monthly wage for unqualified adult workers of 15,500 francs, linked to changes in the cost of living index. Provision was also made for lowering the age of retirement, fixed at 65 years for men and 60 years for women, by one year for employees with 45 years of service (with benefits being fully maintained). In addition, the union centers negotiated with the government a program for accelerated retirement and payment of pensions (prepensions) to males 60 years of age and females 58 years of age who are released by closed plants or employed in plants unlikely to expand. The purpose was to open opportunities to young employees.

## NOTES

1. Guy Spitaels, Le Mouvement Syndical en Belgique (Brussels: Editions de L'Institut de Sociologie, Universite Libre de Bruxelles, 1967), p. 41.

2. World Confederation of Labor (WCL or CMT), Solidarity and Liberation, 28th Congress at Evian, September 25-28, 1973.

3. R. Gubbels, La Greve, Phenomene de Civilisation (Brussels: Institut de Sociologie, Universite Libre de Bruxelles, 1962), p. 211.

4. Cent Ans d'Histoire Sociale en Belgique (Brussels: Edition de L'Universite Libre de Bruxelles, 1972), p. 3.

In the past the Swedes have referred with pride to their industrial relations system and the good relations between management and trade unions. Foreign scholars and politicians spoke admiringly of this association, and some considered it a model for other countries. A characteristic sentiment expressed prior to the 1970s was that "Here has been created a situation of freedom and responsibility, of stability and order that has aroused the admiration and envy of foreign countries."[1]

But this harmony has been disturbed. Evidence of discontent mounts in the form of legal as well as wildcat strikes. Employees have been aroused and are increasingly assertive. The public and politicians are now troubled about the adequacy of the established industrial relations system. They witnessed in 1970 a nine-week illegal strike of miners at the state-owned mining company Luossavaara-Kiirunavaara (LKAB). It was presented as a challenge to union centralism and the neglect of workers' legitimate interests. It attracted much public sympathy and support. There was also the dramatic strike by the Swedish Confederation of Professional Associations (SACO) and the National Federation of Government Officers (SR) in 1971 against public employers. It spread through the entire country and affected railroads, schools, and essential services and threatened to penetrate the defense forces. The government responded through the National Collective Bargaining Board (SAV) with a lockout, a traditional Swedish employer reaction, and then, finally the government itself secured extraordinary legislation for suspending the strike.

These open clashes and the difficulties of resolving differences arising in the periodic renegotiations of agreements, accompanied as they were by threats of bans on overtime and lockouts, raised questions about the efficiency and legitimacy of the entire industrial relations system. People who discounted the importance of these events and characterized the concern as "overreacting" should also note other evidence of tension in the system and demands for change. It appears not as easy now to coordinate and harmonize economic, manpower, and industrial relations policies to achieve simultaneously optimum social reform, economic growth, structural change, full employment, and stability. New realities have intruded that demand new tools for achieving these goals and compromises with tenaciously held tenets of social policy such as egalitarianism, nonintervention-ism of the state into the private economy, and the free collective bar-gaining system. Both the government and the participating organiza-tions are considering new forms and principles of bargaining and the role of labor legislation. The white-collar unions are seeking new arrangements for consolidating their position to graduate to a more independent and coordinate role with the Swedish Confederation of Trade Unions (LO) on the trade union side.

These developments appear to spring from striking changes in the country's economic, political, and social structures and position that occurred during the 1960s. The labor market changed; employ-ment in the public sector increased sharply; blue- and white-collar workers are now about even in numbers; production units are larger; companies are more conglomerate and ownership is more concen-trated; the foreign influence in the domestic economy is greater; and world competition is sharper. The political system that hitherto re-mained aloof from the industrial relations procedures is increasingly being expected to assert itself. Within the trade union movement, some new actors have appeared. The white-collar unions grew in size and are seeking a more independent responsible role. The dominant position of the Swedish Employers' Confederation (SAF) representing private employers is now rather well matched by the SAV and other agencies representing public employers. These phe-nomena are producing pressures for changes in industrial relations structures and for policies that will make the system function effi-ciently and thus retain its legitimacy.

The following analysis presents, first, the fundamental facts of social stratification and the assumptions of the political system basic to the nation's prevailing industrial relations; second, a description of the principal characteristics of the system and the evidences of its malfunctioning; third, a summary of the evidence of the rising volume of social criticism and outright industrial conflicts; fourth, an enumeration of recent economic and political developments affect-ing the industrial relations arrangements and policies; fifth, a list of recent initiatives to change the system; and, finally, our own conclu-sions and projections.

SOCIAL STRATIFICATION: THE BASIS OF INDUSTRIAL
RELATIONS AND POLITICAL SYSTEMS

Social Stratification

The industrial relations and political systems reflect the social
group structure of the country. Though the Social Democratic Party
(SAP) has governed the country for some 40 years and impressive
improvements occurred in the citizen's well-being, since he has attained one of the highest material standards of living in the world,
social group differences persist. They have not spelt an ongoing
bitter class conflict. On the contrary, industrial and political harmony seemed to prevail, impressing the other countries with the
success of the "middle way." What has been distinctive is that the
interest and social groups reached periodic and continuing accommodations of interests with little outright battle.

Sweden enjoys a highly developed industrial system with extensive public services and organizations. Its basic industrial structure
is 90 percent privately owned and dominated by the "15 families,"
index of the high degree of concentration of ownership and capitalist
power.

The active gainfully employed population is unusually high, as
almost four-fifths of the 5 million people aged 18-66 are in the labor
force. Of these, 3.5 million are employees, while 200,000 are
self-employed (75,000 of whom are employers) and another 140,000
are farmers. The 200 largest enterprises employ one-fourth of the
labor force. An examination of the active population by "social
groups" provides a clear insight into the social cleavages in the
country. The three groups are differentiated by type of employment,
level of earnings, and career and are characterized by distinctive
ways of life and outlook. At the top of the ladder are the employers,
higher professionals, and civil servants, mostly with academic degrees. In the middle are white-collar workers and small entrepreneurs and farmers. On the lowest rung are workers, small land-
holders, shop assistants, and workers in the public sector. There
is little social mobility among the three groups. They differ as to
years of schooling, with the highest averaging in 1968, according to
the report of a government commission, 13.2 years and the other
two, 8.8 and 7.2 years respectively. The differences in per capita
property holdings are marked: the middle group's property is valued
at 37 percent of the average of the highest group and the lowest group
is only 14 percent. The respective average annual incomes for 1966
are 31,400 skr, 13,300 skr, and 12,200 skr for the lowest. In an
assessment of the state of nutrition, housing, degree of nervousness,
sight, hearing, teeth, blood circulation, and independence, a uniform

picture was evolved, showing that the degree of disadvantage rises with the decline in social standing.[2]

Social groupings form the basis of the domestic political cleavages. The parties are identified with specific groupings, and the voting pattern of each remains relatively true to this alignment. The degree of voter allegiance to his social group is markedly high, particularly as the country enjoys a highly homogeneous population, and unlike other nations is not troubled by other stratifying forces such as language, race, or religion. The social-economic division is predominant. Each grouping moreover tends to adopt an all-embracing outlook toward most aspects of society.

### The Industrial Relations Organizations Reflect the Stratification

To a greater degree than even the political parties, the national union centers and employer organizations and business associations parallel this social structure and articulate the respective group interests. The labor market is highly organized on the side of the employees, employers, and business interests. Approximately 2.9 million of the gainfully employed belong to a union, while less than 1 million persons acknowledge membership in a political party. The aforementioned 1968 government survey reported that in the population 14-75 years, 5.2 percent were members of political parties and 23.8 percent were members of unions. Whereas 9.4 percent of the respective membership of the political parties attended political meetings, the ratio for union membership was 11.4 percent. The ratios of the membership of the two types of institutions who were organization officials were 3.8 and 9.5 percent respectively. The degree of union membership among the various social groups is unusually high with a higher ratio for nonmanual than manual employees. They are 60 percent for technicians and clerks, 70 percent for blue-collar workers, 75 percent for foremen, and 80 percent for civil servants.[3]

The cleavage between the white- and blue-collar employees is reflected in their various unions. The LO, the traditional dominant base, represents about 1.6 million active workers, largely, but not exclusively, blue-collar workers in both public and private enterprises distributed among 27 industrial federations, 250 local trade councils, 2,300 branches, and 12,000 work clubs. The federations or national unions are responsible for the greater part of the direct bargaining with employers under the guidance of the central body, and their numbers have declined as mergers occur. The "middle-level" white-collar employees belong to the Central Organization of

Salaried Employees (TCO), with 750,000 members. The higher
levels of employees usually join the SACO, with 120,000 members
principally but not exclusively employed in the public service and
including key personnel. The latter two union centers each represent
somewhat more than 20 constituent unions, with more than one-half
of TCO and all of SACO membership belonging to what may be called
craft or occupational unions. SACO, in principle, limits its members
to persons with university degrees. There are also two smaller centers, each with about 20,000 members: SR, collaborating with the
SACO, and the Swedish Syndicalist Union (SAC).

All types and branches of business enterprises are also organized to a high degree in employers' confederations and other associations to promote and safeguard their commercial and political
interests and negotiate with the government on their members' behalf. The SAF had adamantly defended managements' rights to direct
the work force. The employers' organizations are separated by the
form of enterprise ownership. In the private sector, the dominant
one is the SAF, with 25,000 companies employing 800,000 blue-collar
and 400,000 white-collar employees organized in 40 associations.
The cooperatively owned companies are represented through the
Negotiating Board of the Cooperative Union and Wholesale Society
(KFO), and since 1970 the nationalized industries have negotiated
through the Negotiating Organization of National Enterprises (SFO).
In the public sector, the largest three negotiating bodies are the SAV,
the Federation of County Councils, and the Association of Municipalities. The latter three represent bodies employing some 800,000
persons. Table 2 sets forth estimates of the coverage of the agreements among the major employer and trade union organizations, indicating also the total size of the minor agreements and the area not
covered by agreements.

## Collaboration of Organizations with the Political System

One major feature of the Swedish political system is the degree
to which the industrial relations organizations and business associations as well as other special-interest groups are drawn into the
policy development and administrative processes of the government.
Whereas the adjudication of the conflicts of interests in many other
countries is achieved through governmental decisions at the executive
or legislative levels or through outright economic or political battle,
in Sweden it is attained through direct consultations with and negotiations among the parties of interest, and their respective economic
and political bargaining power affects the results. One finds, therefore, that trade unions and employer representatives and spokesmen

### TABLE 2

Estimated Number of Employees Covered by Arrangements by Employer
and Trade Union Organizations, Sweden, 1972

| Trade Union Organizations | Employer Organizations | | | | | Other Contracts | No Contracts |
|---|---|---|---|---|---|---|---|
| | Total | SAF | SAV | Counties | Municipalities | | |
| Total | 2,955,000 | 1,526,000 | 475,000 | 227,000 | 212,800 | 429,000 | 85,200 |
| LO | 1,597,000 | 800,000 | 150,000 | 149,000 | 120,000 | 300,000 | 78,000 |
| TCO | 181,000 | 325,000 | 200,000 | 45,000 | 83,000 | 128,000 | a |
| SACO | 97,000 | 16,000 | 50,000 | 13,000 | 9,800 | 1,000 | 7,200 |
| Other organizations | 25,000 | 5,000 | 20,000 | 20,000[b] | a | a | a |
| No organization | 435,000 | 380,000 | 55,000 | | a | a | a |

a Unknown.

b Included in "No Organization" total.

Source: Data provided by the organizations.

for other organizations not only offer statements of opinions to the
government and parliamentary bodies but also are members of governmental commissions examining specific issues. Their reports
are considered seriously, and their findings are often adopted in toto.
They are also appointed to administrative boards and boards of civil
service agencies at the national and county level, playing an active
role on them. The organizations themselves maintain relatively large
and competent staffs in their national offices for study and analysis of
these problems and to fulfill their many representational functions.
Many important policy and administration initiatives flow from this
participation by the nongovernmental groups. The LO, for example,
is identified as the source of important departures in public economic
and social policies, such as the Swedish manpower policy.

The SAP government supports the consultations and participation as means of moderating political tensions and remaining responsive to new internal developments. Of course, the LO shares other
channels of communication with the SAP government. The SAP and
the LO consider themselves two wings of the same labor movement,
with constant interchange of personnel and formal meetings to achieve
understandings and agreements on policy and strategy. Local branches
of the LO may affiliate with the SAP, and 30 percent of the LO's membership belong to the party through "collective affiliation." Moreover,
a number of LO members are SAP members of parliament. Neither
the TCO nor the SACO has such formal ties, and the greater number
of their members probably vote for the nonsocialist parties.

All central industrial relations organizations are general-
interest agencies that develop policies on the widest range of economic and social problems, including taxation, industrial policy, research, education, and the family.


THE INDEPENDENT COLLECTIVE BARGAINING SYSTEM
IN A SOCIAL-DEMOCRATIC SOCIETY
AND THE EMERGING ISSUES

Independence of the Collective Bargaining System;
Doubts about the "Peace Obligation"

In view of the highly collaborative role of the industrial relations organizations with the government, it is perhaps surprising that
the abiding rule in the Swedish collective bargaining system is noninterference by the government in its operation. This principle is
also observed in collective bargaining between unions and government
bodies. The concept has been formally operative since the signing of
the 1938 Basic Agreement by the LO and SAF at Saltsjobaden. It was

inspired by the parties' desire to avoid further government interference and the growing preference, after the sharp conflicts in the 1920s and early 1930s, for a voluntary system. A special commission organized by the government recommended this course and the parties succeeded in reaching this agreement with the full knowledge of the existing legal framework, particularly reflected in the 1928 collective bargaining legislation. Legal enforcement of collective agreements was already assured and the Labor Court was there to resolve disputes of "rights," the interpretations of the provisions of contracts. Protection was afforded in 1936 for the right to organize. A "peace obligation" forbade resort to economic action, either in the form of strikes or lockouts, during the life of the agreement. The principles were later adopted by other trade union centers and constituents, white-collar groups, and government employees.

Under the Swedish system, the parties within the limits set forth above are free to regulate by agreement other conditions of employment. The state prescribes a limited number of general terms such as working hours, holidays, social insurance, work safety, and of course the conditions for public employees, in the framework of the private agreements. Until the current era, the parties rather zealously adhered to the obligation to respect the public interest. Unions had until recently not insisted on maximum bargaining terms. Employers are reluctant to prosecute strikers, though the SAF from time to time has urged such action. Some people, however, argue that the Labor Court has exacerbated the situation by its decisions.

The Basic Agreements prescribe procedures for negotiations, rules for regulating conflicts dangerous to society, rules respecting the use of economic sanctions, and the procedures for making dismissals or layoffs. Uniquely, the agreements assume that differences will be generally resolved by consultation among the parties, as they, for the period of the contract, strip employees of the use of all power or sanctions to achieve the satisfaction of grievances or new provisions. The "peace obligation" is binding on all unions, by reasons of the 1928 legislation governing collective bargaining. In addition to the Basic Agreement, there are supplementary cooperative agreements covering such subjects as safety, training, works councils, and rationalization.

New voices of dissent are now being heard on the wisdom of maintaining this "peace obligation." Originally it froze the power struggle and was perhaps at the time fairly advantageous to the LO. The critics declare that the "spirit of Saltsjobaden" now calls for worker submission rather than mature cooperation and that the employers are now the primary beneficiaries. In a study of negotiation procedures in labor disputes, Edlund concludes that the employer is "highly privileged" and that it is "hardly conceivable that the system of collective bargaining could function with reasonable efficiency if the employers made maximum use of their rights and resources."[4]

Not only do the employers have institutional advantages but, according to Schmidt, also strategic ones. The lockout, which in Sweden (as in few other countries) is subject to exactly the same regulations as the strike, is a far more powerful weapon. The sympathetic lockout "forms the backbone of the Swedish Employers' Confederation," a counterpart to the trade union use of economic action,[5] which the confederation is prepared to employ.

Moreover, the Labor Court, with tripartite representation, which adjudicates issues of breaches of contract, has tended to have a distinctly conservative influence on industrial relations. The most significant example is its decision relative to article 32 of the SAF constitution, which requires members to include the following article in all collective agreements:

> Reserving the observance of other rules in the agreement, the employer is entitled to direct and distribute the work, to hire and dismiss workers at will, and to employ workers whether they are organized or not.
>
> The right of association shall be left inviolate on both sides.

When the metal workers sought to escape this provision by resisting its inclusion in their contract, the Labor Court ruled that employers enjoy these prerogatives as a legal right and that it was therefore applicable to the entire labor market and even to those relationships that do not specifically include it in their agreements. The SAF over the years has steadfastly maintained this right for management to direct hiring and work arrangements and yielded only to some qualifications of it. The "peace obligation" has therefore forced unions to abandon direct industrial action and not to support individuals or local groups who resort to such tactics.

This position has created the paradox of critical importance on the industrial relations scene. Labor organizations with a powerful position in the area of a national policy determination and administration find themselves very limited in their powers to intervene in industrial or plant policy or administration. Particularly at the local levels, unions and employees can secure adjustments only at the employer's discretion.

In recent years the labor shortage inhibited abuse and promoted more rational personnel policies, but with rising unemployment levels the issue again became critical. The trade unions' acquiescence until recently to this asymmetrical disadvantageous position can be best understood by their dedication to the national economic goals and their trust in the political process and governmental influences to prevent extremely unsatisfactory conditions. Relevant is also the unions' trust in the employers' good will and the ability of workers to overlook marginal aspects of their jobs.

## Fixed Areas of Competence of Parties and New Questions

The demarcation between union and employer areas of competence set by Article 32 and the principles of noninterference by the government into collective bargaining served the parties for many years. Moreover, each respectfully observed and defended the rules and discouraged alterations. Nevertheless, changes are now forthcoming. The suspension in 1971 of the employee's right to strike, of course, severely shook the entire framework.

Unions are now also reconsidering other current lines of demarcation. When bargaining between the LO, TCO, and SAF on workers' representation in management failed, they accepted legislation on the subject, even though it was labeled as provisional. The SACO white-collar unions raised other basic questions in their 1966 and 1971 strikes. They complained that the government through its tax policy and preferences for the low-income groups had unduly discriminated against the higher-paid employees, reducing the differentials. Simultaneously, the government was faced by the ability of the SACO unions in a free collective bargaining system to counteract political decisions to narrow income differentials by securing advantageous agreements through collective bargaining.

## Centralization and Friction among Union Centers, National Unions, and Members

The determination to enforce national objectives and policies not only produced "responsible" positions but also encouraged centralization of authority within each national union and the LO as a union center. Evidence of this development may be found in the following:

1. The principle of the "double veto" was adopted by the 1941 LO Congress. It gave the LO secretariat the right to pass on any strike that extends to more than 3 percent of the union's members and required each union to provide in its constitution for its executive board to have the final word on strikes and matters of contracts.

2. Since 1952, the LO has increasingly become the principal party in collective bargaining negotiating framework contracts with

the SAF and in overseeing the allocation of the negotiated sums in the
separate union negotiations and retaining a hand in the supplementary
separate branch and shop club negotiations. Membership referendums
on contracts have practically disappeared.

3. With the merger of separate unions and the consolidation of
the branches, by 70 percent, the role of the separate union diminished,
and representational forms of participation prevailed. The number
of full-time union officers appointed by the unions' boards increased
substantially.

Many forces besides those enumerated above conspired to this
end. The LO sought not only to assure greater authority for itself to
promote economic growth and stability but also to enforce its preferences for greater economic equality through its solidary wage policy.
Moreover, the SAF encouraged this centralization not only because
the SAF itself was highly centralized and enforced a stringent discipline upon its members but also because the centralization facilitated
the coordination of wage agreements and made possible uniform settlements and promoted national control. Moreover, both parties
realized that this centralization brought with it the danger of more
far-reaching conflicts when breakdowns occurred, but they each believed that this possibility would lead to more responsible bargaining.
In recent years, the LO used threats of bans on overtime and selective
strikes and the SAF used lockouts as tactics in the bargaining process
that were not actually carried out.

To the LO, the centralization of authority is one way to assure
the attainment of a solidary, equitable wage result where workers
neither "overbid" nor "underbid" each other. It is also a form of
"incomes policy" that combines considerations of social responsibility
with freedom from state interference in collective bargaining.

The high degree of centralization has also played a considerable
role in recent wildcat strikes where members protested against national settlements or their failure to get resolutions for their special
complaints. These stoppages invariably produced improvements over
and above the national settlements. In addition, the efforts to enforce
central policies led to the creation of an independent union among
dockworkers (1971). From time to time, individual unions withdrew
from coordinated bargaining, but they received little support from the
LO and encountered increasing difficulties with the SAF.

The central organization of the LO became increasingly aware
of the shortcomings of this process and sought to overcome them with
other communication techniques, such as opinion surveys and "grass-
roots conferences." The "mini-LO" survey gives the LO secretariat
access to members' views. During the discussion of the recent government bill on safety, the LO organizations specifically discussed

the matter with some 4,000 groups, including 75,000 members. It is reported that these reviews had a substantial impact on the final bill. The LO and its constituent unions depend considerably upon their educational programs for contacts with members and for conveying its messages. Moreover, it has relied on and stimulated class solidarity to maintain support for its program.

The problems in the other two large union centers are different. In the TCO the member unions are distributed over a wide range of industries and types of employers. The challenge has been to attain the necessary degree of cohesion to match the LO in their relations with the government and the public administration. Cooperation is achieved through the aggregation of unions into three bodies: TCO-S, for state employees; TCO-K, for municipal employees; and a new organization established in 1973, PTK, the Cartel of Private Employee Unions. The latter is to include some SACO unions. In the government sector, this move to centralization is favored by the government's practice of addressing itself to the central organization rather than the constituent units. With the formation of the PTK, coordination by the TCO of its three principal "political blocs" probably will be smoother, for this structure will better reflect the strengths of the respective interests. It is probable that the central TCO leadership will have less influence on the bargaining policy and tactics of the constituent "blocs."

Centralization in the SACO is more difficult since there is a history of tension between the secretariat and the larger unions. When, in 1968, the secretary general came out on top, the board of directors had to resign. After the 1971 strike, the roles were reversed. The secretary general resigned, and the individual unions are again more actively engaged in bargaining. The SACO unions negotiate separately with the private and municipal sectors, but SACO is the contracting party in the negotiations with the state.

Coordinated Bargaining: Source of Interunion Tension

The issue that is most seriously dividing the union centers and employers is coordination of bargaining. Neither the TCO nor the SACO uniformly achieved this result among their own constituent unions, but the LO consistently pursued this course. Centralized bargaining had coordination as its underlying objective. The centrally negotiated agreement was applicable to all, and the funds assigned to each industry or sector or group or individual were defined in the central agreement. Coordination automatically followed. The "peace agreement" discouraged open dissent in all but a few cases.

The LO also developed an internally consistent economic policy and program for achieving its ends. It advocated an active manpower policy in conjunction with noninflationary fiscal and monetary policies and a favorable posture to increasing industrial efficiency within the plants and in the total economy by supporting the elimination of marginal industries and plants. The manpower programs were to provide for occupational transfers, aids for geographical mobility, temporary public or archival work, aids for temporary production, and a system of company-owned investment funds to encourage industry to dampen investments in boom periods and expand them in recessions. The government would, therefore, not be encouraged to follow inflationary employment policies. Unions would be able to restrain themselves from asking for unstabilizing wage increases. The conclusion of a central formula applicable to all was the answer, and since 1956 they have followed this procedure. To enforce this program and advance the solidary wage program, the LO from 1966 negotiated increases to compensate for part of the wage drift enjoyed by some workers between the dates of contract negotiation and termination for all who did not receive such additions.

While the program was gradually and persistently developed and provisions were secured for its realization, the results have not always been satisfactory. The program has also produced a schism in the union front between the LO and the white-collar unions. The causes are largely to be found outside of the LO in general economic and social developments.

The program rested on the assumption that the LO and SAF would dominate the scene. Two developments called this premise into question. First, new unions appeared, and their size and importance grew, particularly among the expanding white-collar group of employees. Second, the public-service sector also increased in importance and its negotiating bodies pursued policies independently of the SAF. The question became whether the LO and the SAF would lead, or, as history unfolded, whether others would challenge the SAF leadership by taking independent action and resisting coordination.

In the early years, the LO-SAF contract set the pace and the others followed and more or less adopted the resulting package of wages and benefits. When the SACO and TCO showed independence, the LO declared in 1971 that it would not sign its agreement until the formers' contracts were concluded. Only in 1973 did the LO again take the lead. The disparity of views on principles of wage determination had come to light and troubled the LO. The white-collar groups particularly SACO and SR, demanded the "wages-after-taxes" rather than the "solidary-wage" approach. Income differentials became the central issue.

After the 1967 SAF proposal for a new approach to wages, the SAF, LO, and TCO economists studied the issue and brought out a report that offered an economic model for calculating an acceptable

level of increases in labor costs in each sector exposed to foreign
competition and sheltered one.[6] It was received well by the TCO,
guardedly by the LO, and even more coolly by the SAF, and no formal
coordinating structure resulted.

One immediate illustration of the difficulties in getting coordination among the groups was the conclusion of a five-year contract
signed in 1970 by the white-collar unions with the SAF and one for
10 years signed by the journalists with the newspaper industry.
Moreover, the government developed, under the impetus of its electoral commitments to greater equality, renewed dedication to the
solidary wage principle for its own employees. In the 1971 strike,
this view was specifically implemented. The state gave the lower-
income white-collar groups even more than they had expected.

The issue of coordination remains unresolved. Uneasiness
persists about the present competitive stances of the unions, in the
private and public sectors, on wage policy. Recognition exists of the
need for coordination. Many suggestions are being offered. Some
propose a multipartite structure of negotiations; others, round-table
talks; still others, direct participation by the state in the pursuance
of a program of cooperation toward a common income pattern, an
approximation of an income policy. The end of this search is still
not within sight.

### Preference for Parliamentary Social Reform to Militant Union Wage Policy and Industrial Action

The LO in the postwar years favored parliamentary social reform over aggressive union wage policy and militant industrial action.
It considered itself one wing of the labor movement, the spokesman
and organizer of the working class in support of the Social Democratic
Party's position in government and the maintenance of its strength in
industrial relations. The aims were to advance economic growth
and stability and greater economic equality without undermining the
solvency or prosperity of capitalism. Retiring LO Chairman Arne
Geijer in an interview in the summer of 1973 declared that "you
must see to it that industry can flourish in order that you can secure
substantial wage increases and social benefits."

The position of the LO and SAP was to avoid undue direct intervention into the capitalist market economy and limit governmental
action to steps to achieve economic stability and maintain full employment. It did not seek a major change in the power structure in
the economy. The LO had a responsibility not merely to its members but to the entire working class. The collective-bargaining
approach would merely benefit the organized working population and

the strongest groups within it, whereas legislative action would favor all. Militant action would disturb the economy. Workers affected adversely by economic growth should be relieved by social measures and enjoy higher incomes so long as they do not conflict with the principles of the solidary wage policy. Both the industrial and political wings of the labor movement should push for heavier and more egalitarian tax, social security, and manpower policies.

The result of this dedication was an impressive expansion of social programs including various forms of social insurance and public housing. The social programs currently represent an expenditure of about 30 billion skr. If to this sum are added the costs of other programs with a social purpose and the municipal expenses in this field and compulsory insurance fees, the total would be 42 billion skr, or about one-fifth of the national GNP.

Aggressive industrial action was not considered an essential instrument for the conduct of the movement. Arne Geijer declared it "not a proof of a struggling union; rather it is an indication of unsuccessful negotiations." The number and intensity of legal strikes declined during the 1950s and 1960s. Negotiations were the alternative. Where it was not productive, unions had to look to the political arm of the labor movement to force through legislation.

Under the system of industrial relations with centralization and coordination and the "peace obligation," the locals were stripped of much of their power and responsibilities. They did discharge the task of applying the wage sums designated by the negotiating bodies. Their representatives sat on numerous cooperative bodies with management. But settlements of grievances largely depended upon management's good will. Locals could force up issues from the local to union levels and onto the confederation level, but the chances of being considered were minimal. The responsibility to the total society overrode local worker issues.

The dissatisfaction with these restrictions became particularly evident in 1969 and subsequently. Groups protested against the drop in the proportion of personal disposable incomes, the failure to treat local problems, and reliance on manpower policy rather than direct regular employment to solve the unemployment problem. And the white-collar groups also resented the rate of the narrowing of earnings differentials.

### Subordination of Shop-Problem Resolution to Broad Economic Gains

Work was considered by the spokesmen of the labor movement to be a way to realize a higher material standard of living and little

else.  The LO programs up to 1966 did neglect worker concerns about
matters other than earnings and full employment.  The trade union
movement acquiesced to structural changes in industry, payment-by-
result schemes, shift work, and minimal control on short-cycle work.
Gestures toward worker participation in decision-making took the
form of works councils and joint committees, which proved unsatisfactory and inadequate.  Worker job controls were not encouraged.
Rather, the reverse was true.  The union favored management initiative toward greater efficiency to attain higher earnings.  The union
center would not stand in its way of achieving this end.  Works councils should also contribute to higher efficiency.

These positions proved increasingly less viable toward the end
of the 1960s.  Workers reacted adversely to these principles of the
industrial relations system developed jointly by the LO and SAF.
They sought change.

Solidary Wage Policy: Pressures for Further Elaboration

The solidary wage policy became a basic plank in the LO and
SAF programs in the 1950s and remained so in the face of considerable practical difficulties and challenges by employees with higher
incomes and by other union centers.  It proposed to decrease wage
differentials and reward people according to the principle of "equal
pay for equal work" and eliminate low wages.  Job rate differentials
would be set by deliberate evaluation, a goal that has not been
achieved.  Labor, it was argued, was not to subsidize industry with
cheap wages.  Industries unable to afford these rates must be put out
of business and replaced by expanding competitive ones.  Employees
displaced by these national gains should be helped by manpower programs to secure better and more productive jobs.  A highly efficient
competitive private economy would provide these jobs, while training, mobility allowances, relief work, and other forms of employment would be offered for the interim by the National Swedish Labor
Market Board (AMS).  Continued growth would thereby be assured;
the economy would be stabilized; free collective bargaining would
proceed without governmental intervention and without a state-
determined income policy.

LO pressed this campaign against low wages and sought through
collective bargaining to narrow differentials.  Progressively, the LO
in its contracts, beginning in 1964, secured special funds for raising
the earnings of the lower-paying industries, plants, and individuals.
Unions were permitted to negotiate separate funds for advancing
these groups.  The gains enjoyed by some groups through the wage
drift were to be offset by "guaranteed minimum wage drifts" for the

others. There was relentless pressure for this egalitarian end in the negotiations in the private sector, and then the government added its power by offering special concessions to the lower-income groups among government employees. The labor movement stressed and sought to increase "equality" in earnings.

Employers put up resistance in negotiations, but the LO persisted and consistently elaborated the programs in successive negotiations. But in the bargaining at the union level, employers at times managed to maintain established differentials. The LO responded by getting specific funds in the frame contract to be used for this purpose. The wage drift was offset by the abovementioned guarantee of a minimum of such gains to all.

The result has been a decided narrowing of the spread. The differential in average hourly earnings between contract areas declined from 30 percent in 1959 to 15 percent in 1972. In the metal industry, a study shows that individual differences appear to have declined by 10 percent from 1961 to 1971. An intensive inquiry for the period from 1970 to 1972 found that the differences among contract areas were reduced by 23 percent and among individuals by 15 percent. Cautious observers would declare that the solidary wage principle had as a minimum prevented a widening of income gaps among union members.

Without fear of contradiction, it may be concluded that the spread between men's and women's wages narrowed under the relentless pressure of unions. The LO saw to it that women received higher increases than men in the negotiations from 1951 to 1968, and they continued to enjoy the benefits of wage drifts.[7]

Nevertheless, the dispute on the validity of this principle continues, particularly among higher-paid white-collar employees who have determinedly insisted on their rights to the maintenance of their differentials. The 1971 strike dramatized the issue as the SACO and SR in particular protested the diminution of differentials in "after-tax" earnings. The white-collar salaried unions challenged this principle. Both SACO and TCO insist upon the principle of individual salary determination based on the person's capacity and performance and the difficulties of the task.

The TCO's system of job classification sets up 13 groups and 8 hierarchical levels that serve as a statistical reference for wage negotiations rather than as a method of job evaluation for fixing wage rates. Wage agreements provide for general increases in percentages to which are added increases for individuals, which are locally negotiated. Moreover, the SACO and SR continue to insist on the right to maintain "real income" levels for their following and for income to be tested in terms of "life income" and not gross income, as is the mode for lower-paid employees. University graduates start their work careers later and make larger investments in education.

Their group has not enjoyed adequate offsets for inflation and carries a much higher tax burden in a country where income tax rates are progressively higher for the upper-income employees.

But the LO and the SAP held fast to their position. The LO argued that the higher wage increases in sheltered industries in which the low-paid groups are concentrated relate to matters of internal policy in the distribution of incomes and do not raise issues of world competitiveness. True enough, the policy leads to increasing difficulties for the hard-core unemployed, but the response is to liberalize manpower programs and allow them to provide special assistance for people who encounter greater difficulties in securing reemployment. Both educational and social programs necessarily must be harmonious with these egalitarian goals.

Professional economists and conservatives generally remain critical of the policy. They argue that it intensifies unemployment and recessions. The leftists also dissent, for they would like the strategically located workers, like automobile employees, to exploit their bargaining power to secure greater gains. Under the present system the policy merely enriches the internationally competitive industries. In response to this charge, the LO is considering proposing the establishment of "branch funds" made up of the "excess profits" flowing from the workers' restraint to be managed by employees and to be used for reinvestment in expanding and newer industries. This issue came to the fore in 1974, with the marked rise in industrial profits. LO leaders took exception to the action of the minister of Finance who prescribed the use of these higher profits in part for worker-controlled "work environment" funds. They preferred these funds be set aside for periods of economic slackness. Pressure also continues to be applied by the higher-income unionized employees, in some degree within but principally outside of the LO, to maintain their differentials in "incomes after taxes." But the official LO attitude remains that of pressure for a solidary wage policy. The ultimate goal of the solidary wage policy is not to secure the abolition of all wage differentials. It seeks to reduce them and to introduce a system of labor-market-wide job evaluations for a more just wage structure, which takes into consideration differences in job hardships, risk, and other factors. The resulting system of differentials would be markedly different from the one that obtains today.

## SOCIAL CRITICISM AND OUTRIGHT INDUSTRIAL CONFLICT

### Social Criticism

The Swedish industrial relations structure in the last quarter-century was remarkably stable and unchanged. As we have seen, the situation with respect to the solidary wage was different. It evolved from a new conception of what is a fair wage structure, and this goal was substantially realized.

The stability appeared to be based upon the impressive economic gains enjoyed by the population. The standard of living in the first two postwar decades improved. Employment remained high in terms of labor force participation rates and low in terms of unemployment. Wages and earnings developed favorably, and the work week declined from 48 to 40 hours. Vacations doubled in length to four weeks. The material standards of living improved measurably. On the average, 63 percent of all households had a car; 37 percent owned their own house; 78 percent lived in a modern house or apartment; 18 percent owned a second country home. The working class shared in these benefits.[8]

But at the end of the 1960s social criticism intensified and reached a new high pitch. The complaint was that class differences persisted despite all of these gains. The inequalities originating in the work place were carried over into the broader society.

The LO heard the protest that the worker still carried the major load of economic and social costs of industrial change. Politicians like Olof Palme, later prime minister, and LO Chairman Arne Geijer made notable speeches on the topic of social and economic inequality. Geijer said at the SAP congress in 1967:

> Listening to the debate one could get the impression that with fast economic growth all our problems will be solved. That might be correct in a wide perspective, but for the individual this development means a higher risk of increased income differentials. . . .
>
> Dynamic development is a prerequisite for economic and social progress, but we must demand that the additional product created by us all is not used to widen the income gap. . . .
>
> Inequality is documented not only in income statistics, but also in social conditions on the labor market. Those with the lowest wages have also, as a rule, the longest hours, the worst environment, the dirtiest and heaviest jobs and also the highest age of retirement.

In the following elections, the platform of the Social Democratic Party was entitled "Increased Equality."

Concurrently, the unrest expressed itself in an expanding volume of socially critical literature and new political groups and leftist parties. Journalists, writers, and social scientists published articles and books on the physical and psychic impact of the work environment and the influence of a highly organized and increasingly centralized society on man. Work problems that had hitherto been the almost exclusive province of the trade union and labor movements became election-winning political issues. Clause 32 of the Basic Agreement received renewed major attention. The exclusive right of employers to hire and dismiss employees and direct the work force was questioned. Unions were accused of disregarding the underlying conflicts of employers and employees on matters other than wages. Some groups raised the issue of relaxing the restraints of the "peace obligation." Demands began to be made for more rights for the safety stewards to supervise work conditions. A series of articles and books before the 1970 strikes highlighted these conditions. One result of this campaign and the industrial conflicts was renewed interest in industrial democracy, particularly in the labor movement, and in more substantial economic structural reforms.

It would appear that the major impact of the agitation of the leftist groups was upon the subjects of discussions and the formulation of issues, for their political influence was at best minimal. The main political pressure for reform came from the LO and the SAP. None of the new leftist parties drew as much as 1 percent of the vote. The older Communist Party (VPK) gained in votes, but its advances were not impressive.

Outright Industrial Conflict

The rising volume and intensity of social criticism coincided with a growth in the volume of industrial conflict. The industrial scene had been peaceful during the 1950s and 1960s. Except for the big strike in 1945 and some conflicts at the beginning of the 1950s (1951 and 1954), the first 20 postwar years were remarkably quiet. But, from 1969, disturbances kept growing in number. They reached a peak in 1970, causing, according to official statistics, 216 unofficial strikes, but this number hardly tells the full story. Not all strikes are reported. A special study for the metal industry for 1955-67 based on an analysis of stoppages in 46 plants found that there had been in them 34 wildcat stoppages and 60 collective demonstrations. Only 15 were known to the union. The official statistics reported only nine.[9] Nor is this deficiency necessarily due to the exclusion by definition of small strikes, because the regulations do provide for reporting them, and some are reported. In fact, in 1970, the SAF, in trying to combat the rash of wildcat strikes, urged its members to report all incidents and forwarded this information to the Central Bureau of Statistics, which accounts, in part, for the higher volume in later years.

There is, however, no doubt of the soundness of the above generalization about the growing volume of stoppages and conflicts during the recent period. What, however, is equally significant is that the year of the greatest number of strikes hardly compares with the two years of SACO strikes, 1966 and 1971, in work days lost. The proportion of illegal strikes increased, constituting 60 percent of all strikes in 1969; 100 percent in 1970; 93 percent in 1971; and 77 percent in 1972. The duration of strikes rose. Some big wildcat conflicts affected the most prominent companies, such as ASEA, Electrolux, Saab, Scania, and Volvo. The very biggest strike was directed against the state itself. Both private and public employers were hit. Probably the municipal sector was the most peaceful.

A number of changes also occurred in the manner in which the unofficial strikes were conducted. They were better organized. New strikes adopted tactics displayed by prior ones. Meetings were arranged with the workers, with the press and TV in attendance. Greater stress was placed on providing the public with information. The striking dock workers in the fall of 1969 in Gothenburg publicized their grievances and complaints about high rates of injury, casualness of employment, and other unsatisfactory working conditions. They were, thus, the first to obtain substantial public contributions and support, making up for the unions' failure to finance them.

## Miners' Strike (1969-70)

There had been individual strikes like that of the teachers in 1966, which attracted broad attention, but it was the miners' strike against the LKAB company, which started as a complaint against piece work, that really dramatized the phenomenon. It lasted for 57 days and involved 4,700 employees at its peak. The mines are state-owned, and on the board of directors are LO and SAP officials. The workers complained of tightening discipline, a faster work pace, inadequate piece rates, and a lag in wages. Initially, their disgruntlement focused on the contract imposed on one company branch despite its disapproval by the local unions.

The strikers sought higher minimum wages, earlier retirement, better safety regulations, particularly with respect to noise and gas, the abolition of the piece-rate system, and the elimination of the authoritarian style of company leadership. To the fore came regional issues and resentment of union centralization and discrimination against their own local unions within the miners' union, which was dominated by the Social Democrats from the small locals of southern Sweden. The strike forced the national union leadership to respond to the criticism. A campaign resulted in the collection of some 4.5 million skr for assistance and conduct of the strike.

An early compromise was negotiated by the union but was rejected by the workers. The strike was finally settled through mediation of an LO officer who was called in as a "consultant" to the workers. The strike leaders thereafter maintained their independent organization to press for further internal union reform but lost out at the union congress and local branch elections. The "unofficial" strike committee continued to operate as a center of opposition to the official trade union movement and helped finance strikes in other parts of Sweden with the funds that remained from their collection.

Other workers caught the spirit, and wildcat strikes spread. They were irritated by unsolved local issues, inflationary pressure, and new developments and problems. Moreover, they utilized the strike tactic to support their special demands in their negotiations on local supplementary agreements. The rash spread. The SAF tried to get managements to hold fast by offering to compensate them for losses. It proposed to pay them from the first day of the strike, rather than in accordance with the usual period, after one week. It also required the companies to refuse to negotiate with the strikers while they remained on strike and at SAF's request to sue them before the Labor Court. Managements most often tried to settle the strikes along these lines, but with as little public attention as possible and without antagonizing their employees. Accordingly, few cases were brought before the court.

Following the 1974 settlement, a new wave of unofficial strikes hit the economy. It was partially a reaction against the wholly unsatisfactory agreements consummated in the midst of the energy crisis. Rising industrial profits also stimulated considerable discontent. It appears to be laying the foundations for a more enduring pattern of unofficial local strikes being called whenever unsatisfactory central agreements are concluded. The SAF reacted to these acts by encouraging the discharge of "leftist agitators," who took an active part in fomenting these strikes.

## The Public-Sector Conflict (1971)

The official strike among the public employees was another dramatic rupture in the established system of industrial relations. It was the second large-scale reaction of the higher ranks of public employees. In 1966, SACO teachers, and now, SACO and SR, struck, measures that had not been taken by workers in such numbers since 1945. It reflected the tensions created by the unresolved issues of the relations between the LO and the three other union centers and between the private and public sectors as pace-setters. Municipal employees, engineers, social workers, and other white-collar employees went on strike on February 1, 1971. SACO also gave notice

of its intention to take similar action against the national government.
In retaliation, the SAV announced the wholesale lockout of 28,000
SACO members and 2,500 SR members, following the SAF tradition
of meeting strikes or threats thereof by lockouts. Moreover, it also
announced its intentions of locking out other important SR groups, including military officers. Public services, trains, and other utilities
stopped functioning. Underlying the strike was resentment against
the Social Democratic policy of decreasing income differentials by
both tax and wage policies, which had resulted in the narrowing of the
effective earnings differentials between lower- and higher-paid employees. The strikers complained of their inability to gain the special benefits earned by other groups through the wage drift or to
secure offsets against inflation. SACO and SR as organizations were
throughout the strike protesting the government's efforts to force
them to follow a line similar to that adopted in the LO wage policy.

Negotiations between the parties and mediation proved unsuccessful. Then the government took the unprecedented step of asking
the parliament to suspend the employees' right to strike for six
weeks. SACO and SR members returned to work, but the organizations refused to sign the contract. The resentment and embitterment
colored further relations between these two organizations and the LO
and the government.

## THE NEW ECONOMIC ENVIRONMENT, LABOR
## MARKET, AND SOCIAL ASPIRATIONS

The unrest and dissatisfaction with the existing system of industrial relations evidenced in the preceding review springs from
changes in the external economic and industrial conditions. A sense
of frustration permeates the employed population--a feeling that their
problems, needs, and views are not adequately canvassed or met.
They are unduly burdened by the costs of industrial change, and the
rate itself of such charge is excessive. Reformism is being asked to
adapt to a new more dynamic but less profitable era.

### A Period of Economic Sluggishness

Until the recession of 1966-67, the postwar Swedish economy
flourished almost without interruption, suffering only intermittent
setbacks in the rate of economic growth. The situation in the labor
market was more or less balanced; prices and wage increases also
moved in a parallel manner. From 1969, after the recovery, the
economy became sluggish again under the monetary restraints of

1971-72. The rates of economic growth and private investments receded; deficits appeared in the balance of payments in the years 1967-70. Surpluses showed up in 1971-73, but at the high price of a rising volume and rate of unemployment.

Industry, which had been the largest employer, lost its preeminence, to be replaced by the service sector. Per capita GNP, which had grown in Sweden at the rate of 5.4 percent in the first half of the 1960s, somewhat above the 5.1 percent rate for the major OECD industrial countries, dropped back to 3.9 percent in the second half, falling below the 4.5 percent of these OECD countries. In 1971, the GNP recorded no improvement, and in 1972 it was 2.4 percent, less than half of the figure for the OECD countries. Productivity increased by 7 to 8 percent in the earlier period but shrank to 4 or 5 percent in the latter years. Private investments were high in volume in 1958 through 1961, but then the rate sagged and was concentrated on labor-saving rather than expansionary items, largely because of the drop in profits and labor shortages in expanding regions. OECD estimates point to a conclusion that unit labor costs in manufacturing industries were rising more slowly than in other countires, and Sweden gained a competitive edge from the 1973 devaluation of the krona.[10] The price, however, was large-scale displacement and persistently higher unemployment. Industrialists hesitated to invest, to some extent probably because they feared that the government's insistence on "increased equality" would divert or contain profits in private industry.

Questions were being raised about the continued competitiveness of critical industries. It is pointed out that wage and other costs were among the highest in Europe, and public expenditures exceeded the level in competitive nations. Income taxes were unusually high. The 1971-72 recession appeared to reinforce these concerns since it was more severe than in other countries, a relatively new experience for Sweden.

Some business spokesmen and economists questioned whether the supply of new capital would be sufficient to maintain new growth, particularly of the type needed to advance specialized industrial production on which the economy traditionally depended. The government responded by arranging for public investment in industry. A State Investment Bank was established. The National Supplementary Pension Fund will invest part of its assets in private corporate shares, and other investment incentives and aids were also developed. The growth of Swedish foreign investment provided another area of concern lest it reflect the noncompetitiveness of the mother country. Swedish business grew more rapidly abroad than at home. The number of Swedish subsidiaries according to one report increased from 890 in 1960 to 1,806 in 1969, and they are presently growing at an

even faster rate. In 1970, there were 430 Swedish manufacturing
subsidiaries in foreign countries. Investments in Finland increased
markedly, especially in textiles, because of the lower wages. In
1970, new fixed investment by Swedish manufacturing industry abroad
amounted to 22 percent of total new fixed investment by Swedish industry. Multinational Swedish companies showed a rise of employment
in 1965-70 of 24 percent and sales by 80 percent in foreign countries.
In Sweden itself these companies revealed a rise of 45 percent in sales
and an actual decline in employment in manufacturing.[11] On the other
hand, foreign companies have invested in Sweden. The government
also has participated in investments in companies owned partly by the
state in a private Swedish company, and in foreign-owned enterprises.

## Structural Problems Aggravated

The sluggish economic performance aggravated long-standing
economic problems. The North, the western inland areas, and some
parts of the southeast constitute persistent problems. Migration from
these sections has been an ongoing phenomenon. The labor market
authorities facilitated this movement with special aids to migration
and through arranged transfers to public works in populated areas and
retraining. Many migrants actually return to their home areas. Regional economic development programs have become more extensive,
but they have not measured up to the size of the challenge.

The economic backwardness of the area may have been reduced,
but unrest persists in local political contests and appears whenever
other issues arise among workers. The miners' strike of 1969-70
projected these issues and demands for more investments in northern
areas. The longshoremen on the Northern Baltic coast broke away
from their own union to emphasize their concern that the union was
not doing enough to protect their jobs. The charge of the insufficiency
of past efforts to promote regional development was a leading issue in
the 1973 parliamentary election and added to the intensity of dissatisfaction with employment and high taxes.

The strong trend toward mergers presents further sources of
difficulty in the industrial scene. The annual number had been progressively rising from 50 in 1946 to 396 in 1969. After a reduction
in 1970 and 1971, it is presumed that the number moved up again.
These mergers often lead to plant consolidation, with consequent
complaints and disturbances in the labor force.

## Structural Changes in the Labor Market

The number of employed persons, participation rates, and the
number of hours worked rose until the middle 1960s. Since then the

number of employed has continued to increase, in part because of the shortening of the work week ultimately to 40 hours, but working hours remained level. In both 1971 and 1972, when the economy contracted, the number of employed remained stable and working hours declined. The total working hours were below those of every year since 1963.

The importance of industry as an employer also declined in absolute terms. On the other hand, the numbers employed in public employment, particularly at the local government level, expanded. Rural industries shrank and the number of self-employed dropped. Manual workers are decreasing both in absolute numbers and as a percentage of the work force. The number of white-collar employees is growing markedly, and it is projected that they will equal blue-collar employees by 1980.


## The Immigrant Worker

Immigration was until recently a minor political issue. Alien workers numbered 113,000 in 1961, and most of them came from neighboring countries. The additions were modest until 1965, when the number was 146,000. But subsequently, the net additions have been consequential, rising during periods of great industrial activity and then even in the period of high unemployment in 1967/68. The number of alien workers at the end of 1969 was 176,000, rising to 224,000 at the end of 1971 and receding only in 1972 to 218,000. The Finns constitute about half of the total, and the remaining Nordic nationals who enjoy free access to Sweden under the 1954 Common Nordic Labor Market agreement constitute another 12 percent. The remainder consists of persons from Southern Europe, particularly Greece and Yugoslavia. The aliens now total some 5 percent of the labor force and are concentrated in industries such as metal, hotels, and restaurants. They enjoy most of the rights of Swedish citizens and may establish permanent residences. Actually the average weekly wages of LO-organized immigrants are slightly above those of the average native worker. The government's National Immigration and Naturalization Board makes considerable efforts to help these persons acquire a mastery of the Swedish language as well as to adjust to conditions. The National Swedish Labor Market Board (AMS) encourages employers and unions to organize special facilities and committees for helping the immigrants.

The LO has been much concerned about the numbers entering the country, and local branches have exercised their effective veto in the review of applications. In 1973 the labor market parties and the governments of Finland and Sweden entered into an agreement to improve the immigration process both to eliminate abuse and to funnel the movements through official employment agencies. One new requirement calls upon employers to provide 240 paid hours to immigrants from all countries for attendance at free language courses. It is expected that such costs will discourage employers from turning to foreign labor and encourage preference for Swedes and absorb some of the unemployed. Large-scale domestic unemployment and the rising problems of discrimination increased the resistance to the further acceptance of immigrants, and of course the recession reduced the demand for them.

## Large Intractable Unemployed Groups

The unprecedented rise in unemployment for the postwar period and its intractability as well as impact on groups previously relatively immune proved highly disillusioning. Serious doubts developed about the ability of the SAP government and the "active manpower policy" to cope with these issues, as had been their proud boast.

Open unemployment rose in 1968 to 2.2 percent and to unprecedentedly high levels in 1971 of 2.5 percent and in 1972 of 2.7 percent. Despite the marked rise in output in 1973 and the first half of 1974, the rate did not recede satisfactorily. To these rates are added the persons benefiting from labor market measures, including employment relief work and training, who numbered 126,000 in 1971, and 161,000 in 1972; the cumulative rates of unemployment are not particularly favorable in relation to some other Western countries. To these persons one could also add the latent job seekers (persons who would have been looking for work except that they believed no work was available), whose numbers normally exceed those for the unemployed; the resulting picture is one of high unemployment, a relatively novel experience for postwar Sweden. Nevertheless it is important to note the large number of people being assisted by the AMS (Labor Market Board) and other measures as well as the high rate of labor participation.

The magnitude and unusual character of this development is mirrored in other important trends. The average length of unemployment for men increased from 7.8 weeks in 1966, to 10.3 weeks in 1968, and to 15.1 weeks in 1972. The number in the category of "hard-core unemployed" has risen. As the unemployment rates are higher among the working than middle and upper employee classes, by a ratio of 3 to 1, the burden is falling disproportionately on this group. One new aspect of this experience is the comparatively greater rate of increase of unemployment among those in the age group from 16 to 24 and including fresh university graduates, whereas the rise was lower among the middle age groups and lowest in the bracket from 55 to 64 years, for whom the unemployment rate was usually high. Until 1966, unemployment among unionized white-collar employees was below 0.5 percent. The rate for the major insurance funds in 1971, for the first time, exceeded 1 percent, and in 1972 it was at least 0.5 percent higher. Unemployment in the private industries is disproportionately high, since public employees are comparatively sheltered. Rates of unemployment in the northern and forest regions are higher than in the remainder of the country. In 1972, the unemployment rate in the big cities was 2.4 percent, whereas it was 3.8 percent in the forest region. In periods of unemployment, the northern and forest areas tend to be disproportionately harder hit than other regions.

People are also dropping out of the labor market. From 1965 through 1972, there were 25,000 men in the age groups 45 to 65 who were classed as "incapable of working." The benefits or arrangements for them are becoming more generous, reflecting a lowering of the work expectations for them. The invalidity pension system was liberalized in both 1970 and 1972, permitting the granting of a pension to those 60 years of age and over suffering from long-term unemployment. Following the enactment of these provisions, invalidity pension rolls increased by 22,000 in one year. Some 50,000 persons are now employed in sheltered workshops, and more are hoping to enter. Moreover, an increasing proportion of the applicants for vocational rehabilitation are individuals not in the active labor market, 43 percent in 1951 and 89 percent in 1971, indicating that they had dropped out and are seeking to be rehabilitated to enable them to work in industry or in sheltered workshops. Finally, participation rates are declining among middle-aged and older men for a variety of reasons, including the absence of available jobs.

The high rate of labor mobility forced by the dynamism of Swedish industry fosters considerable dissatisfaction and a sense of dependence. An LO study for the years 1963-65 and 1966-68, the first of a boom and the second a recession period, showed that each year about 5 to 6 percent of its members move from one job to another within the company and another 8 to 10 percent are displaced from one employer and seek another. They are then dependent upon their own resources to find another job or must turn to the manpower agencies. A further inquiry into the people's judgment concerning the consequences of this mobility finds them quite disheartened and pessimistic. They generally do not believe that their conditions improved. Fourteen aspects of the job, including wages, are surveyed, and in none of them did a majority of respondents indicate that an improvement had occurred. These are personal responses.[12] But what is important is that these judgments are at variance with the underlying assumptions of LO policy.

Working Conditions and Environment
Arouse Increased Dissatisfaction

With the rising volume of questions being asked about the quality
of the work environment, it has become common for workers also to
join this protest. The 1968 governmental commission studying levels
of living found that workers generally considered their work physically
and psychologically heavy and dirty and the climate at work very bad.
The LO members show even greater dissatisfaction than the working
class as a whole. The commission concluded that the groups employed at what they report are very bad conditions of employment are
"in practically all respects less healthy than the large group that does
not have to undergo any of these hardships."[13]

Decline of Disposable Income and
Regressivity of Tax Systems

Though earnings have risen in recent years, taxes have taken
up a large proportion of the receipts, and public goods and services
constitute a more significant proportion of total consumption, narrowing the individual's range of discretionary expenditures. Disposable
income--personal income after direct taxes--declined considerably,
dropping from 87 percent in 1960 to 77.3 percent in 1972. In the
"preconflict period" 1963-68, nominal gross household incomes rose
by 29 percent, but of this sum 46 percent was absorbed by taxes,
5 percent by individual savings, and the remaining 11 percent by
price increases. Only 38 percent was used for consumption.[14]

The progressivity of the total tax system has also been undermined by the rising importance of municipal and consumption taxes.
State income taxes are progressive, but the system is not as steeply
set against the higher-income groups as is claimed. In 1971, the
actual direct taxes paid by different income groups of gross income
were as follows: 20,000-25,000 skr, 27.5 percent; 40,000-45,000
skr, 35.6 percent; and 70,000-80,000 skr, 39.6 percent.[15] Off-
setting the progressivity of this tax is the doubling of the municipal
taxes, which are uniformly levied on all local residents and are now
on the average 24 percent of the taxable income. The value-added
taxes affecting all purchases including services, which, in 1969, replaced the direct consumption taxes introduced in 1959, are now
about 20 percent and are regressive. Taxes on earnings for social
insurance payments of all types are a uniform percentage of wages
and salaries, but benefits are graded down, according to income so
that higher-income groups do not benefit relatively as much.

The rise in the cost of living has in recent years been especially
burdensome. Food prices are particularly high. The prices of new

homes and the partial release of controls produced a higher housing cost. The new manner and costs of living have encouraged larger participation of married women in the work force, with an increase in the number of two wage-earners in families. The new costs of these higher living levels and demands and inescapable obligations produce a need for continuing earnings. Part of the maintenance of the family is covered by social allowances.

The new demands on family income and the social provisions make for a new group of people dependent upon the state to even out their earnings as they rise and fall with the vicissitudes of the job market. The part of the population receiving social welfare payments in the Stockholm suburbs increased from 2.9 percent in 1965 to 9.2 percent in 1971. The result is a heightened feeling of discontent. The complaints center about the excessive cost of living in certain social settings, the low return on extra earnings, and the dependence on social welfare assistance when reverses set in.

## Aspirations among the People

By the end of the 1960s the debate in Sweden swung to the left, and, in like manner more recently, a reaction to the right has set in. The swing in emphasis and outlook did not change the realities. The same claims for equality and a higher quality of life had been sounded by the labor movement from its very beginning. What happened was that economic and social developments made these issues more pertinent. The costs of growth, workers felt, were falling too heavily and unevenly on them. They insisted on relief. The recession, after decades of relatively constant improvements in living conditions, rising employment, and increased security, had embittered them. Their frustrations triggered political protests and demands for radical solutions, which were, thereafter, partly taken up by the trade union movement itself and partly rejected.

## INITIATIVES FOR RECONSTRUCTION

SAP electoral setbacks in 1970, and later in 1973, the strikes both legal and illegal beginning in 1966, and particularly from 1969 onwards, the internal debates and dissension, the increased discord among the four major union centers, and social criticism, particularly from the leftist groups, prepared the ground for a reconsideration of LO and SAP policies and programs. LO leaders are more inclined to direct their barbs at other union centers, especially SACO and SR, and their political ally, the SAP government. Of course, in the latter case relations continue to be friendly, but the criticism is nonetheless clear in its intent. The new aspirations and expectations within the ranks are perceived by the leaders, and they have changed the course toward more aggressive positions. The new SAP leader Olof Palme and the new LO President Gunnar Nilson are generally regarded as to the left of the positions of their predecessors. New ways are being sought over a wide range of issues. The full range of adaptations in the basic egalitarian democratic credo are still to be defined. But changes in some areas are already evident.

## A More Favorable Attitude toward Legislation
### and State Action

The LO is now more favorably disposed to having the state act on issues it formerly reserved for the private bargaining table. This shift is in part due to the feeling of urgency that haunts the leaders, who need action rather than prolonged negotiations to attain their ends. Where employers resist, the legislature will act. The new 1973 even balance in parliament between the SAP and Communists and the three opposing parties is not likely to change the prospects for legislation. For the present, the LO is pushing, often with the support of TCO, for parliamentary action in a number of different fields. When the employers objected to the LO's formulation for employee representation on company boards of directors, they pressed their objection through governmental channels; legislation was adopted Governmental commissions have considered or are considering other important issues in the industrial relations field such as management's right to hire, direct, and dismiss the labor force, on which some new legislation has been adopted, and methods of settling industrial disputes. Bills are in the hopper relative to job safety and workers' job rights.

The LO is quite ready to consider extending the government's powers to obtain more information on changes in enterprise employment and personnel policies and ultimately even to intervene into the industrial relations field.

## The Need for Greater Government Intervention
### into the Economy and for Tax Reform

The state of high unemployment profoundly troubles the trade union leadership. The 1971 LO congress demanded far-reaching action to stimulate the economy, and the government responded in that year and in the following two years expanded its aid. The LO's traditional opposition to government intervention in the private sector is weakening. The government, with LO support, moved in a number of new directions. It sponsored moves for the state to assume risk-taking responsibilities in industry to assure a higher rate of growth and employment. There is the State Investment Fund and many other aids, grants, and credit institutions. The LO chairman introduced the bill in parliament to enable the Supplementary Pension Fund to purchase corporate stocks, to encourage specific types of enterprises, and to assist enterprises that find it difficult to secure private financing. The present success of the state-owned enterprises may be significant for future plans in this field.

Broader public-sector activities to assure employment to all are being supported. Public employment has risen in 1952-72 at an annual rate of 5.8 percent. The services that were previously privately initiated such as schooling and higher education, medical care, and old-age pension found broad acceptance. The question is what new types of activities should now be initiated. Moreover, the government must also be able to offer employment to the "hard core," of whom only some 8,500 have jobs. The details must still be spelt out.

New public functions must be supported by new taxes and incomes. Already there is considerable discontent with the present high levels. Which groups shall carry the burden, and how shall they be related to the industrial relations system? Shall the low-income groups be further relieved of these costs? Which groups can bear a higher burden? Shall people, particularly in the higher salary groupings, be protected against the erosion of their real income through the tax or wage system, if at all? Shall the SACO position—that net disposable and "life" incomes be the criterion for the judgments on wages—or the traditional gross income concepts be used in wage negotiations? The LO now recognizes that some of its members are as directly interested in better protection of their disposable income as those of the SACO and SR. The chairman of the LO perceived that these decisions also involve questions of the relation to labor negotiations and the state's policy. He said that "a greater equality of income on the Swedish labor market means that the freedom of negotiations has to be yielded to some extent, or at least some small part of it."

Various proposals are being offered on methods of redesigning the tax system. The Metal Workers' Union experts, with by and large support from the remainder of the LO, would shift employee taxes onto the employer. This course could raise disposable income without increasing gross income. The LO rejected a second proposal that would change the schedule of social benefits or taxes for different income groups so that the higher ones benefit therefrom. The SACO view is represented in a third proposal, which would introduce

an index of inflation into the tax system so that the rates would apply
to real rather than nominal income. The last proposal obviously
brings with it a number of problems currently buried in the system,
such as the automatic increase in governmental income with the inflation of values. If these incomes are eliminated, consideration must
be given to alternative types of taxes to compensate for the loss in
income and their incidence.

Answers are now being sought in a much more subdued manner
than when the debate began. The trend is clearly toward a greater
use of payroll taxes. The taxes and the payments for social benefits
by employers will in 1976 amount to about 30 percent of the wage bill.

## Innovations at the Plant and Enterprise Levels

The new design for worker and union rights at the plant and
enterprise levels is more evident. The broad powers delegated to
management by Article 32 are to be limited further. The main points
of this legislation relate to an employer's power to hire and dismiss:
(1) unfair dismissals are to be considered unlawful; job transfers
should first be tried as a solution for misconduct or deficient production; (2) dismissed employees will be entitled to bring their cases to
court and are to be retained during the period of adjudication; (3) in
case of layoffs, preference should be given to older and disabled
employees, with years of service and age being determining factors;
the principle of "last-in/first-out" should be observed; (4) notices of
layoffs must be given at least one month in advance for employees 25
years or younger, and the period successively increases with age so
that it is six months for employees 45 years and older; (5) in case of
temporary layoffs, employees shall be paid their wages and salaries
after given periods of layoff; (6) laid-off employees have prior rehiring rights to their former job and other jobs for which they are qualified; (7) unions shall be provided information about recruitment policy
and labor force planning; and (8) the county labor market board shall
be entitled to information on the wages earned, physical fitness, and
other details of the labor force and to negotiate for the employment
of older and disabled employees where necessary and to order their
employment; the board may order a company to engage its labor force
through the public-employment offices.

While the LO and TCO supported the proposals, the SAF opposed them. The latter contended that these rules restrict the hiring
of the less qualified and increase the likelihood of conflicts between
management and trade unions. Economists have publicly criticized
the proposals as interfering with labor mobility and weighing industry
down with huge costs and the probability of staff demoralization in

view of the protracted periods of advance notice given in case of layoffs. The ultimate measure presumably will seek some reconciliation
of the diverse interests and may contribute to a more orderly and less
capricious internal plant manpower planning system. Another bill
will provide even greater employment security to union officers.

The new law providing for employee representatives on the corporate boards of directors. Local unions representing a majority of
the employees are permitted to appoint two representatives on the
boards of directors of corporations with at least 100 employees, except for insurance companies and banks, for which direct public representatives are appointed. These worker representatives have the same
rights as other directors except in matters of industrial conflict and
collective bargaining. It is estimated that 1.2 million workers will
be affected by this new law. It is also foreseen that unions will shortly
gain the right to appoint their own accountants for examining company
financial statements. These new rights are considered by the LO and
TCO to be only preliminary to the broadening of union and employee
rights on the job and to other changes that may flow from the reports
of a special royal committee examining the problems of the management right to "direct and distribute work." It is anticipated that its
report in 1975 may bring additional changes such as extension of the
area of subjects about which unions may bargain and the strengthening
of the use of local sanctions.

Accompanying the above law is an extension of the government's
own rights to intercede in industry. The government may now appoint
a director to represent the public interest on the boards of certain
holding companies and private economic foundations, in the same
manner as it does in the case of banks and insurance companies. The
county government boards that concern themselves with matters relating to labor market issues will also be entitled to information from
companies about their plans for expansion of production, new installations, closings, and personnel changes and may offer information on
public needs and long-range planning in the public sector.

A third significant development is the expansion of the rights of
the safety steward in the plants. Although LO-SAF agreements exist
respecting the steward's appointment by the union and his rights and
duties and mandate cooperation between employers and unions on
safety matters and although the agreements date back to 1942 and
have been reaffirmed in subsequent agreements in 1949 and 1967, the
steward in fact has had little recourse in the case of disagreement
with management. A new act defines these rights and grants him
access to the needed information, participation in workshop planning,
and the right to order the stoppage of work if he considers health or
safety is endangered, pending an inspection by an official governmental safety inspector. These stewards are trained in accordance with

a program set up by a joint central board, and the costs and lost time
are to be covered by the employer. The trade union and employer
organizations' representatives have been added to the national governing board on Occupational Health and Safety. It is anticipated that a
current commission on work environment will also propose other reforms to improve work conditions within the plants.

Changes within the Structure, Policies, and Practices
of the Trade Union Movement; New Position
of the Member

The trade union movement is also making changes in its opera-
tions. First, there are the relations among the white-collar unions.
The disagreements and conflicts among them could have wiped out the
SACO subsequent to the 1971 strike. But changes have occurred.
Cooperative relations are developing along several different fronts.
The most far-reaching is the agreement for the merger by 1975 of
the SACO and SR. In the public sector, SR, TCO-K, and TCO-S
signed a basic agreement in 1973 with SAV and other public employer.
Both LO and TCO have agreed to cooperate in the municipal employ-
ment area and prepare jointly for the next round of negotiations.

As for the private sector, the 1973 TCO Congress decided to
sponsor, with representation of SACO unions, a new joint organization, the Cartel of Private Employees (PTK) to represent some
350,000 employees. Some eight TCO unions, however, declined to
join this organization. The PTK will establish a significant white-
collar counterpart to the LO in the private sector and increase its
own power within the TCO in relation to the other two organs for
public employees. Already, the CF, SIF, SALF, and LO have joined
in an agreement with the SAF on educational leave. These developments open up the possibility of future closer relations between the
SACO and TCO.

Recent informal ad hoc meetings among the leaders of LO,
SACO, and TCO are described as cooperative. More optimism is
presently being expressed in public about future cooperation and the
possibility of greater understanding and reconciliation of views than
a few years ago. But the LO's high priority for its solidary wage
principles makes it difficult to conceive of the centers' reaching a
united front.

Advances in Employee Earnings and Benefits

Throughout the postwar period, trade union centers focused
their prime attention on improvements in the material returns and

basic working conditions. Wages and salary gains were on the whole satisfactory to the LO and to a somewhat lesser degree also to the TCO. But the SACO repeatedly expressed its disapproval of developments. Nominal wages for male industrial workers increased annually in the period 1951-69 by 6.9 percent and by 7.1 percent for nonmanual workers. The rise in the 1960s was slightly higher than in the 1950s. In the early 1970s the annual rate of increase was over 10 percent, with female employees getting slightly more than men and manual workers more than the nonmanual.

A major achievement of the last decade was the reduction of the work week from 45 to 40 hours. The 30-hour week has already been set as the next goal. In the contract concluded in 1974, the hours for "subsurface" and "shift" workers are set at 36 to 38 hours per week, varying with circumstances. Part-time workers are also to be assured of the numbers of hours needed to qualify them for social security plans.

During the periods when weekly working hours dropped most rapidly, 1958-60 and 1966-68, the annual income of nonmanual employees developed relatively more favorably than manual workers. But in the first half of the 1960s the latter enjoyed more advantageous gains, and again after 1968, the latter's relative benefits improved over those for nonmanual employees.[16]

SACO, representing the higher-income state employees, insists that the best measure of earnings is real disposable income after taxes. The data then reveal that manual workers enjoyed a greater improvement than others and that state employees with university education lost 17 percent in the last five years. The LO and SAP succeeded in reducing the differentials among employees through the combined effects of wage agreements and tax policy.

As for the LO goal of narrowing the differentials between blue-collar and white-collar employees, the 1971 contract for the public sector eliminated the formal disparities. In the private sector, differences continue primarily because of the more liberal pension and sickness benefits for nonmanual employees. Negotiated fringe benefits amount to 12.2 percent of wages for manual workers and 18.4 percent for other employees. But the levies for state-imposed "fringe benefits" are uniformly applied at 20 percent for all.

One major improvement in the 1974 agreement was uniform rules of compensation for all those injured at work or for occupational disease, irrespective of personal responsibility.


PROJECTIONS OF TRENDS


Uncertainties in three major areas, among others, becloud the current scene and make it difficult to project future developments in

the Swedish industrial relations system. First, industry and commerce in Sweden are increasingly concentrated into fewer corporations. The 200 largest Swedish companies, including their foreign
subsidiaries, have a gross product equal to the total national gross
product. Volvo is relatively more significant in the Swedish economy
than General Motors is in the United States. Necessarily, the government, in order to achieve its economic and social policies, will have
to intervene in and help design corporate decisions in various fields
such as investment, finance, industrial relations, and social policy.
It may therefore be said that the socialistic component is increasing
in the mixed economy not necessarily through direct ownership,
though this ratio is rising largely by means of joint private-public
ventures and public industrial investments, but through the government's participation in the decision-making process and in the review
of final decisions. Trade union and public representatives on the
corporate boards are becoming more and more influential. There
would probably be considerable reluctance on the part of the Social
Democratic government to choose international controls of these corporate bodies out of fear that the international authorities would be
more conservative and would not be as dedicated to Social Democratic
goals and policies.

Second, the basis of the present system, the predominance of
the LO in the trade union movement and the class character of the
Social Democratic Party, is being challenged or in the latter instance
found insufficient. Competition among the major trade union centers
threatens to weaken the entire movement. Cohesion and effective
bargaining demands the development among the centers of a mutually
acceptable set of policies and coordination of their bargaining and
institutional practices and strategies. Continued disarray would in-
vite more internal dissension within the major centers and turn back
the pages of history for the LO. The consequence would probably be
greater confusion and more disturbances within the collective bargaining system.

In the political field, the SAP finds it necessary to broaden its
appeal to the white-collar groups; the manual working class no longer
provides a sufficient base for its survival as the government. Moreover, the centrist parties have won over sections among the workers.
Concurrently, the LO is also reshaping its relations with the party.
It is now less inclined to be identified with the day-to-day political
and tactical decisions of the SAP government. There are more and
more occasions when it finds it desirable and necessary to criticize
the government for its policies and practices, which at times run
afoul of the members' interests. This distance has been further
exacerbated by the weakening of LO representation in the parliament.
The new LO president and many important trade union leaders of the

new generation are not members of parliament, a development that contrasts strikingly with past practice. While there is no likelihood of a break, the two wings of the labor movement are seeking a new relationship. Moving into closer relation with the government is the TCO, which finds it essential to seek its support, but the TCO wishes to remain politically independent.

The growing need for a redefinition of relationships between the SAP government and the trade union centers is particularly evidenced in the fields of collective bargaining and economic policy. Traditionally, the government remained aloof. But the state is now increasingly involved as an employer of a substantial part of the working population, as a levier of taxes, and as the formulator and administrator of economic and social policy. These create the environment for collective bargaining and determine the employee's actual take-home pay and reflect the government's views on the appropriate terms for the negotiated agreements. The trade unions, employers, and government are, therefore, becoming intimately involved in shaping agreements, public policy, and private acts. All, therefore, appear to be moving toward a more coordinated and integrated relationship. The government probably cannot remain apart from the collective bargaining process. The SAP government is no longer able simply to respond to the interests of a single class; it must embrace a larger share of all interests in the light of its goals and values. These developments in the SAP government's role are fostering a new system of industrial relations.

Third, the present system evolved during a period of rapid economic growth. Many deficiencies in the treatment of employees were corrected, inequalities in income distribution were moderated, and gaps in the provisions of social amenities and insurance were closed. These were financed by an expanding economy. But one cannot now be sure of the continuance of this high rate of growth. Periods of economic stagnation or lower levels of growth will provide fewer new resources for these purposes. If the private economy is not able to produce full employment, a foremost goal for the labor movement, new policies and programs will have to be initiated. No doubt the success of the nationalized industries will encourage further new ventures.

The difficulties of projecting the direction of future developments in the industrial relations field should now be apparent. The existing system was a viable and beneficial one. The question is whether the environment and institutional relations will continue to favor a progression along established directions and channels or will new ones have to be designed to assist the labor movement to realize the peaceful transformation of the society toward greater equality and an improved quality of life.

EDITOR'S NOTE

Several measures noted above subsequently became law, effective on July 1, 1974, including the Employment Security Act, which protects employees from improper dismissals, and the Employment Promotion Measure, calling for advance notice to employees affected by the curtailment of production, ranging from two to six months, depending on the number of employees affected, and for the promotion of the employment of older employees and those with reduced working capacity. Trade union representatives under another law were assured appropriate time off and a place for the discharge of their responsibilities and priority to employment in case of general layoffs or a shortage of work. A new Labor Dispute Act enlarged the Labor Courts to permit them to deal with the anticipated rise in the volume of disputes. Another law, which became effective on June 1, 1974, required companies to allocate 20 percent of their net profits for the financial year 1974 to an investment fund for improvements in the work environment or working conditions, specifying that the project had to receive approval of a majority of the employee representatives on the enterprise-safety or works councils. An agreement between the LO and the SAF reached in February 1975 under the threat of government legislation allows the economic committee of the union-designated works council to appoint a person from within the company to receive and analyze financial information. If this procedure proves unsatisfactory, the works council may appoint an outside consultant for its analysis.

Further steps were taken by the government to advance trade union views of the economy in the following measures: (1) 500 million kroner in the treasury of the supplementary employee pension fund could now be invested in the shares of private companies, subject to parliamentary review of their use; (2) foreign investments by Swedish corporations could be vetoed if they adversely affected domestic employment by a board containing a trade unionist; and (3) a new government bill would require managements to consult with local trade union branches on all mergers and acquisitions likely to produce unemployment or be harmful to consumers' interests, and such steps could be vetoed by the government.

Swedish economic recovery continued until the end of 1974, bringing unemployment below 2 percent of the labor force, cutting the numbers on work relief and those being given labor market training. Employment in the construction industry remained low. Price increases were below the double-digit level, exports remained high, and the country accumulated a surplus in its balance of payments. High corporate profits prodded the trade union movement to demand a 20.5 percent increase in the opening demands for the new annual round of negotiations. The government sought to deflate this mark of prosperity by requiring corporations to invest 15 percent of the profits in interest free funds in the Central Bank. But time was running out on this favorable trend. The high cost of oil imports converted the surplus in the balance of payments into a deficit, and the Central Bank raised discount rates and tightened credit. The government restored the value-added tax to its previous higher level. The overall effect was to reduce the rate of growth from 4.5 to 2 percent. The rate of consumer price increases began rising, bringing them to a 12 percent level. The 1975 government budget is reflationary in its purpose: to offset the anticipated economic contraction.

The government aided the labor market by reducing the legal pensionable age from 67 to 65 years. Employers who hired women on jobs normally held by men were assured a special subsidy for six months. An occasional wildcat strike is recorded, as occurred at the LKAB mine, where surface workers sought special wage improvements.

## NOTES

1. Nils Elvander, Intressorganisationerna i dagens Sverige (Lund, 1969), p. 29.

2. The 1968 Level of Living Survey in Sweden (published in Swedish by Allmana Forlaget, Stockholm). For a shorter English presentation, see Acta Sociologica 3, 3 (1973): 211-39.

3. The figures for party membership in this survey are lower than those reported by the party organizations.

4. Sten Edlund, Tvisteforhandlingar pa arbetsmarknaden (Trelleborg, 1967).

5. Folke Schmidt, N. B. Aron, K. W. Weddeburn, eds., Industrial Conflict: A Comparative Legal Study (London: Longmans, 1972), p. 65.

6. EFO-rapporten, English summary in G. Edgren, K. O. Faxen, C. E. Odhner, "Wages, Growth and the Distribution of Income," Swedish Journal of Economics 71 (September 1969): 137-60.

7. Rudolf Meidner in Tvarsnitt (Stockholm: LO, 1973). See also R. Meidner, B. Ohman, Fifteen Years of Wage-Policy (Stockholm: LO, 1973).

8. 1968 Level of Living Survey, op. cit.

9. Walter Korpi, "Vilda Strejker" (Stockholm, 1968; mimeo.). Publication of results of this study in English is likely in the near future.

10. OECD, Economic Outlook, no. 13 (Paris: OECD, July 1973), pp. 13-26.

11.  London Financial Times, September 26, 1973.

12.  From a sample survey made by LO, Lilla LO 3, Stockholm, 1969.

13.  1968 Level of Living Survey, op. cit.

14.  Olle Lindgren, Erik Lundberg, "Sveriges Ekonomi i internationella perspektiv," Skand. Bankens Kvartalstidskrift, 1971, 1.

15.  Roland Spant, "Income Distribution in Sweden" (Stockholm: Swedish Institute for Social Research, 1973; mimeo.).

16.  This perspective was developed in a report by Professor Sten Johansson to the Program Commission of SAP, in January 1974.

CHAPTER

# 7

## THE FEDERAL REPUBLIC OF GERMANY: COOPERATIVE UNIONISM AND DUAL BARGAINING SYSTEM CHALLENGED

Joachim Bergmann
Walther Muller-Jentsch

"While most European union movements still see progress in terms of struggle, the Germans have left that far behind. They have not beaten the capitalists, so they have joined them, with the view to a possible takeover."

Eric Jacobs' judgment reflects the prevailing Western image of the trade unions of the Federal Republic of Germany (BRD).[1] They are reputed to be powerful and financially secure, while at the same time using their strength prudently. They are alleged in their negotiations with management to consider the nation's economic capacity. They rarely strike; nor do they endanger economic growth or stoke the tendency toward inflation, but they have gained the highest percentage increase in real wages in Western Europe.

These views are not exactly false, but they miss the point. It is the weakness rather than the inherent strength of the trade unions that determines this behavior. Since the early 1950s, they have been politically on the defensive. Wage increases and improvements in benefits resulted from the high rate of economic activity rather than from militant trade union action. Unions remain weak at the plant level; their membership totals remained relatively stable, and democracy within the unions is poorly developed. Structural deficiencies in the organizations are becoming increasingly evident and members and the lower-level union officials are becoming more critical and more articulate. Wildcat strikes and intraorganizational disputes are no longer unusual. The adequacy of the present collective bargaining system and trade union structures and policies are being called into question.

This increased ferment is not occurring in isolation. Expressions of unrest and demands for other types of change, particularly in the political arena, are also mounting. The student movement, beginning in 1968, rose to a peak in 1969. The Social

Democratic Party (SPD) in 1966 joined a Christian Democratic Union (CDU) coalition government. Then in 1969 it constituted a coalition with itself as the dominant party, accepting the Free Democratic Party (FDP) as the junior partner. Not as spectacular, but nevertheless as symptomatic of the new spirit, were other spontaneous movements. These included those that supported greater citizen participation in local government decisions, particularly on urban planning, bans on local real estate speculation and the demolition of dwellings in the center city, parent groups that demanded improvements in kindergartens and schools, women's groups fighting for emancipation, and leftist groupings with varied objectives, including the reintegration of prison inmates into society or the encouragement of liberation movements in developing countries. The Communist Party of Germany (DKP) was refounded, and left-wing splinter groups appeared. Inside the SPD the Young Socialists, Jusos, insisted upon more socialistic policies than those pressed by the Brandt government. The new politicization of parts of the population became evident when the CDU in April 1972 threatened to unseat the Brandt government. This attempt was countered by large-scale demonstrations and turnouts and, finally, by the great interest shown by the population in the 1972 electoral campaign, which produced a convincing victory for the SPD-FDP coalition.

However different the various groups may have been respecting their goals and motives, they had all become aware of the inadequacy of existing social and political institutions. Opinion polls reported the same phenomenon of a disgruntlement with things as they were. A political conservative polling organization (Institute for Demoscopy) judged that the polls reflected a sense of "increasing readiness for class struggle."

The trade unions appeared for a time immune from this discontent. They seemed to be a stable and reliable institution. But the wildcat strikes of the fall of 1969 changed this picture. If one is inclined to dismiss this eruption as a mere byproduct of the electoral campaign of the year, one has only to observe the recurrence of similar events at the end of 1972 and in 1973. Internal organizational disputes unfolded in the wage negotiations in the metal industries, and another wave of wildcat strikes involved even more workers, forcing significant additional concessions by management and showing up the inadequacies of the existing industrial relations and representational structures.

This paper seeks to clarify the causes for the developing crisis in the trade union movement and collective bargaining and employee representational systems by examining both the external and internal causes of friction and the discontent developing with existing forms of representation, bargaining policies, and results.

## ECONOMIC DEVELOPMENT AND THE UNFOLDING
## OF ECONOMIC GROWTH

Factors of Economic Growth

The economic reconstruction of West Germany after the breakdown of the Third Reich in 1945 followed plans developed from earlier political decisions of the Western occupying powers. The United States in particular sought to integrate the part of Germany occupied by the Western allies into the Western system of defensive alliances. Owing to this decision, the Western allies, soon after the end of the war, abandoned the policy of dismantling industrial enterprises and exacting reparations and stopped attempts at introducing socialist policies. The ensuing U.S. economic assistance proved most effective; the Marshall Plan acted as a pump-primer for economic growth.

Following the adoption of the constitution of the Federal Republic of Germany in 1949, the conservative government saw no reason to challenge the Allies' preliminary decisions since its economic goal was also the restoration of the capitalist economic order, though with some modifications in the field of social policy.

The exceptionally favorable conditions underlying the main phase of the reconstruction period (1950-55) were mainly the following:

1. The relatively limited wartime destruction of the infrastructure and the nation's productive capacity. Estimates place the available industrial capacity in 1947/48 at 105 to 115 percent of the prewar level. [2]

2. Abundance of highly qualified labor.

3. The high rate of self-financing of private investment.

4. An industrial structure able to supply the tremendous world demand for capital goods in the 1950s.

5. Benefiting from growing international political tensions (Cold War) the industrial capacity of the BRD unlike its neighbors-- until the end of the 1950s--was not significantly burdened by the costs of armaments production.

These factors, supported by the nonaggressive wage policy of the trade unions and state economic policy, evoked the ebullient economic growth in the 1950s that earned for this period the label of "economic miracle." Economic growth was maintained from 1950 through 1972 almost without interruption, except for cyclical variations in its rate of growth and structural changes. The total real GNP rose from 1950 to 1972 by 290 percent, the average annual rate being 6.1 percent. Since the end of the 1950s a tendency toward deceleration of the rate of growth was visible that reflected in part the constraint placed on economic growth by the shrinkage of the domestic labor-force potential.

Economic expansion resulted in an ever increasing number of new jobs in the BRD. The working population rose from 21.5 million in 1950 to about 27 million in 1972. Most striking, apart from the increased proportion of foreign labor in the total work force, is the rise in the rate of dependent employees from 68.4 percent in 1950 to 83.4 percent in 1972. Since cessation of the influx of refugees from the German Democratic Republic (DDR), the number of foreign laborers rose, attaining a current total of about 2.5 million.

All through the last 20 years, wages and salaries followed the course of the growth cycles, except for a characteristic delay: the so-called wage lag. Real net wages and salaries per employee tripled over the period from 1950 through 1972, equaling the rise in the real domestic product per employed person. This concurrence in the rate of improvement of both earnings and productivity in effect maintained the basic stability in the income distribution, contributing to a stable social climate for industrial relations and reducing the number of industrial conflicts.

## Keynesianism Supersedes Neoliberalism

Behind the smokescreen of the neoliberal ideology of the "social market economy," promoted by the minister of Economy Ludwig Erhard, the capitalistic system of private ownership flourished. After the monetary reform of 1948, which expropriated personal savings but left the ownership of real capital untouched and with the abandonment of price controls, the government pursued policies favorable to the further accumulation of private capital to promote economic reconstruction and expansion. Measures to achieve these ends included tax exemptions, liberal depreciation rates, direct subsidies, and incentives for promoting exports. Corporate profits remained tax free or subject to preferential tax rates as long as they were not distributed and reinvested. The proportion of self-financing by private business amounted to 50 percent in the 1950s, compared to 20 percent in 1965.[3]

Toward trade unions the government pursued a policy of "moral suasion" and public denunciation to get them to reduce their wage demands, continuously asserting the priority of price stability. It appealed to the public's fears of inflation to keep down union wage demands. Where such appeals had no effect, it denounced trade unions as being a "state within the state," as furthering the interests of its class at the expense of the nation, thereby endangering the free market economy and democracy. The prevailing militant anticommunist mood of the country forced trade unions into a politically defensive position. Workers were contented with the modest wage improvements, for their aspirations had been deflated by war and postwar deprivation and the fears of inflation remained strong. High profits and growth rates in the 1950s allowed ample scope for concessions in wages or working time to satisfy the dependent workers' immediate interests.

Toward the end of the 1950s and at the beginning of the 1960s, a change was in the making in the orientation of the government's economic and finance policy. While it had previously been determined by neoliberal tenets, it was now increasingly replaced by Keynesian principles. After full employment was attained in 1959, the impulses to growth weakened. Only with the recession of 1966/67, which for the first time after the war brought the economy to a standstill, did the leadership in economic policy pass into the hands of a Keynesian, Karl Schiller. The federal minister of the Economy in the Grand Coalition in 1966 could, for the purposes of the control of the macroeconomic process, make use of a number of instruments and institutions that had been conceived and developed in the preceding years. These were (1) annual reports on economic developments and the prospects for the individual components of national income, presented for the first time by the federal minister of the Economy in 1963; (2) the so-called concerted action, recommended for the first time by the Council of Experts in its second report in 1965/66 and institutionalized by Schiller in 1967, seeking to harmonize the policies of management and trade union groups with those of the federal and financial governmental authorities; and (3) the 1967 Law for Promoting Stability and Growth in the Economy, which provided the government with a wide range of instruments to stabilize the economy: a stabilization council of the federal government, Lander, and local governments; medium-term financial planning of public budgets; investment programs; and discretionary power to vary tax and depreciation rates. By virtue of these instruments, and with the support of the trade unions, which abstained from making wage demands, the Grand Coalition succeeded in reversing the economic decline. This union policy proved, however, to be a costly political step giving birth subsequently to an internal union crisis and to industrial unrest. Moreover, these policies were not equally effective in containing inflationary pressures. Inflation, no doubt, is today the main economic problem of the BRD. The rate of price rises since 1966 exceeded those in former years. The government is now faced with the same dilemma as most other developed countries--namely, to curb inflationary trends without endangering full employment, on which depends

the loyalty of the masses. It seeks like other governments to escape
the dilemma by a combination of restrictive financial and monetary
policies and by "moral suasion" of the trade unions.

## CHANGES IN DGB POLICIES

The Munich Program of 1949: Espousal of
Alternative Social Order to Capitalism

The German Trade Union Federation (DGB) at its founding
Congress in October 1949 in Munich adopted a program that was anticapitalist in orientation--as many programs were at that time. It
did not mention the trade unions' traditional aims and strategies but
instead defined the principles of a new economic and social order.
The Munich program was, in some measure, only a belated
programmatic statement on a new democratic economic order, belated inasmuch as the Allied powers had already set the course for
the restoration of capitalism and because militant anticommunism
had become the dominant ideology, as a consequence of the Cold War.
The fundamental principles of the new order, formulated in the "economic principles," called for the following.

1. An economic policy, which, while guarding the dignity
of free men, guarantees the full employment of all willing to work,
the productive utilization of all economic productive forces, and the
satisfaction of economic needs.
2. Co-determination by organized employees in all personnel, economic, and social questions arising in the management and
design of the economy.
3. The nationalization of key industries, especially of mining, iron and steel, chemicals, power, the principal means of transportation, and credit institutions.
4. The attainment of social justice through the appropriate
participation of working people in the total returns of the economy
and the assurance of adequate sustenance to those incapable of working because of age, invalidity, or sickness.

Realization of such concepts calls for a central economic
planning system to prevent private interests from prevailing against
the needs of the entire economy.[4]
In this list of demands, economic planning, public property,
and co-determination constituted the basic planks. Together, they
constituted a socialist economic order that, by dissociating itself
from the centralized planning system of communist countries and in

its emphasis on self-management as a decisive principle, identified itself as a "third course." Realization of any one of these objectives by itself, for example, co-determination, would not change the capitalist economic system, as subsequent experiences have shown.

To justify this program of social change, leading trade unionists developed a vehement critical analysis of capitalism, based on Marxian theories as well as their own living experiences, according to which wage policy no longer could be the exclusive function of the trade unions. The destruction of workers' organizations by the Nazis had dramatically shown that even the workers' immediate interests could be effectively promoted only by securing an overall democratic order. By questioning the institutional framework of contemporary capitalism, the DGB became a political association.

## Defeat and Retreat

Unlike the experience in 1918/19, there were after 1945 no radical tendencies evident among the working class. During the early days of the restoration of the organizations, trade unionists found the majority of employees to be disoriented and demoralized, as a consequence of the destruction of workers' organizations by the Nazis. Workers had lost touch with socialist traditions and were no longer accustomed to collective action. The pseudopoliticization through fascist mass organizations had led them to distrust all political engagements. True enough, workers actively expressed their disgruntlement with hunger, the dismantlement of factories, price rises, and unemployment, but the strikes and demonstrations of 1946-49 were essentially protests and defensive moves. They, however, could not serve the trade unions as a basis for conveying their visions of anticapitalistic reform. The DGB hoped for their realization through the newly elected federal parliament. This policy seemed reasonable at the beginning since most other political parties' conceptions of the new order, as laid down in their programs, were in line with those of the trade unions. Besides, the trade unions expected the SPD to win at the polls. But the SPD did not gain a parliamentary majority; neither was the private capitalist economy shaken by a crisis nor questioned by the people, as was expected by the fathers of the Munich program. Hence, trade unions shelved their anticapitalistic reform programs.

The last major trade union fight occurred in 1951. The conservative majority in parliament sought to abolish the co-determination parity system of labor representation on the supervisory boards in the coal-mining and steel industries, which had been introduced by the Allies on the occasion of plant dismantling.

Not until unionists threatened a mass strike in May 1951 did the parliament confirm by law co-determination in this industry.

The union center's fight against the new works council law
in 1952, which consolidated the power of the entrepreneurs and evicted
trade unions from the plants, was only half-hearted. The government
of Konrad Adenauer had denounced the trade unions' threat of a general strike as unconstitutional and an illegal attempt of a nonparlia-
mentary group to impose its will on the parliamentary majority.
Thus, the situation became so tense and conflict so bitter that one of
the DGB's theorists remarked privately that the Bundestag ought to
be chased into the Rhine or, else, to stop all action.[5] The DGB decided to avoid a conflict with the parliament and called off the projected strike.

With the electoral reverses of the SPD in 1953, a process
began of pragmatic adaptation to a stabilizing capitalist society. The
socialist program of the DGB, which originally was approved by the
rank and file because it stressed measures to satisfy the immediate
needs of the postwar period, was bound to fade in urgency and plausi-
bility at a time when the flourishing capitalist system granted economic and social concessions that satisfied the relatively low expectations of the workers.

In the prospering economy, trade unions reverted to a traditional wage policy. With their 1955 action program, which essentially was limited to the demands of the day formulated in terms of
the existing system, the Munich program lost its relevance for practical action, but the 1955 program was not revised until 1963.

## The Dusseldorf Program of 1963:
## Adaptation to Neocapitalism

John Maynard Keynes, and not Marx, was the godfather of
the new platform adopted in 1963 by the DGB. Instead of calling for
a fundamental change of the capitalistic economic and social order,
the foremost goal became the modernization of economic policy to
secure economic growth and full employment.

In adapting their wage policy to the realities of the economy
at the end of the 1950s trade unions adopted the theories of Keynes
and his school. Bound to calculate the macroeconomic consequences
of their wage policy and to consider the limited scope of action trade
unions learned earlier than the official governmental economists,
who still adhered to neoliberal principles, to analyze economic
events in terms of the more advanced theories. It is therefore not
surprising that the first section of the program dealing with the
"principles of economic policy" reads much like the basic tenets of

the economic policy pursued after 1966 by Economic Minister Schiller. The program outlines the following aims of economic policy: (1) full employment and continuous economic expansion; (2) a just and equitable distribution of incomes and wealth; (3) stability of the currency; (4) prevention of the abuse of economic power; and (5) international economic cooperation.

This list of objectives, being general in nature, no longer includes the central points of the Munich Program and is, on the whole, equally shared by the state and private management. The only important challenge may be found in the demand for a just and equitable distribution of incomes and wealth, especially in face of the explicit "claim for the employees' participation in the already accumulated wealth." No reference, however, is made to the probable conflicts among the goals--for instance, between economic growth and redistribution--although the trade unions knew from their experience in the 1950s that they were not in a position to change the existing distribution of income in their favor. At other places in the program they accepted the entrepreneurs' right to control the use of their capital for investment. Being placed between two "common good goals," the aim of redistribution suggests illusory expectations as respects an active wage policy and the state's tax policy. The program, therefore, seems to imply that income redistribution, as compared with the goals of full employment, economic growth, and stability, would hold only a secondary position.

The instruments proposed for achieving the economic goals were essentially those common to the modern capitalist state: (1) national economic overall planning in the form of a national budget, prescribing targets for the economy for stated periods (these guidelines are considered binding on state economic agencies but only indicative for private economic groups); (2) fiscal and tax policy to be directed toward expanding public expenditures and serve as a force for cyclical stabilization; (3) controlled investments to be effected through tax measures, credit policy, and systems of depreciation allowances; and (4) policies to promote market competition. In addition to these Keynesian instruments, the program proposed the use of others, including the extension of publicly owned and cooperative undertakings, control of economic power, and workers' co-determination. Some of these means, of course, are liable to jeopardize the consensus with the capitalist state and the private entrepreneurs. But as they are to be employed only in case the ultimate goals cannot be attained by other means, the threat of conflict is primarily theoretical in nature.

To sum up, the Dusseldorf program projected an image of West German trade unionism being essentially in conformity with the existing system. The objectives of the Munich program--planning,

nationalization, and co-determination--remained in it but only in
subordinate positions or to be made to conform to the existing economic order. The concept of an inherent antagonism of interests
yielded to the view of the coexistence of a plurality of interests amenable to reconciliation. Earlier declarations pronouncing the "absolute identity of the state and the economy"[6] were replaced by a view
that the state was the instrument for achieving the general welfare
and therefore could command the loyalty of trade unions. The notion
of a crisis-prone capitalism tending to threaten the existence of
democracy and political freedoms is now superseded by a techno-
cratic model of a prosperous planned capitalism capable of doing justice to the workers' interests and compatible with political democracy. The Dusseldorf program offered a base for trade unions cooperation with the state and the management to achieve the stated
objectives within the existing institutional framework.

## THE BARGAINING PARTIES: THEIR
## STRUCTURE AND POWER CENTERS

### The Trade Unions

The German postwar trade unions are based on two principles: a unitary central organization of industrial national unions.
The common resistance of Christian, Social Democratic, and communist trade unionists against the Nazi regime had prepared the way
for a unitary trade union organization, independent of political or religious affiliations. In October 1949 the founding Congress of the
DGB took place in Munich. The more than 100 separate trade unions
consolidated into 16 new industrial unions, the constituents of the
new top federation. All occupational categories: manual workers,
white-collar employees, and civil servants in the same industry or
civil service were to belong to the same trade union, according to
the principle of "one enterprise, one trade union."
The DGB now consists of 16 national trade unions with some
7 million wage and salary employees. They amount to at least 80
percent of all unionized employees. Other organizations not affiliated
to the DGB include the German Civil Service Union (DBB) with
720,000 members and the German Salaried Employees Union (DAG)
with 460,000 members. There are also several smaller unions for
civil servants and white-collar employees, including the Christian
workers' trade union, which rarely exert any influence on the collective bargaining process. Discussions about merger between the DAG
and DGB are being carried on, as their economic and sociopolitical
objectives are now similar.

The 16 DGB unions differ in size, varying from 35,000 to 2.3 million. The absolute numbers of employees affiliated with DGB unions increases regularly, but the ratio of organized members of the total employees shows a tendency to decline, dropping from 35.9 to 29.8 percent in 1970. This drop may be ascribed principally to the shift of employment to white-collar employees and civil servants, with the latter tending to join the DAG and DBB, if they organize at all. In 1969, about 40 percent of the blue-collar and 20 of the white-collar employees were organized either in the DGB or the DAG. [7]

The DGB as the national trade union center represents its constituents primarily in the political area and is their spokesman in the European Community. It serves as a coordination and arbitration agency among the member unions; it has little authority to coordinate the collective bargaining policies of the member unions. The individual national unions are completely independent in this basic field of action. * Prior efforts, especially by the right-wing unions, to endow the DGB with more authority in the wage field, reflected an attempt to make wage policy an instrument of state economic policy (incomes policy). They failed because of the resistance of the largest union, IG Metall.

The DGB and its member unions have similar structures with three organizational levels. At the bottom is the local branch of a national union. Its organs are the member meetings or meetings of representatives and the administrative boards (local presidium). The local presidium, which consists of officers, both paid and unpaid, is elected by the members or delegates meetings. In some unions, the executive officers are nominated by the national presidium and are confirmed at the delegates meetings.

The locals are joined into district organizations, which may or may not coincide with the boundaries of the Lander, depending on their size. Their main organs are the district conference of delegates from locals and its presidium. The district presidium, which also consists of both paid and unpaid officers, is elected or confirmed by the district delegates. The organs of the federation are the trade union congress and the national or central presidium. The congress, which meets every three years, is the primary body of every trade union; its delegates are elected at the locals. Its decisions are binding on the presidiums and all other organs of the union. The congress elects the presidium, which also consists of paid and

---

*In 1963 the Union of Construction, Stone, and Clay Workers abandoned the active wage policy aimed at income redistribution, as called for in the DGB program, in favor of the productivity-oriented wage policy advanced by the government and management, without being threatened with sanctions.

unpaid officers. An advisory council, attached to the presidium, performs the congress's functions between meetings and must be convened several times a year.

The formal organizational structure, a democratic system of delegates operating according to the principle of "democratic centralism," is in practice affected by strong tendencies toward bureaucratic administration and centralized control. This is particularly evident in the conduct of collective bargaining.

According to the statutes the presidium has the authority to make all decisions with respect to wage policy. Negotiating committees only have the right to present "position papers" and "recommendations" to the presidiums. Hence, the wage policy is jointly dealt with by the presidiums and the district leadership. During the postwar years, wage policy more and more became the concern of the central authorities; members and lower-level officers today exercise but minimal influence. It is only in case of a threat of strikes that the membership must be brought into the process of decision-making to vote on the strike referendum. But the presidium again decides on calling such referenda. In addition, the presidium has other means for furthering its views. It oversees the spending of the organization's income and financial reserves, which enables it to select and employ the experts of the organization who are likely to be people who will reinforce its views before the lower organizational levels. All educational programs and the recruitment of officers are under their charge. Through the selection of editors and the definition of the policy for the organizations' official newspaper, they have a most effective mass communication medium. Major local activities are guided by policy statements developed by the presidiums and their advisory councils, particularly as regards local educational activity, selection of candidates for the works councils, and activities of shop stewards.

As experience has shown, the congresses, though the top organ, do not act effectively as a counterbalance to the presidium's authority. Their control functions are limited; their recommended policies always tend to be confined to past practices. Ratification of present policy and reelection of the presidiums have been their main functions, even though much criticism was voiced in the discussions.

Only the shop stewards could constitute a counterweight to the established authorities. But it is only recently that they have gained sufficient autonomy and importance within the intraorganizational relations of some unions. The shop stewards represent the trade unions' base in the enterprises. They are unpaid honorary officers, the most active, and often the most politically oriented among the union members in a work place. Their function is to communicate and explain union policy and to inform and mobilize the passive majority of the members in cases of disputes and strikes. While they have no formal place in the structure of policy-making, the shop stewards often constitute the backbone of the internal opposition within industrial centers.

## The Employers' Associations

After several years of discouragement by the occupying powers, the employers founded two general central organizations. One is the Federation of German Industry (BDI), which deals primarily with economic issues, particularly before the federal and Lander governments. The second is the Federal Union of German Employers' Associations (BDA), which is preoccupied with matters relating to social policy and collective bargaining, including wage issues.

The BDA represents about 80 percent of all private enterprises organized in their industrial associations; they employ about 90 percent of all engaged in private industry. Thus, West German entrepreneurs are organized to a much higher degree than employees. The employers' organization is a union of actual or potential competitors forming a cartel against their common adversary, the trade unions, and a pressure group before the parliament and the state administration. In 1971 the BDA consisted of 44 national associations that had 385 Lander and regional associations.

Negotiations with unions are conducted by the regional or Lander associations in the case of regional bargaining and the central national industry associations for national bargaining. Employers prefer national negotiations to prevent unions from making use of the full economic margin for wage increases in the individual districts or from picking out militant districts to enforce their demands. In national negotiations, macroeconomic arguments and global economic considerations become central concerns.

While the BDA is empowered only to make recommendations to its member associations, the central authority of several large employers' associations, including metal and chemicals, has grown to such an extent that they have become the primary negotiators. Where unions seek decentralized regional negotiations, the employers in fact counter by organizing a "core commission," which appears at all regional negotiations consisting of the same persons, employing the same arguments and strategy. In the metal industry a survey[8] estimates that 50 persons who are in leading positions in Gesamtmetall and at the same time representatives of large undertakings determine the policy and the strategy and negotiations for the entire industry, which employs some 4 million persons.

## CONSTRAINED DUAL INDUSTRIAL
## RELATIONS SYSTEM

The entire industrial relations system in the Federal Republic is built on a highly developed series of legal regulations. The aim
is to check the conflict of interests and to avoid the resulting political risks. These ends are being achieved, for one, by having the
state itself regulate matters that are amenable to autonomous collective bargaining, as for instance the relations between employees and
management within the enterprise, and for another, by legislation
and juridical prescriptions laying down structural conditions and
principles for collective bargaining and the conduct of industrial disputes. Through general legal regulations of the relations within the
enterprise, the unions are denied the right to represent the workers'
interests within the enterprise. They are limited to collective bargaining with the employer associations beyond the enterprise level.
Thus, the system of industrial relations in the BRD assumed its specific dual character, and this, above all, accounts for its flexibility
and ability to absorb social conflicts.


### Employee Representation in Enterprise:
### Works Councils--A Separate Arm

The 1952 BVG law (adopted in parliament against the opposition of the SPD) extensively defines the relations between management
and employees. * It provided for the establishment of autonomous
works councils elected by all employees rather than only by union
members. It defines the veto power and the rights of co-determination of the employees, and their representatives. Some council members in larger enterprises are released from their job activities, devoting full time to their duties. The unions have no rights to represent employees' interests within the enterprise and, at best, may
serve as advisors to the works council.

The works council is the legally designated representative
of employees in the enterprise for co-determination and participation
in the regulation of social and personnel affairs. (The discussion of

---

*The present Works Council Law is patterned after the 1920
Works Council Law, which established the dual character of industrial relations system. The Works Council Law was passed by the
parliament in 1952, over the objections of the SPD. In 1972, it was
reformulated by the Socialist-Liberal Coalition, without substantial
changes.

the works councils must not be confused with the well-known system of co-determination in the management of coal and steel industries.) Among the more important of these matters are the determination of the forms and principles of methods of wage payment, especially in the case of incentive systems; regulation of working time and over-time; personnel changes and dismissals; arrangements of the physi-cal work place; setting of bonuses and premiums (above basic wage rates); and all fringe benefits (compare paragraphs 87, 90, 91, and 95 of the Law on Enterprise Statutes). As for economic decisions, the works council is entitled only to get information, and the manage-ment is in no way limited in its power to make decisions (para. 106). In cases of curtailment of production or the closing of an enterprise the council may only demand prescribed payments to compensate the dismissed employee for the damages done (Social Plan) (para. 112). The most significant right is joint decision-making with management on matters relating to the wage incentive system and the bonuses and premiums. The general enterprise agreements on these matters are binding on the parties but may be unilaterally revoked (para. 77). The council is not empowered to negotiate on basic wage rates or working conditions; these are reserved to the unions.

However, these rights of co-determination of the works council, though quite numerous and also effective, are subject to a general clause of "trustful co-operation" with management "for the welfare of the employees and enterprise" (para. 2). It is bound by a "peace obligation" and may, according to the BVG, in no instance resort to "measures of labor conflict" (paras. 74, 2), to calling strikes or demonstrations.* Consequently, it has a narrow range of bargaining power with management. Bound by the "peace obligation," it can in negotiations underscore the possibility of conflicts, but it is in no position to guide open conflicts, such as spontaneous strikes. It must count on the pressure exerted by the employees to gain its advances, without being able to utilize fully the opportunities offered by outright wage conflict. Works councils generally are an instru-ment of mediation between employees and management.

Its importance as the representative of employees in the enterprise should nevertheless not be underestimated. It has--by reason of the rights accorded it by law--a substantial impact on the level and distribution of the local wage additions to the general con-tract, particularly in the large enterprises, where there is scope for an autonomous wage policy within the enterprise. The internal enterprise wage policy enables the council to generate much local

---

*Indicative of the desire to contain plant-level conflicts is the absolute prohibition of any political activity within the enter-prise (distribution of leaflets, political agitation) (para. 74).

loyalty among employees, alongside and independently of the unions. Its following is indicated by the evidence that council members usually are reelected. Pertinent studies have shown that employees by now view the council as a necessary form of representation of their interests and often even identify it with the union.

The works council does tend--particularly in large enterprises--toward bureaucratization and professionalization, toward setting its members apart from the employees. The reason is not only the full-time preoccupation of its members with their duties, the long terms of office, the necessity to specialize in certain issues (wage incentive systems, job evaluation, social expenditures, and so on), and the concomitant importance of expert knowledge but also the obligation to respect its obligation for the "welfare of the enterprise"--that is, to regard the interests of management. It is there to promote the interests of the employees but is, at the same time, bound up in the enterprise's system of social welfare without having a voice in the major decisions of the management.

Also the trade unions are unable fully to curb this tendency toward the works councils' becoming autonomous bodies. Two means might be employed by them. First, they control the selection of candidates for election to the works councils, and, in fact, the overwhelming majority of all works council members are union designees. * Second, active union members are forcing works councils to prove their legitimacy. While shop stewards formerly have been an arm of works councils and a "school" for future works council candidates, numbers of them have in recent years become more independent and able to monitor the work of these councils.

Nevertheless, the works councils and the trade unions are not competitors. The great majority of the council members are loyal union members who realize that their effectiveness in the council depends on the activities of union members within the enterprise. Yet by virtue of their legal status and the loyalty of the employees, works councils are relatively autonomous, and their members enjoy a special position within the trade union organization, as will be further explained.

By reason of its legal status and privilege to negotiate with management, the council helps determine the union's influence within the enterprise. The council is influential in determining or mapping out the activity of the shop stewards, arranging the recruitment of new members and the distribution of the union newspaper, and so on.

_____

*In 1972 about 78 percent of all works council members were members of the DGB unions, but this percentage was below the level of 83 percent registered in 1965.

By reason of these functions, and above all the recruitment of members and the collection of union dues, the works councils became an indispensable and a "second main arm" of union organization. Their extraordinary influence makes itself felt through the generalized mechanics of the election process, in the selection of delegates to superior levels of the union organization. Consequently, their members usually constitute at least a relative, and often the absolute, majority not only in the local presidiums but also in the negotiating committees and district presidiums and at the union congresses.

### Collective Bargaining System: Its Constraints

Banished from enterprises, trade unions are confined to the formal system of bargaining with employer associations outside of the enterprises. They deal with such matters as general wage systems, job supplements, vacation allowance rates, job evaluation systems, working time and conditions, bonuses and premiums, and other terms of employment. Agreements on these subjects may be concluded for varying lengths of time ranging up to several years, with the wage contract itself applicable for a shorter period, such as 8 to 18 months.

The collective bargaining contracts have two characteristics that severely limit trade union bargaining power.

First, most contracts cover a whole Land, or several Lander, and frequently more than 100,000 employees. They embrace a varied number of branches differing in size and economic conditions. The metal industry, for instance, includes shipbuilding, car manufacture, machinery construction, as well as the optical industry, precision machinery, and musical instruments manufacture. Wage contracts covering broad heterogeneous areas* are necessarily oriented to average output or even to marginally profitable firms rather than to the more profitable large enterprises. They tend to overlook changes in business conditions developing during the course of the contract year, the effects of the specific methods of wage remuneration on actual earnings, and the local labor market conditions. Under this system of collective bargaining, wage agreements do not tap the industry's full capacity to grant wage increases. The result is a permanent wage drift. During the 1960s the real earnings per year increased by 2 percent in excess of those in the contract (see Table 3). The wage drift was, of course, highest in the

---

*The large collective bargaining areas date back to the wage system of the fascist regime and were retained after the war.

more profitable industries, rising to 40 percent in the metal processing and 30 percent in the chemical industries.* These additional wage
increases enable management to make local plant concessions to meet
local bottleneck problems in the labor market and to provide for specific local incentives; this procedure increases an employee's attachment to the firm.

TABLE 3

Wage Drift, Federal Republic of Germany
(increase in percent)

| Year | Contract Wages and Salaries per Hour 1 | Actual Wages and Salaries per Hour 2 | Wage Drift (2 minus 1) |
|---|---|---|---|
| 1960 | 7.5 | 8.9 | 1.4 |
| 1961 | 8.7 | 12.0 | 3.3 |
| 1962 | 8.8 | 11.6 | 2.8 |
| 1963 | 5.8 | 8.2 | 2.4 |
| 1964 | 6.4 | 8.8 | 2.4 |
| 1965 | 7.8 | 9.5 | 1.7 |
| 1966 | 7.1 | 7.7 | 0.6 |
| 1967 | 4.0 | 5.3 | 1.3 |
| 1968 | 4.0 | 6.0 | 2.0 |
| 1969 | 7.0 | 10.3 | 3.3 |
| 1970 | 12.9 | 14.9 | 2.0 |
| Average annual rate of increase, 1960-70 | 7.3 | 9.4 | 2.1 |

Source: Bretschneider, Husmann, Schnabel, Handbuch
einkommens--und vermogenspolitischer Daten. Koln, Table C-52.

---

*These figures are in an unpublished study of the Institute of
Social Research in Frankfurt/Main. The available empirical data
indicate that the increases in the wage contracts are additions to
effective earnings, which means that job differentials remained as
before.

As a consequence of the BVG and the collective bargaining system, trade unions see themselves as being kept at a distance from the enterprise. The works council, not the trade union, acts as the partner of a contract with the local management. The unions are no longer able to demonstrate their wage policy to be an effective instrument for labor representation as long as real earnings are considerably higher than those in the contract, as is the rule in large enterprises. Although there are no legal barriers to enterprise bargaining, few such attempts are made, and few such agreements are consummated. Employers stoutly oppose them, being unwilling to abandon the instrument of enterprise bargaining, the works councils. Many support the latter openly or secretly in preference to direct bargaining with unions.

Enterprise wage policy, the counterpart and supplement to union wage policy, lends great flexibility to the system of industrial relations in the BRD, allowing for adaptation to economic conditions, freezing or even reducing supplements in periods of recession, without violating the collective agreement. Unions are left with no effective means of resistance and are restricted to moral protest. Neither works councils nor the workers have legal redress to prevent the reduction of supplements, as occurred in some plants in the recession of 1966/67. Wildcat strikes involve great risks during recession periods. During prosperous periods, wage additions permit adaptation to local labor market conditions and a personnel policy directed to the specific needs of the enterprise.

The second characteristic of the German system is that agreements after being signed may be extended to an entire industry, according to a procedure laid down by law. These extensions of wage agreements have become the rule in the BRD, since it is in the employers' interest to ensure fair competition. As for the trade unions, this means that the unorganized profit from wage increases, which the unions negotiate, and that successful wage bargaining will not necessarily induce the unorganized to join the union.

The labor courts in 1967 ruled against the Textile and Garment Workers Union and the Industrial Union of Construction, Stone, and Clay Workers, when they tried to limit benefits to their members or to secure through special contracts special benefits for the latter. The Federal Labor Court (BAG) declared differentiation between union members and nonmembers to be inadmissible, recognizing the customary procedure--that is, that contract wage rates are minimum wage rates. As a result of this decision, the union scale has become the minimum for the entire Federal Republic.

A Restrictive Legal System

The principle formulated by the above decision of the Federal
Labor Court, that no one shall be required against his will to join an
association and shall not be disadvantaged thereby, is but one example of the antiunion bias of the juridical system. This tendency has
been observed since the reestablishment of the labor courts in the
early 1950s.

Most significant among these decisions is the Sozialadaquanz
principle of "social appropriateness" of labor disputes, which means
that the strike must correspond to the "moral social order of the society as it developed historically" as well as "to the principles of collective labor laws." This principle, actually a vague formula open to
arbitrary interpretation, has been defined in many cases in a conservative spirit. The tests are that (1) the strike aims at the improvement of working conditions: political strikes are unqualifiedly illegal;
(2) it is conducted by the legitimate bargaining partners as defined by
law, which rules out wildcat strikes; (3) it is a measure of last resort, with evidence presented that alternative methods of negotiations
have been exhausted and with arbitration procedures mandatory; and
(4) it is conducted "fairly," thereby excluding the use of force or economic destruction of the adversary. The initiators of illegal, "socially inappropriate" strikes, namely the unions, may be held responsible for the consequences. Unions are thereby prevented from
taking an active part in spontaneous strikes. They may neither negotiate on behalf of wildcat strikers nor support them with financial
assistance from the union strike fund and may not initiate wildcat
strikes. They are expected to try to persuade strikers to return to
work, a responsibility inherent in the collective agreement.

In addition to the principle of "social appropriateness" the Federal Labor Court, in accordance with an abstract liberalistic pattern
of conflict, ruled that strikes and lockouts are equivalent instruments
in labor disputes. This finding in effect was enunciated despite provisions of the federal constitution and its "social state" clause designed to protect the socially weaker groups in society. Employers'
associations have repeatedly used the lockout, particularly in the
metal strikes in 1963 and 1971, when they locked out all employees
of all enterprises within the area covered by the collective contract.
They sought to place a severe drain on the union's strike funds and
force a quick termination of the strike.

To complement the restrictive definition of the right to strike,
the court decided that the so-called peace obligation, the prohibition
against unions taking any aggressive measures, obtains while the
contract is in force. In a legally doubtful however binding interpretation in a case involving the metal union, the court ruled that the

conduct of a strike vote was itself an "aggressive measure"--that is, a transgression of the responsibility for maintaining peace (1958). (The IG Metall was held responsible for the damages caused by the strike and was ordered by the court to pay DM 30 million. The IG Metall was relieved of the fine in an agreement with the employers' association.)

This finding made the process of democratic decision-making among union members not at all touching on the relations with the bargaining partners at the moment of the referendum a violation of the "peace obligation."* A referendum as well as the preceding mobilization campaign among the members, no doubt, may exert some pressure upon the employers. The process of decision-making within mass organizations inevitably is going on in public and has in itself the effect of promoting democracy. This is not true of the decision-making process in the employers' organizations; for instance, the decision to lock out usually is made without any publicity. Here, as elsewhere, the principle of the "equivalent instruments" is working to the disadvantage of the unions.

The trade union movement has not battled these restrictive decisions by the Federal Labor Court for several reasons. For one, prior to the recession and the SPD's participating in the government, public opinion, the mass media, and the federal governments were antiunion. Other moves were being made within the parliament to establish legal compulsory arbitration (1953 and 1957); the early government drafts of emergency legislation (1959/60) practically provided for the suspension of the freedom of organization in crisis situations. Had the unions tried to counter the court decisions, they would have been left on their own, not knowing whether a majority of their own members would support them. Moreover, owing to the marked legalistic attitude of the German unions, which reflects this generation of union leaders' experience with the outlawry and arbitrariness of the Nazi regime, they are inclined strictly to observe the law and legal decisions, even if they may prove disadvantageous to the union movement.

In consequence of the restrictive court decisions and reflecting their legalistic attitude, German trade unions usually agree to provisions for voluntary arbitration in their agreements, normally calling

---

*As a consequence of this decision, the IG Chemie included a provision in the statutes declaring that no referendum is required before a strike is called. In 1974 the DGB Federal Committee recommended that unions determine for themselves whether strike votes were needed for strike action; negotiations with management would be needed only if considered productive.

on neutral arbitrators. The process of arbitration in effect calls for
a cooling-off period, which may reduce the members' readiness to
strike.

One consequence of the comprehensive legal regulation of industrial relations is that trade unions have lodged responsibilities
for decisions with the presidiums, which in fact are authorized to
decide on collective bargaining and labor conflicts. The institutional
and legal conditions of the unions' range of action as outlined above
have accounted until recently for the relatively undisturbed climate
of industrial relations in the BRD.

RISE AND DECLINE OF COOPERATIVE WAGE POLICY

Conversion of DGB Unions from an Active
to a Cooperative Wage Policy

Wavering between active representation of members' interests
and adaptation to the requirements of economic stabilization is a
fundamental characteristic of West German unions' wage policy. [9]
This behavior is not accidental; it results from the pragmatic course
followed by the unions' leading bodies.

Economic conditions and the memberships' interests are the
two major determinants of trade union behavior. Unions, since the
end of the 1950s, sought to realize their members' interests by
adapting their policies to economic requirements--namely, by limiting their demands essentially to increases in productivity. This
strategy was possible owing to the high level of economic prosperity
that allowed for regular increases in real wages, and the existence
of a politically passive and acquiescent membership, whose expectations rarely went beyond the levels being negotiated. These factors
made for the cooperative policy, which later easily meshed in with
the institutional framework of the state incomes policy.

The cooperative wage policy, developed in the 1950s, is the
product of wage conflicts in which both parties learned to look for a
common and mutually agreeable platform for their goals. The employers accepted the necessity of providing annual wage increases,
and the unions renounced the claim of effecting a redistribution of
incomes by way of wage policy, agreeing to the necessity of a
productivity-oriented wage policy.* Though most unions officially

---

*In the IG Metall this process was brought to a head later than
in the other unions, virtually only with the 1963 strike. This was
the last strike with redistribution as a goal. Following lockouts and

speak of the goal of income redistribution by means of an "active wage policy," this claim has over time become mere ideology. Only the right-wing union of construction, stone, and clay workers, in accordance with established policy in 1963, officially acknowledged the concept of a productivity-oriented wage policy, expecting redistribution by "wealth formation by workers" to be promoted by the state.

Evidence of the conversion of the DGB unions toward being cooperative organizations is further provided by the decline of strike activities since 1958, the process of reorientation apparently coming to a halt toward the end of the 1950s. During the period 1950-58, each year witnessed at least one large official strike. But in the 1960s official strikes became a rarity.

The diminution in the scope and number of strikes is in contrast to developments in other countries, where strikes tended in the 1960s to become more extensive and involved larger numbers of employees than in the 1950s. Strikes in the BRD had also been politically oriented in the 1950s and often combined both economic and political demands. They were aimed against the enactment of the BVG and involved a two-day printers' strike. Another series was called in 1955, in defense of the co-determination provisions in the mining and steel industries, and involved some 600,000 metal and mining workers. In 1956/57 a 16-week strike of metal workers sought the equalization of payments in case of sickness between blue- and white-collar workers. The same period also witnessed campaigns endorsed by unions against atomic rearmament and the expansion of the military forces. In retrospect, this period seems to represent a peak in the unions' struggle for the workers' economic and political demands.

In contrast, the union-led strikes in the 1960s and early 1970s sought exclusively to prevent wage cuts or to support demands for wage increases. They occurred during the cyclical downturns in 1962-63, 1967, and 1971, which underscores their defensive nature. Characteristically, the offensive strike waves in the boom years of 1969 and 1973 were unofficial movements.

Integration of the Cooperative Wage Policy into National
Income Policy and Its Consequences: Wildcat Strikes

When in 1966/67 the Grand Coalition under the leadership of Minister Schiller inaugurated Keynesian economic policies to counteract the developing recession, it found the trade union movement

---

government intervention, the IG Metall, however, yielded to the rule of income distribution in line with the principles of the economic system--that is, wage increases are related to rises in productivity. This rule has in practice not seriously been questioned since then.

prepared and a willing supporter. Through its bargaining experience and the Dusseldorf Basic Program of 1963, the movement was well prepared for "concerted action."

With the Dusseldorf program, unions had accepted the principle of general economic planning and the use of economic analyses for the guidance of policy within a market economy. They assigned the highest priority to the achievement of economic growth and full employment and, at the same time, accepted the principle of allowing employers the freedom independently to employ their capital.

Since the mid-1950s the unions followed the principle of orienting their decisions on wage policy to macroeconomic data. The centralization of collective bargaining negotiations permitted the top leaders to enforce the decisions without much difficulty among the members. The unions were therefore well-prepared to act the part assigned to them by the state crisis management: to exercise wage restraint in the national interest in order to overcome the recession.

The idea of "concerted action"--that is, cooperation of the state, the unions, and the employers' associations--originated with the 1965 second annual report of the Council of Experts. It called for a "coordinated adjustment of behavior (of unions and employers) with a view of a progressive containment of the inflationary trend." Unions and employers declared themselves ready to cooperate. However, the initiative failed as the government refused to call for quantitative economic goals and omitted from its draft of the stabilization law the principle of accommodation of behavior by both the state and economic groups. When the SPD entered the Grand Coalition, it secured the inclusion of the provisions for "concerted action" in the final version of the "Law for Promoting Stability and Growth in the Economy."

Paragraph 3 of the law provides that "in the case of a threat" to the goals of economic policy--that is, "price level stability, high rates of employment, external economic equilibrium under conditions of a constant and adequate rate of growth"--the government shall make available "guidelines for the purpose of achieving simultaneously coordinated behavior (concerted action) of regional organizations, unions and employers associations." "The procedure calls for the presentation of relevant macro-data emphasizing the economic interdependencies." According to the wording of the law and as the practice has shown, the "concerted action" is an instrument of information and consultation; no decisions are binding on the parties.

The immediate aim of the first meetings in spring 1967 was to coordinate wage policy with the program of economic expansion. The federal government had adopted two investment budgets amounting to DM 11 billion and other measures including special liberal depreciation allowances. The unions were urged to restrain their wage

demands, not to puncture the entrepreneurs' improved profit expectations. Unions were promised a later settlement, which would include these delayed wage increases and restore "social symmetry."*
The unions agreed to this program for a number of reasons.
First, they were keen to see an early end to the recession. Second,
they felt that with the SPD in the government they would be assured
of a better hearing and guarantee of workers' interests. Third, they
accepted the principle of "social symmetry." Fourth, they were re-
assured since the minister had acknowledged the need of prescribing
wage increases within the defined limits. Fifth, they had incorporated
the essential elements of this "new economic policy" in their own
Dusseldorf program.

During the first two years (1967 and 1968) of the operation of
the plan, the unions observed the level of wage increases set down in
the orientation materials. In the first year they achieved an increase
of 3.5 percent, exactly on the target, and in the second, 4.3 percent,
which compared with 4 to 5 percent in the orientation data. The third
year, 1969, showed an increase of wages of 10.3 percent, whereas
the orientation data indicated 5.5 to 6.5 percent.[10] But this disparity
resulted from events outside of the unions' control.

The period of wage restraint facilitated the attainment of the
fast economic upswing. Moreover, unions concluded agreements
for longer than the customary 12 months. But the growing discrep-
ancy between wage and profit developments during the economic upturn and intensification of management's drive for higher efficiency
built up dissatisfaction among the rank and file; the promise of "social symmetry" had not been kept. Wildcat strikes broke out in the
fall of 1969 in parts of the steel, metal, coal-mining, and textiles
industries, and in the public service, with at least 140,000 workers
participating, enforcing a revision of the unions' restraint wage
policy.

The wave of spontaneous strikes in September 1969, an event
quite unprecedented for the German trade union movement, strongly
affected the unions' wage policy and their organizational structure.
It brought about a reversal of the state incomes policy and also endangered the established institutionalized cooperative representational system.

The wildcat strikes freed the unions from their obligations
under the state incomes policy, and thereafter it played only a minor
role in shaping actual wage policies. The new militancy, which expressed itself in other than official union action and indicated dwind-
ling confidence among the rank and file in the official organizations,

---

*This slogan was coined by Minister of the Economy Schiller
and became popular in the discussion of economic policy.

revealed latent forces that had to be taken into account but might also
be made use of by union organizations in their future bargaining
policy.

The experience produced a debate in which the presidiums of
the two most involved unions took different stands. The presidium of
the Mine and Power Workers Union argued that the strikes in the Ruhr
and Saar regions had been of no use to the workers and had not
strengthened the unions' bargaining power against the employers and
that they had been precipitated by communists and radicals. The
presidium of the Metal Workers Union did not explicitly approve the
strikes but found in them support for their earlier warning to employers that there was unrest among the employees and considered them
justified. It also saw that they might force employers prior to the
termination of the contract to enter into negotiations with the union
and to make wage concessions.

Critical voices among members and officers looked upon the
September strikes as an inevitable consequence of the cooperative
bargaining policy practiced by the unions. They interpreted the
strikes as support of the criticism of the "concerted action" made
by other lower- and middle-rank officers at union congresses before
1969. In the eyes of this group of members and officers the decision
of the leadership to support cooperation with the concerted action
showed them to be desirous of observing the "rules of the capitalist
system," which was in conflict with their own conception of union
functions.

Without giving up the prior policies for limited member representation, trade unions drew more of the active union elements into
their policy-making forums, steering toward a more active wage
policy to demonstrate their legitimacy.


DECISION-MAKING AND MEMBERSHIP
PARTICIPATION IN UNIONS


The policies of the German trade unions, which, since the end
of the 1950s, justify calling them cooperative unions are not derived
from the pursuit of member interests but rather flow from the acceptance of the requirements for capital accumulation in the economy.
One major focus of an analysis of intraorganizational developments
within cooperative unions therefore must be on the role of the membership and the membership's interests in the process of decision-
making.

Structure of Decision-Making in Cooperative Trade Unions

In general, members do not take an active interest in the organizations' activities, in particular in the process of decision-making

Except for strike situations, rarely do more than 10 percent of the members stay in constant and close contact with the organizations. Nevertheless, the attitude of members cannot be characterized as completely indifferent. The vast majority of members as well as nonmembers (80-90 percent) do consider the unions absolutely necessary to the defense of their economic interests. In general, their attitude may be described as passive, but they offer willing acquiescence.

These empirical findings reflect the fact that is characteristic of a cooperative union, that the participation of members in decision-making is not really necessary and is at times an impediment. Demands are determined by the prevailing economic situations (such as rate of growth, growth of productivity, and market conditions). They may be defined by the rules of the Keynesian economic policy--that is, by "technical rules" that do not call in question the "institutional frame" of the social system or the existing alignment of power or the distribution of income and property. The application of these "technical rules" to wage policy does not call for a discussion of the standards of social justice.

Nevertheless, the process of decision-making is not irrelevant to the relationship between the organization and its members. The prevailing policy must at all times produce sufficient consent to enable the members to accept the organization as the legitimate representative of their interests. Only in this case will they be truly bound to collective-bargaining decisions, and only if decision-making procedure is sanctioned democratically by the people will the organization secure the members' loyalty. Legitimation of union policy by its members is all the more important since cooperative unions must also be able to mobilize members at least temporarily for strikes and to activate passive members and make them the executors of their own interests.

The process of decision-making in collective bargaining in cooperative trade unions obviously faces a specific dilemma. On the one hand, it must be screened from open and uncontrolled articulation of members' interests and discussion of the underlying standards of social justice; articulation of members' interests is to be limited both as to quantity and quality. On the other hand, the screening and limitation must be achieved without disciplinary or repressive measures, for otherwise decision-making could not be identified as a democratic process, working without pressure, and thus would lose its decisive function of legitimation.

The problem is solved by restrictive mechanisms, lest the organization be required to offer its policy for approval by the unregimented discussion of members' interests. In controversial cases, the policy is sanctioned by the fact that members do not revolt and leave.

Restricted Membership Participation
in Organizational Processes

Collective bargaining committees are the union organs of
decision-making as to the goals and strategies of the wage policy.
Despite their crucial importance in the organizations' activities,
they are standing committees of local delegates' meetings, not being
directly responsible to the rank and file and its representative organs. They are only entitled to present "position papers" and "recommendations" in the formative process of drafting of wage demands,
to agree or to reject the bargaining results and projected referendums
and strikes. Due to the necessity of maintaining a consistent strategy,
the formal and final right of making binding decisions is reserved to
the presidiums, to prevent the centrally organized employers' associations from playing off union collective-bargaining groups against
each other. Hitherto, the presidiums in general followed the recommendations of the collective-bargaining committees. Except for
cases of referendums, the latter represent to the membership the
only authority for the democratic legitimation of wage decisions by
the central organs.
     The members of the negotiating committees get their demo-
cratic mandate from the regional delegates' meetings, though the
latter's election is determined by the requirements of general union
policy rather than by those of the wage policy. Owing to the mechanics of election, the collective bargaining committees tend to be dominated by members of the works councils, and, in particular, those
of large enterprises.
     The lower-level officers, especially the shop stewards, are
not brought into the process of decision-making, and the collective
bargaining committees are not under any obligation to accept the demands of shop stewards and active members. Thus, the members
of the works councils play a crucial role in decision-making in the
collective-bargaining committees. By reason of their position, they
do not tend to favor an aggressive wage policy, which would involve
the risk of wage disputes and would curtail the scope of the autonomous plant level wage policy. Instead, they are inclined to promote
"moderate" wage increases according to average rates of profits and
productivity gains. Their own positional interests coincide with the
aims of a cooperative wage policy adapted to economic growth. They
are the "natural" partners of unions pursuing a cooperative wage
policy.
     The presidiums exercise their influence, save for occasional
variations, according to the following pattern: They communicate
their views together with supporting arguments by experts to the
bargaining committees of the individual districts, thus shaping the

discussion beforehand. Slightly modified but accepted and approved by democratic vote in the form of "recommendations" of the negotiating committees, these views are returned to the presidiums for final formal sanction. Should the committee's proposals strongly deviate from those proposed, the presidium is likely to seek a revision, referring to the necessity of a single consistent strategy. Actually, they ratify the internal orientation data introduced by them into the process of decision-making.

It is obvious that only strong pressure on the part of members and shop stewards could break up this partnership of the presidiums and works councils. Owing to the membership's passivity, such pressure, indeed, is in general unlikely in the decisive phase before wage negotiations. Dissatisfaction is usually given voice only ex-post-facto as a reaction, after acceptance of a wage contract. It may express itself in verbal criticism, in abstinence from voting and adverse votes at the election of lower-level officers and works councils, or in the form of demonstrative withdrawals from membership or in wildcat strikes. Criticism usually is limited to individual groups of workers, plants, or organizational areas. Apart from large wildcat strikes, they do not affect the organizations' policy, for reactive criticism cannot endanger intraorganizational decisions, which are considered to have been democratically formulated. In case of conflicts between presidiums and individual groups of members, criticism is rejected by referring them to the approval of the democratically elected bargaining committee and to the failure of the members to participate in the preparatory phase of the bargaining process.

Nevertheless, this process of legitimation is imperfect, for members who are dissatisfied with wage agreements are not likely to accept them as being in accordance with their interests. They will merely put up with the decision since they have no means, or there are no means, for revision within the organization. Legitimation of controversial decisions in general is negatory; it does not rest on a positive agreement but only on the absence of an alternative practicable means of action.

The legitimacy of representative organs, however, is seriously called into question if a union wage policy is subordinated to the directives of incomes policy and if the members, in particular the active members and the lower-level officers, become aware of that. In this case, decisions of the representative organs no longer may be considered autonomous and therefore not democratically sanctioned decisions. Wage restraint, which is usually synonymous with incomes policy, is no more than the adaptation of the trade unions' wage policy to the purposes of the state economic policy and cannot be justified by the standards of just distribution, which the trade unions cannot forego. It is this inner contradiction on which trade union cooperation with incomes policy has foundered to date. The wildcat strikes not only originated from the divergence between growth-oriented wage increases and membership interests in higher feasible raises, but just as much from the conviction of lower-level officers and active members that cooperation with the incomes policy nullifies their rights to autonomous employee representation.

As long as the trade union wage policy is not completely integrated into the incomes policy, one cannot speak of a "reversal of the process of decision-making." A deliberate cooperative practice has also to consider the vital interests of the membership, irrespective of the manner in which they are introduced into the process of decision-making by the members themselves or by their immediate representatives, or by the bargaining committees and the leadership, depending on their judgment as to their urgency. They are filtered, limited, and selected with regard to their compatibility with the specific requirements of the processes of capital accumulation. They are adapted to economic capacities, a practice born from the insight gained in the limits of wage policy. The unions' veto power is hardly sufficient to counteract inflationary trends and unemployment brought about by the management's decisions on prices and investments.

The rationality remaining in a cooperative policy is further nullified, for the membership is not allowed to participate in the determination of the organizations' goals. Only calculable participation at the time of wage bargaining, on the occasion of strike votes and strikes, "quasi-participation" as it were, is compatible with a cooperative policy; it is acceptable as long as it strengthens the organization's bargaining power without reducing the leaders' scope of action. Membership participation in the event of strike votes and strikes is indeed defined in the statutes in a very restrictive way. Members are not granted the autonomous right to express agreement or to reject proposed strikes. Strikes can be called only if they are supported by a positive vote of 75 percent, a restriction that may be described as almost prohibitive. This applies particularly to the second vote, for which at least 75 percent are required to reject an agreement if the strike is to be continued; consequently, a dissenting minority of only 26 percent is able to end a strike. The aim is to make the strike "calculable," to make strike votes and strikes computable instruments.

Deficiencies in the Union Representation System

These limitations on membership participation create serious defects in the intraorganizational processes, with far-reaching consequences for the trade unions' representational system. One consequence is that the established institutional forms of workers' representation have become inflexible; membership interests that are not compatible with them or are causing difficulties are ignored. An example is the demand for a "plant-level wage policy"--that is, for plant wage contracts that would legally safeguard supplements and social benefits. Although called for by the congresses of the IG Metall and IG Chemie, there have to date been only half-hearted attempts to put them into practice. They foundered on the opposition of the works councils in the large enterprises and the presidiums. Plant-level wage policy no doubt would strongly reduce the influence of the present decision-making bodies, the bargaining committees, and the union centers, in favor of the shop stewards. The membership evidently is interested in seeing their actual earnings legally secured. The achievement of the goal would mean effective control by the membership of wage policy at the enterprise and also of the hitherto independent policies of the works councils. It would strengthen the trade unions' position in the plants but would produce a conflict with the leadership of many works councils.

Due to low levels of membership participation in union affairs, the organization is also becoming less capable of perceiving changes and shifts in the interests of the membership. The leadership tends to overlook virulent dissatisfaction with trade union wage policy, as it did in the case of the September 1969 strikes.

In the discussion on co-determination, too, there is a gap between the leaders and the membership. Empirical studies point out that workers tend to understand co-determination somewhat differently than the official interpretations. Workers view it as their means of securing veto powers on working conditions, on forms of wage compensation, and other matters where management exercises unilateral power. This disparity has as yet not been perceived by the centers of the unions, as is made evident by the official arguments for extension of the parity system to the supervisory boards of the firms. While in the years after 1945 trade unions were able to act bona fide in fighting for co-determination at the management level, they cannot do so today.

Demands for co-determination at the work place, brought forward by groups of trade unionists even in the middle-level leadership, undoubtedly are closer to the thinking of the workers than co-determination in the management of the enterprise. Workers naturally have an interest in co-determination relative to concrete working conditions, speed of work, supervisors' competences, plant rationalization, and forms of wage compensation. Nevertheless, even before a discussion within the organization could have been opened, presidiums rejected this proposal, referring to the danger of "group egoism"

and "syndicalist splintering." Similarly, they disregarded the issue
of wage incentive systems, though it is the oldest mechanism for the
stabilization of management power in the plant and the intensification
of the efficiency of labor. The principle of monetary compensation
for bad and unhealthy working conditions was first questioned in principle in the labor conflicts in 1973, when the demand was made for
their elimination.

The current system of workers' representation as well as the
intraorganizational processes are, so to speak, operating above the
memberships' heads. Leaders prefer to take up obvious interests
related to immediate subsistence, as otherwise members would oppose the organization's policies. But they do little to articulate latent
interests; debates on these subjects are impeded and often stopped.


THE CRISIS OF TRADE UNION POLICY


Evidence


In recent years, particularly since the strikes in September
1969, changes have occurred that may render the intraorganizational
distribution of power unstable. Decisive action in this direction
originated among shop stewards. In many larger enterprises of the
automobile, metal and steel, and chemical industries, the shop stewards outgrew their role as helping hands of the works councils, gaining both independence and an ability to oppose the works councils and
the union's leadership apparatus.

1. The new independence and greater activity of the shop stewards made itself felt through more effective control of the works councils. Conflicts between shop stewards and the old, established works
councils members have become frequent. Close cooperation of works
councils with plant managements in matters of plant-level wage policy at times produced charges of corruption. Disputes arose on the
occasion of the 1972 works councils' elections. In some large enterprises in the industrial centers, shop stewards used their right to decide for themselves as to who would be on the list of candidates. In
several cases works councils members' reelection became doubtful
as they did not receive a safe place on the voting list, whereupon in
some cases competitive lists of candidates of former members were
presented, which was against the rules. In some large plants in the
automobile and chemical industries, long-time members of works
councils were voted out of office and shop stewards replaced them.[11]

2. Internally, the new independence of the shop stewards is
demonstrated mainly by criticisms of the centralized wage policy.

The demand for a wage policy oriented more closely to the needs of the employee on the workshop floor was the nucleus around which an intraorganizational opposition crystallized at the last two congresses of the IG Metall (1971) and the IG Chemie (1972). In numerous motions presented at these congresses, the following demands were made; however, none except for the first one passed.

a. Shop stewards should be granted binding rights by the statutes, in particular, to participate in the election of members of the bargaining committees and should be empowered to require these committees to justify their action. (This resolution was adopted at the 1972 congress of the IG Chemie. The IG Metall statutes do not grant any rights to the shop stewards.)

b. In addition to the works councils, the shop steward bodies should have a decisive voice in the wage policies, in particular as regards the determination of incentive pay systems and premiums, speed of work, design of the physical work place, and the selection of supervisors--demands that implement the concept of co-determination at the work place.

c. There should be a plant-level wage policy, which ought to be exactly defined, calling for institutionalization and legalization of trade union negotiation procedures at the plant level, which would safeguard real earnings by wage contracts and exploit the unions' bargaining power to improve the wage agreement.

d. Each regional contract should be submitted for approval by the membership and be binding only on their acceptance.

3. The increased activity of the shop stewards in recent years brought into the open internal union disputes over wage agreements. Examples are to be found in the IG Chemie and the IG Metall. In the chemical industry shop stewards in 1970 sought to secure plant wage contracts. When the influential members of works councils in the bargaining committees instead accepted the exceptionally high wage offer made by the employers' association, they faced heavy criticism from the rank and file. In the following year official strikes were conducted on a selective plant basis only, allowing several large plants to remain untouched, while in other plants strike actions showed a strong tendency toward radicalization. Finally, the union presidium, at the government's insistence, ended the strike without calling for a vote. The strike, its course, and the manner in which it was terminated produced sharp intraunion disputes, as did also the issue on the works councils' policy of social partnership in the chemical industry.

The wage contracts signed by the IG Metall in January 1973 gave rise to considerable dissatisfaction among the members because of the insufficiency of the rise. In the iron and steel industry, members voted to strike against the contract, but the strike was called

off and the presidium recommended acceptance of a new employers'
offer. Differences developed over this offer in the bargaining committee and a minority of about one-third rejected it. At a subsequent
vote only 26 percent of the votes cast by union members were in its
favor, but the presidium proclaimed acceptance, as permitted by the
statutes, though only a minority had voted for it. The shop stewards
in the industrial centers who openly pleaded for rejection of the compromise were largely responsible for this clear-cut vote of no confidence against the recommendations of the bargaining committees and
presidium. Immediately following the conclusion of the contract,
wildcat strikes broke out in the steel industry, which could only be
settled by additional above-the-contract increases. In 1974 unions
insisted upon and secured wage settlements averaging 12.5 percent
reflecting the leaders' efforts to meet member expectations.

4. The steady and rapid increase of spontaneous strikes in recent years, particularly within the area of the IG Metall, has made
apparent the crisis in the trade union representational system and of
the internal decision-making procedures. A study of strikes covering the period from 1948 through 1968 found that 83 percent of all
strikes in the years from 1964 to 1968 were wildcat strikes and that
two-thirds of the strikers engaged in wildcats.[12] The proportion is
likely to be much higher for later dates, since the years 1969, 1970,
and 1973 witnessed an upsurge of wildcat strikes.

The spontaneous strikes in 1969 resulted from the protest
against the trade unions' cooperation with the incomes policies.
Workers felt they had been discriminated against on finding that profits were rising perceptively whereas wages were lagging behind. Empirical studies of these strikes indicate that in-plant trade union officials initiated and managed them.[13]

While the spontaneous strikes in 1970 flowed from the official
wage bargaining in the metal industry and helped to secure a favorable contract, those in the spring and summer of 1973 were the immediate consequence of the unsatisfactory wage contract in the metal
industry in January 1973. The 8.5 percent wage increase was much
less than the members had expected, and the rise in the cost of living in the following months obliterated the real gains. The subsequent boom, with the resulting shortage in the labor market and high
profits in the industry, created growing dissatisfaction among workers and caused a number of concerns to grant voluntary increases
beyond those called for by the contract. As a result workers in other
plants followed with wildcat strikes, often lasting several days, to enforce payment of inflation supplements. Almost 200,000 metal workers were involved in the unofficial strikes during the months of June
through August 1973.

5. Characteristic of the spontaneous strike movement of 1973
and quite a shock to great parts of the public was the militant partici-

pation in them of a large number of foreign workers. In several plants of the automobile industry they took the initiative in determining the course of the strikes. The one-week strike in the Ford plants at Cologne, much discussed in public, was called the Turkenstreik (Turks' strike) because 12,000 of the 24,000 Ford blue-collar strikers were Turkish workers. And, in fact, two-thirds of the strikers were foreign workers.

The Ford strike showed two distinctive features, as compared with the usual spontaneous strikes of 1973, which are paradigmatic for strikes in which foreign workers play a leading role: (1) The strike goals were not limited to demands for wage increases on account of the rising costs of living but also included demands for slowing down the speed of work and for longer rest periods; and (2) The organization and the development of the strike were completely beyond the control of the unions and their plant-level representatives. By their militant activities (permanent occupation of the plant and daily demonstrations right across the workshop floors) and by the election of an autonomous strike committee, which incidentally did not include any shop steward, the foreign workers' actions moved beyond the usual framework of strike strategy and tactics.

This behavior is to be accounted for by the specific social situation of the foreign workers in the BRD, which may be characterized as one of social discrimination, social isolation, and insufficient union representation. They are performing activities not requiring special qualifications, are in low-wage occupations, and have poor housing accommodations, more than one-half of them not having a flat of their own.

The unions in the BRD have hitherto not objected to the employment of foreign workers. They indeed were successful in organizing one-third of them (this corresponds to the ratio of organization of the German workers). On the other hand, the resentment of the foreign workers against the unions may be quite justified. Some allege that the unions have a greater interest in increasing their membership figures than in developing an effective employee representation system directed to the correction of the specific situation of the foreign workers. Only rarely do foreign workers hold union posts. At the beginning of 1970 about 10 percent of the IG Metall membership consisted of foreign workers, but their percentage among shop stewards was under 5 and that of works councils' members only slightly over 2. At the last congress of the IG Metall in 1971 only one of the 470 delegates was a foreign worker.

## Causes

Apart from the economic and collective bargaining conditions enumerated above, the crisis in union representation is being aggravated by a number of specific structural deficiencies in the bargaining and representation system.

1. The centralized cooperative wage policy and the resulting system, though relatively successful in the postwar years, left a number of obvious structural gaps in the bargaining system. Unions were excluded from the shop floor. First, the central industry and regional bargaining system did not fully capture the individual enterprise's potential for granting wage increases, particularly in the case of the larger ones. More or less autonomously, informal plant wage policies therefore developed. Second, the overall general agreements prescribed quasilegislative standards and general directives to be applied and implemented at the plant level by the works councils. As a result, the overall industry agreement lost much of its significance to the individual worker, for the more crucial agreement was that negotiated for the plant between the management and the works councils. Despite this rise in its responsibility, the works councils gained no new bargaining tools. They were precluded by law from engaging in real economic action and had to rely on their negotiating skills to get good terms. They could not effectively take the initiative to enforce or defend wage additions, secure improvements in working conditions, or prevent their deterioration. Active and militant groups developed to fill the gap left by the inability of the works councils to satisfy local expectations. They responded by organizing spontaneous strikes.

2. Shop stewards were increasingly being placed in an anomalous position. They had a critical role to play in the union machinery. In case of referendums and ballot votes on strikes, they were responsible for informing passive members of the issues at hand and convincing them of the union's position and the justification for the demands and their realizable nature. They were therefore expected to be completely identified with union policies and support the organization's strategy. But many of them had become dissatisfied with the cooperative wage policy and therefore had become less effective agents for the union itself. If they were disgruntled they tended to be among those who took the stronger positions and were the most sensitive to the weakness of the cooperative wage policy and be critical of the compromises reached in the agreements. They therefore had become less reliable. They became the focus of much local friction between members and union leadership.

3. Changes are also evident in the prevailing attitudes among workers toward wage policy. According to recent empirical research the standard for wage demands has shifted. Tests for wage increases are no longer related to the traditional standards of sustenance and physical efficiency, as was the case in the 1950s. Instead, economic

growth has become the determining factor. In particular the younger age groups, those spared the experience of the economic crisis of the 1930s and of the immediate postwar period, regard an adequate share of the growing social wealth a legitimate claim. The former general fixation on price stability also is being moderated among workers. The vast majority of employees is no longer willing to forgo wage demands on the grounds of price stability. This change of attitude toward wage policy coincides with a new attitude toward unemployment. As empirical studies have shown, unemployment is no longer accepted as inevitable by the majority of workers and lower-level union officials. Skepticism is indeed rather common as regards the ability of the system to function without crisis, but people believe that the state's economic policy is capable to regulate the economic processes to avoid large-scale unemployment. The guarantee of a work place for all is considered a legitimate claim, which the state economic policy can satisfy.

These changes in the workers' thinking have a real basis in the social and economic developments of the past two decades. The experience of continuous economic growth with a high rate of employment and the ease with which the recession of 1966/67 was overcome evoked and strengthened the claim for appropriate participation in the social wealth and the expectation of a secure work place.

Empirical findings on the new "wage consciousness" are confirmed by the unofficial strikes of 1973. The strikers sought compensation for the loss in real wages caused by inflation and, second, an adequate share in the high profits of industry during the boom phase. The unofficial strikes of 1969 reflected this new type of thinking. In the summer of 1973, the legitimacy of the trade union wage policy was seriously challenged.

4. The increased wage demands by wage earners met head on the reduced industrial margins for wage increases, resulting from the altered position of the economy, producing sharp industrial conflicts.

a. Since the 1960s, structural limits on economic growth have become visible. The extraordinary factors conducive to the "economic miracle" in the 1950s have been exhausted. Growth is now principally dependent upon increased productivity of labor, but the transition from extensive to intensive expansion in output is impeded by the deficiencies in the national infrastructure and the past inadequacies of the investments in employee training and research. To overcome these deficits large governmental expenditures are now required. That people in the Federal Republic are becoming aware that the need for reforming the social system is in part a reflection of these needs for modernization. The SPD, which was elected on its declaration that it is a "party of reform," is planning to increase the government's portion of the total social product from 1970 to 1985 from 28 percent to 34 percent. To finance these projects, increases in taxes are required, and these are to be imposed on consumption rather than investment goods, thereby slowing down the rise on the employee's income.

b. "Secular inflation," which is being stoked by the worldwide monetary crisis, as well as the apparent shortages in crucial and strategic commodities and the ability of producers of some commodities such as oil to exact strikingly higher prices, have become major problems for the government. To maintain its favorable position in the world, it must control domestic inflation. But a government that accepts the principle of an employer's freedom of action is limited in its ability to influence the entrepreneur's price policy. It is therefore apt to turn to wage policy as its primary lever for fighting inflation. The greater the problem that inflation presents, the greater the temptation to seek to have unions contain their wage demands and forgo increases in real wages. Proposals are therefore discussed among economists and in bureaucratic circles about reactivating in one form or another a state income policy and limit, if not abolish, the principle of the freedom of wage determination. The older "concerted wage" policy, which involved the discussion of orientation data, would therefore be replaced by binding wage guidelines adapted to the requirements for economic stabilization and growth.

The development of the West German trade unions as outlined above is paradigmatic. The system of trade union collective bargaining and the corresponding internal processes as they unfolded since the mid-1950s, were attuned, on the one hand, to the conditions of an expanding economy, and, on the other, to widespread apathy among the membership. It finally resulted in the growing autonomy of the leadership structure. Nevertheless, by prudently adapting to prevailing institutional and economic conditions, unions were able to espouse effectively the immediate interests of the membership. The increasing tendencies for active members to pursue their interests more militantly, if necessary even by unofficial strikes, are bound to collide with the established intraorganizational procedures. Owing to the inherent incongruities, the organizational structure is incapable of satisfying the members' interests in greater participation and their broader aspirations. It is also equally incompatible with the growing militancy among workers. Drastic changes are needed in the trade union structure, as are systems of collective bargaining and employee representation to avoid the frictions and internal union and industrial conflicts that these developments portend. For the trade unions to continue to serve with the present structure seeking to enforce a cooperative bargaining relations would produce even greater strife for they would become an instrument for the manifest regimentation of the wage-earner and employee, a status he is unlikely to accept.

Response to Crisis

The spread of wildcat strikes and the formation of union opposition groups might ordinarily provoke fundamental changes in union policy and structure. But the trade union leaders were reluctant to act. Nor was the rank-and-file pressure continuous or strong enough to force these innovations. As a result the organizations made tactical changes in procedure and modest concessions to meet the issues raised by internal unrest.

First, there was more disposition to decentralize wage negotiations. After the September strikes, the IG Metall granted its districts more autonomy in their wage policies. Moreover, the same national union gradually adopted the warning-strike technique involving specific areas or plants as a leverage for improving the final terms of its agreement. The unofficial 1970 warning strikes of 300,000 metalworkers had the tactical support of the union and demonstrated the workers' readiness to fight for their demands. The pattern for the 1971 wage round was set by a three-week strike in Baden-Wurttenberg. A six-week strike in the same area in 1973 secured improvements in the general agreement respecting wages and working conditions. In the 1974 decentralized wage negotiations, a three-week strike in the Underwesser district crystallized the terms for this wage round.

The strike strategy was also taken up by other unions. Special note must be made of six other major official strikes called from 1971-74 to secure the basic demands. The IG Chemie led one in June 1971 in the chemical industry, the first in 50 years and then again one in October 1972 in the grinding materials industry. The paper and printing union (DGB) led one in its industry in April 1973. The wood and plastic union did the same in January 1974. And, finally, the three civil service unions (public service, postal workers, and railroad workers) conducted one in February 1974.

A third development was the changes in the nature of the demands. As to wages, unions are now combining across-the-board percentage increases with demands for minimum wage increases for the low wage groups, a type of proposal first offered in the September strikes. The proposals currently being presented to management for bargaining include regulations respecting working conditions, vacations, regulations, and work pace and similar concerns affecting the speed of work and job strains. They were prominent in the unofficial 1973 strikes and became issues in the official bargaining by the IG Metall in 1973, and it was successful in making gains in the field.

On the other hand, the unions have been less tolerant of internal dissidents. They have been particularly harsh with initiators of rank-and-file movements and independent tactical moves. Procedures are being introduced and on occasion employed to exclude such people, dismiss troublesome local union activists and officials, and dissolve troublesome elected local bodies. Most DGB unions have adopted resolutions allowing for action to be taken against left-wing radical groups that might be infiltrating and otherwise challenging the established structure. The resolutions are broad enough so that they might also be employed against other disturbing minority groups.

While the trade union movement has made modest modifications both in procedure and demands in response to the rising unrest among the rank and file, it has not brooked insurgent movements, which would challenge and change the cooperative wage policy and the prevailing superior position of the works council in the plant as compared with a rank-and-file union shop steward structure. While these policies and dual structures persist, the German industrial relations system rests on an unsteady base.

EDITOR'S NOTE

Collective bargaining at the end of 1974 took place in an adverse economic environment. Though Germany fared better than most industrial countries, with consumer prices rising less than 7 percent and the surplus in the balance being maintained at high levels, economic reverses set in. Unemployment rose beyond the 3.5 percent level to 5.1 percent in January 1975. A number of industries experienced a sharp drop in activity, including automobiles, metal, apparel, and construction. To reduce the permanent work force, a number of large companies offered the golden handshake, particularly to foreign workers, hoping for them to resign and leave the country. The government, in November 1973, banned the further entry of non-EEC nationals and introduced legislation authorizing heavy penalties to be imposed on employers procuring or employing illegal foreign labor.

In this setting the government through its consultations with unions and employers under the "concerted action program" appealed for wage increases to be kept below the two-digit level. The settlement for the steel industry, one of the active ones, provided a 9 percent increase, plus fringe benefits, plus two lump-sum payments to share the industry's unusual prosperity. A later agreement for the basic metal industry called for a 6.8 percent rise. The stormy petrel of the beginning of the year, the public employee union, responded by requesting a modest package and agreed to a 6.48 percent rise for 13 months. The railroad settlement was also conservative—6 percent for 13 months.

A wildcat strike at the time of the Ruhr metal industry negotiations (February 1975) protested the delay in negotiations and the employers' refusal to increase their offer.

The IG Metall followed other unions by having its congress authorize its presidium to expel actual or suspected extremists without an inquiry and defeating amendments offered by its radical wing.

The Mitbestimmung legislation is winding its way through the parliament despite employer opposition. One much-publicized example of trade union influence on corporation decisions is that the board of supervisors of Volkswagen decided not to proceed with the construction of an assembly plant in the United States as the union members of the board sought to prevent further inroads in German automobile employment.

The government itself responded to the spreading recession by taking positive steps to reflate the economy. At first it expanded its expenditures to help the hard-hit construction industry and depressed areas. Then in December it announced a full program of stimulation by increasing expenditures sharply and providing investment incentives to private industry and liberalized unemployment benefits. The program also extended the maximum period for the payment of these benefits and offered job mobility allowances to those securing jobs away from their regular residence. Employers were offered premiums to hire the jobless. New personal income taxes relieved the burden on low- and middle-income groups and increased them for the top-income groups. Some of the costs of these programs were to be funded out of the reserves built up through taxes paid in the more active periods. The money supply was also increased by the Central Bank. These steps were taken in part at the behest of the trade union movement for its cooperation in maintaining a moderate wage movement.

## NOTES

1. London Sunday Times, April 20, 1973.
2. Deutsches Institut fur Wirtschaftsforschung, Sonderhefte N.F. no. 42, Reihe A: Forschung, Anlagevermogen, Produktion und Beschaftigung in der Industrie im Gebiet der Bundesrepublik von 1924-1956 (Berlin: von Rolf Krengel, 1958), p. 94.
3. Annual Report of the Council of Economic Advisors of the Federal Government (Sachverstandigenrat), Printed Matter of the Bundestag V/2310, no. 484 and Table 36.
4. Minutes of the Founding Congress of the Deutscher Gewerkschaftsbund of 1949 (Koln, 1950), p. 318.

5. Theo Pirker, Die blinde Macht, part 1 (Munich, 1960), p. 282.

6. Victor Agartz in a speech delivered before the DGB-Congress of 1954; Minutes, op. cit., p. 435.

7. Walter Nickel, Zum Verhaltnis von Arbeiterschaft und Gewerkschaft (Koln, 1972), p. 119.

8. Claus Noe, Gebandigter Klassenkampf. Tarifautonomie in der Bundesrepublik Deutschland (Berlin, 1970), p. 198.

9. The reflections that follow have been developed more systematically by Walther Muller-Jentsch in his essay "Bedingungen kooperativer und konfliktorischer Gewerkschaftspolitik," Leviathan, 1973, no. 2, p. 223.

10. Quoted from Hermann Adam, "Konzertierte Aktion, politische Willensbildung und Tarifautonomie in der Bundesrepublik," in WWI-Mitteilungen 1972, nos. 2/3, p. 12.

11. See three case studies made at the time of the last works councils election, in Gewerkschaften und Klassenkampf, Kritisches Jahrbuch 1973, edited by O. Jacobi, W. Muller-Jentsch, E. Schmidt (Frankfurt, 1973), p. 43.

12. R. Kalbitz, "Die Entwicklung von Streiks und Aussperrungen in der BRD," Gewerkschaften und Klassenkampf, Kritisches Jahrbuch 1973 (Frankfurt, 1973), p. 174.

13. M. Schumann et al., Am Beispiel der Septemberstreiks. Anfang der Rekonstruktionsperiode der Arbeiterklasse (Frankfurt, 1971), p. 162; J. Bergmann, "Neues Lohnbewubtsein und September-streiks," in Gewerkschaften und Klassenkampf, Kritisches Jahrbuch 1972, edited by O. Jacobi, W. Muller-Jentsch, E. Schmidt (Frankfurt, 1972), p. 171.

CHAPTER

# 8

**FRANCE: ELITIST
SOCIETY INHIBITS
ARTICULATED BARGAINING**
Jean-Daniel Reynaud

## GROWTH AND ITS CONSEQUENCES

The economic and social changes in France during the last 25 years present few unique features in comparison with those of other industrial countries. A fairly regular and high rate of growth in France's GNP produced the expected results: a large reduction in the actively employed population in agriculture, which, between 1946 and 1968, decreased by one-half in absolute numbers and continues to decline; an increase in the secondary sector, at first rapid, then leveling off, despite the stress placed by the Sixth Plan (1970-75) on industrialization; and a more rapid increase in the tertiary sector. Furthermore, there was an increase in the proportion of wage-earners in the active population, due to the reduction in the numbers of self-employed, and a further differentiation in the categories of employees, with the most rapid increase occurring among those with higher or average skills. The proportion of women in the working population slightly diminished, if agricultural employment is included. There is little doubt, however, that the rate of employment of women in nonagricultural occupations is rapidly increasing today. Finally, as in most industrial countries of Europe, the need for immigrant manpower has become pressing, all the more as the reserves of young agricultural workers are being exhausted.

At the same time, household consumption progressed regularly at a rate of 4 to 5 percent a year. This increase changed in a predictable manner the relative importance of different provisions of the budget. Most important for us is the very perceptible rise in savings, frequently invested in housing, and the acquisition of durable consumer goods.

Let us repeat: The above facts are, in themselves, neither surprising nor original. Economic growth accounts for them and,

with differences of degree, Germany, Belgium, and Holland have
shown similar developments. Whatever surprise there is comes from
the banality of this development. For about 10 years after the war,
economists and sociologists (not to mention statesmen) strove furiously to explain why France did not, like the other countries of Europe,
enjoy "normal" growth. At a time when their explanations had become
more or less convincing, they were no longer relevant. Along with
the German miracle and the Italian miracle, there was a French miracle, or rather, there was no miracle at all. The country of small
family enterprises and an all-powerful administration no longer lived
on local time and in the shadow of its subprefects. It underwent rapid
growth, the most rapid in its history for so long a period of time--
exactly like its neighbors.

We know, moreover, that the French themselves took a long
time to come to believe in their own capacity for growth. It was a
point of debate in each election. Their newly acquired conviction,
heightened by the projections of the Hudson Institute and the OECD,
still has something fragile about it.

But that is not the principal paradox. In 1948 it was undoubtedly
difficult to foresee the economic development of the succeeding 25
years. Supposing, however, that it had been foreseen, it would have
been still more difficult to project that this development would not
bring about a general easing of conflicts and social tensions. Who is
the sociologist or political scientist who, if by some miracle he had
secured the above economic data, would have predicted the following
political and social developments: (1) the continuance of a powerful
Communist Party, which receives approximately 20 to 22 percent of
the votes and controls the majority labor union, which maintains its
own position; (2) the decline of the Socialist Party (despite an upturn
since 1970) and even more of labor unions with Socialist sympathies;
(3) the recurrence of grave, at times violent, conflicts, in one case
even culminating in a general strike that lasted several weeks and
threatened the very political system; and (4) the appearance of an
extreme left, more "radical" than the Communist Party, weak in
numbers and influence insofar as votes are concerned but significant
because of the considerable number of militants that it inspires,
notably in social conflicts. Carrying the paradox to an extreme: It
would have been easier to predict the political developments, the difficulties of decolonization, even the collapse of the Fourth Republic
when faced with the decisions exacted by the war in Algeria, than the
strong fundamental forces of political and social life revealed in the
1968 explosion and the radicalization of the French Democratic Federation of Labor (CFDT).

Certainly, some of the contemporary phenomena are direct
consequences of 1968, results of this upheaval. And, certainly too,

an explosion like that in 1968 has all the characteristics of an "event --that is to say, in which converged, in part accidentally, two different lines of development. No internal necessity linked the student manifestations with the workers' occupation of factories, and, in fact, the two movements scarcely communicated with one another. In this sense, it was a major but unpredictable accident, both in its beginning and its consequences. Should one be astonished at not having imagined the new face of a town after an earthquake? In the same manner, the France of 1974 bears traces of the cataclysm. But there is no reason to link them with any persistent tendency or to believe in their permanence.

Therefore, we must examine what is persistent and what is ephemeral in today's social conflicts.

## STRIKES, DEMANDS, AND ACTIVISM

### Strikes

France is one of the few countries in Europe where the annual average number of days lost by strikes from 1969 to 1972 is not much higher than from 1964 to 1967. One has only to omit the experience of 1968 to disclose a picture of a relatively peaceful society (in any case, much less affected by strikes than England or Italy), perhaps even of a society that is growing more peaceful. Is it necessary, however, to emphasize how arbitrary the picture would be? It does enable one to draw a conclusion, both as to method and substance, from this observation; namely, it is not very instructive, especially in the case of France, to analyze statistically the total numbers of strikes, to speculate on annual variations, and to try to derive long-term trends. Actually, strikes occur in cycles. It is absurd to add together units that are neither homogeneous nor independent and the whole of which assume the characteristic of an overall political event. Very long-term tendencies doubtless can be discerned. But their usefulness in explaining contemporary tendencies is, on the other hand, less certain. One may even wonder if they are stable.

Figures on strikes suggest that, except for 1968, their volume is not exceptional neither before nor afterwards, nor for their excesses nor shortfalls. It would not be reasonable to conclude much more.

Could we, on the other hand, try to identify the characteristics of the strikes that appear to be developing? There is some risk in doing so, as the conclusions would generally be based on a small number of cases, and their selection is determined by the hazards of journalism rather than their intrinsic importance. Moreover, the

unions publicize the conflicts that interest them, usually selecting
them by the newspapers' tests of significance or the strikes' exem-
plary nature. Such a collection hardly provides a representative
sample.

With this reservation, and we are not unaware of its importance,
a few characteristics may be noted.

First of all, there is the increasing importance of the enterprise
or more precisely the plant strike in a system in which the essential
part of the negotiations is on an industrial basis. The strikes that
impressed popular opinion each have a name: Renault in 1971 and
1973 (and more precisely Le Mans and Flins), le Joint Francais or
Les Nouvelles Galeries at Thionville in 1972, Lip or Pechiney-
Nogueres in 1973. Of course, it must not be overlooked that three
days of strikes at the SNCF (French National Railways) weigh more
heavily in the statistics, and probably in their economic consequences,
and that other conflicts that got less publicity are perhaps just as
significant--for example, the strike by Parisian garbage workers in
1972. In short, a strike in an establishment attracts greater attention in the media because it is often more spectacular and offers a
story to be told with surprises, climaxes, and endings. What remains indisputable is the effort made by the unions to sustain and
popularize such events.

These strikes, or at least the better known among them, have
another characteristic, more disturbing to employers and to a part
of public opinion. They often challenge the law or custom. They are,
in their development, irregular or extreme. The strike at Le Joint
Francais in St. Brieuc began with the occupation of the plant by the
workers, or more precisely a majority of the workers. The police
then expelled the strikers. At the aluminum foundry in Nogueres
in July 1973, the strikers stationed pickets at the factory entrance.
The management directed a sheriff to take note that emergency and
safety squads had been refused admittance. The conflict was so bitter that the electrolytic vats had to be stopped, thus causing considerable damage to the equipment.

Finally, is it necessary to recall the case of the Lip conflict
(summer 1973)? It was a strange conflict, in which the workers in a
bankrupt enterprise occupied the buildings to protest against the poor
managerial performance of their former boss and demand a reorganization of the business. They took possession of the funds on hand
and the stock of watches already produced, sold them, and paid themselves wages out of the cash on hand and the money brought in by sales.
It goes without saying that the actions of the "strikers" showed little
respect for the laws of bankruptcy.

These infractions of the law, this breaking of rules, were not
initiated from a higher level of the unions. On the contrary, in most

cases they resulted from pressure from below, or at least from the
militants at the base, with the support of the mass of workers. They
stem more from a call for direct action, little troubled by juridical
complications, than from revolutionary ardor. And, in fact, they
occasionally embarrassed the central organizations.

Finally, these strikes made little use of economic pressure.
The strikers at the Joint Francais could hardly hope to bring the
powerful Compagnie Generale d'Electricite (CGE) to its knees. They
succeeded primarily because they transformed their case into a sym-
bol of the fight against regional discrimination, which they proclaimed
endangered the very future of Brittany. The low wages at Joint
Francais proved that Brittany was underprivileged.

The most striking illustration of this use of public support is
the Lip strike. The organization of the "rapport of forces" by the
local employees obviously was not intended to apply economic pressure on management. For in fact, what economic pressure can
workers exert on a bankrupt factory? It sought the support of local,
and especially national, opinion to persuade the public authorities to
take action to save the plant.

It would be easy to exaggerate the influence of the extreme left
groups in these strikes. Even where the Unified Socialist Party
(PSU) had a corps of followers among the union militants who exerted
some influence on the course of the conflict, their impact was rarely
significant enough to direct the development. Nevertheless, their
activities reinforced the tendencies toward direct action, which was
rooted in a variety of other causes. As for the other leftist groups,
even though they made a show of strength here and there, their power
was very limited. But they served a function, despite their internal
struggles and doctrinal differences. They expressed in an extreme
manner a discontent that reflected a widespread feeling among employees. They may be truly characterized as witnesses much more
than actors in the situation.

The extreme left groups were thus able on occasion to express
the impatience among employees with the archaic working conditions
and the constraints of shift work and their determination to obtain
immediate redress without an intermediary in the form of an increase
in wages or the loosening of the organizational constraints. But,
even as for this function of creating a channel for expression particularly in cases of extreme impatience, the extreme left proved to be
of limited importance. The existing trade union organizations have
spelt out the major themes of workers' concern and led or guided the
important strikes. Even if it is true, and it seems well established,
that there is today more initiative and militancy among the employees
themselves, it is, nevertheless, a fact that strikers turn to these
unions for information or advice. And, equally significant, union

militants generally provide the leadership for local action. The CFDT, and to a lesser degree, the Confederation of Labor, Force Ouvriere (CGT-FO), tried to absorb the leftist moods. The CGT barred the leftists from their operations. But all three, in different ways, maintained control of the local situations.

Thus, many new forms and variations of conflict appeared. Did the nature and content of the demands also change?

## Demands

For several years after 1968, it became fashionable, especially in leftist circles, to contrast "quantitative" demands (wages, bonuses, hours of work) and "qualitative" demands (power, quality of life). Management circles also took up this distinction, in a more philosophic form, comparing the demand for "having" to that of "being." And, of course, nothing prevents people--and many do--from translating these demands into terms of dissatisfaction and satisfaction or personal hygiene and motivation.

These contrasting terms had the merit of drawing attention to new patterns of conduct and of enlarging the concerns and the field of responsibility of unionists and personnel directors. In the reality of industrial relations, however, if taken literally, there is a considerable risk that they may lead to grave errors.

In the first place, no factual data support the use of these two terms as opposites or alternatives. Demands concerning the rhythm of the work speed or the material conditions for its performance are inextricably intermeshed with the problems of bonuses, wages, and amount of pay. It would be absurd to apply to the reality of collective relationships a schema, like that of Maslow, which describes the growth of individual personality. In other terms, we know of no case in which one may usefully distinguish, in the form of demands, the factors of personal hygiene and motivation. The wages factor is always present. When one lists the reasons for dissatisfaction or the desires, one will include erratic and poor ventilation, breakdown of machines, and overly strict supervision by the foreman. It is natural, and in itself not very instructive, that the sum total of concerns mixes up the different categories. More precisely, the distinction does not permit one to sort out the different demands, either for the purpose of establishing priorities or predicting the results to be expected from their satisfaction. The logic of the demand quite naturally leads the union apparatus and individuals to give priority to what is measurable and verifiable, to do first that which one is most confident can be secured, which lends itself to objective definition, and which one can control with some assurance. In this sense, the idea

that "higher" needs should take precedence over "lower" needs ig-
nores the very logic of the adversary relations and the nature of negotiations in industrial relations.

To reject such opposites, however, is not to deny that new demands appeared. On the contrary, it serves to define more precisely
their nature, origin, and extent.

The area of grievances was enlarged. In certain cases, traditional demands are presented in a sharper, more urgent manner.
Thus, dissatisfaction about shift work is not new. Unions traditionally
concerned themselves with this issue; they oppose shift work when
justified by economic reasons, not technological ones.

As the workers' pressures grew stronger, sometimes expressing themselves abruptly, managements discovered in an increasing
number of cases, for example, that it was not technically essential
to maintain night shifts and sought more actively to automate the individual processes of production. A demand that is not new in these
circumstances gets a higher priority and, for this reason, poses new
problems to the employer.

The same interpretation could be applied to the increased importance assigned to material conditions of labor. Of course, personnel delegates and health and safety committees have always been
concerned with these matters. The novelty was simply in the urgency
or in the impatience surrounding the demand for correction. Compromises based on a wage bonus became less acceptable.

In this very vast domain of working conditions, however, appear two new types of demands. One is for a shorter grievance procedure. In this case, the grievance is not separable from negotiations. The second is to participate in the decision-making process
before rather than after the change has been made.

It is we who speak of the necessity for shorter procedures.
What seems, in fact, to exist is a mistrust among employees of centralized negotiations, of what transpires during the long journey of a
grievance from the plant to the enterprise to the industry organizations and back again. At times there is a distrust even with enterprise negotiations because they do not take place in the plant where
the problem arose. In other words, at least in a number of cases,
events appear to reflect a desire on the part of those involved to keep
their hands on the procedure and to demand, in fact, a short circuit
for negotiations and a grievance procedure that would return negotiations to the plant for handling.

In the second place, and this is why we don't distinguish between grievances and contract negotiations, the demands, even local
ones, at times call for preliminary consultation and not just the right
to protest after the fact. Is it impatience, as in the preceding case?
Perhaps, but it is an impatience that may have far-reaching conse-

quences for established relationships. If we recall that in France, as in most of the countries of continental Europe, the possibilities for workers and their organizations' controlling working conditions and practices are generally very limited, one may understand the importance of such a change.

Moreover, the demands express a new desire for greater equality or at least for a reduction of social distances and hierarchies in remuneration and power. Although it is neither very new (historic precedents abound) nor isolated, this theme is today becoming more important. At times, it is expressed in wage demands such as an across-the-board increase for all employees, or at least, a uniform increase of part of the raise. Of course, this demand is not unanimously supported by all groups. The Confederation Generale des Cadres (CGC) is, very naturally, opposed to it. The CGT has serious reservations. At other times, this move becomes a demand to equalize the social benefits of different groups in the enterprise. This is the object of the demand for employee status for manual workers (mensualisation). Finally, this widespread dissatisfaction is expressed in the disapproval of the elaborate hierarchy of management in the plant of subforemen and the "little chiefs"; and also in the technician's criticism of their superiors and the manner in which the latter supervise their work, and even of lower management toward higher management.

Did these issues truly raise the question of equality, or is the issue really the appropriate relationships of employees to authority? Both are doubtless closely related. But this latter theme should not be forgotten. If, as M. Seeman showed in a study made just before 1968, one of the characteristics of the situation of the French worker in comparison with that of the Swedish and American samples is a very strong feeling of powerlessness, it is evident why the explosion of 1968 occurred as it did, at least in a few privileged cases where higher white-collar workers took part, in terms of demands for power.[1] Specifically, rank-and-file workers wanted to have a say in the shop over the organization of the work and the design of jobs; the higher echelons wanted to be consulted and to participate in the decision-making. Admittedly, these are ambiguous demands, since they confuse the desire for a more just distribution of power with the claim that it will increase efficiency. It combines a demand for democratization and one for modernization. But perhaps this ambiguity makes it all the more effective in getting management to make concessions. The development of modern management methods were certainly stimulated by the demands of 1968.

For all that, is it necessary to interpret these claims as a willingness to have access to management? The CFDT, since its congress of 1970, lists the demand for self-management (autogestion) among its long-term objectives. Although it is difficult to measure its appeal, it is probable that this proposal touches a sensitive point, at least with the militants. How precisely has this call been expressed? Has it progressed much further, for the moment, than a vague dissatisfaction with being kept out of important decisions and the equally vague desire for a different structure of the enterprise? As for us, we doubt it, and the very manner in which the CFDT endeavors to identify this term with an aspiration rather than a program seems to confirm this judgment.

Finally, new groups are engaging in militant action. Semi-skilled workers have provoked much talk about themselves in the last five or six years. They were at the base of some of the great strikes of the period, including strikes at the two Renault plants where the issue was the problem of the classification of the semiskilled (O.S.). Although the prominent role of the skilled workers should not be overlooked, the important new development is the initiative of the semiskilled. It may open up new possibilities of action.

It seems equally true that traditionally "peaceful" categories of employees are today taking a more active part in social conflicts. These include women, both manual workers and sales clerks, and perhaps even immigrants. In the last 20 years, it is true, as V. Scardigli shows convincingly, that there was a strong negative correlation between the volume of strikes in an industrial branch and the percentage of female employees.[2] On the other hand, there is none at all with the proportion of unskilled workers. But these general findings say little about recent tendencies. Nor do they remove the possibility that the propensity to strike while still lower than the men's rate, has increased among women.

Besides strikes per se, dissatisfactions are often daily expressed in other ways. Industrial enterprises have more difficulty, it seems in recruiting manpower, particularly among young workers. Personnel managements conclude that they are unhappy with industrial work, since the same phenomenon does not appear in the offices. We know of no general collection of data on absenteeism or on labor turnover, but the figures for a good number of enterprises show a limited increase. Disciplinary difficulties are also generally reported by management. Foremen, for very different reasons than was true during the 1950s and 1960s, have again become a problem and a group causing much concern.

But this list of dissatisfactions and strikes reveals only a part of the situation. The paradox is indeed that in spite of all the above difficulties, or perhaps because of them, collective bargaining since 1967 has developed impressively.

## COLLECTIVE BARGAINING STRUCTURE WITH
## A MISSING LINK

Collective negotiation, if one judges by the number of signed agreements, has undergone several phases since the enactment of the law of February 11, 1950, which gave to the parties the freedom to negotiate: a rather slow beginning, until 1954; rapid development from 1955 to 1958; a sudden drop in 1959, followed by a rise until 1963; a slowdown in 1964; and then a rise, which was rather slow at first and then which became rapid beginning in 1968 (Table 4).

The last period is the one on which we will focus. But, to understand its implications, it is necessary to distinguish, beyond the overall figures, the different levels and areas of bargaining.

### The Development of Interindustry Negotiations

Unlike the Scandinavian countries, interindustry bargaining between a confederation of employers and confederations of workers and covering practically all economic branches is not traditional in France. The law does not favor it. The first such signed agreement on the complementary pensions of executives of 1947 had only doubtful validity. It took an ordinance in 1958 to validate it. Only in 1971 did the reform of the law give it a solid juridical base. Moreover, the central management organization, the Council of French Employers (CNPF), did not approve of this type of an agreement. Faced by union demands for these agreements, it contended that it was not qualified to negotiate them, except with the express mandate of all management federations. It is only with the internal reform of 1969 that the CNPF explicitly acquired the right to do so, and even then its range of authority omitted the field of wage determination.

But, in spite of these obstacles, this type of negotiation corresponds to deep characteristics of the French system of industrial relations. The propensity for centralization, which is so marked in French society, could not be excluded for long from this sytem. Moreover, the collective agreement has always been considered more of a regulation jointly adopted by the parties in the industry than a contract. It was therefore natural to undertake to regulate in like manner more general issues and to adopt programs complementing, or substituting for, social security, or even elaborating general pieces of social policy.

The goal may appear unduly ambitious or, in any case, singular in this context. Does not such an accord presuppose a consensus between the partners, at least on some general principles? Is it not evident, on the contrary, that such a consensus can scarcely be said

## TABLE 4

### Annual Distribution of Collective Agreements and Amendments in Nonagricultural Industries, France

Category of Agreement

| | National Collective | | Amendments for the National Collective Agreement on Retirement and Welfare of Executives (period from 12 Feb. 1950 to 7 Feb. 1959) | Regional Collective | | Local Collective | | Establishment Collective | | Total |
|---|---|---|---|---|---|---|---|---|---|---|
| | Agreements | Amendments | | Agreements | Amendments | Agreements | Amendments | Agreements | Amendments | |
| 1950 | 14 | 6 | 10 | 11 | 2 | 7 | 7 | 9 | 8 | 64 |
| 1951 | 17 | 44 | 14 | 10 | 24 | 11 | 36 | 11 | 14 | 181 |
| 1952 | 12 | 19 | 22 | 7 | 11 | 12 | 21 | 18 | 26 | 148 |
| 1953 | 6 | 34 | 8 | 4 | 14 | 14 | 24 | 12 | 19 | 135 |
| 1954 | 12 | 44 | 7 | 8 | 21 | 36 | 56 | 11 | 29 | 224 |
| 1955 | 30 | 95 | 4 | 31 | 59 | 76 | 283 | 73 | 135 | 786 |
| 1956 | 23 | 113 | 1 | 27 | 80 | 43 | 251 | 89 | 169 | 796 |
| 1957 | 24 | 201 | 11 | 17 | 123 | 46 | 413 | 45 | 212 | 1,092 |
| 1958 | 28 | 218 | 9 | 15 | 180 | 44 | 538 | 32 | 249 | 1,313 |
| 1959 | 11 | 167 | 1 | 8 | 109 | 27 | 301 | 42 | 222 | 888 |
| 1960 | 8 | 200 | -- | 6 | 171 | 18 | 426 | 50 | 228 | 1,107 |
| 1961 | 8 | 209 | -- | 5 | 180 | 28 | 510 | 51 | 261 | 1,252 |
| 1962 | 9 | 284 | -- | 8 | 198 | 14 | 507 | 52 | 378 | 1,450 |
| 1963 | 4 | 307 | -- | 10 | 248 | 23 | 605 | 47 | 336 | 1,580 |
| 1964 | 12 | 200 | -- | 9 | 197 | 30 | 363 | 55 | 235 | 1,101 |
| 1965 | 12 | 232 | -- | 5 | 209 | 18 | 423 | 48 | 347 | 1,297 |
| 1966 | 12 | 248 | -- | 6 | 275 | 20 | 493 | 44 | 309 | 1,406 |
| 1967 | 9 | 255 | -- | 14 | 315 | 36 | 538 | 56 | 352 | 1,567 |
| 1968 | 25 | 454 | -- | 15 | 332 | 39 | 760 | 52 | 529 | 2,205 |
| 1969-70 | 23 | 478 | -- | 10 | 315 | 31 | 553 | 91 | 493 | 1,999 |
| 1970-71 | 14 | 421 | -- | -- | 289 | 30 | 496 | 84 | 574 | 1,918 |
| Total (1950-71) | 313 | 4,237 | 87 | 224 | 3,352 | 604 | 7,604 | 972 | 5,125 | 22,510 |

Note: The figures report total number of agreements and amendments concluded in the course of each year; no allowance made for terminations of these documents.

Source: Ministry of Labor.

to exist between workers' unions that declare that they want to see
management disappear and a federation of employers that affirms the
virtues of economic liberalism? Isn't it also clear that the reasons
for supporting interindustry negotiations are radically different for
the respective parties? For employers recognize in this instrument
a way to escape from the constraints imposed by public authorities,
to get out of the strait-jacket of social security and its principles, to
introduce elements of the liberal society they wish to establish. The
unions, on the other hand, see in these agreements an opportunity to
obtain supplements or new advantages, to improve employee security
and guarantees, to participate in the administration of these programs,
and even to overcome individual industry resistance or even "global-
ize" the problems. One of the lessons to be drawn from the French
experience of the last 15 years is that it is possible, without complete
consensus, to reach a high degree of agreement on specific subjects.
After 1947, additional supplementary retirement systems were created for various intermediary categories and industrial branches
(textiles, for example), and finally, in 1957, an interindustry accord
was signed imposing uniform basic standards. The development of
these accords and the institutions that administer these funds resulted
in a jointly administered quasiuniversal system of complementary
retirements funds for workers.

A further step was taken in 1958 with the accord on complementary unemployment benefits covering a greater number of workers
than the public system. The parties asked for and obtained reforms
in the latter. The joint system, gradually increased its responsibilities, for example, by extending it to those who are starting to work
and to migrants from agricultural occupations.

A new group of accords was signed about 1968. At the very
outset there was the agreement, modest in itself, on benefits to be
paid by the enterprises for partial unemployment (January 1968), and
then after the "events," an accord on employment security (February
1969), the declaration in principle favoring mensualisation (April
1970), the accord on vocational training (July 1970), and its subsequent clauses concerning higher white-collar employees (April 1971).
Finally, negotiations are now taking place on working conditions.

Without describing the details of these accords, three principal
characteristics may be noted:

1. First, in all cases they are based on a close collaboration
between the "private" partners and the public authorities. This fact
in itself is not really new in France, where it is traditional for the
state to intervene in the handling of social problems. But the manner
in which it intervenes is new. It is close to the established pattern
when it proposes objectives to the negotiators, as in the case of the

accords on employment and on <u>mensualisation</u>, both of which originated with the government. But the government limited itself to indicating the direction for discussions. It was not to legislate, even when it would have been possible for it to do so. The procedure departs most strikingly from the traditional one when it accepts proposals from the parties for the reform of the system of vocational training and lets them develop the detailed regulations for the application of a law; in fact, it seems to turn over to the parties part of the public responsibility, by asking them to negotiate a mutually acceptable set of rules. Even when it appears to be returning to its habitual role, it offers the parties wide areas of self-government. When the law of July 1971 generalized and codified a system of continued training defined by the accord of July 1970, the government allowed the law to be framed in general terms, to permit the parties considerable initiative and leeway to develop jointly agreed upon rules.

2. These accords not only provide common rules but also stimulate branch negotiation by providing it with a framework. It is evidenced in the case of <u>mensualisation</u>, in which the national confederations limited themselves to adopting a declaration of principle and referred the task of applying them to the industries, which were expected to develop their specific agreements. In the case of the agreement on employment security, the industry agreements did not limit themselves to adapting the general text to the particularities of the industry but made it more precise and elaborated the provisions.

The CNPF therefore very consciously played the role of orchestra conductor for the world of management. The interindustry accords had already in the first period served as a stimulant for industry bargaining (except for the accord on unemployment benefits), as in the case for complementary retirement benefits. But it was expanded in the second period. The CNPF has assumed the responsibility for defining a broad range of social policies.

3. What is really involved is the development of broad economic and social policy. The 1958 accord on unemployment benefits signed in a period of economic uncertainty (inflation ultimately led to the devaluation of the franc and a policy of economic retrenchment) also sought to facilitate structural changes in industry. The social agreement for the Lorraine Iron and Steel Industry, at the industrial level, organized a program for meeting the problems resulting from the anticipated reduction in the number of workers caused by the modernization of the steel industry. The accord on employment should also be viewed in the light of the concurrent concerted drive at the reequipment and the further rationalization of industry. The accord on vocational training sought to answer the sharply felt need for qualified manpower and open up the possibilities for internal advancement.

The "social security" accords progressively organized a coherent system of coverage of personal risks, which in management's views did not suffer from the same defects as traditional social security. The 1967 reform of this system paid close heed to the criticism voiced by the employers. It did so all the more easily because complementary institutions already existed.

Finally, the great accords strongly favored the development of joint union and management long-term policies because they prepared the way for frequent discussions between the parties. The accord on employment not only set up a system of severance benefits but also, and more importantly, created joint committees responsible for the continued study of the problems of employment by branch and region. The accord on training is important notably because it granted workers rights to training, but perhaps even more so because it inaugurated the system of joint continuing study in this domain. Although, in both cases, the committee meets for the purposes of discussion only and has no decision-making powers, this limitation may in fact only be a precaution to prevent formal rules from interfering with the possibilities of reaching an understanding in an environment and on subjects in which cooperation is not yet firmly established. It also means that the accords are programs; their effectiveness will be ultimately gauged by their actual application.

Industry Agreements: Advances,
Limitations, and Weaknesses

The novelty of the procedure and the provisions of the inter-industry accords should not obscure the importance of the industry accords, which remain the backbone of the French system. Their development has been important and productive. But their course has not been without difficulties and failures. Two illustrations will suffice to indicate them. The negotiations in the chemical industry stopped for more than one year (until October 1973) because the minister of Labor had invited to the joint committee the French Confederation of Labor (CFT), a union with which the other unions refused to be seated. They considered it to be a "yellow" union. In the metal industry the discussions on job classifications have been going on for several years without the parties' reaching an agreement.

But the successes of the system are more numerous. Although the work week had remained practically unchanged for 20 years in France, aside from a few fluctations due to economic conditions, it has regularly been reduced since 1968, though the economic situation indicated a different direction. The effectiveness of the negotiations is here indisputable. Similarly, in a society characterized by the presence of many social distinctions, which cultivates differences in status and privileges, mensualisation has since 1970 progressed rapidly. Thereby, the differences in the status of the worker and the white-collar employees (lower white-collar employees, technicians, foremen) were substantially narrowed through collective agreements. Even if the equalization is not complete, the changes instituted were important because they went beyond current practices and in fact introduced new ones.

To increase the effectiveness of the system they introduced changes in the structure of negotiations. In the metals industry, where negotiations had hitherto been limited to regional units to avoid confrontations that would have been too vast and too global, they agreed to national negotiations on the length of the week of work, mensualisation, and employment security. In this very large industrial group, including all metal work, a close articulation was established among national and regional agreements, and this process is continuing to expand.

But the regional negotiations retained complete responsibility for wage negotiations. The least change occurred at the last item. As a result of the inflationary pressures, it had become the practice periodically to revise wages even before the 1971 law required it. Since 1968 both nominal wages and real wages have risen rapidly. But the negotiation on wages was restricted and confined in the principal branches (metals, construction) to the review of minimums. Actually, employers and unions in France do not negotiate on wages. They negotiate only minimums, which protect the workers in marginal enterprises but which have only a minimal effect on most employees. It is even doubtful that this indirect effect is very significant. The minimums record and ratify past wage movements much more than they determine future movements.

The determination of actual wages, both in principle and in fact, remains within the jurisdiction of the enterprise. In a certain number of cases, genuine wage agreements are negotiated in the enterprise, but they rarely, so far as we know, fix wages in francs. Generally, they limit themselves to guaranteeing percentage increases in wages. But even this practice is not general. For most wage-earners the actual wage is not a subject of negotiations.

This gap in the negotiations system is serious. It weakens the unions' standing with their following. It explains the omission of discussions on economic issues in French contract negotiations. This absence of bilateral negotiations impedes the development of a full incomes policy. The pressure of the public authorities on employers to limit wage concessions as occurred in 1963 when the stabilization plan was being applied in effect eliminated the last vestige of relevance from the minimums but did not reach actual wage developments, which proceeded quite independently of the discussions of the minimums.

Finally, there are the broadening differences between the privileged branches, the ones in which negotiations are organized, frequent, effective, and the underprivileged branches, in which negotiations are purely formal, if they even take place. In the former, the importance and the number of matters dealt with during recent years in fact created a condition of continuous bargaining during which one can scarcely escape discussions, and differences of interpretation are resolved through negotiations. In fact, without saying so, reasonable commitments are made because they can be kept, and, in case of difficulties, they can be adjusted. In the second group, on the contrary, meetings are rare, and the results are meager. The passivity of the workers is great, with resulting recurrent explosions of anger. It is among these industries (clothing, commerce) that one can find leftist federations of the CFDT. The contrasts in views are considerable. These differences are, moreover, reflected in the union organizations themselves.

Bargaining in the Public Sector:
"The Progress Agreement"

Certain enterprises belong wholly or substantially to the state but are characterized by no distinctive procedure for negotiations (for example, the Regie Renault, Air France, the national aerospace industry, and the national petroleum companies). They are covered by the same collective agreements as similar enterprises in the private sector. Some have played a pioneering role in their industry, as is certainly true of Renault. But neither by reason of legal regulations nor by practice is this role different from that of a private enterprise.

On the other hand, other sections of the public sector merit special attention. They are not subject to the law of February 1950, governing the general system of collective agreements. The personnel of these companies are covered by a specific statute. The principal ones are the French (national) Electricity and Gas (EGF), the French National Railway Society (SNCF), the French coal industry, and the Paris subways and buses (Regie autonome des transports parisiens, RATP). The existence of a statute makes them similar to civil servants, who since 1948 are covered by a law for the civil service.

Workers and trade unions viewed the enactment of the statute immediately after the Liberation as a significant achievement in that it fixed the principal conditions of employment. The guarantees granted in the law acquired the permanence and the stability of a legislative or regulatory act. The advantages were considerable.

They provided total security of employment, regular progression in seniority, objective rules for promotion, genuine protection against arbitrary acts thanks to an extensive system of joint committees, advantageous retirement plans, and numerous social advantages. Finally, depending on the various procedures in each case, workers' representatives gained the right to intervene effectively in the determination of wages.

The disadvantages of the arrangements developed progressively. The representatives of employees in management councils rapidly lost their effectiveness, both for circumstantial reasons (the violent conflicts at the end of the 1940s, at times involving the exclusion of the CGT and reinforcement of state control) and for basic reasons (the conversion of national into state enterprises). The statute appeared to become a rigid rule, and it was difficult to adapt to the needs of new situations. The relative advantage of public over private employment crumbled away. In the new situation where there was a shortage of manpower, job guarantees became less meaningful. The improvements of social benefits in the private sector and the complementary systems of retirement benefits reduced the differences in benefits. Finally, under the pressure of economic difficulties and especially of inflation, government control of wages in the public sector increased. A decree of 1953 confirmed an existing practice, requiring all increases in wages in the public sector to receive prior approval of the minister of Finances. Negotiations on this point became difficult and indirect. Unions complained that the management had no power and that they had no access to the people who really made the decisions.

Frequent short work stoppages, generally limited to one or two days, expressed this growing discontent. The great strike of the coal-miners in 1963 forced the problem into the open. With the settlement of the strike, thanks to the intervention of three "wise men" named by the government, in a manner essentially satisfactory to the strikers, a study of the arrangements was entrusted to a councilor of state. The Toutee report (1964) recommended a new procedure for the determination of wages. Its principle was simple: In each enterprise, a joint committee presided over by a high civil servant was to ascertain most wage developments; the government, after consultation with the unions, was to decide the total percentage wage bill increase, and management and unions were then to negotiate the distribution of the increases.

On the whole, the unions were unhappy with the result. They felt locked in by a constraining and authoritarian procedure (especially in the second phase), but they realized that the Toutee procedure at least required the parties to define the principal wage problems and take an overall view of same. When it was abandoned after

1968, it opened the way for more direct negotiations between the parties.

Developments in this new direction occurred under the supervision of the Chaban-Delmas government (1969-72) and the counselor for Social Affairs of the prime minister, Jacques Delors. Desirous of giving greater autonomy to the managements of the national enterprises, it was possible to give the managements more responsibility over wages and to relax the degree of government control.

The "contracts of progress" were not achieved without conflicts. The conclusion of the first contract, that of Electricite de France, was aided by the failure of a strike. It was ambitious, since it was valid for two years; it partially linked wage increases to the progress of productivity in the enterprise; it limited the possibilities of recourse to a strike and led to a veritable wage policy, granting a larger increase to the lowest-paid employees. The CGT refused to sign and organized a referendum in which 53 percent of the voters turned it down, but the other unions signed the contract and it remained valid.

It had been preceded in October 1969 by an accord in the civil service, improving especially the wages of the two lowest categories of employees. And it was followed by a series of other accords (SNCF, Coal, Alsatian potassium, and so on). But these extensions contained important modifications. The clause that restricted recourse to a strike disappeared; the linkage of wages to productivity is absent from most contracts; the clauses permitting or requiring the revision of wages during the term of a contract in a case of rapid rise in the cost of living was made more precise and was elaborated. Largely satisfied with the basic provisions, the CGT signed most of the new agreements.

The progressive changes in the "contracts of progress" certainly diminished their effect. But the essential elements remain: The public sector discovered the advantages and constraints imposed by real negotiation of wages. The CGT could even feel that it succeeded, by its obstinacy, in canceling any political advantages the government could have hoped to have derived from the action. It willingly entered into the negotiations.

Direct negotiation between management and unions was not limited to wages. The best example is the modernization agreement signed at the SNCF, which facilitates the transformation of management and the equipment of the railways by giving guarantees to the workers. The success of these accords is notable, especially in an enterprise that is in the process of reorganization but, even more significant, is experiencing a large reduction in the work force.

This profound transformation of practices took place with no reference to the legal foundations for the procedure. Since they are neither collective agreements in the sense of the law of 1950 nor regulatory decisions, it is most difficult precisely to define their juridical status. Actually, nobody bothers to ask the question. Pragmatism is not a traditional virtue in French negotiation. Yet this approach is striking in this case. Need it be recalled that the clauses that raise wages in the event of an increase in the cost of living almost peg wages to changes in the cost of living and that this provision is forbidden by law?

The pragmatic approach resulted in bringing closer the situation in the nationalized industries to that prevailing in the private sector. Without removing the guarantee of statute, the unions are now negotiating with the managements by following practically the same procedures as in the chemical and metal industries.

How durable is this achievement? It is impossible, after five years of experience, to provide a firm answer. Does the strike in the SNCF in October 1973 and the unilateral decisions on pay increases made by managements suggest the end of the contractual policy? In any case, these developments have caused a setback. But it is doubtful that an experiment of this type can be abandoned without leaving many traces. It is unlikely that, supported by a very satisfactory system for handling complaints and demands and joint examinations of disagreements on the application of the agreements, negotiations in the public sector can return to earlier practices without risking grave reactions.


The Missing Link: The Absence of Company Bargaining

The law of 1971, by granting to the enterprise accord the status of a collective agreement, indicated a desire to encourage negotiations at this level. Moreover, the discussions in the Economic Council revealed a substantial agreement on this position between the social partners. As previously indicated, progress in this direction has been modest.

The need for such enterprise agreements is, however, clear, and the strikes we described provided a few examples of the problems they would help answer. Not only do industry agreements not really regulate wages, they do not deal effectively with the problems that have acquired new significance, such as material conditions of work, pace of and interest in the work, and opportunities for promotion and training. These issues are now posed in a concrete manner in industry. These demands and the movements, in their support, like the efforts of personnel management, to deal with them create a vast range of subjects for discussion, conflicts, and agreement.

Are they not discussed? They are dealt with but in a scattered
and relatively incoherent manner. The discussions on these issues
assume neither the clear form of a confrontation nor the solidity of
a contract.

The successive waves of legislation, as well as the requirements of a multiple union structure, led to an accumulation of institutions designed to assure representation of personnel. There are
elected personnel delegates, chosen by a vote in the establishment
who present individual or collective demands (1936); elected delegates
who constitute the works council (1945), which administers social
benefits and must be informed and consulted on enterprise policies;
union delegates designed by the union (1968) who collect the dues and
represent the union in the plant; and, finally, the union, which is
authorized to negotiate agreements with management. (It is unusual
for the union section in the enterprise to perform this function.)
Workers' demands may pass through all of these channels without
necessarily observing the minute division of labor imposed on these
distinctive agencies by law. If it is a question, for example, of
working conditions, personnel delegates may make a demand on management. But the works council may also do so since it is consulted
on organizational issues and technology. The health and security
committee may also pursue the issue. The union delegate can find
it a matter for union action. Several routes are possible. None are
compulsory.

Also, the negotiations are usually informal and scattered. It
would be false to conclude, considering the documents and the additional clauses signed, that there are few negotiations at the enterprise level in France. But they rarely assume the form of a real
accord or a collective agreement.

Here again, the current solution is very pragmatic and fragile.
Recent inflation and prosperity facilitated the conclusion of arrangements between the parties. But with the deterioration of economic
conditions, these practices become less satisfactory. Their insufficiency has become more apparent. Not only does one not always
know what to expect nor what is the import of the agreements, but
their relative priority is determined rather haphazardly. Very often,
local conditions, or the employer, if he has a coherent personnel
policy, determines the choice. In both instances the unions play only
a minor role.

This weakness of the system of negotiations at the enterprise
level is perhaps one of the major deficiencies of the French collective
bargaining system. Certainly, it is a long-standing failing, but the
shortcoming is now more seriously felt. This is the significance of
the above limited development in enterprise bargaining. It still affects few workers in the work place, and it is they whose dissatisfaction has in recent years set the tone for industrial relations.

## THE UNIONS: IDEOLOGY, STRENGTHS,
## AND WEAKNESSES

Two features characterize French unionism: pluralism, ever
strong and even tending to reinforce itself, and class-oriented organizations, focusing on overall worker interests rather than the defense of their narrow economic interests, such as those concerned
with a particular craft or job.

Three large confederations represent the workers. The General Confederation of Labor (CGT), the largest, is of Marxist persuasion and has privileged links with the Communist Party. Its secretary
general is a member of the bureau of the party. The French Democratic Confederation of Labor (CFDT), the name assumed in 1964 by
the French Democratic Confederation of Christian Workers (CFTC)
is currently free of all ties with the Catholic Church and its social
doctrines. It is second in size certainly in relation to the private
sector. Its orientation has progressively moved to the left, and today
it claims a socialist point of view. The third is the General Confederation of Labor-Labor Force (CGT-Force ouvriere), which in 1947
split from the CGT and is particularly strong in the public sector.
It is considered to be a member of the socialist family of organizations but insists on its independence. There is the CFTC, which consists of persons who in 1964 separated from the CFDT and maintains
its Catholic orientation. For the management category of employees
(foremen, engineers, administration), the General Confederation in
Management Employees (Confederation generale des cadres, CGC)
is a separate organization. Unions or autonomous federations exist
in various industries. The largest is the National Federation of
Education (FEN), which unites the majority of teachers (primary,
secondary, higher). It includes people of diverse political views.
Finally, independent unions have in recent years appeared, at times
with management support. These organizations are in general rejected by the others, which refuse to sit with them in bargaining sessions. The largest is the French Confederation of Labor.

In spite of their diversity, these organizations have a common
feature: whatever importance they assign to collective negotiation,
they consider themselves to be more than the managers of the interests of their members. They lay claim to wider visions, as reflected in their statutes and the convention discussions. Their ambition is to define an ideal of society. Weak in numbers, organization,
and resources, if they are compared with German or Scandinavian
unions, they are strong in their sensitivity to worker needs and demands and have the capacity to articulate and express in concrete
form what is happening among workers at the plant level; when necessary they have the ability to mobilize their following in support of

these demands. They rely on a corps of militants rather than on an administrative apparatus, on conviction, devotion, and ideology more than on organization and discipline. In a period of great change, these characteristics appear to become assets rather than defects.

## Memberships and Influence

It is impossible to report the exact numbers of members of the principal organizations. The CGT states that it has 2.3 million members, including retired persons; the CFDT, 700,000, which is doubtless fairly exact; and the CGT-FO, 800,000. The FEN is no doubt the most important federation in France, with perhaps 450,000 members. It would be useless to challenge these claims by offering estimates offered by other groups, which are usually considerably lower. The rate of unionization among employees as a whole ranges probably between 20 and 25 percent.

Not only are these figures not very exact, their significance is uncertain. The average union member of the CGT makes somewhat less than eight monthly dues payments per year, explained by withdrawals, new additions, and omissions in payments. It is probably not different among the other unions. The line of demarcation between the member, the sympathizer, and the apathetic is quite vague. In many cases, the strength of a union is commonly judged less by the number of its members than on the number of those that it can mobilize for an activity.

Of course, there are many exceptions to this general picture. The percentage of membership is very high in certain categories (teachers, dock workers), in certain branches (merchant marine), and in certain enterprises (EDF, SNCF). Dues are paid very regularly, it appears, by civil servants. Considerable effort has been made in the last four years by the larger organizations to raise the amount of dues and to improve the regularity of payment. It is probable, although it is difficult to verify, that the numbers of members have increased since 1968, but this increase in any case is not impressive.

At least as important as membership is the union's influence. It can be measured in the private sector by the number of votes cast in the elections for members of the works councils, but only if we recall that this statistic relates only to enterprises that have more than 50 workers and elected a council. Besides, the exclusion of the public sector tends to understate the CGT-FO's position.

These figures show that in 1970 and 1971, the CGT candidates received 52 percent of the votes for wage-earner and employee committeemen; the CFDT, 20 percent; the CGT-FO, 7.8 percent; the

CFTC, 2.3 percent; and the other unions, 7.1 percent. The vote for candidates unaffiliated with unions was 12.5 percent. As for foremen, technicians, and lower levels of management committeemen, the CGC received 24.6 percent; the CGT, 16.4 percent; CFDT, 16.7 percent; CGT-FO, 6.8 percent; CFTC, 3.2 percent; and other unions, 12.3 percent. Twenty-two percent of the vote was for committeemen not affiliated with any union.[3]

Another measure of union influence is the number of union sections in enterprises, created since the 1968 law. Forty percent of the covered enterprises in 1973 had at least one union section. In all there were 20,700 sections and 23,800 union delegates. The CGT had 42.7 percent of the union sections, and the percentages for the other unions in descending order were CFDT, 25.3; CGT-FO, 10.8; CGC, 10.2; CFTC, 4.5; CFT, 1.9; and other unions 4.5.

Although we have no precise data on the distribution of the memberships by status, we may note that the workers' confederations seek to enroll technicians and the lower level of management by creating special unions for them as well as the importance of the CGC. The figures for unionization among the civil servants is relatively high, as illustrated by the case of national education. In brief, white-collar unionism has existed for a long time. Some growth has no doubt taken place, but such organization is scarcely a novelty and presents no new frontier to conquer.

The statistics on the elections for the works councils confirm the spread of union support in the various industrial categories. Although nonunion candidates get more votes in the elections for the technicians and lower-management employees, they tend to receive one-fifth of this total vote, and support for them among the wage-earners is about one-eighth of the total vote.

Organization: Role of Confederation and Federations;
Weaknesses of Plant Union Sections

The basic union unit is the local union, which usually represents one industry in one city. It belongs to a national industrial federation and an interindustry union for the Departement. Federations and the latter constitute the confederation.

The confederation retains its paramount role within the organization. Although the responsibility for collective bargaining belongs to the federation and the unions, it is in the confederation that information is concentrated and from which it is distributed, that strategies are elaborated, and that the most important public positions are taken. The central group is strong, although it is not authoritarian. The CGT-FO grants the greatest degree of autonomy to the federations.

The CFDT seeks to gain conformance and observance with its views
and programs by promoting intense internal discussion. The CGT
reinforces its own effectiveness by using the parallel apparatus of
the Communist Party (PCF). But, more generally, in a union movement in which doctrine, ideology, and overall strategy direct daily
action, it is natural that the strategy should be elaborated at the summit and that, at least, the unity of the movement should prevail over
the divergent tendencies in the individual industries and categories of
employees.

For all that, the confederations do not maintain a powerful administrative apparatus. Their resources are modest. On the average, dues correspond to one hour of work per month, though the
CFDT decided to raise them up gradually to 1 percent of the wages.
The portion of the income paid to the confederation varies from 4 or
5 percent in the CGT to more than 15 percent in the CFDT. The latter is the only one with a confederal fund, which serves both as a
strike fund and a fund for the organization of new sectors. There
are few permanent positions, though the number is larger in the civil
service and nationalized industries, in which a number of employees
are regularly engaged in union activities and retain their regular
salaries. Their wages are modest, generally equal to that of a
skilled worker. Militants at the base are generally volunteers. Some
who have elective plant positions are enabled to spend a few hours a
week from their work on these duties. They are spurred on by their
dedication and convictions and a sense of responsibility rather than
by a personal ambition to rise in the organization. The strong moral
authority of the confederation is more generally concentrated with
the person holding the principal permanent positions and not the bureaucracy.

The regional organization (interindustry) of the unions at city,
Departement, or regional levels plays an important role, particularly
at times of bargaining. It is called upon to support the weakest organizations, in conjunction with other local groups. This role however declined in the 1960s, to the advantage of the federations, particularly in the CFDT. It is nevertheless possible that this trend
was recently reversed, as the strong local militant activities became
more significant.

Another force strengthening the role of these local organizations is the emphasis on paraindustrial demands such as transportation, housing, and quality-of-life items, which must be translated
into improvements at the local level. It is for this reason that the
CFDT endeavors, in this sense, to create basic interprofessional
unions for the localities that are more decentralized than the UD's
(Departmente interindustry labor unions) and would take over the responsibility for greater coordination of union activities in a section
of a city or small city.

The training programs for the militants seek to furnish them with tools for action. But it is also one of the elements that holds the organization together. In these training sessions, they acquire some knowledge of law, economics, and the responsibilities and skills of the personnel delegate. But they are also involved in the elaboration of ideas and major orientations, which assure the unified set of views within the organization. The unions spend a considerable sum of money on this activity. The overall responsibility for the program and the actual training is entrusted to the confederations, but the local centers and national federations share in these responsibilities and activities. The unions receive some assistance from the public authorities. The training serves not only to equip the staffs to deal with the outside and employers but also helps to build a greater cohesion within the organization.

### Strategies and Principles: Socialist Orientations and Response to Rank and File

The CFDT, originally a union of Catholic orientation with a moderate social philosophy, with its strength largely concentrated among the white-collar employees during the last 25 years experienced profound changes. Its center of gravity moved toward industrial and blue-collar categories; its positions have stiffened. During 1964, it rejected all confessional references. The events of 1968 accelerated the evolution and its further radicalization. The convention of 1970 affirmed its socialist objectives, social ownership of the means of production, democratic planning, and self-management.

Because of these changes, it may be said that all three principal federations claim to be socialistic. Anticapitalism is a long-standing point of agreement among the unions. The great social commotion of recent years sharpened and reinforced this attitude. Certainly, profound differences remain among the organizations. The democratic socialism of CGT-FO is very different from that of the CGT, which is close to the Communist Party (PCF), while the CFDT, in adopting the principle of self-management, coopted and modernized earlier anarchistic views.

These approaches had one common result. All rejected the vague proposal proffered since 1958 by the governmental majority for "participation." Each had its own rationale for this opposition. The CGT-FO rejected it in the name of contractual freedom; the CGT, of the class struggle; and the CFDT, of self-government. They regarded the offer with mistrust. They were not particularly attracted to other suggestions, including profit-sharing, established by the ordinance of 1967, and worker stock-sharing plan, or even the designation of

workers' representatives to the management boards of directors of
large companies.

But there were wide disagreements among them. They are
revealed in the position on negotiations. The CGT-FO was on the
whole the best supporter of the government's contractual policy and
management's agreements policy. The four main accords covered
domains in which the CGT-FO had long demanded joint discussions,
as was true for employment security and vocational training. In
their negotiations, it has played a prominent role. It placed great
stock on honoring agreements. It rejected the offer of participation
because it viewed industrial relations largely to be a system of contractual relations between management and trade unions.

The CGT and the CFDT currently share the common view that
an agreement is a state of truce, stressing its character in the continuing struggle between labor and capital. They do not refuse to
negotiate. But their emphasis is upon demands to present and claims
to press. The trade union should not be converted into a guardian of
the agreement and the agent for worker discipline. Moreover, their
own weak position and tenuous hold on their membership makes it
impossible for them to discipline their members or other employees.
The constant need to press new demands would in any case make it
quite impractical for them to make any serious "peace pledge."

The principle of self-management serves to protect the CFDT
from seriously considering the suggestions for "participation" and
of co-determination and inspires a continuing effort to inculcate militant attitudes among its following. It reflects the deeply felt need
for a change in the power relationships within the enterprise organization. This goal is widely shared in Europe but expresses a more
deeply felt need and is conducive to more explosive reactions in a
stratified, hierarchical, and authoritarian society, such as is found
in France. On the other hand, the CGT regarded this entire proposal
with distrust and even repugnance.

It would not be sufficient for the proper understanding of French
unions to evaluate them solely in terms of doctrines. Traditions
have a great influence as organizations feed and absorb them. But,
to understand them fully, one must see how the doctrines are actually
applied. The distinctive characteristic of the present situation is not
only the emergence of new demands, the intermittent spontaneous
strikes, and the militancy of the workers but also the change in the
locus of the initiative and the power in organizations, particularly in
the unions. At the CGT, the watchword is "democratization"--that
is, "Let us increase consultation, encourage discussion in the union
sections, pay greater attention to what is happening at the base, and
require the permanent leaders to exhibit more flexibility and open-
mindedness." In like manner, the CFDT is seeking to apply ideas on

self-management to its own administration. Although the conventions of 1973 strongly reaffirmed the necessity of union organization, condemned too "spontaneous" formulas for the self-government of strikes, it called for all to respect local initiative and responsibilities, and the elimination of authoritarian decisions. Its behavior in the strikes that have been described illustrate this view.

Unions and Political Parties:<br>Political Union of Left

The social situation we just described affects in two ways the relations between unions and political parties. First, they reinforce the total labor movement--that is, the awareness of a common social basis for both political and union activities and an agreement on their ultimate objectives. Second, they foster greater differentiation in their respective roles.

The first trend is admittedly not new in the CGT. But it allowed the confederation to emphasize more openly, as it did in the convention of 1971, the common set of ideas that links it to the Communist Party. The second is more important. The CGT in the late 1940s and early 1950s stressed the problems of international politics in its slogans for activities and mass demonstrations. In the 1970s, the CGT wants to become a mass organization, concerned with following very closely and flexibly developments in the nature of the new needs and demands, stressing its distinctiveness from the party. The latter is oriented to eventual governmental responsibilities, electoral strategy, major decisions on orientation. The union, in line with Lenin's concepts, is not to be the vanguard of the working class. It is to include all who are employed. The objective is to organize and achieve their unification, stressing at the beginning their immediate needs.

Actually, the CGT probably persuaded the Communist Party to adopt a freer position as regards the lower levels of management. It inspired other changes in its programs and stoutly maintained a coherent policy of collective bargaining.

The problem for the CFDT is different. Formerly linked with the Christian Democratic Party (MRP), it always maintained an independent position even before the MRP disappeared under the shock of Gaullism. Currently, it is seeking a partner within the small Unified Socialist Party (PSU) and even more recently, in the Socialist Party (PS), which has become stronger since 1970. The PSU adopted the idea of self-management, and the PS is favorable toward it.

The election of 1973 confirmed this interpretation. The Socialist and Communist parties agreed on a common program that provided the substantive basis for the electoral alliance. The CGT supported the common program without hesitation or reservations. The CFDT, while urging its members to vote for the union of the left (and more and more firmly as the date approached) nevertheless kept its distance regarding the program. It took this position first because the program assigned little place to its views, but also, and it is probably more important, because it believed that to pledge support for a five-year program was contrary to the very spirit of unionism. Its highest priority was to express workers' needs, and it should not compromise its position in a manner that would limit this responsibility.

The other organizations observed a strict neutrality in elections. The CGT-FO emphasized its traditional refusal to take sides, the more strongly in this case because it was quite hostile to the rapprochement between the Socialists and the Communists.

These confederal positions do not enable us to predict how their members will vote. If a survey in March 1973 is correct, 87 percent of the members of the CGT voted for the parties of the common program, 63 percent of FO, and 51 percent of CFDT. The vote among the latter's members is particularly distinctive for the high proportion who voted for the PSU (11 percent, the national average being less than 3 percent) and for the majority or the center (38 percent in total).[4] This dispersion of the votes may in part explain why the CFDT was hesitant about supporting the common program.

International Attachments

As is logical, the CGT belongs to the World Union Federation (WFTU), the CFDT to the World Labor Confederation (WCL), and CGT-FO to the International Confederation of Free Trade Unions (ICFTU). But the new developments must be sought below this distinction.

First, the CGT and the Italian CGIL made an effort to get and secure recognition by the EEC. Without giving up its opposition to the EEC, the CGT now accepts its existence and participates as an official internal opposition group within the organization. It is further evidence that these European institutions have significance for the people of the Continent.

In the second place, the CFDT has been moving to broaden its international affiliations beyond the WCL. Its Federation of Metallurgy is now a member of the International Federation of Metallurgical Workers. The Federation of Chemical Workers and the Federation of Food Product Workers did likewise. The recent creation of the European Trade Union Federation by the ICFTU national centers and its acceptance of members of the WCL, including the CFDT, is another case in point.

## EMPLOYERS AND THEIR ORGANIZATIONS

Employers and their organizations are also being transformed under pressure of many new forces. France yielded its system of protection, especially due to its membership in the EEC, and moved to a more open economy. Particularly important to this change have been the growth of international trade, the large number of mergers that produced a group of larger corporations, and the appearance of a new generation of management, trained in economics and the discipline of modern management, who are steadily taking over the direction of enterprises. The effects were felt in the 1960s in the organizations of employers and their social policy. Stimulated by enterprise initiatives and study groups, the trade industry associations showed a greater capacity for initiative and long-term thinking.

The events of 1968 contributed substantially to this change. The fear that they inspired brought about more advances than regressions, toward the protection of the enterprise spirit and the affirmation of collective bargaining rather than to a defensive and conservative attitude. The divisions became stronger between traditional small management and the self-employed, on the one hand, and the companies, particularly the large companies, which supported expansion, on the other. And it is the latter that took over the leadership of the movement.

### Employers' Organizations

The industry organizations have roughly the same structure as those of the workers. There are local branch associations connected with industry federations or national associations, on one hand, with local interassociations, on the other. At the top, a confederation, the National Council of French Management (CNPF), combines both types of organizations. The CNPF provides both economic and social representation for employers.

But, internally, the associations deal primarily with economic matters while the larger industrial federations (the Union of Metallurgical and Mining Industries, Union of Chemical Industries, and Union of Textile Industries, for example) handle the social issues.

The powers of the CNPF were originally highly restricted. The reform of 1969 extended them. They increased the president's authority and provided for his election by a general assembly. The statutes now give him the right to define a social policy after the appropriate internal discussions and agreements. His contacts with his adherents are more direct. Current subjects including issues such as vocational training are discussed in sessions arranged for

general debate. The stress has shifted from a defense of management
interests to the development of the enterprise.

A flexible apparatus of committees supported by well-staffed
services gives the CNPF and the main associations a means for
making well-researched studies and for publicizing well-prepared
statements on positions and policies. Internal consultation is extensive and continuous. It is now generally agreed that the president
and the executives of the association have the effective ability of leading the organization.

Despite the increased authority of the CNPF, its competence in
certain matters is circumscribed. In the matter of wages the constituent industry federations are completely independent. They remain responsible for the widest range of issues in social policy.

Enterprises retain a considerable autonomy from the association and even total independence in the matter of pay. The tendency
is probably toward increasing this autonomy. The great industrial
corporations extending over several industries and regions retain even
greater freedom to act, particularly on wage and social matters.

A confederation combines small and medium-sized owner-
operated enterprises (CGPME). Formerly it belonged to the CNPF
but kept its distance. A huge loose rather than a disciplined organization, it represents the traditional little manager and expresses
vigorously his worries and his wrath against the state, the "big ones,"
the unions, rampant socialism. In competition with it, other associations appear from time to time among artisans and shopkeepers,
which express, at times violently, the revolt of the shrinking categories of businesses, affected by recent economic developments.


Philosophy and Orientation


Though united in trade associations, with some well-known exceptions, management is composed of groups with diverse views and
different interests. In the association, one may find both old aristo-
cratic companies and the young construction entrepreneurs, steel
and clothing companies, banking and electric industries. Their social
origins, outlooks, and beliefs vary greatly. In face of this diversity
it is difficult to formulate a single French management philosophy.
The CNPF usually takes the cautious middle road. In the last five
years, however, it sought to improve the employers' public image.

In the first place, liberalism is no longer a discreet or slightly
shameful conviction. It has been accepted and publicly vindicated
against the traditions of corporatism, deeply rooted in the Catholic
faith. In its new active role the CNPF pronounced its view before the
1973 elections and criticized (a departure from past practices) the

program of the left, without, however, implicating itself directly in the electoral campaign. In 1973, the president of the CNPF took the opportunity of some large and serious strikes to clarify management's position respecting them.

In the preparation of the Sixth Plan, management, collectively and in specialized committees, championed economic growth and industrialization. It publicly took exception to the advocates of the zero growth rate. It concurrently joined the fight against pollution and the destruction of the environment. It endeavors to incarnate not only economic rationality but also the general benefits to be expected from expansion.

### Social Policy: Union Sections Bypassed for Works Councils

The principal results of the social policy of management have already been reviewed in the paragraphs on collective bargaining. The CNPF participated directly in the interindustry agreements and indirectly in the industry agreements that resulted from the former. These agreements developed and enlarged upon the 1968 Grenelle proposals, drafted in the hope of putting an end to strikes.

But, as has been pointed out, similar developments have not occurred at the plant level. The president of the CNPF had, however, publicly declared that negotiations take place at three levels: interindustry, industry, and enterprise. It is perhaps useful to take a closer look at the policy followed at the latter level.

Two major accords, employment security and vocational training, contemplated their further implementation at the enterprise and plant level. In both instances, the works council and not the union section was chosen as the relevant institution. This was a crucial decision, since it gave preference to the consultative organism legally incapable of negotiating, to the detriment of the union and, of course, the formal agreement.

The de facto situation certainly favors this solution. The works council includes among its responsibilities a concern for employment and training problems. It must be warned of a reduction in the number of employees and, more generally, of employment situations. Therefore, it was natural to strengthen its present role. Moreover, employers see in the works council an elected body, closing out the debate on the importance of the individual unions. Management could thereby meet with a single representative, whereas there were always a variety of unions.

There are perhaps other reasons for this position. Some are circumstantial. Employers had long resisted granting official recognition to the union in the enterprise. They had accepted it in the discussions that led to the law of December 1968 only in order to keep the promises made in the heat of the great May strikes. Thus, the employers gave preference to the works councils, which they had regarded with mistrust for a long time, to avoid assigning too much importance to the new institution, the union section.

There were also deeper reasons. The employers were not ready to construct an integrated complete system of bargaining with the possibility of an appeal being carried from one level to the next higher one. In a situation in which the contractual commitment is limited, they prefer more flexible formulas, permitting discussion (and, in fact, negotiation if need be) without having any obligation to reach a real formal agreement. The unions, on the other hand, were not anxious to negotiate agreements on reductions in the work force and were very uncertain about the responsibilities that they could effectively assume in the matter of training. This arrangement, therefore, facilitated the discussions but, on the other hand, reduced the role of bargaining.

The limited development of the plant agreement therefore reflected not an opposition to discussion in principle (though there were such cases) but a pragmatic step by the parties to serve their own ends. But it left the bargaining structure incomplete, and this gap can have serious consequences in a crisis.

### Personnel Policy Underdeveloped

Personnel policy is generally considered a management prerogative. So it is hardly thought of as a function of the industry association. But it is today sufficiently important that we must include it in our review.

It is the weakness in this area that partly explains the difficulties of enterprise bargaining. Personnel policy is still not very advanced in most French enterprises. In spite of the exceptions, the number of which is increasing, in spite of the efforts of a professional association such as the Association of Personnel Directors (ANDCP), this field neither receives the funds nor attracts the qualified personnel nor secures the necessary authority for its proper functioning. Decisions in this domain are made with little information, little study, and little consideration of long-term consequences. Intuition, common sense, knowledge of men, compensate only partially for the technical weakness. Industry negotiators rarely have access to well-informed persons with appropriate authority within the enterprise to aid them in their negotiations or to help them understand the problems likely to arise in the implementation of the agreements.

Is it necessary to underline the consequences of this weakness? For the average worker, as for the militant at the base, the elaborate policies worked out at higher levels never appear to be real, as little effort is made to apply them at the enterprise level.

## THE PUBLIC SECTOR: AREA OF INNOVATION

The changeover from the Fourth to the Fifth Republic in 1958, by changing the relationships between the executive and the legislative, also altered the ways in which unions and industry organizations could influence decisions on economic and social policy. Appeals to parliamentarians lost their effectiveness, consultations with the executive gained; support from public opinion is becoming more effective when it is more global.

The appearance since that time of a stable parliamentary majority (generally considered to be right-center) also contributed to and reinforced the power of the executive and freed the unions from the constraints previously imposed on them by the government of parties close to them. Lacking highly placed allies, they turned toward direct negotiations. Finally, the shift diminished the importance of institutions for collaboration such as the plan, developed on the margins of the political system.

### Decline of the Plan as a Means
### for Achieving Agreements

At the end of the Fourth Republic and the beginning of the Fifth, the plan played an important role in providing both management and trade unions with a meeting place for discussion of economic and social policy. In the first place, it was a way of escaping the constraints and uncertainties of a crumbling political system; in the second, it was a substitute for political debate, at a time of weakened political parties and Congress; in both, an implicit ideology of growth helped to find a consensus in spite of the ongoing conflict. The commissions on modernization (and even the Superior Council of the plan and the Social and Economic Council) became for several years the centers of political and economic innovation. Representatives to these bodies could participate as individuals without officially binding their organizations and were, therefore, able to reach semiofficial, and effective, agreements on important matters of policy to which the government paid considerable attention.

The effort in 1963 to devise an incomes policy represented the high point of this era of collaboration and heralded its decline. The study of the issues revealed quite sharply to the unions and employers the new constraints that would thereafter bind them. No matter whether it be contractual or indicative, such a policy would assume a degree of centralization of decision-making the organizations were not ready to accept. It called in periods of rapid inflation for a degree of discipline of the manpower market that the parties found unattractive and difficult to enforce. Moreover, the gap between the proposal and the means for effectuation had to be considered. At the most elementary level, it became evident that knowledge of incomes was too limited to permit one to go beyond a simple restraint to slow down the pace of increases and to contemplate even selective controls.

At the same time, perhaps because the government first reached the same conclusion, it announced at the end of 1963 without prior consultation of the parties a stabilization program based on classical conjunctural measures. To the unions, the stabilization plan appeared to shelve the collaborative procedures developed under the plan; that system was no longer operative.

All interests began to realize that the plan could no longer be considered separately from other political issues. The very importance assigned to the plan by the government and General de Gaulle and the arrangement they introduced calling for prior vote by the parliament on basic choices for levels for growth in response to the demand for more "democratic planning" made the plan part and parcel of the political system. This new procedure revealed the sovereign character of the government's decisions. Moreover, the trade unions became increasingly aware of the tenuousness of the consultation procedure, the limitations of their headquarters staff for this task, and the distance between the locus of union decision-making and the rank-and-file members and their daily concerns. Their means were insufficient for such an ambitious undertaking.

The climate in which the Sixth Plan (1970-75) was prepared was definitely different from that of the preceding ones. Committees were downgraded to consultative functions. Trade unions no longer considered them to be adequate channels for obtaining information, a position always held by the CGT. The CFDT reacted so strongly against this change that in the middle of the period of the development of the plan, it withdrew its delegates from all further association better to denote its severance from the plan.

For all that, planning is not moribund. It has even been technically improved. It now concentrates on more precise objectives and prepares more adequately documented programs with a carefully outlined calendar for its development. It has become a better instrument for analysis and projection. But it lost its political function, which had made it a meeting place for the development of new social relations and new powers for decision-making.

Not only the institutions but also the objectives were being called into question. The necessity for growth was still approved,

but there was increasing uncertainty about the benefits to be expected
from it. Modernization no longer appears as the magic key to achieve
a new society. It left untouched questions of income distribution,
stratification in society, and the traditional distribution of power. In
20 years of growth, the work week had not been reduced, but in the
three years following 1968, despite the very high level of economic
activity, collective bargaining produced a substantial reduction in
hours. Economic growth, it became clear, does not automatically
provide the basis for a consensus. In fact, it helps create new stakes
for conflict and issues for negotiations.

### Industrial Policy: Trade Unions Excluded
### from Development

A second illustration of the tendency to revert to traditional
methods of bargaining is provided in the field of industrial policy.
The government spelt out its principles of industrial policy in the
analysis of the Fifth Plan. It sought to give greater weight to manufacturing industry, encouraging enterprises to merge to create large
corporations of international stature with greater financial resources,
capable of financing their own growth. Provision was also made for
the creation of the National Foundation for Instruction in Management
Disciplines (FNEG) to promote the use of modern methods of management. But the plan committees in which the trade unions were represented lost all control of the projects. The unions had fewer and
fewer opportunities to present their views on policy and were increasingly restricted to negotiating on the personnel consequences of the
policy itself. A case in the iron and steel industry will serve as an
illustration.

The Iron and Steel Planning Commission had thoroughly analyzed the economic difficulties of the industry. It was encumbered
by excessive debt, arrears in modernization, and a scattering of
enterprises. But the solutions for these problems were negotiated
directly between the employers and the public authorities. In fact,
the iron and steel association had worked out a program for investment at the time that a plan was elaborated for the progressive concentration of the industry into two large corporations. The association negotiated in 1966 an agreement with the government on the conditions for financial aid. One condition was that the association
would reach an agreement with the trade unions on the social problems created by the reorganization and most particularly, the closing of establishments and the reduction in the size of the work force.
In conformity with these principles the parties in 1967 signed a
Social Agreement for the Lorraine Metal Group.

The negotiations were difficult, reflecting the seriousness of the issues and the care devoted by the parties to the discussions. The final agreement provided social guarantees for the workers and, what was a most important precedent, the preferential rights to transfer from one enterprise to another, with the maintenance of seniority rights as well as other accumulated rights to benefits. Provision was made for vocational retraining, with guarantees of employment and for early retirement privileges. The agreement provided for the treatment of the industry as a whole.

The trade unions were, however, displeased with the announcement of the agreement between the employers and government and the need for them to bargain on conditions prescribed by this contract. While the consummation of a social accord was a condition for the validation of the financial pact, they were not themselves involved in the financial decisions. The unions could discuss the ways in which the principles could be applied and negotiate the agreement relative to their impact on the work force, but they could not seek changes in these financial agreements themselves. In their view the discussions in the Iron and Steel Planning Commission had been stopped and thereafter pursued without them in a different forum.

They drew two lessons from this experience. First, the unions were no longer involved in the three-party discussions. The second lesson was that the traditional collective bargaining procedure despite the obvious limitations (they had to accept the number of workers to be laid off as a premise, and they could not negotiate this number) had nevertheless proven reasonably effective. Though they were not entirely satisfied, the unions were pleased with the results and the new precedents. The traditional bargaining relations, even involving, as it did in this case, a strike during the negotiations, had regained their confidence.

This change in attitude was particularly pronounced for the CFDT. It had previously carefully analyzed the procedure for collaboration and had developed great hopes for its results. Now it had to make striking changes in its attitudes. The CGT, which had been distrustful of the entire procedure, felt that it had been vindicated and reinforced its emphasis on direct industrial action. Industrial policy was now the preoccupation of employers and the government and no longer a common undertaking of all parties.

## Social and Contractual Policy

"Participation," the key word in Gaullist policy, automatically provokes support from the deputies of the majority party and opposition among the unions and perhaps also among employers. It

covers a variety of projects. The 1967 ordinance required enterprises to set aside part of their profits for workers in the form of
assets to be frozen for five years. It is an element of an incomes
policy that can only have a long-term impact. Regarding workers'
stock, the public authorities set an example by initiating in 1973 such
a program at Regie Renault and then with the banks and nationalized
insurance companies.

The policy respecting employment security and vocational training developed through the joint action of the public authorities and
both parties. Unemployment benefits are in part underwritten by
public allowances, which have been revised recurrently to extend
their coverage and complemented by a voluntary system provided in
the 1958 agreement. The same is true of partial unemployment benefits. An adult training program was established in 1946 to facilitate
changes in employment and to guide labor toward industries needing
manpower. The National Association for Adult Vocational Training
(AFPA), which administers this program, has joint advisory committees composed of industrial associations and union representatives
organized under the authority of the minister of Labor. The National
Employment Fund (FNE, 1963) pays retraining and transfer allowances to assist in the changes in occupational qualifications and transfers to new locations of employment. Both the assocations and unions
are in advisory positions. A joint commission examines the agreements signed with the individual enterprises. In 1967, the National
Employment Agency (ANPE) was organized to improve placement
facilities. The 1970 interindustry agreement and the 1971 law implemented a vast program for job and continuous training.

The division of responsibilities appears quite complex. For
one purpose, an agreement provides for a jointly administered system to complement the public one. For another purpose, the public
authorities initiate and foster negotiations, as in the case of employment security. The prime minister after the ordinance of 1967 wrote
a letter to the CNPF and the trade union confederations proposing the
subjects for voluntary negotiations and they resulted in the 1969
agreement. In another connection, two laws, those of 1966 and 1968,
preceded the national agreement of 1970 on vocational training, which
extended the program and granted workers new rights for training.
The 1971 law codified existing arrangements and introduced a special
tax to assure adequate financing for the system. The parties have
considerable leeway for initiative in the application of the law and
are encouraged to consult and negotiate further agreements concerning same.

It is too early to assess the results, but it is possible to evaluate the procedures. The public authorities followed a flexible and
pragmatic course. They assumed the responsibilities where it was

difficult or impossible to expect an agreement between the parties. Where they considered the possibilities of such agreements favorable, they delegated the responsibilities to the parties, retaining rights to intervene and advise them to help overcome difficulties in the negotiations and administration. In still other cases they entrusted the parties with the administration of the organizations. The legislation permits and sometimes favors such delegations of responsibilities.

Whereas the form of collaboration represented by the planning committees is on the decline, the new form based on negotiations and coordination of initiatives is growing.

The government appears to be trying to intervene in the same manner in the field of working conditions. It is seeking to limit the use of governmental regulation. It established a public agency (1973) charged with the responsibility for collecting information and financing studies and even experiments in the field, and, thereafter for providing reports to the interested parties. But the parties retained the responsibility for reaching an agreement.

In spite of the changes since 1968 in the political scene with turnover of ministers and programs, social policy remained quite stable. The Chaban-Delmas government developed it most extensively and called it a "contractual policy." Its principles are simple. It accepts the existence of major divisions in French society. There is not only a variety of organizations but also a diversity of ideologies and social programs. The state should therefore not impose a single pattern and regulate everything from a central headquarters. Rather, it must recognize that the industrial associations and the trade unions should be allowed to discharge their responsibilities. The state should therefore "seek a system of rules which respects the philosophic autonomy of each partner, while permitting them to collaborate and enter into agreements on social progress."[5]

We have already examined the manner in which these principles have been applied in the public sector, their results and limitations. No doubt it would be too optimistic to expect the "rules of the game" to have by now been firmly established. Neither the political nor social circumstances would permit this degree of progress. The means were not adequate for moving toward these goals. But what is most significant is the change of approach. The new program is more realistic, and its achievements are considerable. Management, for its part, has taken steps in the direction laid down by this new approach. While the trade unions are reluctant to endorse the concept of the "new society," they have been willing to enter into negotiations, and agreements developed on the basis of these new procedures.

PROSPECTS FOR THE FUTURE

However summary is our description of developments, it should make clear why it is difficult to project the future. We have observed several important innovations in the field of collective bargaining, a special type of collaboration among the public authorities, employers, and employees, along with the radicalization of union position and the intensification of industrial conflict. The country enjoyed a period of government stability, previously unknown in France, and a continuity of economic and social policy and a stable majority in the elections, associated with the continued operation of a vigorous Socialist and Communist opposition, which would not compromise its positions to attract votes from the center, as usually occurs in a bipolar political system. In addition, leftist pressure, though commanding a small vote, was nevertheless vocal and significant. The nation enjoyed a high continued rate of growth that profoundly changed the society but sharpened the dissatisfaction with backward conditions of daily life and the persistent social inequalities. It has been an era of cooperation without consensus, and prosperity accompanied by social and ideological divisions. What future may we expect?

Since the mid-1950s, France dedicated itself to economic growth. At first the goal was the privilege of a few, but it mobilized the energies of management, high-ranking civil servants, and even, to a degree, though rarely explicitly, the unions. It may have even reached a good share of the population. It offered, if not a final goal, a necessary objective that permitted traditional problems to be examined anew. The goal was partly realized. Perhaps because the effort commanded such intense dedication, there is considerable disillusionment because of the new difficulties met in the further advancement of the country. Economic growth is still needed, but it has ceased to be the general overriding objective.

In part the new doubts spring from the fact that the movement finally was led and managed by a small elite. A similar centralization of powers and decision-making authority continues and is characteristic of recent changes. It is not an accident that expansion of collective bargaining started with an agreement at the highest level, and the revival of the contractual policy resulted partly from governmental policy. We have already emphasized the point that there are few means for delegating responsibility down to the lowest levels.

The results therefore are rarely deeply rooted. Their impact on daily life is still weak. The average man does not have the feeling that he is better able by reason of these changes of institutions to deal with the problems with which he is directly confronted.

At the same time, the average man has greater powers for securing a hearing for his views, for protest, and for insisting upon his
views being respected. The shift of power to the lower levels does
not immediately produce a mature rounded system of local democratic
participation. On the contrary, because intermediate levels of regulation are missing between the rank-and-file initiative and broad social controls, the situation is characterized by an excess of powers
at the lower levels.

This excess has paralyzing effects on the organization. It provokes much agitation and provides few answers. The demands have
grown and have become stronger but are poorly dealt with by the political system. The expanding array of demands challenge and
threaten the system but do not necessarily bring about decisions and
changes.

The situation is not unique. Its causes and forms of expression
are replicated in a number of other European countries. Nevertheless, in a highly centralized and fractionated country, its effects
bear directly on the whole political system. The future of industrial
relations in this country will be determined in large part by the manner in which the political system will be able to face this challenge.


EDITOR'S NOTE

Industrial tension increased particularly at the national level
and in the public sector. With the support of the government a new
interindustry agreement signed by the five major union centers provided for almost 90 percent pay for one year to persons displaced by
companies going out of business or by economic contraction. But a
subsequent one for strengthening the retraining procedures was signed
only by the CGT-FO, subscribed to in principle by two additional
unions (CGC and CFTC), and rejected by the major ones (CGT and
CFDT) and is now in effect.

Two general one-day strikes called by the two major union
centers affected primarily the public sector. The first in November
was serious enough to be likened to the May 1968 events. The wage
and employment issues were most preeminent. In the months of
October and November, strikes in individual sectors ranging from
the postal service to the gas and electric industry, railways, and
coal-mines added heat to the confrontations. But by the beginning
of December, they were settled; and a short period without strikes
prevailed, only to have the tension reawakened by the December 12
general strike.

Rising prices reaching a rate of increase close to 15 percent,
growing unemployment attaining a level of 700,000, with common

projections of a million unemployed in the winter months, fed popular discontent. Severe restraints on the consumption of energy added to the complaints. The balance-of-payment deficits continued, resulting from high oil costs. Both employers (CNPF) and the trade union centers urged the relaxation of the restrictive economic policies and actual reflation. The government responded first with increases in the minimum wages, higher pensions, and family allowances and, later, the liberal unemployment benefits contained in the interindustry agreements and the reopening of negotiations with unions in the public sector for the 1975 contract. In February 1975 the Finance Minister offered a program of selective supports for the stimulation of the economy. Immigration restrictions continued severe, but to moderate the discontent among the foreign population more funds and services were announced for training and social programs.

## NOTES

1. M. Seeman, "The Signals of 68 Alienation in Pre-crisis France," American Sociological Review 57 (August 1972): 385-402.

2. V. Scardigli, Societe francaise et conflicts sociaux, multi gr., Credo, rapport no. 4209, 1973, chapter 8.

3. Yves Delamotte, in Revue francaise des affaires sociales, October-December 1972, p. 73.

4. Sofres, in Le Nouvel Observateur, March 28, 1973, National Sample. Since the number of union members surveyed is small in relation to the national population, the figures should be read cautiously.

5. Jacques Chaban-Delmas, "Speech to Parisian Metal Management" (April 28, 1970), cited in Jean Bunel and Paul Meunier, Chaban-Delmas (Paris: Stock, 1972), p. 283.

# CHAPTER

# 9

## CANADA:
## POSTWAR CHANGES
## AND CURRENT FERMENT
George Vickers Haythorne

Many changes have occurred within the industrial relations
system in Canada since World War II, but no alteration has taken
place in the system itself. General satisfaction with its performance
and the achievement of substantial economic and social progress contributed to widespread complacency. Ferment is now developing
among some unions; new dynamic forces emerging in society are
shaking traditional attitudes and practices. These developments
create major new issues, some of which originate within the field
of industrial relations, while most have their origin outside. Whatever their source, these issues must be tackled realistically. In so
doing, changing modes of behavior, attitudes, and interests point to
the need for new directions in industrial relations.

### CHANGES WITHIN THE INDUSTRIAL
### RELATIONS SYSTEM

Before the end of the 1940s the industrial relations system took
definite shape. Backed by many years of experience and legislation
the system that then emerged remained essentially intact under both
federal and provincial jurisdictions for the next 25 years.* Meanwhile

---

*The principal features of the industrial relations system in
Canada combine the compulsory conciliation of disputes arising in
the negotiation of collective agreements, a distinctive Canadian characteristic tracing its origin back to the early years of the century,
and a requirement, first developed in the United States in the 1930s,
that employers must bargain in good faith with certified unions, for

extensive changes took place in the size and structure of worker and employer organizations, the scope of their periodic negotiations and agreements, and the nature and extent of government intervention in industrial relations.

## Worker Organizations

Unions in Canada added 1.5 million members to their strength from 1951 to 1973. This increase, which brought the total to 2.5 million, while substantial, was not spectacular. Both the economy and employment grew rapidly, and, even in 1973, organized workers still comprised only 28 percent of the labor force.

The most notable recent advance in employee organization occurred in public administration. Before bargaining rights were introduced in the federal government in 1967, a total of 125,000, or 30 percent of all public servants, were reported in unions. Most of these were provincial and municipal employees. By 1972 their number had increased to 348,000, or 66 percent of all Canadian public servants. Of these, 44 percent were in the federal administration. The two largest bodies in this public sector of the economy, the Canadian Union of Public Employees and the Public Service Alliance of Canada, had grown to over 100,000. The Canadian membership of two "international" unions had also risen to over 100,000 in that year. These, the United Auto Workers and the United Steelworkers of America, had, in common with other unions at this time, increased their numbers through mergers and achieved wider industrial coverage as well through plant expansion. In the mid-1950s two major union federations, the Trade and Labour Council of Canada and the Canadian Congress of Labor, united to form the Canadian Labour Congress (CLC), which in 1973 reported over 1.8 million members. The second largest federation, the Confederation of National Trade Unions (CNTU), had 165,000 members.

Other structural changes in unions occurred. The most significant of these was the movement, sharply accelerated during the

---

designated bargaining units, and vice versa. Other important elements are the provision of penalties when either party is found to have committed unfair labor practices specified in the covering legislation, the right to strike or lock-out if the third-party mediation or conciliation process proves unsuccessful in resolving interest disputes, and the final settlement through arbitration of rights disputes arising out of the interpretation or application of agreements during the periods these are in force.

past decade, toward the autonomy of Canadian locals within their parent international bodies. The close "binational" (United States-Canada) linkage had provided strength and stability when Canadian locals were small and relatively weak. As they increased in size, their capacity for independent action increased. Besides, the rapidly expanding associations of public servants, nearly all of which were Canadian-based, joined with other previously organized all-Canadian bodies in pressing for national autonomy in union affairs. Among the latter were the widely dispersed Canadian Brotherhood of Transport and General Workers.* Two other developments encouraged still further independent or at least autonomous Canadian union action. One was a wave of protectionist tariff sentiment emerging in the U.S. labor movement. Union members in Canada strongly opposed this move. The other development was a more conscious recognition that Canadian unions must take their own position, along with those of all other countries, in dealing with the mounting number of multinational corporations and intergovernmental world bodies.

### Business and Industrial Organizations

Major shifts in the size and organization of firms and industries accompanied the steady growth of the Canadian economy during the quarter century following World War II. One of the changes that had an important impact on industrial relations was the definite trend toward larger operations. As in case of unions, this resulted from

---

*The practical expression of greater autonomy has taken many forms. In some cases--for example, the Steel Workers of America--the Canadian sector, while remaining an integral part of the international, virtually runs its own affairs. Much the same applies with the United Automobile Workers except that bargaining is now conducted by both the UAW and the automobile companies across the U.S.-Canadian border. In pulp and paper, on the other hand, the 52,000 Canadian members of the United Paperworkers International Union decided by referendum in February 1974 to establish a completely separate entity. The creation of this new body, known as the Canadian Paperworkers Union, received full support from the UPIU while this decision was pending. The CLC at its 1974 convention called for greater autonomy for Canadian districts of international unions, permitting them to elect Canadian officers, formulate policies on national affairs, elect Canadian representatives to speak for the union in Canada, and designate Canadian representatives to International Trade Secretariats and independent participation in the social, cultural, economic, and political life of the Canadian community.

mergers as well as business expansion. In manufacturing, for example, the peak number of 38,200 establishments, operating throughout the country, was reached in 1955. By 1969 the number had dropped to 32,700. Expressed in another way, the average annual value of output per manufacturing establishment increased from $700,000 in 1961 to $1.3 million in 1968. An even more striking indication of growth and consolidation was revealed in an analysis of information specially assembled for the year 1965 from 170,000 corporations in all industries. It found that 174 firms, or only slightly over 0.1 percent of all corporations, accounted for 25, 40, and 50 percent, respectively, of total sales, profits, and assets in that year. At the beginning of the 1970s foreigners owned 58 percent of the manufacturing industry.

The rapid increase in the influence exercised by multinational corporations contributed greatly to these changes. The book value of direct annual investments by U.S. firms alone in Canada rose from an estimated $3.6 billion in 1950 to $11.2 billion in 1960 and to $22.8 billion in 1970. Moreover, in 1950 there were 225 subsidiaries in Canada of 187 multinational corporations with headquarters in the United States. By 1967 the number of subsidiaries of these same multinational corporations had increased to 443. This number did not include other multinationals based in the United States, Europe, or elsewhere that had operations in Canada.

Several important internal organizational changes accompanied the growth in the size and scale of the operations of business enterprises. One of these, especially in large firms, was the rapid spread of specialized personnel, industrial relations, and research departments. Another was the divorce of the ownership and management roles in big enterprises, which continued to be combined in most small firms.

Many new industry and trade associations on both a national and regional basis appeared during these years. Usually created for broader business purposes, these bodies frequently appointed staff members, or named special committees to deal with industrial relations. The two principal national employers organizations, the Canadian Manufacturers' Association and the Canadian Chamber of Commerce, did similarly.

## Collective Bargaining

The number and range of items included in Canadian collective agreements increased steadily over the postwar period. To the provisions relating to wage rates, hours of work, and employment conditions were added new variations of union security, improved safety,

pensions, shortened work week, paid vacations, training, technological change, and the sharing of benefits for productivity improvements.
The rapid pace of new technology led to the most difficult bargaining
issues. The introduction of diesel locomotives on the railways, containerization in the ports, and computerized mail services, for example, each resulted in serious impasses in industrial relations.
These and other prolonged disputes centering around the impact of
technological innovations gave rise to new employment security provisions in collective agreements, including advance notification of
layoffs, stepped-up training and retraining plans, supplementary unemployment benefits, and severance pay.

While numerous new provisions were added to labor-management
agreements, little modification occurred in the pattern or structure of
negotiations themselves. One of the few changes in the latter was a
trend toward industrywide and broader geographic bargaining. This
took place, for instance, in meat packing, steel fabrication, automobile production, and construction. The initiative in the first three
cases sprang mainly from trade unions to improve their bargaining
strength. In construction the move to pool industrial relations resources came primarily from employers, who, faced with already
strong building trades unions, sought to secure greater stability and
uniformity in labor costs.

The emergence of personnel and industrial relations departments in firms as they grew large was due mainly to a conscious
need to counter tough union demands for increases in pay and fringe
benefits. Industrial relations departments were also designed to
help strengthen management's resistance to the erosion of their
rights and prerogatives. More positively, they contributed to increased order and stability in labor relations. Besides, employers
frequently took the initiative in improving in-service training programs, manpower utilization, safety provisions, and productivity.

Numerous interactions between the expansion of firms and that
of unions occurred during this period of rapid growth in the economy.
For example, it was no coincidence that the four largest enterprises,
together producing over 90 percent of all the motor vehicles in the
country in 1965, all had strong and unified workers' organizations.
A similar situation applied in that year in the manufacture of beer,
tobacco, and men's hats. Conversely, in meat-packing, demands
by locals for improved wages and working conditions, firmly backed
by a large and widely represented parent union, contributed to the
closing down of small, low-productivity plants or to their purchase
by larger and more effectively operated enterprises.

The existence of large firms did not necessarily lead to their
employees' joining a union. To help avoid organization, it was still
not uncommon for firms to establish employment conditions and

levels of earnings at least equal to or better than those in unionized
enterprises. Moreover, not all large firms with unions bargained
on an enterprise basis. Some companies producing steel and electrical products did in fact develop master contracts with their unions,
which, with local variations, applied to all their individual plants.
The practice, though, of local multiemployer bargaining remained
common. In these cases, however, bargaining typically covered a
variety of trades and production occupations grouped in a single
union. In the construction industry, and to a lesser extent in transportation, bargaining between employers and workers continued in
most cases on a craft-by-craft basis.


Public Involvement in Industrial Relations

The federal and provincial governments normally through their
Departments of Labour continued to discharge mediation and conciliation roles in industrial disputes when the parties themselves were
unable to resolve their differences. Aside from introducing greater
flexibility in their timing, these services changed little over the
years. An extension of economic analysis and research facilities
took place in the Canada Department of Labour in the 1940s. Later
similar agencies were created in provincial departments. These
research branches assisted in evolving a positive approach on the
part of governments to industrial relations. This was done through
supplying, on an objective basis, data to both unions and employers
for collective bargaining. Research on current issues helped also
in developing public labor policies and in assisting with the resolution of potential disputes. *

In 1965, Canada adopted a Labour Standards Code. While restricted to employees under federal jurisdiction, this code set a pattern for higher standards than those that previously existed under
provincial legislation. It covered minimum wages, maximum daily
and weekly hours, statutory holidays, and paid annual vacations.
While the code was designed primarily to protect unorganized workers, it formally recognized the improved working conditions already
obtained through collective bargaining.

Other established forms of public intervention bearing on industrial relations were either expanded or initiated. The government

---

*Both employer associations and trade unions built up their re-
search services to aid their subsidiaries, and universities and private industrial relations agencies organized special services in the
field and expanded their educational and consulting efforts.

sponsored and serviced joint union management committees in plants
and other establishments. Begun as wartime "production" committees, these were later converted into "consultation" committees. By
the early 1970s over 2,500 of these joint committees operated throughout the country. Although deliberately kept distinct from the processes of collective bargaining, many became channels of communication and discussion and aids in resolving local plant problems arising between workers and employers during the term of their collective agreements. A Manpower Consultative Service introduced in
1964 assists unions and employers in dealing with technological innovations. Technical education and employment facilities were also
extended and improved during the 1960s as part of a positive manpower program.


## COMPLACENCY VERSUS RESTLESSNESS

While changes of a far-reaching character occurred within the
industrial relations system in Canada during the postwar years, an
impressive degree of complacency persisted among both workers and
employers. Despite periods of unemployment and inflation, the parties had grown to live with each other. They were content with their
industrial relations system, enjoyed the substantial material benefits from their labors, and for the most part agreed that government
intervention in their affairs should be kept to a minimum.

Some concern was expressed by the unions about the power of
corporations and particularly of multinational corporations, but then
some unions, too, had become powerful in their own way. As long
as both groups were able to serve their own interests on the basis of
"power" meeting "power" and on occasion "power" joining "power,"
there was little reason to rock the boat. There were moreover "rising expectations" to be met for the employed and seemingly less need
to be concerned about those who were not, as a result of the much
improved social security measures. This state of affairs suited governments as well as employers and workers. It led to a widespread
feeling that all was basically well, and there was little thought of
fundamental change.

But then pervasive discontent among the youth, women's,
consumers', and "native population" groups became more vigorous, and a searching analysis began. These developments each
had an impact, but at the time they were not generally considered
as directly affecting industrial relations policies. In the field
of industrial relations an extensive review undertaken over the years
1966 to 1968, by a task force composed of university personnel, produced no strikingly different blueprint for the future.[1]

Behind this prevailing aura of comfort and complacency, however, some signs of restlessness began to appear. These took several forms. With the continuation of prolonged and deep-seated inflation in the late 1960s and early 1970s the government became less certain of its ability to manage the economy and less confident in the free play of market forces to provide acceptable economic and social answers. It had also become increasingly obvious that powerful groups, be they corporations, managements of institutions, unions, or governments, operate to their own advantage with little serious regard for broader domestic or global responsibilities. Moreover, they resist all attempts to become engaged in responsible policy-making and administration, which would involve them in new types of relationships and in major institutional changes in the collective bargaining field. They are ever ready to recommend restraints on adversaries, while proclaiming the righteousness of their own positions and activities. Few consider intensively developing new alternatives to tackle current and projected problems, preferring to be defensive rather than positive. Even unions retreat to utopian far-reaching proposals for structural change to achieve their stated goals, without formulating transitional proposals for immediate implementation. Though Canadian trade union centers belong to international bodies where new ideas and programs are actively being discussed, union leaders have made little effort to coopt or adapt them to domestic conditions for advocacy or for discussion, or, in fact, to develop realistic new approaches themselves.[2]

The inability of governments to deal effectively with many contemporary questions or to engage the full cooperation of employers and unions in doing so raises widespread uncertainties and doubts. Some major problems, including inflation, glaring income inequalities, resource depletion, and monetary instability, require new and comprehensive international measures, but this fact does not remove the necessity for more determined steps to cope with them in Canada. Delays in doing so only lead to more and deeper anxieties. In the case of inflation, to take just one of the problems, Canada is faced with an urgent need for strong and concerted action at a time when the federal government, most unions, and employer groups remain opposed to, or equivocal about, any tough comprehensive restraint programs.[3] As long as this dilemma, which inevitably has a close bearing on industrial relations, remains unsolved, it will continue to be a breeding ground for individual and social ferment.

Changes in attitudes and outlook of some segments of the population contribute to impatience and protest. One expression of such social unrest has occurred in Quebec, where the French Canadians, deprived economically and socially over a long period, pressed strongly during the more prosperous years of the 1950s and 1960s for separation from the rest of Canada or at the very least for equality in language and position with English Canadians. Generally acknowledged as sound in conception, if not in all its objectives, by the rest of the country, this "nationalist" movement was led mainly by middle-class intellectuals, including union leaders. Through becoming deeply involved in this broader population movement, unionism itself was deflected. The movement remains a force, but, meanwhile, vibrant collective voices have also been raised in other parts of the country and a broader form of nationalism has emerged.

Sectionalism present in the western provinces for many years has become particularly pronounced. This sentiment does not spring from the large numbers of "new" postwar immigrants, many of whom settled in these parts; it rather emerges from "old" Canadians living in the "west" with a long, deep antipathy to the economic power exercised by the "east," especially that represented by the financial and industrial interests concentrated in the Toronto-Montreal axis. * More recently these sentiments have been further aroused by a concern that measures taken on behalf of French-speaking Canadians, again largely located in the central and eastern regions, may be detrimental to all Canadians. The stirring in the west is associated also with radically different forms of political expression. These range from the socialist New Democratic Party to the conservative Social Credit Party, both of which were born within the region.†

The new nationalism is built in part on the principle that the country's resources should benefit primarily Canadians rather than externally based multinational corporations or other foreign interests. This pro-Canadian emphasis is vigorously supported by Westerners who see an opportunity to develop a more balanced regional economy. By diverting a larger portion of the revenues from the production and export of their rich oil, gas, and mineral resources, they hope to stimulate investments in secondary and tertiary industries in their provinces. This is also reflected in a new drive for

---

*A strong regional feeling of unfair discrimination has also been present in the four east-coast provinces and especially the three older "Maritime Provinces." This animus is directed also against the two Central Canadian provinces, but it has become less vocal in recent years as the provinces enjoyed extensive federal assistance under various federal-provincial shared-cost programs.

† (The New Democratic Party governments are currently in power in three western provinces: Manitoba, Saskatchewan, and British Columbia. In the fourth province, Alberta, the Progressive Conservative Party forms the government, replacing in 1971 the Social Credit Policy, which had been in power continuously since 1933.)

"Canadian identity" and patriotism. This new nationalism is also expressed, as already noted, in the movement toward autonomy gaining momentum among unions.

There are other signs of agitation in the unions, particularly among public service employees, where a younger and more militant leadership has emerged. One evidence of this ferment is a radical change in leadership that occurred at the 1974 biennial convention of the Canadian Labour Congress. It was in fact public employees who played a prominent part in breaking a long-standing tradition by overthrowing some officially backed leadership candidates. Another indication of deep feeling and frustration is the sharp increase of rejected settlements over the postwar years by members of public service unions who demand a more equitable share of the fruits of the country's recent rapid development.

The agitation that has developed in the public service is not all one-sided. When disputes arise in government activities, they usually have wider consequences than when they occur in private operations. A shutdown of the postal service, for example, affects everyone in the country and many outside. This creates much more disturbance and potential public annoyance than a work stoppage in a single plant, where those affected are normally limited to the immediate vicinity. Governments too are directly involved as employers, and this raises added problems in distinguishing clearly their role in this respect from that of serving as an impartial third-party mediator in disputes. Some of the most difficult and intractable disputes in recent years have in fact involved public employees under both provincial and federal jurisdictions. Steps taken to settle these may satisfy citizens generally but can aggravate workers, especially if what appears to them to be tough legislative settlements are imposed.* Many public servants, including teachers, and other professional groups have, moreover, distinctive views about their own demands. With an aroused awareness of the increasing role of government and of their collective strength, they will continue to press their claims in many ways. The militancy of public servants will probably also "rub off" on other groups.

---------------

*In Quebec three major unions involved in a bitter strike against the provincial authorities in 1972 not only sought widespread support to defeat the government's position but openly defied the law. The tactics pursued were opposed by part of the union membership. This led to a split in their ranks, the failure of the union leadership, and in the end full, although reluctant, conformity to the law.

MAJOR ISSUES CONFRONTING
INDUSTRIAL RELATIONS

The signs of restlessness throughout the country point up more
sharply major issues for workers, employers, and governments.
These are not always clearly defined or well understood. Nor is
there broad agreement about their relative importance within any
one of the three groups, let alone among all three. There is even
less agreement about the action needed to deal with them.

### Multinational Corporations and Nationalism

One set of issues relate to the increasing power exercised by
large multinational corporations. This power represents a challenge
and a threat to industrial relations and to the economy generally.
The issues involved have been heightened for Canada, as for other
countries, by the worldwide energy crisis beginning late in 1973.
Out of this emerged a broader consensus that the development and
use of resources and the revenue yield from them can no longer be
left in the hands of large and often externally based corporations.
But equally, in a highly interdependent world, many more decisions
affecting the welfare of all nations must be made collectively. In
the past, multinational corporations have been left largely free to
pursue their own interests on the loose assumption that this was also
in everyone's interest. Governments have begun to lay down acceptable ground rules for action by multinational corporations within
their borders, but the formulation and application of these rules present new problems for these governments and also corporations and
unions. The extension of these rules through appropriate international bodies is rapidly becoming necessary to ensure acceptable
global behavior by corporations, unions, and governments.
The related issue of nationalism has both positive and negative
features. Developing policies that attempt to balance greater domestic control with a continuing inward flow of investment funds can
create major difficulties for management, workers, and owners of
individual industries. Past commitments made in good faith have to
be respected. Canadians also value highly their close and mutually
beneficial associations with other countries, and especially with the
United States. As satisfactory practices emerge for dealing more
effectively with international economic and social matters, the new
Canadian nationalism should become less inward-looking. In the
meantime many pressures pro and con a "Canada-first" policy will
continue. In industrial relations, however, the "pro" pressures have
been reduced substantially by the progress already made in achieving
union autonomy within the country.

### Abandonment of Traditional Values and Attitudes

A different issue, and also one confronting all Canadians, is the rejection of long-established values and attitudes toward practices and institutions. This abandonment of traditional values and standards leaves most people and particularly the youth unable to depend on the past. They have greater flexibility and freedom in facing the future but have the difficult and responsible task of rethinking their attitudes, determining what values are important and setting new standards. The rapid advance of technology, improved living conditions, and higher levels of education also contribute to a revolution in conventional patterns of family and individual behavior.

Translated into the field of industrial relations, this new freedom of thought can make for more vigorous and creative action, but this cannot be easily or quickly accomplished when many institutions and practices of unions and management are entrenched and rigid. Few leaders in the past in either group have displayed any serious interest in evolving new patterns of relationship. Most have been content to perpetuate their traditional adversary roles, but there are a select few employers and union leaders who read the signs of the times and see the necessity of reconciling the admittedly narrower interests of their groups with those of the public as a whole. In addition, the current ferment is raising more basic questions about the nature and character of worker-employer relations and their place in a rapidly changing society.

### Management of the Economy

The steadily growing participation of government in the management of the economy poses another major set of problems for industrial relations. The need for greater public involvement is more widely recognized and appreciated today. This changed view is due in large part to the fulfillment of war and postwar commitments by governments to provide more generous social and economic security measures and promote growth and full employment. Nevertheless, the extension of the public role inevitably produces conflicts with special-interest groups and traditional industrial practices. Its acceptance is not easy for those employers and workers who have long supported a completely free market economy. New problems are also raised for governments that have not in the past wished to become more directly involved than necessary in industrial relations.

Some government-sponsored programs have been generally welcomed. This was the case, for example, with the broadly based winter employment program introduced in the 1950s and the greatly

expanded technical education facilities in the 1960s. Others, such
as the extension of labor legislation, are usually more rapidly accepted by workers than employers, while the reverse was true, for
instance, with the national productivity improvement program in the
early 1960s. More recently the antiinflation program proposed in
1969, while conditionally accepted by the employers, was not welcomed with any real enthusiasm by either party.

The proliferation of public planning, operating, and advisory
agencies is also changing traditional concepts of public service and
administration. Of necessity, many more national and regional policies require close consultation with and often the active cooperation
of employers and unions. While most are ready to be consulted, cooperation is not always forthcoming. Their hesitancy is due in large
measure to the fact that they still see public intervention as a threat
to their long-cherished and stoutly defended freedom of action in pursuing their own economic interests.

## Industrial Democracy

Still another issue that bears directly on labor relations is industrial democracy and, particularly, the extent to which it should
be encouraged and practiced. An increased role by employees in
decision-making in a plant or firm, which "industrial democracy"
implies, has not gained wide support in Canada. Both unions and
employers have usually concluded that they would each lose more
than they would gain by following such a course. More specifically
there is an underlying fear that industrial democracy would weaken
collective bargaining, built as it is with the adversary principle as
its cornerstone. Some of these strongly held attitudes are being con-
tested, but the basic problem of how to reconcile an evolving industrial and social democracy with changes required in worker-employer
relations remains to be solved.

## NEW DIRECTIONS NEEDED

There is little consensus about the steps needed to deal with
these issues currently facing Canadian workers, employers, and governments or even about the new directions necessary for the future.
Yet satisfactory and broadly acceptable solutions to these questions
are becoming increasingly urgent.

Some new patterns in social and economic behavior that are inevitably influencing the role and place of industrial relations are,
however, emerging. One of these that has been increasingly evident

in public policies and programs over recent years is the recognition that there must be closer consultation and participation among governments, employers, and workers in dealing with major common problems. Collaboration has been initiated not only by governments. In textiles, rubber footwear, and construction, for example, where difficult internal industry problems have arisen, proposals made to the federal government by employers and workers have led to positive, three-way follow-up action. These various joint programs are also leading to a growing interdependence between industrial relations and other broader policies.

Another pattern of behavior that is becoming clear is the disappearance of hard lines, drawn in the past among unions, employers, and governments. Each is now more ready to concede its dependence on the other two and all of them on the general public. Each in the past claimed that it also serves, at least ultimately, the public interest. Today, a more enlightened and critical public is no longer ready to accept these claims without question. They are insisting that they be proven or amended. Democratic processes, armed with greatly improved communication facilities and educational programs, support the public in this position.

The developing joint programs, a wider consensus on the need for planned and coordinated national policies in the interests of the country as a whole, and the ferment demanding changes in outdated attitudes and practices all point to the need for a concerted and critical examination of industrial relations and of the system in which they operate. It can no longer be assumed that the system, even though painfully created and generally effective in the past, should continue without change.

It is timely that there is new leadership in the labor movement and that union members are looking for strong and positive action. There are other signs within employer groups, unions, and governments of rethinking the bases of bargaining and their separate joint roles, defining more sharply common interests in industry and society, and developing new methods to resolve conflict.

Yet it must be repeated that many built-in rigidities remain in the industrial relations system. Because of this, basic changes are unlikely to take place easily or from within the system. New approaches are more likely to come from a combined attack by governments, employers, and unions on common problems facing all of them and the country, such as inflation, allocating the nation's natural resources, and sharing the benefits of the economic progress at home and abroad. Of the three parties, public authorities are in the best position to provide the leadership required. As a first step toward determining realistic new directions, the federal government could initiate an urgently needed critical examination of the industrial relations system and the interrelation between it and national and international policies. This might be done by inviting all parties concerned to share in the closer identification of major issues facing the country, to play their part in considering and developing short- and long-term policies and programs to deal with them, and to participate as appropriate in the execution of agreed policies and programs. Those participating would require flexibility in outlook, especially concerning the present and potential roles of major groups in the functioning of the economy. They would need also to be persons able to take part in an objective and responsible manner whether at the national and provincial or at the shop and office level. The new directions and policies developed, moreover, could not be expected to succeed unless they, along with the issues they were designed to meet, were clearly articulated at all levels and fully reconciled with acceptable collective bargaining procedures.

NOTES

1. Canadian Industrial Relations, Report of the Task Force on Labour Relations (Ottawa: Queen's Printer, December 1968).

2. An experienced observer of industrial relations and a full-time union officer had written, "The goals of organized labor [are] admirable, and its function of redistributing the nation's wealth indispensable. But its internal conservatism is appalling. Its sentries patrol the ramparts of Fortress Labor, ready to repel invaders armed with Dangerous New Ideas." Ed Finn, "Labor's Love Lost," Macleans (Toronto), May 1974.

3. A broad-ranging prices and incomes policy involving joint participation by federal and provincial governments, employers, and unions was proposed in 1969. After preliminary discussions the unions withdrew. Following this the employers agreed to participate along with governments for one year in a modified program directed mainly against price increases. See "Prices and Incomes Policy: The Canadian Experience, 1969-1972," by the author, International Labour Review, December 1973, ILO, Geneva.

# THE UNITED STATES:
# A TIME FOR
# REASSESSMENT
Sumner Rosen

## HISTORICAL ROLE OF UNIONS
## IN THE U.S. ECONOMY

U.S. labor unions have adapted themselves over a long period of time to the requirements of institutional survival and effectiveness in a private enterprise economy. In the modern era, unions success-fully converted themselves, with the help of the state, from a small, narrowly based group rooted in the elite of the blue-collar labor force--the skilled workers--into a mass organization based in the major industries of the economy. Previous efforts had been made to establish such a mass base; some had limited success, but none endured. By contrast, the mass unionizing movement of 1935-45 succeeded.

Some observers and participants believed that the age of mass unionism would usher in an era in which mass action, based on working-class issues and working-class consciousness, would come to replace, or at least complement, the "job-conscious" unionism found in the older unionized sectors. They saw U.S. capitalism in disarray as a result of the depression and believed that a new union movement was being created that would take up working-class strug-gles in ways similar to the pattern found in Europe where socialisti-cally oriented trade union centers hold an anticapitalistic orientation and support reformist social-democratic parties.

These expectations were incorrect. They failed to take ac-count of the deep roots the older union forms and outlooks had estab-lished in the American soil. The unsuccessful struggles waged in earlier periods, by the Socialists, the Industrial Workers of the World (IWW), and others to dislodge the American Federation of Labor (AFL) and craft unionism from their dominant position were

historically decisive. While John L. Lewis and the other founders of
the Congress of Industrial Organizations (CIO) broke with craft unionism as an organizing principle, they did not break with other fundamental principles of unionism established in the period from the
founding of the modern trade unions in the 1850s and the formation of
the AFL in 1886 to the organization of the CIO in 1935. These included (1) a commitment to collective bargaining with employers on
terms of employment as the central instrument for winning gains for
workers; (2) acceptance of private enterprise as the dominant form
of economic organization and the source of employment of workers;
and (3) recruitment of union leadership from the ranks of workers.
Political action was conceived of at most as a supplement to the bargaining process, not as its replacement or as a means for extending
benefits secured through collective bargaining to the entire working
population. Unions did not resort to general strikes, political
strikes, and other forms of action not related to unionization of the
unorganized, the settlement of contract disputes, or the correction
of specific injustices in the work place. The achievement of short-
run improvements in wages, hours, and working conditions mattered
far more than advancing the long-run interests of the working class
as a whole or changing the capitalistic system.


## UNIONISM TODAY: A DEFENSIVE POSTURE

Compared to the pre-CIO era, unions have successfully established themselves, often in the face of strong opposition, as a major
force in the economy and in political life. Mass unionism was made
possible by the enactment of the Wagner Act in 1935, which placed
the protection of federal law behind efforts to organize and establish
bargaining relationships in the major industrial sectors. By the end
of World War II, public opinion had changed; unions were perceived
as having achieved too much power. The Taft-Hartley Law (1947)
and the Landrum-Griffin Act (1959) sought to curb and contain that
power. As the study of labor economics expanded, some economists
and members of the public came to support the view that union bargaining power was an important factor in producing "wage-push"
inflation.

When the Wagner Act was passed, and in the years that followed, business spokesmen, political leaders, the press, and many
scholars predicted the coming of a "laboristic society," to use a
phrase of Professor Sumner H. Slichter, in which power would shift
away from business hands into those of union leaders controlling or
manipulating millions of workers. Today, the numerical strength
of U.S. unions is at an all-time high. Yet, in a recent analysis,

Neil Chamberlain observes, "Management acts, the union reacts. . . . labor unions are the dependent variable in the set of economic relationships. Business holds the initiative. . . . the large corporation is the dominant institution. "[1]

While unions have become strong, U.S. business has more than matched that strength. Industrial relations must be evaluated against the backdrop of power relations that now prevail in the U.S. and the world economy. As they have in other major industrial societies, the forces of management and ownership have learned not only how to survive unionism but how to profit from it and, in many cases, how to prevail over it. Unionism in the United States is on the defensive and is likely to remain so. It is striking how little recognition or concern is expressed about this condition by the elected leadership of the U.S. labor movement and its unofficial spokesmen. On occasion, unions will be urged to develop, in J. B. S. Hardman's phrase,[2] a "new sense of mission," but the prevailing view among leaders and friends appears to be confidence that the union movement will survive and prosper and will learn to adapt in the future as in the past and that there is no real basis for concern. When Jerry Wurf, president, American Federation of State, County, and Municipal Employees (AFSCME) submitted a resolution at the 1973 AFL-CIO convention calling for the establishment of a commission to study the state of American unionism and to recommend methods to strengthen and protect the institution, he was soundly rebuked and his proposal was buried by the leadership; the resolutions committee found it "unnecessary and unwise" and rested its full confidence in the executive council.[3]

Wurf's proposal focused on issues of structure and procedure within the AFL-CIO. The problems to which he pointed include jurisdictional conflicts and confusion, the need to merge or amalgamate in order to bargain effectively, inadequate organizing efforts, and poor relationships between the union movement and other groups interested in social, political, and economic change. An admirer of the large and relatively powerful central bodies that govern the labor movements in a few European countries, Wurf clearly was treading on sensitivities in urging more consolidation, more rational jurisdictional boundaries, more effective control of jurisdictional contests, and a stronger central body.

It is true that progress along these lines, if it could be made, might well improve the ability of the unions to deal with the problems they face. But the really difficult problems are those beyond the control of the unions, which no amount of exclusively internal reconstruction can affect. The difficulties confronting U.S. unionism derive from the weakening of collective bargaining performance at the job, plant, and company levels, which are the basis for American union organization and action.

One of Wurf's complaints is that unions remain divided and
competitive even when they face major corporations with massive
economic power.  Since the mid-1950s, U.S. corporations have
metamorphosed into new forms and structures.  In the process, they
tend to leave the unions far behind.  This is particularly the case
with the group of industrial unions that became the dominant force in
American unionism as a result of the impetus of the CIO organizing
efforts of the 1935-45 period.

The forms the unions took at that time were adapted to the need
to confront effectively major corporations, specialized by industry
and linked to one another within the industry and using collective bargaining methods.  Unions developed these methods into a highly sophisticated and effective instrument for regulating the relationships
between management and unions, between the mid-1930s and the
mid-1950s.

When corporations diversified their holdings to reach into varied industries, unions with the encouragement and support of the
AFL-CIO Industrial Union Department formed over 70 coalitions of
constituent unions of the major corporations to create "coordinated
collective bargaining."  This arrangement overcame some deficiencies
in the existing system but did not fully answer the demands for concerted action.  Moreover, it suffered from the continued suspicions
and tensions produced by union rivalries and different union traditions.

As shifts continued in the structure of the economy and the distribution of employment, unions were unable to establish significant
bases in many areas of major economic growth.  They retained their
strongest footing in the slowest-growing sectors--industry, transportation, and contract construction.  Between 1958 and 1973, the number of blue-collar workers increased 28 percent from 23.3 million to
29.9 million.  During the same period, white-collar employment
grew from 26.8 million to 40.4 million, an increase of 50 percent.
The growth sectors have been in trade, finance and insurance, services, and government employment, particularly state and local government.  Together, these sectors accounted for 68 percent of nonagricultural employment in 1973, compared with 54 percent in 1958.

Manufacturing was the frontier and then the heartland of industrial unionism, but today's growth industries are health, education,
recreation, banking, and other services.  Membership figures show
the results.  While union membership has increased, the labor force
has increased faster.  In 1951, of the nonsupervisory work force, 47
percent were union members; by 1971 the percentage had fallen to 42
percent.  Unions of public service employees are the fastest-growing
unions in the country, but in 1970 only 19.6 percent of all local government employees were union members, well below the 37.4 percent in durable goods manufacture, 44.8 percent in transportation

and utilities, and 39. 2 percent in construction. In all sectors, including those where white-collar jobs predominate, the proportion of white-collar workers in unions (9. 8 percent) is far below that of blue-collar workers (39. 3 percent). Craftsmen (42. 7 percent unionized) and operatives (40. 4 percent unionized) are the union bulwarks in the occupational structure, but they numbered only 30. 6 percent of all employed persons in 1970, a percentage that continues to decline. [4]

## THE POWER OF U.S. BUSINESS

American business has built a position in the society and the political system much different from the situation during the formative period of the modern union movement. The New Deal period legislated important new social protections for workers, farmers, and others; it also imposed many controls and limits on business freedom. Labor legislation was among the most important of these measures. The Wagner Act, resisted bitterly but unsuccessfully by business interests, protected union organization and compelled employers to recognize and to bargain collectively with unions. Union leaders were welcome participants in political decision-making.

The entry of the United States into World War II ended this period of business defensiveness. Business leaders were called on to help lead the economic effort to build a war economy. That economy itself virtually eliminated unemployment and vastly improved the earnings and living standards of millions of workers and farmers. War prosperity served both to subordinate the reformist movements of the 1930s and rehabilitate the reputation and standing of the business system. Since then, business has built itself into the position of holding the major levers of economic and political power in the economy. This consolidation of power has fundamentally altered the relationships between employers and unions in the corporate sector.

Business strength is expressed in several important ways: (1) corporations have built collective patterns of cooperation and collaboration; (2) they have strengthened their economic power through diversification; (3) they have established international power and profit bases; and (4) they have increased their managerial effectiveness vis-a-vis workers and unions. Most U.S. unions have not been able to respond effectively to any of these developments. Each of them has left the union movement relatively weaker in the struggle to achieve and sustain effective bargaining leverage.

### Collaboration

Patterns of collaboration and cooperation among corporations grew during the war effort of 1941-45, which involved corporate managers in close cooperation in managing the war economy. These patterns have been reinforced by several other factors. One was the rising influence of the professional schools of business, which train new generations of managers and also bring together those at middle and upper levels for intensive study of management methods. A second was the increase in political influence of the business groups, following the war. Business used instruments of consultation and collaboration, such as industry advisory councils and political work through the Chamber of Commerce and other groups, trade associations, and in direct relationships with the executive branch. These efforts bore fruits in such union-control measures as the Taft-Hartley and Landrum-Griffin bills. The Business Advisory Council became, particularly in the 1950s and early 1960s, a major forum for exchange of views between top business and top government officials, from which both the press and labor were excluded. Trade associations in the aerospace industry developed powerful lobbying pressures in support of continued high levels of military spending, and counterparts were developed around highway spending, support for housing construction, maritime subsidies, and other public policies important to business. The latter efforts often had union support.

## Economic Power

Following the consolidation of corporate strength in the 1920s, the rapid advent and consolidation of mass unionism in the major industries during the later 1930s and early 1940s and the greatly expanded regulatory role of the federal government appeared to reduce the economic power of large corporations. In retrospect, this view was highly exaggerated. The purchasing power accumulated by U.S. consumers during the war, when housing and consumer durables were in short supply or unavailable, launched an era of economic prosperity, which, reinforced by the Korean War, was sustained with only limited interruptions through the decade of the 1950s. Big business was able to consolidate and increase the bases of its economic power during this period.

The merger movement of the 1960s described by Fortune magazine as "longer and . . . bigger"[5] than those of the 1890s and 1920s, increased corporate economic power. The merger movement had many important consequences for the economy--among them, the fact that the economic strength of the corporations began significantly to overbear that of the industrial unions with which they, or their components, had dealt.

Other forces besides the corporate merger movement have contributed to this development. Market power itself, as practiced in the concentrated and oligopolistic industries, has led to significant expansion and the development of an unprecedented capacity for financial control. Major corporations in the 1955-65 period were able to establish and sustain rates of return on net worth that far exceeded, and were more stable than, those of the past. This made possible steady expansion of plant capacity from both retained earnings and bank loans, giving the corporations significant reserve production capacity that could be used to make up quickly any production lost in strikes.

Diversification has also favored business bargaining power. High rates of retained earnings stimulated the search for diversification opportunities. The conglomerate corporation of the 1960s represents this new face of U.S. corporate practice. Stretching across product and process lines, these firms found it possible to deal separately with unions organized by traditional market categories, to orchestrate their negotiations in order to maximize their ability to avoid or resist the major union groups, to make it more difficult for unions to secure common expiration dates, and in other ways to limit union negotiating effectiveness. A study of collective bargaining at Litton Industries' Royal typewriter plant concluded that "under appropriate conditions the new corporate structure can make the old bargaining structure obsolete, and their new unconventional administrative procedure can make the traditional bargaining procedure unworkable."[6]

## International Activities

Many large corporations have moved from a national to an international basis; what is called the multinational corporation is a most important new development in U.S. business. Utilizing the leverage once available in a dollar-dependent world, U.S. corporations acquired major shares in the industrial economies of many major industrial nations and built plants in many of the less developed countries. This provides a greater choice of production sites and enables them to shift the balance between domestic and foreign-made goods without jeopardy to profit, alter the foreign-domestic division in the production of finished goods from raw materials or components, and assign different shares of profits to foreign-based and domestic operations in response to tax or other changes, including union pressures. This is a formidable new array of instruments with which to confront single-industry, domestic unions. Except for Canada--and, even there, affiliates have recently made moves to greater independence or separation--U.S. unions have not been able to follow the corporations abroad in order to confront them with

international solidarity. The trade secretariats are still weak instruments for such coordination, though in a few cases--such as
metals and chemicals--they provide some assistance to national
unions through international coordination of information and occasional resistance to stepped-up production.

The domestic employment impact of the multinational corporation is very much a disputed question. [7] On the one hand, they are
among the most dynamic firms in the economy, with high rates of
growth in overall employment. On the other hand, they have been a
factor in the growth of U.S. imports and the successive devaluations
of the dollar that have occurred in recent years and alarmed some
national policy-makers and union leaders alike. Available evidence
appears to support the view that multinational corporations have reduced employment of lower-skilled workers whose interests are of
direct concern to unions. They are thus a factor in some industries,
shifting the balance of bargaining power against unions representing
these workers. Unions in turn have sought to counter this tendency
through political action in support of legislation to curb multinational
corporations, but these efforts made no progress.


### Increased Managerial Effectiveness


Business has changed internally as well as externally. Sophisticated new methods of management and control have been developed
and installed in major enterprises. Corporate management has
adopted new goals and has worked hard to find the means to achieve
them. In the past, two different philosophies toward unionism were
in contention in professional discussion and management thinking.
Firms like General Motors and General Electric, different in many
ways, shared a commitment to a consistent hard line toward unionism. (The recent Lordstown strike against General Motors, heralded
by some commentators as the beginning of the revolt of the younger
workers against corporate discipline, in fact testifies to the continuation of this traditional posture by the employer.)

U.S. Steel symbolized a different approach, that of management seeking to build a partnership with the union, viewing the union
as an instrument to serve management's goal of building a stable,
contented, and productive labor force. This posture, still true of
U.S. Steel, has been accepted by the national leadership of the United
Steelworkers and praised by the AFL-CIO. [8] The first approach followed the bitter organizing struggles in autos and electrical machinery; the second owes much to the relatively peaceful process by which
unionism was established in the major steel-producing firms, built
as it was on the conversion of company unions to independent unions.

As the balance of power steadily shifted in favor of the employer side, it became an increasingly plausible employer strategy to seek supremacy over the unions. Corporate management has generally moved to contain unionism and reduce its effectiveness, using newer and more sophisticated methods. Some of these were developed in the 1950s on the base laid by work in the behavioral sciences in the 1930s and 1940s. The period since then has seen the development of a large arsenal of methods for analyzing the sources of worker discontent, for motivating workers, training managers and supervisors, reorganizing or restructuring jobs and job content, and building more effective organizational structures to achieve corporate control.

On the whole, the business system has shown great readiness to take advantage of new opportunities. Many managers still believe that workers require discipline and that a highly structured setting, strong supervision, and authoritarian hierarchy are natural and necessary, but they are pragmatists, ready to utilize new methods and approaches if these offer the prospect of reducing costs and increasing productivity, without being deterred by ideological considerations. Personnel staffs and line supervision far outweigh the union shop organizations. Their coordinated activities and greater skills and indoctrination help them to offset or mute many initiatives by workers and shop stewards whose preparation is usually too limited and aid from national organizations too spotty to deal with the sophisticated methods used by the other side.

## CHANGES IN THE POLITICAL CLIMATE AND THEIR EFFECTS ON UNIONS

The period of greatest union growth and the institutionalization of the labor movement occurred when the political climate was highly favorable. But beginning with the wave of postwar strikes in 1946, the climate shifted sharply, and this shift continued through most of the 1950s; following a reversal during the Kennedy period (1961-63), it resumed.

Despite some interruptions, the war and postwar periods produced unprecedented and sustained economic prosperity, sufficient to dilute interest in further social reform. Anticommunist hysteria in the late 1940s and early 1950s, which led to the purge in the CIO, divided the industrial unions. The appearance during this period of structural unemployment along with price inflation stimulated the development of theories of "cost-push" inflation, which assigned a major responsibility for price rigidity and price increases to the bargaining power of unions. The investigations of the special Senate

committee on labor racketeering in the mid-1950s revealed a pattern
of financial abuse and manipulation of the laws governing labor organizing activities, which further soiled labor's reputation.

The two major acts of federal legislation since World War II,
the Taft-Hartley Law (1947) and the Landrum-Griffin Act (1959), both
restricted union bargaining effectiveness and the ability to organize
and liberalized the rights of employers to oppose union organizing efforts. In part as a consequence of these new restrictions, union membership actually declined between 1956 and 1961 for the first time
since the early years of the depression of the 1930s.

The reversal of public opinion and the erosion of political support that began to take hold in the late 1940s reinforced moves for the
absorption of the weakened CIO into the AFL through the merger that
took place in 1955. The predominance of power in the new organization rested with the AFL branch, and that predominance was solidi-
fied in the years that followed, strengthening the influence of the conservative elements in the central organization.

The 1960s were dramatic as well as decisive in setting the
unions into the political mold these events had prepared. A series
of major issues confronted the society, of which two stood out: the
eruption of black discontent and anger, and the trauma of the Vietnam
war. The black revolt spread throughout the South, and then into
northern cities. The massive march on Washington in August 1963
was a milestone of one kind; the urban riots of 1965-67 marked one
of a different kind. While some unions, particularly those formerly
associated with the CIO, identified themselves with black demands
for equal justice and economic opportunity, many were indifferent
or actively opposed, especially to those demands that directly affected the distribution of job opportunities within their jurisdictions.
Unemployed or underemployed blacks picketing urban construction
sites became a frequent event in major cities. While the national
AFL-CIO supported civil rights laws to provide equal legal rights,
individual local unions and some nationals offered little support for
enforcement of black economic demands; indeed the building trades
successfully resisted efforts to integrate the skilled construction
labor force and conceded only limited access to apprenticeship for
young blacks and other minority members.

When the civil rights struggle turned its attention to integrating
northern schools and housing, workers as individuals were strongly
represented among those who responded with hostility, often active
and militant. The tradition of mutual distrust between the trade
union movement and the black community, which had been partially
bridged during the CIO period, widened again.

On the Vietnam war, the AFL-CIO, personified by President
George Meany, stubbornly and totally resisted any effort to enlist

the trade union movement in the movement in opposition, which began slowly in the wake of the 1965 expansion of the war and grew steadily in the years that followed. Individual union leaders and union groups supported the antiwar movement; a conference in Chicago in 1968 was supported by several major union figures and attracted several hundred regional and local leaders, but the great majority of AFL-CIO and independent unions remained silent or actively supported U.S. policy.

This position deepened the isolation of the labor movement from important political movements in the United States. Liberal and intellectual support was critical during labor's period of major growth; its diminution or loss has not threatened labor's ability to survive, but it has exacted an important cost by weakening the movement's ability to overcome the widespread skepticism or hostility that took root among many parts of the general public in the 1940s and 1950s.

Antiintellectualism has deep historic roots in the labor movement. Unions depend heavily on the special skills of professionally trained people, but these people generally occupy modest positions with little real formal power. During the early CIO years, many intellectuals and professional people were attracted to unionism as a career. While they were primarily employed because of their professional skills, their motivation included a commitment to social change; the unions were a new force that would help make change possible. They helped to articulate and extend the CIO's adoption of wider social goals, such as racial justice, economic justice, welfare reform, and health insurance. In recent years, the AFL-CIO, its constituent national unions, and the independent unions, have made relatively little use of its internal staff or outside persons to help appraise and redefine their orientation, policies, or tactics in the light of the new external developments or their overall functions and responsibilities in the nation and the world.

## WORKER "AFFLUENCE" AND INSECURITY

The wave of union organization in the 1935-45 period focused on industrial workers. Their organizing success, often against bitter resistance, and their effectiveness at the bargaining table enlisted broad public support, partly because the new unions were able to curb the power of large corporations and partly because the workers themselves were so badly exploited. Each new negotiating advance moved them and their families one step more out of poverty, toward decent levels of income and job security.

Two decades later the picture had changed. While far from affluent, many workers had joined at least the lower levels of the middle class. Median earnings of unionized year-round full-time blue-collar workers in 1970 were $8,664, nearly $2,000 more than those of nonunionized blue-collar workers. The margin of union over nonunion earnings in construction was more than $3,300.[9]

These are impressive achievements; they also have important consequences. Public sympathy is far less readily available to workers seeking higher wages and benefits through collective bargaining when they already equal or surpass the income levels of most Americans, than it was when workers were poor and struggling to achieve minimal gains.

Workers are less ready to strike, because the impact on their economic situation is far more severe than it was before the era of mortgage and installment payments, college expenses for children, extensive vacations, and so on. Their leaders echo this reluctance. Paul Hall recently spoke for his union:

> We in the maritime unions know we have the guts and muscle to fight if we have to. But maritime strikes have outlived their purposes. One maritime strike is too many, for whatever stated reason. If the maritime industry is to be rejuvenated, there must be no strikes, no work stoppages, no interference with the flow of ships and their cargo.[10]

The number of workers involved in stoppages, and the percent of time lost, have indeed remained at low levels in recent years, even though tensions and frustrations in negotiations have increased, compared with the first two postwar decades.

Workers' concerns have been affected by their changed economic status. While the old worries about income and job security persist, workers at the upper-income level have new worries as well, some of which they share with others in the middle class. Inflation jeopardizes the prospect of continuing increases in real incomes. Possible skill obsolescence is a threat. Agitation for racial justice, which appears to threaten the basis of their job security and their hard-won status relative to the poorer elements of the working class is challenging. Young college people who disparage the work ethic and appear to impugn workers' ethnic identity are offensive.

These changes affect workers' political attitudes and expectations. They identify more with mainstream or middle-class political views and have increasingly cooled to demands voiced in the 1960s on behalf of blacks and other minorities. Workers' support of the Vietnam war on traditional patriotic grounds was resistant to change. By 1968, union members, particularly those earning between

$5,000 and $10,000 per year, were more likely than others to have
voted for George Wallace.

An increasing distance opened between unionized workers and
the disadvantaged, particularly those in racial minorities and those
on welfare. For some--particularly the skilled workers in the building trades--black demands appeared to be a direct threat to their
self-interest and the unions through which they have controlled access to jobs. While racial animosity is a factor, concern about relative status probably is more important. This was reflected in the
success of the Wallace effort in 1972 and of Nixon campaign efforts
directed at workers. Until Nixon demonstrated that it could happen,
many were unable to believe that blue-collar workers would deviate
from their long-term Democratic allegiance in response to a campaign that stressed the work-ethic values and patriotism. These
themes echoed the anxieties and dissatisfactions many workers have
felt as their hard-won entry into the ranks of the middle class appeared to be jeopardized, on the one hand, by threats from below
and discredited, on the other hand, by advocates of the new cultural
values, associated with youth, which developed so rapidly in the
late 1960s.

In order to conserve their gains, groups of workers and some
local union leaders are increasingly willing to support those who
share their concerns about racial pressures, "unpatriotic" antiwar
agitation, welfare burdens that appear to support the idle at the expense of those who work. Peter Brennan, a construction union leader, later appointed secretary of Labor, came to the attention of then
President Nixon as a result of the massive demonstration by construction and other workers in support of the Vietnam war that took
place in New York in May 1970.


## UNIONISM AND STRATIFICATION AMONG WORKERS

Bargaining success since the mid-1950s has not benefited all
workers equally. Those in the stronger bargaining positions--highly
skilled workers and unionized workers in concentrated industries--
have been the chief beneficiaries, while others have fallen behind.
Analysis of the trend in earnings among different groups in the labor
force shows that the ratio of upper to lower earnings has increased
steadily throughout the post-1945 period and somewhat more rapidly
during the past decade. In addition, organized workers have secured
negotiated improvements in fringe benefits greater than those won by
unorganized and less well-organized blue-collar workers.

In the initial phase of mass unionism, advances were relatively widely shared. Since the 1950s, however, the divergence has been

substantial. These relative differences within the working class have important psychological and institutional consequences. Those at the upper levels have less reason to identify with those below. Stratifying tendencies undermine the roots of solidarity and deepen differences based on industry or on occupation. Where these differences correspond to a different distribution of workers by color or sex, the psychological distance increases still more.

In this respect, the trade union movement, vastly larger than was its nonindustrial predecessor represented in the AFL, has come nevertheless to resemble the pre-merger AFL. Organized workers in the economically stronger industries are an emerging elite of the labor force, just as the labor aristocracy of the past consisted of the skilled workers organized into crafts; "status bargaining" replaces "deprivation bargaining." This helps to explain the similarity between cultural and political postures expressed within the AFL-CIO today and those of the AFL unions in the pre-CIO and pre-merger years. Men like George Meany and I. W. Abel, based in dissimilar unions, speak virtually the same way in their public statements on unionism, collective bargaining, and industrial strife.

## THE CHANGED SETTING IN THE WORK PLACE

In his detailed and insightful examination of labor-management relationships in the steel and automobile industry, Richard Herding argues[11] that since the 1950s, the industrial unions have shifted from reliance on "labor power" to the use of "union influence" in responding to workers' needs and problems, particularly those that are direct outcomes of changes at the work place. The celebratory discussion of a maturing system of industrial relations by U.S. scholars in the 1950s tended to focus primarily on economic advances, the achievement of stability in the employer-union relationship, and the replacement of stoppages by orderly processes for settling disputes and grievances. Herding argues that the evaluation that flows from this focus is incomplete. It largely overlooked the question of what was happening at the work place.

Mass unions that represent the entire organized work force in a plant cannot deal with all work-related problems that arise in each of the many different job settings. By contrast, a craft union normally deals with problems common to workers with similar jobs and tasks. The mass unions rely on overall protections such as seniority clauses and general processes for dispute settlement through adjudicatory mechanisms, such as the grievance procedure, to deal with the consequences of change. Change that threatens to eliminate elements in the work process is a direct challenge to craft unions because it threatens the self-interest of their membership. Technological changes in an industrial setting affect work assignments, work pace, work location, and other variables: Only sometimes do they reach skill content. Unions can negotiate over the impact of these changes and seek an appropriate quid pro quo for those affected. So long as industrial unions have the power to limit management's unilateral acts and secure concessions through negotiation, the overall interests of the mass of workers can be effectively protected.

Seniority clauses, for example, control the impact of change on workers but do not truly limit managerial decision-making. They determine the order in which workers are affected by using such criteria as age and length of service in the plant or department and protect the employee's rights to transfers, rehiring, and other rights. In this way, they balance the rights of different membership groups and resolve intergroup conflict. The wide diversity of occupations and employee groups in industrial plants produces internal union debates on the priority to be assigned to each group's needs and demands. The skilled group in the automobile industry provoked a serious internal dispute in connection with the ratification of the 1973 settlement.

Division among blue-collar workers grows proportionately as more nonwhites than whites occupy the lower-level blue-collar jobs. They in turn elect increasing numbers of nonwhites to be shop stewards and to local union offices. Aggrieved employees, both union and nonunion, have appealed outside of the bargaining system to federal agencies for relief, and an increasing number of companies and associated unions have been required to eliminate discriminatory practices and to compensate those injured by past patterns of discrimination.

Local union leaders must face internal divisions which reflect skill level, status, sex, and racial dimensions. Their established constituencies are built on older groups within the union, usually the more skilled male whites. But changes in the composition of their membership present a real source of internal tension.[12] Individual leaders may accept a "responsible" relationship to employers as the necessary price of survival. They increasingly speak for those whom Herding calls the "hard-core employed," but this course is conducive to internal division. He sees an

> emerging pattern of feudalization, hierarchiza-
> tion, and efficiency intensification [which] forms
> the common substantive rationale for management
> and "responsible union leadership," and its more
> or less articulate rejection provides a common
> platform both for intra-union opposition and for
> those at the fringe or in the core of exclusion
> from the new workers' paradise.[13]

348 WORKER MILITANCYWORKER MILITANCY

## MANAGEMENT INITIATIVES

Management consistently seeks to acquire greater control over the production process in order to improve efficiency and reduce costs. Moving beyond the long-established techniques of wage incentives and job evaluation, disciples of modern management employ new techniques of organizational change that drastically change traditional methods of production. These include job enrichment, team-building, and similar departures developed through extensive research and development.

The union response to the newer management methods has been mixed. In national conferences on work redesign, for example, while some union spokesmen have adopted the traditional approach of mistrust, others have participated actively in such discussions with employers. It is of course true that worker resistance to total control can never be overcome. Early studies in nonunion settings showed how effectively workers resist efforts to speed up work or improve efficiency through changes in methods. Where worker leverage is greatest, unions can effectively support and organize this resistance, slowing the introduction of new technology or improved efficiency. But where new technology or new organizational patterns are pervasive, unions cannot prevent their introduction. They negotiate on the impact of change, seeking to protect or compensate the affected group as a whole. The negotiations are between the two institutions-- management and union. The focus shifts from the shop floor or work setting to the pay envelope, the seniority list, layoff provisions, transfer and retaining clauses and similar measures.

When these efforts fail, as in the late 1960s, workers express their disapproval with union performance through wildcat stoppages, contract rejections, and support of opposition candidates, particularly in local elections.

There is little objective evidence that management success in the effort to contain unionism has weakened workers' basic commitment to their unions. Data from National Labor Relations Board (NLRB) deauthorization elections show that the number of dissatisfied workers has been small--never more than 30,000 in a year-- and that few large establishments have been involved.

This is because the labor movement has in effect a monopoly on the methods by which the issues of struggle in the work place are defined and the instruments tested and utilized. No other institution pretends to contest this role. As long as this is the case, unionism will remain the indispensable instrument for expressing workers' attitudes, responses, and desires with regard to work and its rewards. Conflicts between generations, among racial groups, and between different skill and status levels will continue and even

increase in importance, but these struggles will be fought and resolved within the union and between union and employer.

In their discussion of worker responses to management methods, Sumner H. Slichter and his colleagues demonstrated that, despite occasional dramatic episodes, neither worker nor union resistance has had any significant effect in limiting management's ability
to introduce new methods or other efficiency-raising changes. Outside of the craft unions, they reported "no evidence of serious concern" about union or worker response to these changes. [14] And while
they found few cases of labor-management collaboration to improve
productivity, there is now increased activity of this kind led by the
United Steelworkers and the steel industry. Similar efforts to secure
higher productivity and limit work stoppages are being recorded in
parts of the construction industry.

Industrial workers are subjected to constraints and controls
that are as rigorous and oppressive as any in the past, and their response is no different than in the past. Unions respond to worker
resistance to change by establishing or revalidating the union's right
to negotiate its impact on employment, job and skill levels, pay, and
production standards. Once this is done, resistance tends to recede,
though sporadic outbursts do occur. In this respect, industrial relations patterns and practice have not changed in recent decades in industry.


## EFFECTS OF CHANGES ON UNIONS


The new dilemma of U.S. unionism is the fact that collective
bargaining, which has always been the primary instrument for the
achievement of worker and union objectives, now faces important
constraints that limit its effectiveness and usefulness. But the union
movement is so fully specialized in this approach that unions may
find it difficult to adapt successfully to a new environment.

Industrial unionism successfully exploited the favorable economic conditions that prevailed during the war and postwar periods:
In effect they exacted a share of the gains of the large oligopolistic
firms in major industrial sectors. High demand was maintained in
part by major federal programs--building a large federal highway
system, developing a massive military machine and production capa-
bility, and underwriting a large-scale expansion of suburban hous-
ing--which helped to extend and consolidate the commanding position
of large corporate entities. These measures helped to stabilize the
economy at low levels of unemployment, masked only by the emergence of structural and area unemployment.

The craft unions held their own by maintaining their traditional ability to negotiate from the strength of limited numbers of members holding needed skills, where the costs to management from concessions were outweighed by those that would result from shutting down the work site, which in industrial settings meant loss of all production.

In these circumstances the collective bargaining seemed to work well. Employers, many of whom had feared and resisted the unionization of their work force, found positive merits in unionism, advantages that management could realize. The professional literature of the postwar period reflects this view. Economists pointed out that unionism often offers concrete benefits to management. The National Planning Association sponsored a long-term study of 30 separate labor-management relationships to establish principles that would explain, as its title indicates, The Causes of Industrial Peace Under Collective Bargaining. Models of collective bargaining relationships were offered, which suggested a natural progression from hostility through stability and then, hopefully, in the direction of labor-management cooperation. A consensus emerged that the best national policy was to leave the parties free to work out their own relationships and settlements. The Taft-Hartley provisions regulating and limiting strike action in national emergency disputes were increasingly perceived by professional writers as cumbersome, rigid, and ineffective. Public opinion supported the view that free collective bargaining, though imperfect and sometimes disruptive, was the necessary and appropriate process for resolving labor-management disputes and that the system that had developed was an integral part of the U.S. economy. This has become the "conventional wisdom" endorsed by business, government, labor, and academic spokesmen.

By the late 1950s and early 1960s, a few dissenting voices began to express doubt or concern that the progress that had been made could be sustained.[15] More recent experience has provided added reasons for doubt and concern. Eight important factors can be cited:

1. Industrial management has successfully resisted union efforts to expand the scope of bargaining and to secure substantial new benefits. Over the 1965-73 period, real spendable wages of factory workers with families increased by less than 1 percent per year and declined in five of the eight years. By contrast, real spendable earnings between 1960 and 1965 rose every year, at an annual average of 2.4 percent. And while existing benefits have been improved, only a limited number of new items of major importance, such as prepaid dental benefits and earlier retirement at age 62, have been added to the range of established fringe benefits. Even the lifetime employment guarantee won for the typesetters on New York City newspapers recalls similar earlier achievements for crafts on the railroads.

2. Nonunion or minimally organized sectors have become dominant in the economy. Organizing efforts are only beginning to have a national impact in state and local government and have scarcely made any national headway in such major sectors as health and hospitals, banking, insurance, recreation, and so on. In these industries, outside of a few strongly organized subsectors, management can operate unilaterally or with minimal consultation with employee groups.

3. Free collective bargaining and the right to strike are increasingly unacceptable to broad sectors of public and political opinion; indeed, many workers, and some union leaders, share these views. Thus unions are increasingly inhibited in pushing negotiations to the point of impasse, where, in the past, strike action was both plausible and effective in securing concessions from employers.

4. The pressure of imports and the decline of U.S. export strength in the industrial sector pushed unions increasingly to seek tariff and other protection through federal legislation and action. This leads unions and their industries to act together in seeking help. Even the United Automobile Workers suggested limitations on imports. This collaboration in turn undermines the independent posture that is necessary if unions are to exert their full leverage at the bargaining table.

5. Slowed rates of productivity increase lead labor and management in search of mechanisms for joint action to improve productivity, even though this also must alter the traditional posture of independence at the bargaining table. The steel industry and the United Steelworkers have taken significant steps in this direction, and others are watching this effort with interest.

6. Recent inflation created a situation that severely limits the freedom of unions and employers to set their own terms. Wage and price controls were imposed once and could be again. In periods of strong governmental pressure, official or unofficial, on wages, unions lose their freedom of action.

7. Unemployment rates, except during the height of the Vietnam war, rose above the levels that prevailed during the 1947-57 period. Even more important, conservative economic policies and pronouncements increased public tolerance of rising unemployment rates above 4 percent, arguing that efforts to reduce unemployment may increase inflation and thus have weakened the basic labor market situation facing many unions.

8. Unions in some industries face added economic difficulties. Technological change has undercut the power of the typesetters and other crafts in the printing industry; nonunion competition has grown substantially in construction; aerospace unions face declining demand; and legislation to protect the environment and control pollution may curtail jobs in a variety of unionized industries.

Unions like those in the maritime industry long ago learned to look to state action for help, but for the bulk of U.S. unions, this dependence is new and raises serious difficulties. Unions are a political minority in a period when the balance of political power has moved to the side of business; public opinion accepts unionism as legitimate and necessary but opposes further increases in the economic or political power of the union movement. Critics of unionism have focused on shortcomings within the labor movement without being sufficiently sensitive to the changing circumstances that face the unions and make adjustment increasingly difficult.

As collective bargaining proves increasingly less able to function with freedom and effectiveness, further economic advances for workers depend increasingly on the actions of outside agencies. Unions must seek recognition and help from the state; their political effectiveness, not their militance or their economic leverage, becomes the key to success. This reduces their political independence; their political choices are conditioned by the need to preserve and increase their ability to secure political objectives, far more than was true in the past. Until the imposition of wage and price controls in 1971, periods when the route to wage and benefits increases led through Washington were confined to special, temporary situations, such as World War II and the Korean War. Now this process is becoming more often the normal one; periods of free unfettered bargaining will be the exception, not the rule in the future.

This new relationship to the state carries with it a price. Those who wield political power can reward or punish client groups according to whether the political behavior and posture of these groups meets the needs of the power-holders. In the past the trade union movement, and in particular the industrial unions, have acted on the whole as a liberal force in society. They were committed to programs of social change and reform and to the use of the power of the state to curb and control corporate power and to improve the welfare of the poor and the powerless. They worked for more progressive taxation, higher minimum wages, and generous welfare and income support policies. They sought a larger role for the state in providing, financing, and monitoring health care, education, and social services.

The energy with which these positions and commitments are pursued, except as they directly reflect members' interests, may be reduced with the continuing dependence of unions on state action and corporate largesse. Collaboration with employers in improving productivity, curbing the "excesses" of the consumer movement, and opposing the job-threatening aspects of the environmental protection movement will become acts of self-interest. The need to protect jobs against erosion has been a major reason for the consistent support of high levels of military expenditures by the AFL-CIO. Efforts to reduce highway spending meet the opposition of the automobile, trucking, and construction unions.

This pattern will become more characteristic in the future now that the federal government appears to have become a permanent participant at the bargaining table. Unions will need to develop a special relationship with both the executive and legislative branches of government, to assure steadily rising incomes and employment protection to the organized sector of the labor force. It leads in the direction of the erosion of the trade union movement's historic identification with the underprivileged and the powerless and of its commitment to social change and social reform.

As the issues of social reform came increasingly to life and to the political forefront during the 1960s, the constraints that had already begun to take hold exerted their influence on labor unions and helped to shape the union response to these issues. Labor's role--sometimes divided, sometimes aloof, on the issues of racial justice and the war--help to explain the erosion of the larger base of liberal and public support the labor movement had established through its struggles and successes in 1935-45 and the increasing isolation of the trade union movement from the newer forces of social change that emerged during these later struggles. They illuminate the defensive posture of the unions, the failure to organize, the concentration on protecting gains already won rather than seeking to break new ground.

But, as we have seen, these efforts could not prevent stagnation for many workers on the primary issue of improving real wages and benefits. The strength of the corporations, the indifference or hostility of the state, the inability of the unions to secure effective action to reduce or control inflation led to a standstill for many unionized groups, to an increasing sense of frustration and concern, to doubts about the viability of the institution itself.

In this situation, why did not the union movement recognize that the struggles of the 1960s offered an opportunity to them to take a leadership role, to build a coalition of forces that would move the struggle to improve workers' incomes, benefits, and status away from the bargaining relationship, where it had stagnated, to the larger political and economic arena and there to confront the economic and political power of the employers and their allies?

We noted at the outset the absence in U.S. labor history of an institutional commitment to the concept of class struggle as necessary for the liberation of the working class. At the work place, class struggle has been as intense and serious in the U.S. setting as in any other, and more so than in most Western countries, but its focus has always been local. Instances of class struggle in

American labor history lack a cumulative or unified character; each
new confrontation yields a pragmatic accommodation; it is not perceived as a new stage in the conflict between two classes on the stage
of history. Without a long tradition of working-class struggle or a
tradition that links individual conflicts to a shared set of goals of the
working class as a whole, the conclusion of an individual struggle,
even one of major proportions, like the 1959 steel strike or the
dramatic 1972 Lordstown strike, leads the parties back to the pattern
of case-by-case accommodation. The energies of workers and their
union focus on the proximate causes of their dissatisfaction--a wage
increase denied, a new method unilaterally introduced, an arbitrary
act of discipline--and the struggle slackens when that specific obstacle has been overcome. The fight is at the level of plant and not
over the pattern of ownership or control that prevails in the industry;
its focus is on the specific instruments of exploitation or abuse, not
on the class or group on whose behalf they are utilized. The U.S.
trade union movement has not developed the capacity or the vocabu-
lary that would make it possible to confront employers as a class in
political struggle over those issues of direct interest to workers that
cannot any longer be satisfactorily dealt with through collective bargaining.

This lack of an ideological framework for struggle is not unique
to the trade union movement; it has affected and ultimately limited
other serious efforts at social or economic change, including the far-
reaching efforts made by U.S. blacks in the 1960s.

## FORCES FOR CHANGE IN AMERICAN UNIONS

Unions of blue-collar workers, predominantly industrial and
in the private sector, have been the mainstream of the U.S. labor
movement. Until recently white-collar unions and unions of public
employees were small, weak, and unimportant, and efforts to organize farm workers have repeatedly failed. In recent years some
writers have argued that the U.S. economy has been changing from
an industrial to a service society. Among other changes, this means
that nonmanual workers outnumber manual workers in the labor
force; they work in smaller settings than are typical in industry;
they were employed where control of work content cannot be centrally planned and controlled to the degree found in industry, where
technology and economies of scale have less application, work content cannot be as fully routinized, and workers themselves are more
visible, and closer to, those who use the services, than is the case
in industry. And many work for public or nonprofit employers,
while most workers in the long-unionized sectors are employed by
privately owned, profit-seeking employers.

In recent years unions of public employees have grown far faster than others and have become the focus of public discussion of labor policy issues, as were the industrial unions in the 1930s, 1940s, and 1950s. These unions bring new sources of energy and vitality to the labor movement. They also raise important issues about the future of the labor movement, of collective bargaining, and of political action in promoting workers' objectives. Blue-collar and white-collar workers are in some important respects different, as may be their unions. Relationships and reciprocal perception are still evolving, sometimes with strain and tension, as this new sector of organized labor develops its own shape and faces its special problems. Clerks and sales workers, hospital aides, social workers, and teachers work in different settings and often behave and think differently from industrial workers. Their large-scale entry into unionism has only recently begun. Relatively few have so far been involved in serious confrontation with employers reacting to their efforts to organize. Leaders and members of older unions often regard these efforts skeptically and find it difficult to identify with them, though there has been some wholehearted support.

In recent years these newer unions have begun to assume greater importance within the labor movement. Two officers of the major public-employee unions--the AFSCME and the AFT--were elevated to the executive council of the AFL-CIO. Dramatic struggles, like that of the garbage workers in Memphis in 1968, in which Martin Luther King Jr. lost his life, and the hospital workers in Charleston in 1969 have won respect and support from the older unions. Farm workers, led by Cesar Chavez, struggled for several years without much union support, but their stubborn persistence and dedication brought the AFL-CIO officially to their side.

These unions face serious obstacles. No general federal law protects the rights of public employees or farm workers to organize and bargain. Public employees must proceed state by state, often facing hostile legislatures. Recognition is often conditional, and union rights are severely curtailed. A 1972 survey, analyzing 286 agreements covering 613,490 public employees, found:[16]

- a majority contained no-strike provisions;
- only 40 percent provided a union role in disciplinary proceedings;
- only 55 percent provided for binding arbitration of grievances;
- only 58 percent dealt with procedures and criteria for promotion;
- only 17 percent provided for any form of union security and, among these, the most frequent was the weakest, an agency shop provision.

Yet these unions show great organizing and negotiation energy.
Their potential growth and strength has clearly impressed the leadership of the labor movement, and they carry increasing weight in the
inner councils.

These workers are increasingly found in what may be termed
"consumer-intensive" industries, like public and nonprofit services--
health, education, government services--or private firms such as
banks, stores, insurance offices, and so on. In these areas, employees often must collaborate with customers and consumers, and vice
versa. In supermarkets, doctors' offices, outpatient departments,
schools and colleges, customers--or clients or patients--perform
many activities that affect or determine the outcome of the activities
of the enterprise.

This requires a different management approach to issues of
productivity and control. In industry, engineering and technical attention is focused on the product or the process. In service industries, management success depends on its ability to enlist the cooperation of employees and to secure appropriate behavior, often in
direct relationship to the client or consumer. Here industrial engineering methods are of less use than those derived from psychology,
organizational theory, group dynamics, and similar disciplines.

Another important difference is the concern of some groups of
public and service sector employees with the content of their work
and the quality of the service they provide. Issues in this area are
becoming important in negotiations in education, are frequently invoked in social services and mental health, and are discussed by
unions of health and hospital workers. In part this interest stems
from the identification of such workers with the service, in part
from the fact that they bear the brunt of dissatisfaction and discontent when the public finds reason to complain or distrust what is being offered. If people buy cars that are shoddy or soup that is tainted,
they blame the firms that make them, but when the garbage is not
collected or children fail to progress in school, they blame the garbage collectors or the teachers. And because public employees work
in institutions directly supported by tax funds, the public expresses
its views more directly than is the case even with bad telephone service, which is privately provided.

A third important difference is the absence of a fundamental
conflict of interest between the immediate public employers and public employees and the presence of some major common interests between them. Public employers are not profit-makers. While they
must deal with issues of cost and productivity, these issues take a
different shape than in the private sector. It is not the marketplace
or stockholders but political constituencies to whom they are accountable. The relationship between them and their employees is often

one of mutual survival and dependence, with issues of supremacy or power secondary. The logic of the service sector, particularly public service, is in the direction of consent and collaboration. In the private sector, the fundamental interests of workers and owners are opposed. But, in the public sector, the basis for this conflict of interests is absent in most work relationships. Both employees and public institutions have a stake in overcoming the lack of respect shown to the public sector. Rising tax loads in cities and counties, and increasing discontent with the quality and level of many public services, have put the public sector even more sharply on the defensive in recent years. Proposals or concrete steps have been taken to contract school services to private firms, to make public and private schools compete, to establish quasipublic corporations to run major public services, and in other ways to give the private sector a larger role. Such steps threaten both employees and public institutions; both have an interest in restoring confidence in the ability of local government to perform. Finally, the refusal by Congress and the executive to provide the support needed by large cities has raised major fiscal problems for them, calling into question the ability of their governments to provide necessary services and posing a serious threat to the job security of city employees.

To deal with these problems, coalitions of employee groups and the governments that employ their members are needed. More is at stake than self-interest. The cities are where unresolved issues of race, social injustice, and inequality are most sharply posed and most concentrated. Increasingly the public employees are members of racial and ethnic minorities, just as once public employment was an important avenue to opportunity for white immigrant groups. This new membership base provides added motivation for public employee unions to take an active part in dealing with the urban issues of our time. Many of the leaders of these unions take as their model of unionism the social commitment of the CIO during the 1930s and 1940s. But they have an institutional as well as a personal motivation for an activist role. Solving urgent problems of housing, education, income maintenance, and racial inequality is critical to the very survival of the cities in which they and their members must work and live.

This does not mean that all public-employee unions are socially activist. Indeed some of the horizontal unions resemble the craft unions of the private sector in their racial and social attitudes; for them the primary struggle is still to preserve their relative advantage over those of lower status and less pay. But many public employees are organized in vertical unions on the industrial model; they find it natural as well as necessary to take up the burden of legitimizing major new national commitments to the solution of the problems of

the cities, in collaboration with other urban-based groups and with
city governments. Because they have found it necessary to develop
political effectiveness, they also have at hand some of the necessary
tools for waging this struggle on the state and national scenes.
AFSCME in recent years has provided several important examples
of activities of this kind.

At what is still an early stage in the development of public-
sector unionism, these comments are admittedly speculative to a
degree. Public-employee unionism is still weak. More important,
large sectors of the services sector are mostly or totally nonunionized; millions of workers in banks, insurance companies, and wholesale and retail trade are outside union ranks. Their collective self-
interest as they see it may well diverge sharply from that of the organized public employees whose unions often seek to model themselves on the social activism and egalitarian ethos of the CIO. In
the service sector, we are very far indeed from serious mass unionization and cannot predict how long organization will take or what,
when it comes, its political and ideological direction will be. Public-
employee unionism is, however, a reality; its record to date, while
not conclusive, and its likely development in the future cannot be ignored.

## UNIONISM, POLITICS, AND THE FUTURE

At the present the trade union movement is divided and isolated
from liberal, women, minority, and youth groups. The convergence
of separate union groups around the increased need for political effectiveness is still in its early stages. The ending of the older political direction, in which labor was firmly allied to the liberal wing
of the Democratic Party, began to emerge clearly in the mid-1960s,
when many union members were alienated or threatened by the pressures of the black community for jobs and housing; while many unions
worked closely with black leadership in the 1963 march on Washington, the conservative elements in the leadership of the AFL-CIO had
already begun to distance themselves from the new black activism.
By the 1968 presidential election, the inroads made by George Wallace
of Alabama, deliberately playing on working-class fears and concerns
in the North as well as the South, showed how far polarization between nonblack workers and blacks had gone; it took extraordinary
efforts by the AFL-CIO to hold a large labor vote for the Democratic
candidate.

By the 1972 election the labor movement was fragmented as
never before in modern history; some of the liberal unions supported
George McGovern, but most union leaders followed George Meany's

lead in stating their neutrality, and some actively supported the
Nixon candidacy; among them, notably, was Frank Fitzsimmons,
Hoffa's successor in the International Brotherhood of Teamsters
(IBT).

This repudiation of traditional support for the Democratic
Party was only in part a hedge in the face of the evidence that blue-
collar workers opposed McGovern and his domestic program. If the
political stakes for the trade union movement had not appeared to be
so high, there would have been less resistance to McGovern, more
of an effort to modify some of his views and program emphases in
order to mollify worker wariness and hostility, and a higher propensity to risk defeat for the sake of preserving labor's role on the liberal side of the ongoing national struggle between liberal and conservative values. But the concrete issues at stake for important
groups of U.S. labor did not appear to justify taking this risk.

The decision to keep open the door to a Nixon-controlled administration rested on the belief that achieving organized labor's
central objectives requires action by the federal government. These
goals include wage increases, pension protection, job protection,
protection of workers against job-related hazards, control of escalating health-care costs, and possible federal assumption of such
costs that are not negotiated as part of the bargaining package. As
the focus shifts away from the bargaining table to the actions of
Congress and the administration, organized labor's energies begin
to shift and change. After wage controls were imposed in 1971, many
unions experienced delay, reduction, or denial of bargained increases
at the hands of the federal wage control apparatus. They learned the
importance of a political counterpart to bargaining effectiveness.
Controls were lifted, but the lessons of that experience remain a
warning for the future. Similarly, unions have tried in vain to exercise direct control over the ability of conglomerate and multinational
corporations to control job location and the division of production;
many groups have experienced losses in membership and stiffened
economic resistance in bargaining, as a result of increased corporate
strength and flexibility. Unions saw that only federal action could effectively protect their members and help them to counter the threat
of moving jobs, functions, even whole plants out of union reach. The
same considerations apply to the struggle, which unions have not been
able to win, to protect negotiated pension rights against the risk of
plant closing, inadequate funding, excessive administrative costs that
water down benefits, and other well-documented abuses. And even to
mount a research and development effort of the scope needed to restore important lost ground in the competitive edge of U.S. industry
will probably require expenditures of a level and scope that require
federal action.

For all these reasons, the industrial and manual unions have been changing their relationship to the national administration from one of relative autonomy to one of increasing collaboration. In turn this frees the conservative, probusiness administrations that have dominated national political life in recent years from the need to balance their biases in order to limit the political risks that would be posed by labor-liberal opposition. Similarly the conservative elements in the trade union movement need take less heed of the views of the more liberal groups to maximize the unions' effectiveness in their dealings with the national government.

Certainly Nixon was not slow to recognize and exploit these needs and constraints in his 1968 and 1972 campaigns, the latter being enormously successful. He understood that the importance of state action made it possible for his administration to divide the unions, manipulate labor's fears and insecurities, and in the process begin to create a version of the corporate state with the central government playing the dominant role.

The 1972 election results indicated that significant progress had been made in this direction and that major segments of the union movement had been delivered into his hands. Though events thereafter destroyed Nixon's power to move any further in this direction, the basic constellation of forces has not been changed by Watergate and its many aftermaths; more skilled, more secure successors will still hold many of the keys to the resolution of labor's goals and difficulties and will therefore have major power to shape and control how labor's energies and strength are deployed, at the bargaining table as well as in national political life.

The picture is complicated, however, by the fact that the newer unions, led by the public-employee groups, are also beginning to assume an important position in national political life. For them too, success depends on the actions of the national administration and the Congress. Because they have always needed political success, such a role, even on the national level, comes naturally. They too face the need to protect their ability to negotiate wage and salary increases from either wage control or erosion through inflation and to safeguard the health and welfare benefits negotiated for their members. To this extent, they share the agenda of the older private-sector unions. But they have other needs that tend to move them in political directions that differ from those of the private-sector industrial and manual unions. Their need to restore the fiscal and economic viability of the nation's cities requires that they be linked to other important groups whose fate rests on the success of this effort; these include the major racial and civil rights organizations as well as important segments of the intellectual and liberal community, two groups that have increasingly been alienated from the trade union movement over the postwar period. Thus it was not surprising that the United Automobile Workers, the major exception among industrial unions to the drift away from liberalism, and the AFSCME took the lead among the coalition of unions that opposed Meany's decision not to support the 1972 Democratic candidate. Those allied with them included unions that feel less the threat of imports or job export on the one hand, and those--like the Communication Workers of America (CWA), the Amalgamated Meat Cutters, and Amalgamated Clothing Workers-- whose leaders have traditionally been offended by or independent of Meany's leadership.

The younger leadership of the newer unions has a more natural affinity with activist liberal writers and political figures and the constituencies whose goals they articulate. They are less threatened by the liberal intelligentsia. They believe that the welfare of the workers they represent is connected to that of blacks, the aged, the working poor, the welfare population, and others in the nation's cities, and that they must build coalitions and political movements with those groups. Finally, their membership now and in future will include nonwhites and Spanish-speaking workers as major components, on whom they will depend for support.

Thus, while political effectiveness holds the key to the future of U.S. unionism, there is more than one direction in which this need leads its component groups. While the progressive elements are a minority, their strength is growing and their vigor contrasts sharply with the relative somnolence of some older elements. Their decision during the 1972 campaign was vindicated by the subsequent collapse of the Nixon-Agnew group and thus of the commitments that were assumed to flow from labor's decision not to oppose them. But as long as conservative, probusiness forces continue to dominate political life and to control the levers of national power, the self-interest of the trade union movement means continued dependence on actions and decisions of the state. The incipient forces of social change that gathered strength and momentum in the 1960s remain scattered and disorganized. The debacle of the Nixon-Agnew group was led and controlled by conventional political groups, not by liberals; the opportunities that might have been offered in this period of disarray to reconstitute the liberal coalitions and to restate with renewed emphasis the liberal agenda remained unrecognized and were not acted upon. After a period of unprecedented inflation, which eroded workers' incomes and shifted income distribution sharply in favor of corporate profits, the strength of the corporate sector remained unimpaired and unchallenged. The trade union movement in the 1968-73 period was unable either to restore its power at the work place and bargaining table or to assert its strength and influence in decisive national issues at the political level.

One cannot conclude without a reminder that the trade union movement has appeared in the past incapable of responding to new conditions and new challenges yet has emerged in retrospect with important achievements and with new relevance to the lives of workers and the needs of society. There is reason for cautious hope that this will again be the case. In his penetrating study of Western painting[17] John Berger describes our situation as "the industrial society which has moved towards democracy and then stopped halfway." While there are many candidates who profess the ability to help complete that process, the union movement is the one indispensable component of the struggle.

## NOTES

1. Neil W. Chamberlain, "Collective Bargaining in the Private Sector," in The Next Twenty-Five Years of Industrial Relations, ed. Gerald R. Somers (Madison, Wis.: Industrial Relations Research Association, 1973), p. 19.

2. "The Labor Movement: A Re-Examination," a conference in honor of David J. Saposs, January 14-15, 1966, University of Wisconsin, p. 18.

3. "The Labor Movement," American Federationist 80 (November 1973): 19.

4. U.S. Department of Labor, Bureau of Labor Statistics, Selected Earnings and Demographic Characteristics of Union Members, 1970, Report 417 (Washington, D.C.: Government Printing Office, 1972), Table 2.

5. Gilbert Burck, "The Merger Movement Rides High," Fortune 79 (February 1969): 80.

6. Charles Craypo, "Collective Bargaining in the Multinational Conglomerate Corporation: Litton's Shutdown of Royal Typewriter," manuscript, p. 41.

7. A recent analysis of these questions, including a critical analysis of such major studies as those of the U.S. Tariff Commission, the U.S. Department of Commerce, and the Brookings Institution, is found in "The Employment Impact of Multinational Corporations," Institute of Public Administration, January 1974, a report to the Manpower Administration, U.S. Department of Labor. See also chapters 7 and 8 of Duane Kujawa, ed., American Labor and the Multinational Corporation (New York: Praeger Publishers, 1973).

8. "Steel Pact Cited as Model for New Bargaining Era," AFL-CIO News, April 7, 1973, p. 1.

9. U.S. Department of Labor, Selected Earnings and Demographic Characteristics of Union Members, op. cit., pp. 2-3 and Table 6.

10. Nation's Business, September 1973, p. 39.

11. R. Herding, Job Control and Union Structure (Rotterdam: Rotterdam University Press, 1972), pp. 116, 121-22.

12. Ibid., p. 347. The Coalition of Black Trade Unionists organized in 1972 claims that 15 percent of the U.S. trade union membership is black, and the Coalition for Labor Union Women established in 1974 estimates that women compose 20 percent of the membership. Both seek higher proportion of representation in the leadership and the promotion of their specific interests and views both in collective bargaining and the legislative and administrative programs and activities.

13. Ibid., p. 36.

14. Sumner H. Slichter, James J. Healy, and E. Roberts Livernash, The Impact of Collective Bargaining on Management (Washington, D.C.: Brookings Institution, 1960), p. 265; cf. also pp. 670-68.

15. Solomon Barkin, The Decline of the Labor Movement (Santa Barbara, Cal.: Center for the Study of Democratic Institutions, 1961); Joseph A. Beirne, New Horizons for American Labor (Washington, D.C.: Public Affairs Press, 1962); Paul Jacobs, The State of the Unions (New York: Athenaeum, 1963); Sidney Lens, The Crisis of American Labor (New York: A. S. Barnes, 1959); and Richard A. Lester, As Unions Mature (Princeton: Princeton University Press, 1958).

16. U.S. Department of Labor, Bureau of Labor Statistics, Municipal Collective Bargaining Agreements in Large Cities, Bulletin 1759 (Washington, D.C.: Government Printing Office, 1972).

17. John Berger, Ways of Seeing (London: Pelican, 1972), p. 148.

SUMMARY AND
CONCLUSION:
REDESIGNING COLLECTIVE
BARGAINING AND CAPITALISM
Solomon Barkin

The economic and social changes of the third postwar decade are producing significant alterations in Western European nations and less fundamental ones in the two North American countries. The structures, locus of power, and rules of conduct of capitalism in Europe are being modified. At the economic-political level, two trends are significant. One is the growing interdependence of national economies, at a time when governments are seeking to become more effective operators of their internal systems. Monopolistic prices are frustrating national efforts at attaining stability and growth. The second is the basic revision in the industrial relations systems. Employees and trade unions* in most countries are acquiring greater rights to participate in decision-making. Employees and unions are receiving more information on the enterprise as a business operation and on matters affecting personnel. Bilateral (with management) or multilateral (with both employers and government) bargaining rights are now applicable to an expanding range of subjects at the job, plant, company, industry, and national economic levels. Trade unions are also aspiring for similar rights in shaping European economic and social policy and administration.

Recent advances in labor and social standards, earnings, benefits, and working conditions in Europe and in Canada are narrowing the historic gap between the high achievements in the United States and those in these other countries, and if the full range of public services is included, the current difference may be very small for

---

*Throughout this chapter, "union center" or "confederation" refers to national associations of industrial, category, craft or other unions or federations.

countries such as Canada, West Germany, and Sweden. The new economic power won by labor and trade union aggressiveness is forcing governments--but least of all that of the United States--to fashion more equitable responses to current economic challenges.

In response to the new restlessness, militancy, and broader expectations shared by the established work force, trade union leaders and labor movement (broadly including the labor and socialist parties) are relinquishing the complacent attitudes that marked the decades since 1945. Now a humanistic socialism characterizes these movements, favoring increased unity through cooperation or mergers of national union centers. A more independent political stance supports their advocacy of policies and negotiations for them with governments and political parties. And a new confidence also prevails that stems from greater coherence within the movement, the large popular base, and the conviction that their efforts are essential to a more equitable and effective system.

Governments responded to the new demands and pressures by legislating some expectations into existence, particularly where employers and their associations resisted voluntary advances. As employers of a substantial proportion of the work force and having the responsibility for devising programs to attain national socioeconomic objectives, governments have also become more intimately involved in the processes of collective bargaining. Employers and their associations have modified their position on some issues though hardly in areas affecting their basic prerogatives of ownership; it was here that governments have interceded to achieve domestic tranquility, though as yet with limited consequences.

As confrontation with the intense problems of inflation, commodity shortages, and international payments become more pervasive and as the issue of the maintenance of living standards becomes more central, nations are likely to look to greater coordination and collaboration of employers, trade unions, employees, and governments in their solution. Trade unions are demanding as a quid pro quo greater participation in bilateral and multilateral decision-making and socially equitable programs.


## NEW ACTIVISM

Vast changes are flowing from the unrest pervading the industrial world. Governments more than employers have realized that these were imperative. Canada and Great Britain have conducted extensive reviews of their industrial relations systems. Even conservative governments were ready to act, but where they sought to restrain trade unions, they soon learned, as in Great Britain, that

only a constructive and nonrepressive course could win labor's cooperation. Here too the United States was an exception, for the Nixon
government did not seek contacts with the major union centers.

To understand the nature of labor discontent, one must first examine the activist groups as indicators of the new forces and then
identify the specific strains and frustrations pervading the work force.
No statistical measures are available objectively to rank the dissident
groups by importance; moreover, individuals may belong to several
such groups.

## Groups of Activists

Among those being considered, youth clearly deserves to be
first. Raised in the confident postwar years in a time of "rising affluence uninterrupted by major economic dislocations," it was not
satisfied merely with what was available. It tended to prize humanistic goals, including free speech and social-political participation.
This sentiment was almost universal among young people of all economic and social categories.[1] Workers among them became active
participants and often leaders in strikes, demonstrations, and protests demanding further advances.

Foreign labor, including illegal entrants, perceptibly increased
to 9 million in Europe and to possibly more than half of that number in
the two North American countries. This work force plays an important part in the economy of most industrial nations, constituting nearly
9 percent of the working population of northern Europe. Considered
second-class citizens, they have suffered discrimination and exploitation and lived under the threat of deportation. Their complaints,
even if heard, were not regularly processed by works councils or
trade unions.[2]

Their early submissive attitudes in time gave way to overt protests. Tending to follow native workers who went on strike, they
learned the value of initiatives that would secure remedies for their
complaints. They often received the support of youth, radical groups,
and indigenous employees. Over time, their protests increased in
number, and the range of complaints broadened.

National migrants and minorities suffered from similar problems. Southern Italians constitute a substantial part of the Northern
work force, and their difficulties have reinforced industrial turbulence since 1968. Significant strikes among minorities also occurred
in Belgium and Sweden. In the United States, Puerto Ricans and
Chicanos often protested and struck to advance their interests. So
did the blacks. Many of them joined unions and became active unionists, ultimately forming a Coalition of Black Trade Unions (CBTU)
to promote their cause.

Sectional labor groups based on linguistic, ethnic, religious, or geographical identities took similar action in Belgium, Canada, and Italy. They sought primarily correction of regional economic backwardness or the equalization of rights and wages. In Canada, local unions of U.S.-based international trade unions secured greater autonomy or set up their own national organizations.

Women also joined the activists to achieve the implementation of legislative and political commitments to equal pay for equal work or to get communities to appropriate funds for child care and other special services that would ease their lot as workers. Legal protection of women against discrimination was rare outside of the United States. Dramatic strikes on women's issues are reported in both Belgium and France. In the United States, female employees formed a Coalition of Labor Union Women (CLUW) to secure their ends and to organize women into the existing union structure.

White-collar employees both in private and public sectors in traditional and expanding industries also contributed to the volume of disturbances. Working in the new milieu of increasing equality, they sought their share of the benefits and working conditions favorable to their special interests. In Sweden their strike dramatized the demand for the maintenance of the differentials in real disposable earnings, opposing the equalitarian pressures of the LO and SAF and the SAP government. Canada, France, Germany, Italy, Sweden, United Kingdom, and the United States reported such strikes, a substantial proportion of them occurring in the public services.

The revival of radicalism further stimulated union activism. While few organized radicals were active in industrial affairs, some did penetrate worker ranks, recruited supporters among them, and at times counseled shop leaders. Their efforts reawakened some once-dormant dissatisfactions, but their active role remained for the most part limited. Most European official trade unions coopted the movements of discontent. Northern America's radicals had little if any following in industry. But they made some contribution to industrial disturbances in Belgium, Denmark, Germany, Italy, the Netherlands, Sweden, and Great Britain. In the last, for instance, they persuaded some shop stewards about the advantages and needs for direct action. Some of the radicals became key union leaders and comprised an increasingly influential "leftist" faction. Their main contribution was to force discontent to the surface, articulate issues, and, on occasion, provide local leadership. The dominant union leadership maintained its basic commitment to change through progressive advances, thereby continuing the efforts to change that the radicals often had let lapse in the 1970s.

Nonetheless, many gains were won by protesting groups. Trade unions established or intensified work among the youth, foreign, and

national blocs, and women and white-collar employees. The needs of
these groups became special articles of the union programs. Their
representatives were recruited as local leaders, and some reached
important leadership positions. Laws were liberalized to allow for
the election of foreigners to works councils, and special council
representation for youth was assured. Regional and sectional representatives received greater autonomy in such national movements as
Belgium and Canada. The ICFTU's charter of rights for foreign
workers guides national union centers and furthers the cause of foreigners in international circles. Communities are organizing for-
eigner consultative councils better to program assistance and services
for them (Belgium, Germany, and the Netherlands). Indeed, the
awakened sense of injustice and insistence on equalization of rights
and benefits established a strong foundation for continuing industrial
restlessness, and it added to that already present in the general
working community.

## Impatience with Rate of Change

Improvements in economic and social conditions in all countries
were impressive. But the social fabric felt the strains of the tugging
inequities in the distribution of benefits. Concessions to entrepreneurs for economic growth and innovation, which appeared rational
when introduced, skewed the distribution of capital ownership income
and power. Social services intended to promote equity and opportunity often disproportionately served the middle and higher socioeconomic groups, which were in a position immediately to benefit from
them. When the masses sought their share of such services, they
faced the unpreparedness of the institutions to make effective delivery
as well as the issue of public funding. The services call for massive
public expenditures. Conservative groups resist higher taxes. Administrators and established interests in higher education protested
the dilution of their "elite" services. They were not prepared to
offer a curriculum appropriate for the more popular use of the institutions. As for housing, low-income groups enjoyed few priorities
in countries such as the United States. In national public-health
care, as contrasted with the fee-for-service systems, more democratic standards prevailed. In Sweden, LO Congress delegates complained that workers carried the major costs of industrial change.
Social cleavages thus persisted in provoking social protest.

## New Sources of Frustration and Uneasiness

Recent developments have further intensified the frustration
and uneasiness in the work population. To be sure, the ascendancy

of the left in political life forced centrists in many countries to yield their dominance. Furthermore, minority and coalition governments became prevalent. But demands for expanding social services and equities continued to precipitate controversy, producing delays and disappointment. The vision of a united Europe faded, as national governments resisted the transfer of power to the projected regional federal state.

A relatively smooth rate of growth and price rises became less attainable. Higher rates of unemployment developed intermittently in several countries and threatened to become more common. But the rising rate of inflation was even more disturbing in countries where manpower programs provided adequately for the unemployed, which was general in Europe. Extraordinary increases in the prices of some basic commodities followed by large jumps in oil prices produced two-digit inflation; this was intolerable to the working population and others. Chronic deficits in international payments now became persistent problems for many countries, with the resulting need to adapt domestic policy to this new reality. If there had been any doubt about the influence of inflation on unrest, the experience of 1973 and 1974 dispelled it. Strikes increased as workers sought protection through large wage increases and contract escalator provisions.

A new problem developed as governments perceived that their national growth rates would drop. "Slumpflation" loomed as a real threat. People became troubled by talk about curtailing consumption or, at a minimum, not improving real income. Workers pondered whether they again would carry an unequal part of the cost as they believed that they had not equitably shared in the gains. It became a common question whether governments would continue to support a high-employment economy. Within the industrial relations field, job and structural changes continued at a high rate; these meant displacement, at times relocation, and, in many cases, retraining. Fears of change and queries about facilities for adjustment, maintenance of earnings, and new employment remained widespread.

As routines were upset, the number of complaints moved upward. An awareness grew of the deficiencies in the systems of handling grievances and methods of securing redress. Agreements and union structures stressed stability and not responsiveness to workers' complaints. Union officials and works councilors had become removed from the workers. One recourse was a system wherein workers and local unions would deal directly with the issues affecting them and share in the decision-making process. But the right had yet to be won. The second solution was direct action, which could also serve to gain these aforementioned rights. And in some countries, like Great Britain, national unions condoned local action as the effective way of handling the issue.

Older systems of wage settlement disintegrated in many countries. The Netherlands' long-standing formal plan of wage restraint gave way to newer arrangements. Wage controls elsewhere did not long survive. Economic calculations upon which agreements were based at times proved mistaken. Workers often took the initiative in securing adjustments through direct appeal and stoppages. As these proved more and more effective, resort to such tactics increased; so did waves of unrest and resultant worker protest.

Political action appeared even more necessary than before; workers realized most poignantly that the government was setting many policies and making decisions that controlled their very lives as well as the conditions and terms of employment. In Italy, on the other hand, unions looked to collective bargaining to compensate for governmental shortfalls.

## OBJECTIVE EVIDENCE OF UNREST

### Economic Evidence: Strikes, Absenteeism, and Labor Turnover

In Western democracies where strikes are either constitutionally sanctioned or, under certain circumstances, appropriate instruments to secure redress or, where wildcat and spontaneous strikes occur though they are officially banned, their volume offers an index of discontent. It is not the only index, and it is in fact a faulty one, since the data are not necessarily complete or reliable or fully comparable among countries.

The 1968 outbreaks in France prompted a wave of strikes. They followed a period of declining strikes, reflecting an earlier era when consensus prevailed. But after 1968 the volume of strikes was on the rise. An International Labor Office survey of 14 European and North American countries for the five-year period (1968-72) showed the rate of loss of work days from stoppages to have been highest in Italy (1,912 per 1,000 persons employed), followed by Canada (1,724), the United States (1,534), the United Kingdom (968), Ireland (964), and Finland (916). Six additional countries reported rates below 100 work days lost per 1,000 employees, and Luxembourg had no strikes at all (Table 5). A most cautious review of the data concluded that "industrial conflict had been increasing in the latter portion of the decade in many countries."[3] The peak year in work days lost differed, with three establishing it in 1969 (Canada, Ireland, and Italy), five in 1970 (Belgium, Denmark, the Netherlands, Norway, and the United States), four in 1971 (Finland, Germany, Sweden, and Switzerland), and one in 1972 (the United Kingdom). Data for 1973

TABLE 5

Days Lost through Industrial Stoppages per 1,000 Employees, by Selected Countries

| Countries | 1960 | 1961 | 1962 | 1963 | 1964 | 1965 | 1966 | 1967 | 1968 | 1969 | 1970 | 1971 | 1972 | 1973 | Average for Five Years 1963-67 | Average for Five Years 1968-72 |
|---|---|---|---|---|---|---|---|---|---|---|---|---|---|---|---|---|
| Australia[a] | 380 | 330 | 280 | 320 | 480 | 410 | 360 | 320 | 460 | 860 | 1,040 | 1,300 | 840 | 1,030 | 378 | 900 |
| Belgium | 210 | 60 | 160 | 140 | 250 | 40 | 320 | 90 | 230 | 100 | 840 | 720 | 180 | 500 | 168 | 414 |
| Canada | 310 | 510 | 590 | 330 | 560 | 790 | 1,570 | 1,200 | 1,670 | 2,550 | 2,180 | 800 | 1,420 | 1,650 | 890 | 1,724 |
| Denmark[b] | 100 | 3,340 | 30 | 40 | 30 | 400 | 30 | 20 | 20 | 80 | 170 | 30 | 40 | 4,020 | 104 | 68 |
| Finland | 130 | 50 | 30 | 1,410 | 80 | 20 | 150 | 410 | 250 | 200 | 280 | 3,320 | 530 | 2,510 | 414 | 916 |
| France | 160 | 330 | 220 | 770 | 280 | 100 | 240 | 430 | e | 200 | 190 | 430 | 290 | 330 | 364 | 277[f] |
| Federal Republic of Germany | -- | -- | 30 | 140 | -- | -- | -- | 30 | -- | 20 | 10 | 340 | -- | 40 | 34 | 74 |
| Ireland | 140 | 590 | 320 | 760 | 1,620 | 1,720 | 1,420 | 520 | 910 | 2,170 | 490 | 660 | 590 | 420 | 1,208 | 964 |
| Italy | 540 | 870 | 2,270 | 1,150 | 1,270 | 540 | 1,710 | 580 | 930 | 4,160 | 1,730 | 1,060 | 1,680 | 2,280 | 1,050 | 1,912 |
| Netherlands | 260 | 10 | -- | 20 | 20 | 30 | 10 | -- | 10 | 10 | 140 | 50 | 70 | 330 | 16 | 56 |
| Norway | -- | 570 | 130 | 360 | -- | -- | -- | 10 | 10 | -- | 70 | 10 | -- | 10 | 74 | 18 |
| Sweden[c] | 10 | -- | -- | 10 | 10 | -- | 110 | -- | -- | 30 | 40 | 240 | -- | -- | 26 | 62 |
| Switzerland | -- | -- | -- | 50 | -- | -- | -- | -- | -- | -- | 10 | 10 | -- | -- | 10 | 2 |
| United Kingdom | 240 | 220 | 440 | 140 | 170 | 220 | 170 | 220 | 370 | 520 | 740 | 1,130 | 2,080 | 570 | 184 | 968 |
| United States[d] | 750 | 650 | 730 | 630 | 850 | 860 | 880 | 1,430 | 1,590 | 1,390 | 2,210 | 1,610 | 870 | 770 | 930 | 1,534 |

Notes: Industries covered are mining, manufacturing, construction, and transportation.

[a]Including electricity and gas; excluding communication.
[b]Manufacturing only.
[c]All industries included.
[d]Including electricity, gas, and sanitary schedules.
[e]Not available.
[f]Average for 1969-72 only.

Source: United Kingdom Department of Employment Gazette (derived from information furnished by the International Labor Office).

show a further decided pickup in work days lost from stoppage,
though declines from 1972 are indicated for Canada, Ireland, and the
United Kingdom. Serious escalation occurred in Denmark, Italy,
France, and Netherlands. Again in 1974 stoppages may prove larger
than 1973.

Among the distinctive characteristics of the strikes of the period, six require special attention. Unofficial stoppages became
more significant even in countries with relatively stable patterns of
industrial relations. Data for the United Kingdom indicate they
represented from 1968 through 1972 95 percent of all strikes. In
Sweden, in 1970 all strikes had been illegal, and the figure for the
subsequent two years was 85 percent. All but two of the 171 stoppages from 1965 through 69 in Denmark and 22 out of the 23 strikes
in Norway for the period fell into this category. In Germany, the
percentage for 1964-68 was 83.3 percent and possibly higher for
later years, until the trade unions began systematically to recognize
them and seek official legal sanction for individual "warning strikes."
Strikers were in fact protesting against the restrictiveness of the
industrywide bargaining system that neglected local issues and
against the legal restraints imposed on most types of strikes. Direct
action became a tool for rectifying these deficiencies and inadequate
works council settlements or a method of supporting the negotiators'
seeking higher settlements. Among the countries in which they occurred are Belgium, France, Finland, Germany, Italy, the Netherlands, Sweden, Switzerland, and the United Kingdom. After the
early wave of unofficial strikes, union leaders increasingly shifted
from a negative or passive to an active leadership role.

Second, an impressive proportion of the strikes occurred among
public employees (Canada, France, Italy, Sweden, the United Kingdom, and the United States) who also used the weapon of the demonstration. Third, other techniques for collective action, such as
work-to-rule, going slow, and banning overtime were on the increase.
Fourth, plant occupations were reported in a number of countries
including Belgium, France, Great Britain, Italy, and the Netherlands.
Primarily employed in plants threatened by closure, they dramatized
the workers' reaction to finding their life investment in a firm eliminated. In some instances, workers responded to announced closings
with work-ins, as in France and the United Kingdom--that is, by
continuing production to demonstrate that profitable operations were
feasible. And employees did score some victories; governments
either arranged for their placement with other companies or the
continued operation of the plants themselves. Fifth, a number of
contributors to this volume observe that strike administration improved as the number of strikes increased. Sixth, unions shortened
and staggered strikes in Germany, Italy, and the Netherlands to
make them more effective and less costly to their strike funds.

There is no overall measure for unrest; reports of absenteeism as well as labor turnover can therefore provide additional insight. They reinforce the conclusions about the prevalence of a high degree of on-job frustration. An OECD conference of management experts found that absenteeism considered acceptable at 5 to 7 percent had "since 1965 and still more recently according to the region grown rapidly, often reaching 10 to 12 percent and sometimes 35 percent." The experts concluded that "absenteeism and staff turnover are thus important phenomena not only because of their relative size but because of their rapid increase . . . [and] significance."[4]

## Trade Union Growth

Resurgent labor militancy at the end of the 1960s and in the 1970s revitalized the trade unions. In most European countries, membership had stagnated during the first half of the 1960s and some unions suffered setbacks.[5] The enthusiasm generated by strike action, the new demands, and accelerated gains brought many resisters into the ranks. Increased membership in European countries, however, was not of such dimensions as to raise the ratio of organization of the likely potential, as the size of the labor force also increased. Among the nine EEC countries, the EEC Commission estimates the ratios remained stable at 42 percent from 1958 through 1972, with only slight improvements in Belgium and Ireland. The highest ratio of union organization, 70 percent, is reported in Belgium and Denmark; with the 50 percent level in Ireland, Italy, Luxembourg, and the United Kingdom; 40 percent in Germany and Netherlands; and 20 percent in France. Independent estimates place the ratios at the 70 percent level for Austria, Norway, and Sweden; 30 percent for Canada, Switzerland, and the United States. Increases in North American union membership came primarily from among public employees (Table 6).

It must be added that the effective influence of trade unions is affected by a number of factors in addition to numerical size and percentage of members to the potential. These include strategic economic location of members, geographic concentration, overall national economic activity, and legal or contractual rights to participation in decision-making.

## NEW PREMISES OF THE TRADE UNION MOVEMENT

The new militancy stimulated the revision and reorientation of the views of a number of national trade union centers in Europe.

TABLE 6

Trade Union Membership, Selected Countries
(thousands)

| Country and National Center | Membership | |
|---|---|---|
| | 1960 | 1972 or 1973 |
| Austria | | |
| Federation of Austrian Trade Unions (OGB) | 1,501 | 1,560 (1973) |
| Belgium | 1,700* | 2,200* (1972) |
| General Federation of Labor (FGTB) | 706 | 937 (1972) |
| Confederation of Christian Unions (CSC) | 762 | 1,046 (1972) |
| Federation of Liberal Trade Unions (CGSLB) | 100 | 145 (1972) |
| Canada | 1,459 | 2,500 (1973) |
| Canadian Congress of Labor (CLC) | 1,123 | 1,800 (1973) |
| Confederation of National Trade Unions (CNTU) | | 200 (1973) |
| Denmark | | |
| Federation of Danish Trade Unions (LO) | 740 | 909 (1971) |
| Federation of Civil Servants and Salaried Employees (FTF) | 148 | 187 (1972) |
| France | | 3 to 5,000 |
| General Confederation of Labor (CGT) | | largest |
| French Democratic Federation of Labor (CFDT) | | middle |
| French Federation of Christian Workers (CFTC) | | small |
| General Confederation of Management Employees (CGC) | | small |
| General Confederation of Labor-Force Ouvriere (CGT-FO) | | middle |
| The Federal Republic of Germany | 7,500* | 8,200* (1972) |
| German Federation of Trade Unions (DGB) | 6,378 | 6,986 (1972) |
| German Salaried Employees' Union (DAG) | 450 | 469 (1972) |
| German Civil Service Union (DBB) | 650 | 713 (1972) |
| Ireland | | |
| Irish Congress of Trade Unions | | 547 |

| Country and National Center | Membership | |
| --- | --- | --- |
| | 1960 | 1972 or 1973 |
| Italy | | 5 to 6,000 |
|   Italian General Confederation of Labor (CGIL) | | largest |
|   Italian Confederation of Labor Unions (CISL) | | middle |
|   Italian Union of Labor (UIL) | | small |
| Netherlands | 1,400 | 1,700 (1973) |
|   Netherlands Federation of Trade Unions (NVV) | 487 | 633 (1973) |
|   Netherlands Catholic Trade Unions (NKV) | 400 | 395 (1973) |
|   Protestant National Federation of Trade Unions (CNV) | 219 | 236 (1973) |
| Norway | | |
|   Norwegian Federation of Trade Unions (LO) | 545 | 606 (1973) |
| Sweden | | |
|   Swedish Federation of Labor (LO) | 1,486 | 1,771 (1972) |
|   Central Organization of Salaried Employees (TCO) | 394 | 804 (1972) |
|   Swedish Federation of Professional Associations (SACO) | 57 | 122 (1972) |
|   National Federation of Government Officers (SR) | | 20 (1972) |
| Switzerland | | |
|   Swiss Federation of Trade Unions (SFTU) | 437 | 441 (1972) |
|   Swiss Federation of Employees' Societies (FSSE) | 90 | 126 (1972) |
|   Swiss Federation of National-Christian Trade Unions (SFNCTU) | 90 | 98 (1972) |
|   Swiss Federation of Protestant (Evangelical) Trade Unions (SFPTU) | 15 | 14 (1972) |
| United Kingdom | 9,800 | 11,317 (1972) |
| United States | 17,000 | 19,400 (1972) |
|   American Federation of Labor-Congress of Industrial Organizations (AFL-CIO) | 14,000 | 15,300 (1972) |

*Estimated

Sources: Individual country chapters and other sources.

These adjustments reflected the broader aspirations and expectations shared by workers and leftists as well as a new determination to use a broader set of social instruments, economic and political, national and local, to achieve their ends. The unions now sought to treat directly with a host of issues, extending from internal ones, such as closing the gap between union officials and members, to external ones, such as developing an effective tool for dealing with multinational corporations and laggard governments.

## Humanistic Socialism (WCL and Belgian, Dutch, and French National Centers)

Long denominational in character, the Christian trade union movement espoused the sociocooperative outlook of the Catholic Church enunciated in encyclicals from 1891 onward. One dramatic expression of the new trend was the transformation of this movement to a more humanistic socialistic orientation. In the mid-1960s, Christian trade unions both through their international agency, the World Confederation of Labor (WCL), and in a number of national centers particularly in Belgium, France, and Netherlands adopted an anticapitalistic and revolutionary outlook. They would replace both the capitalistic and Marxist state socialistic societies by more decentralized, self-governing economic and social units coordinated through democratic planning, shared in by all governed groups themselves, and based on the social ownership of the economy. Trade unions would be a major force in the transformation. They would lead in the battle against abuses to improve the lot of man, train workers in their new responsibilities as participants in work-place self-management, and sharpen both class awareness and identity. Democracy, the devolution of power, and socialization of the production system became central themes. The autonomous trade unions had to be models; they must observe democratic principles and decentralize power within their own institutional structure. Individuals should be guaranteed their needs and security as well as possess opportunities for self-fulfillment and freedom of conscience. The WCL favored cooperative activities among the national centers and world trade union confederations, and it acted on this proposition.

In 1974 the Belgium FTGB convention, a "free" trade union center, took such a position with its 1971 congress resolution on "workers' control." It advocated "self-management of the enterprises exercised within the frame of a political democracy [which] will give workers maximum control over their labor as a stage toward mastery over their lives." The Dutch "free" NVV took a similar position in adopting in 1971 the Universal Declaration of the Rights of Mankind.

### Labor Reformism: Legislation for Greater Union-Worker Participation (Swedish LO)

The Swedish LO had a history of progressive gains over several decades through agreements with management. At its 1971 Congress, the issue of industrial democracy was taken up with renewed intensity. Instead of accenting long-term goals, the LO endorsed industrial democracy and considered methods for achieving it as an aspect of a new society. Reflecting its determination to pursue this position, the LO was now prepared to turn to legislation, when management would not make substantial concessions, a course it previously eschewed. The LO now sought to broaden worker participation in decision-making at the job level, thereby limiting management's historic prerogatives to direct and allocate work without prior negotiations with the union. Trade unions would deal with matters of job design, work environment, plant conditions, and manpower policies. More adequate information, both in amount and quality, would be needed by workers; they might need their own auditor to prepare them for negotiations and decision-making. The authority of the works councils would be strengthened and members would engage in their firm's long-term budgeting and planning efforts. Workers and union representatives, though a minority on the corporation's board of directors, would present their judgments and be better prepared for direct negotiations later within the company. The LO program called further for "active participation of citizens in deciding national economic and social priorities in order that the society may be shaped more and more in accordance with the fundamental principles of social democracy." Political and social goals would be integrated with economic objectives in the management of the economy.[6]

### Laborism: The Social Contract (British TUC)

In preparation for the ultimate political electoral challenge to the Conservative government of Edward Heath, the Labour Party and the British TUC joined in a February 1973 "social contract" statement outlining an agenda of economic and social programs. (The 1974 TUC Congress supported this understanding.) In 1974, the Labour Party assumed the reins of a minority government; this agenda then guided it. In the industrial relations field, the government secured the repeal of the Industrial Relations Act and then prepared an Employment Protection bill defining workers' rights, developing an independent conciliation and arbitration service. It contemplated a new Companies Act incorporating the TUC program for equal trade union representation on the boards of directors of nationalized industries and on the supervisory boards of larger private enterprises. But the autonomy of the trade unions would persist. In return the TUC offered voluntary wage restraints, which ruled out increases in real income, and recommended that its affiliates limit wage increases to cost-of-living adjustments, provisions for reasonable minimum wages, the elimination of discriminatory wage levels, reforms in the job pay structure, improvements in job security, and better fringe benefits, including a four-week annual holiday. Constraints on prices would be part of the plan. The TUC saw this "social contract" as an agreement voluntarily observed by its constituency in their own and the national interests. Later developments revealed the TUC difficulties in getting its constituent unions to abide by these principles.

## Economic and Social Reformism
### (Italian Trade Union Movement)

Italian trade union confederations look upon their organizations not only as leverages for the protection and promotion of worker interests in the shop and as employee bargaining for his share of economic gains but also for the attainment of his broad economic and social expectations and to redesign the national economic and social structure. Their methods for achieving these ends are collective bargaining at the local level, mass pressures, and demonstrations, the critically powerful forces in democratic societies. Rising real employee benefits and earnings, more intimate participation in decision-making on the floor as well as in higher echelons of the enterprise, and improved working conditions are accepted functions. In addition, their responsibilities include gaining an improved social infrastructure, eliminating class differences, and securing the development of backward areas. Their economic strength is to be employed to get the government to undertake these programs. Where the latter fails, the trade unions are directly to impose this responsibility on big private and public business, getting it to invest in the South, in research and development to create new jobs, better local transportation, nursery schools, continuing education, and lower food costs for their employees, hoping in part that these new corporate responsibilities would convert them into active partners in a movement to make the government more active and effective in these areas. Unions are also insisting through the same pressure tactics that the government pursue more equitable economic policies in dealing with the problems of deflation, by shifting the burdens primarily to higher-income groups. These are practical tactical measures for progressively changing the society.

## Other Aims and Programs

The principles underlying the above four trends--humanistic socialism, labor reformism, laborism, and economic and social reformism--are similar. They would enrich the traditional trade union goals with an insistence upon democratic rights in industry and society. They reflect a desire to gain thorough information about the enterprise by participating directly in the business policy agencies, to enjoy real participation rights in decision-making at the job and plant levels, and to accrue powers for bilateral or multilateral bargaining on all direct workers' issues. Trade union influence would extend progressively to the national levels, where the organizations would negotiate overall agreements or social contracts with employers and governments. They are ready to follow the course of legislation where their political influence is sufficient to be effective and management resists change and concessions granting broader rights to workers. Egalitarianism is the pervading principle for trade unionists, rejecting disparities in economic returns and opportunities. However, organized higher-income employee groups have resisted plans that they considered unduly favorable to lower-income groups (as in the Netherlands and Sweden). The state would if necessary be the mechanism for realizing these ends. Social goals should play a central role in determining choices and priorities.

The trade union centers continue to stress their autonomy and the voluntary nature of all agreements. They believe that directly negotiated contracts with government or managements assure better understanding, more balanced, and equitable solutions and greater compliance with the agreements. In the new environment, they view themselves not as social partners but as interlocutors, or negotiators on behalf of employees.

In relation to the political party system, the trade unions also emphasized their strength and independence, a position that contrasts sharply with their former subordinate stance. They have political allies with whom in varying degrees they share outlooks. But they increasingly follow their own course and recognize the possibilities and the reality of the two being at odds on specific issues. They have succeeded to an unprecedented degree in many countries in influencing political programs and legislation. In Great Britain, industrial relations policies divided the two major parties, with the Labour Party following the TUC positions.

The emphasis on humanistic democratic ideals also reawakened the unions' needs of maintaining closer contacts with their membership. The means of communication from the bottom to the top and vice versa had to be improved. New techniques for ascertaining worker attitudes are being used, such as opinion polls, educational conferences, invitations for direct responses to specific questions, and frequent conferences and seminars. Sectarianism appears to be an anachronism, as denominational influences and political differences wane. Cooperation and mergers among the dual and plural unions are more common in policy formation, political action, and bargaining.

Trade unionists, moreover, do not readily accept restraints on wage increases in the interest of price stability. Their experience has taught them that price movements are not necessarily related to wages and costs and that restraints on prices must be extensive and intimate to be effective. Other economic homilies appear also to have lost much of their acceptance by workers and union national policies. Consequently, they seek direct negotiations and agreements in these fields rather than reliance primarily on market forces. Moreover, workers accept the wisdom that governments are able to underwrite full employment, if the private sector fails.

### Managements' Reassessment

No such far-reaching changes took place in the ranks of management. Largely preoccupied with operating problems, they remain troubled by employee unrest, expressed by strikes, absenteeism, high labor turnover, and difficulties in achieving discipline. They respond to these issues primarily with proposals for mechanical rearrangements on the job site, such as job enlargement and enrichment, job autonomy, or other variations in job design. The social environment and organizational structure tend to be ignored or introduced in isolated experiments. Indicative of their difficulties is their inability to deal with wage incentive systems, no longer truly useful in advanced countries. Indeed, in some cases, incentive systems even subvert the impulse to greater output or provide little stimulus to higher productivity where the financial rewards are minor and workers are primarily concerned with improvements in the job or more rights in decision-making, and become inflationary where national wage policies are in effect. But managements do not scrap them, except where they are long recognized as being obsolete, as on assembly-line operations. To be sure, dysfunctionalism produces tension, but remedies of a fundamental nature did not emerge.

Management is increasingly amenable to giving more information and to extending the areas of consultation to employees and unions but reluctant to agree to bilateral decision-making. Nor does it wish to grant workers power in the corporate decision-making organs. Proposals for an articulated bargaining system from top to bottom arouse opposition: Management sees them solely as of a new system of contract enforcement by which to coerce local employers. In countries where industrywide bargaining shielded management from contacts with individual trade unions at the shop level, employers resist close contacts, turning to works councils as a last resort. But the new industrial leadership of the Italian employers' association is more favorable to collective bargaining on a company basis to promote a positive relation with the trade unions for meeting worker aspirations while preserving the private enterprise system and jointly prodding the government to undertake more adequate local public facilities and services.

## MAJOR CHANGES IN INSTITUTIONS, UNION GUIDES, PROCEDURES, AND ACHIEVEMENTS OF COLLECTIVE BARGAINING

Labor's impatience, frustrations, and uneasiness generated a wave of industrial unrest. Following the strikes and industrial disturbances supporting the new trade union principles and programs came significant changes in industrial relations institutions, union short-run objectives, and collective bargaining. Some are already in evidence; others loom on the horizon; and still others are in process of development. The gains made in one country become the targets of other countries.

### Institutions

#### Trade Unions

Not the least among the institutions affected by changes were the trade unions themselves. Two trends were at work. One favored greater centralization through mergers or closer coordination of national and regional federations and unions. The other sought more intimate membership participation in activities as well as improvements in the informational and decision-making process.

Centralizing Tendencies. Consolidation was in evidence in the trade union movement at many levels. Within the national trade union sector, the advantages of a united single national center are well-known; and clearly recalled is the high price of division during the 1930s. Single dominant organizations existed at the end of the war in several countries (Denmark, Ireland, Norway, Sweden, and the United Kingdom). Two efforts at consolidation made in the postwar recovery period survived (Austria and Germany). In the mid-1950s the AFL and CIO merged. A merger is planned between the Netherlands

Trade Union Federation (NVV) and the Netherlands Catholic Trade
Union Federation (NKV). Mergers in other countries have been
thwarted by ideological or policy differences (France, Italy) or the
conviction, as in Belgium, that it would be politically undesirable.
In such countries, in the 1960s, national centers developed procedures
for consultation and collaboration on policy statements, presentations
to government bodies, economic action, and political demonstrations.
These procedures are not necessarily successful or smooth--witness
competitive centers, as in Sweden--but they do promote coherence.

     At the regional level, the free trade union movement through
the ICFTU evolved a system of regional organizations. In 1973 it
organized the European Trade Union Confederation (ETUC), which
was joined in 1974 by the European Organization of the WCL (1968-74)
(EO-WCL). In July 1974, the CGIL was accepted, thereby enlarging
the regional organization to 30 trade union centers in 17 European
countries with 30 million individual members. In January 1974, discussions between a number of European national union centers and
the WFTU for closer collaboration under the auspices of the ILO
Workers' Group produced an agreement to sponsor a joint conference
on problems of workers' health and safety in the enterprise. AFL-CIO
opposition to such contacts in part explains its withdrawal in 1969
from the ICFTU. In addition, the national union centers in the Scandinavian countries maintain regional organizations. Furthermore,
trade secretariats exist at the regional level usually as offshoots of
the international secretariats and now include Christian unions.

     In a third trend, smaller national unions merge with other
unions, or general workers' unions swallow up small unions within
the same national centers. Where such consolidations are not concluded, coordination is being accelerated to meet the realities of
collective bargaining. Where multiple unions share the same jurisdiction or are present in the same plant or operate in plants of the
same company or in what is defined as an industry unit for bargaining
purposes, they are setting up liaison committees, industrial federations, joint industrial councils, coalitions for bargaining, or other
devices for cooperation and mutual support. National unions in one
center in the Netherlands that share similar views on policy and
bargaining, as in the chemical, metal, and textile unions, created a
single bloc. Unions are also consolidating their small locals to create regional units for better administration.

     Centralization is a trend parallel to consolidation. More author-
ity is being ceded to or coopted by union centers and national unions
depriving national and local unions of considerable discretion. The
rising volume of negotiations with the government and the growing
number of national basic agreements with management reinforce this
trend. In Great Britain during the period of wage controls, the TUC

assumed responsibilities for reviewing wage claims of its constituents to forestall harsher statutory controls; and it continues to advise individual national unions that encounter difficulties in applying national TUC policy. In countries with overall national collective agreements or "social contracts" or "social programing," such as Austria, Belgium, Netherlands, and the Scandinavian countries, the national centers usually possess some powers for implementing their obligations. Having an adversary status in the economy and society, unions are under compulsion to reach and maintain a consistency of doctrine and strategy among constituent organizations and members. Therefore, this authority is increasingly ceded to the national center to direct--once policies are pronounced. Implementation of such policies is generally left to agencies below the national center level. Another development strengthened in recent years, though not of recent origin, vests additional authority in the executives of either the national center or national union. In a number of countries, they are empowered to consummate agreements without the affirmative action of the membership. Such a course was encouraged in Germany by the severe legal penalties imposed upon those violating the "peace obligations" presumed by the courts to be contained in agreements. The DGB in 1974 authorized constituent unions to determine for themselves whether strikes could be declared without prior negotiations.

In France and Italy, with long traditions favoring community labor federations or bourses, local federations recently gained new importance. They coalesced trade union forces for more local public amenities or local or regional planning. But in the present economic environment with its concentration on national action, these community federations, except in Italy, are unlikely effectively to compete for influence with national unions.

Decentralizing Tendencies: Internal Union. Countering these centripetal forces are similar strong ones emphasizing the need to improve internal communications between the worker and the union, to strengthen the union organization in the shop, to expand the role of the works councils and to enable the union to assist, guide, and, if necessary, supplant the works councils. The wave of spontaneous strikes since 1968 reinforced these trends. Most of them occurred without union guidance and in some early cases, in defiance of the union. Workers sought better conditions of employment, redress of grievances, and also greater union presence in the shop to improve their chances for dealing effectively with immediate issues.

Unions are now trying to achieve improvements in communication through better training of union officials and more frequent contacts with the membership and canvasses of their views by one means

or another. Unions in recent years secured broader recognition of
their representatives in the shop, greater freedom for these officials,
and job protection for them (France, Germany, and the Netherlands).
In France union shop sections are formally recognized. The Swedish
LO increased the responsibilities of its factory clubs, the union's
shop outpost. Shop stewards in the German unions seek to negotiate
directly on behalf of their local constituency. The United States and
Canadian systems are built on an active and aggressive shop union
steward system. In practice, British shop stewards act quite independently with minimal surveillance from the union itself. Probably, the
most far-reaching change occurred in Italy, where the post-1969 trade
union movement rebuilt its structures on the union shop organization
embracing delegates and workers' assemblies. Finally, rank-and-
file groups are seeking more rights for local self-determination to
counter, if necessary, decisions by national leaders. The unofficial
strikes are often led by independent ad hoc committees, which rarely
survive the event.

Decentralizing Tendencies: Works Councils. Most troublesome in
the industrial relations field is the relation between unions and works
councils. The latter grew out of the demand for workers' representation in the shop, employers' resistance to adversary relations with
unions, and the desire of governments for cooperative attitudes between the parties. They came into existence in World War I, and
thereafter laws in continental countries required the establishment
of works councils while governments in Canada and the United Kingdom encouraged their formation, or national collective agreements
prescribed them, as in the Scandinavian countries and Italy. Though
legally required, they remained weak in most countries, often were
not actually constituted, and in some withered or disappeared. In
any case, their responsibilities remained limited to nonbargaining
issues. Management tended to influence them and limited their operations. In Germany, however, works councils assumed increasing
importance. Their local agreements with management, nominally
set in the framework of general industry agreements, constituted a
regulatory system that paralleled the collective agreement. Their
influence within Germany's shops was sufficient to create a dual bargaining system that restrained the union's preeminence and limited
its role in bargaining on a wide range of issues. The arrangement
produced an unsteady basis for industrial relations. Recently,
French employers deliberately revitalized the works councils to negotiate with them and thereby avoid dealing with union shop sections.
     The ambiguous positions of the councilors is one source of
confusion beclouding the system. On the one hand, the former have
to maintain a nonadversary attitude, often prescribed by the enabling

legislation, and, on the other, they are usually loyal union members.
As union officials, many help formulate union policies and maintain
union organizations in the shop. Workers recognize that their gains
flow from their organized power, but agreements are negotiated by
an independent body, at times including nonunion members and directly dependent on management largesse.

Unions remain in an ambivalent position respecting works councils. They see the councils as aids to developing intimate knowledge
of the shop, in obtaining greater rights for workers, and in securing
a role for workers in decision-making on matters that managements
resist giving to unions. Councils are often a means of securing gains
unobtainable in direct bargaining. But, at the same time, unions
recognize works councils as barriers to their own deeper penetration
into the shop. They, therefore, simultaneously pursue three courses
intermixed in different proportions at various times: First, to increase the rights and competences of the works councils; second, to
enhance their own role in the councils to the point of controlling their
operations; and third, if possible, to displace councils by union shop
bodies.

The fight for increased rights and competences produced gains.
Councils acquired the right to deal with many issues formerly reserved to management, including distribution and organization of
work and working hours as well as the operations of the assembly
lines. Safety committees, comparable in their own field to works
councils, also received more powers to investigate and to take initiatives, including cessation of questionable operations. Works councils have to be furnished regularly with more adequate economic and
financial data about the enterprise, and in some countries they even
obtained the formal right to their own auditor examining the data
(Belgium, France, and Sweden). Areas for bilateral decision-making
have been enlarged, and prior notices of change in operations by
management are now more widely required. Councilors received
more protection from layoffs and greater independence in the conduct
of their business. As the issues grew more concrete, affecting the
workers directly, union members became more searching about
council candidates and, at times, openly challenged veteran candidates by nominating new ones.

From the start, unions had preferential rights in selecting
candidates for the councils and usually took this responsibility seriously. They spent much money on the elections and devoted much
time and funds for their training. Currently, several nations require
employers to finance union training of councilors. These activities
led to an overwhelming proportion of union members on the councils.
Unions also sought and acquired the right to act in an advisory capacity to councilors or to be present, as in Austria and the Netherlands,
at their sessions.

The ultimate union goal is to replace the works councils with union agencies. Issues, such as the goal implied, should be bargained rather than unilaterally resolved by management, even when consultation exists. There have been some successes. Italy's shop committee supplanted in fact, as well as by agreement, the older works councils in many industries. In Belgium, union representatives regularly intercede on issues where they find the councils are inadequate. In Austria, the councils have been converted into union agencies. The same trend is perceptible in the Scandinavian countries. The framework for a continuous articulated structure for industrial relations based on direct union-management relations is evolving and replacing the former dual arrangement, whereby unions bargained at an industry level while works councils consultation and some bargaining assisted at the plant level.

In both Canada and the United States, union shop stewards never acquired the authority or experience of dealing with the business and economic problems of the firms, except in extreme cases of closures and programs for deliberate union-management cooperation. The extension of union activities to safety and health problems now encounters serious resistance. The system therefore is limited to negotiations on matters involving broad worker interests, though presumably unions could expand their impact through demands and struggle.

## Employers: Individual and Associations and Personnel Practices

Multiplication of the large national and multinational corporations for a time threatened managements' industry-wide national representational and bargaining structure. Large corporations ventured into the industrial relations field. But these corporations, particularly those of U.S. origin, learned that withdrawal from the agreements deprived them of the benefits of the "peace obligation" and that the contracts in fact prescribed only quasilegal minimum changes that rarely intruded seriously into the actual operations of the plant and in fact shielded the managements from direct contact with union representatives. They joined or rejoined the employer associations, except for U.S. corporations in the United Kingdom.

Significant for the industrial relations field, the authority of the French National Employers' Council (CNPF) was enlarged in 1970, permitting it to enter into interindustry agreements with trade unions and the government. In Italy, regional industry assocations are now more actively engaged in collective bargaining with unions. A similar tendency to increase the importance of industry associations as compared with overall national employer associations was

also observed in the Netherlands. German and Scandinavian employers associations already enjoy vast powers over members. Multiemployer bargaining in the United States in recent years made no
impressive advances. In all countries professional staffs are occupying increasingly more important roles in the associations.

Industrial relations and personnel activities had in the past
played only a minor role in European plant management, as most
serious issues were handled by the associations. In some countries,
companies dealt primarily with works councils, which they learned
to contain or manipulate. But the recent surge in worker militancy
and the greater bargaining leverage of workers in the tight labor
market, their insistence on correctives for local conditions, the increased authority of the works councils, the growing presence of
unions within the plants and, finally, the mounting volume of company bargaining with unions as illustrated by developments in Italy,
Belgium, Great Britain, and the Netherlands, brought to the fore the
need for modern sophisticated personnel policy and highly competent
personnel staffs. Many managements, recognizing this need, either
individually or with the aid of trade associations and the governments
began training personnel and sponsoring research in the field. Staff
was necessary in order to bring information to the executives for
policy-making and bargaining, to develop competent negotiators, to
apply decisions and agreements in plants, to meet employee complaints, and to moderate the diverse sources of unrest.

The British Government developed the Code of Practice for
management and urged employers to develop a formal comparable
manual for individual plants. Much of the new European industrial
relations and personnel techniques and procedures was borrowed from
the United States. But, in time, individual companies and research
bodies in Great Britain, the Netherlands, and Sweden forged ahead,
making significant contributions in theory, policy, and practices.
Improvements followed in the handling of personnel dealings with
unions and actual conditions within the plants. In the United States
and Canada, however, there have been no recent outstanding innovations. But the professionalism of lower-level staffs improved, enabling companies to deal effectively with and generally to outclass
trade union personnel both inside and outside the plants.

## Public-Sector Bargaining Institutions

With the spread of collective bargaining for employees in publicly owned enterprises and the civil service, governments established their own bargaining organizations. Illustrative of this trend
is Italy's agency for publicly owned corporations (Intersind), which
in its agreements often sets the pace for those in private industry.

In Sweden, a Public Enterprise Bargaining Organization (SFP) exists
for this purpose. Some states and municipalities in the United States
have also established such special bodies. The Canadian Government
has such an agency in the Treasury Board. In France and Great Britain, bargaining is done directly by the individual public corporation,
with the central government overseeing the offers and final terms.

## Union and Worker Participation in Decision-Making

The earlier description of union efforts to influence decision-
making at the plant and job levels has its parallel in efforts to develop
procedures for determining governmental and enterprise (company)
policies and programs. Currently, the primary focus is on union-
government negotiations on socioeconomic matters, positions on
boards of directors of enterprises, and negotiated employee capital-
formation schemes.

### Government Level

Before World War II, Western nations expanded their consultations with unions on governmental economic and social programs.
During the war, collaboration was extensive, and many trade unionists occupied critical ministerial and administrative posts. During
the postwar reconstruction, unions played a central role in productivity drives. Consultation continued at the European regional level
through advisory bodies to the OECD. One trade unionist was a member of the High Authority of the European Coal and Steel Community
(ECSC), and another was a commissioner of the European Economic
Community. Trade unionists constitute one-third of the Economic
and Social Committee and are members of many EEC consultative
bodies and are observers to others. They are associated with but
not part of the organization. EEC and the commissioners recently
have emphasized the need for increased participation of the "social
partners" in the economic and social decisions of the Community. At
present the unions' impact is largely felt through their ability to persuade individual member nations to promote their views.

At the national level unions in most countries participate in
many consultative agencies. Some are institutionalized, formally requiring trade union representatives; others are ad hoc in nature. The
number and significance of these consultative bodies vary with the
political establishment in a given country; conservative regimes tend
to curtail or even eliminate them.

Economic planning was one area trade unions counted upon to
offer them opportunities for considerable influence. But this

expectation proved overly optimistic in most countries. Several planning agencies became exclusively technical in nature though trade unions were usually represented on the advisory boards reviewing agency findings. In other countries, advisory economic boards with union representatives develop policy proposals, submitting them to the government. Their impact varies from country to country and time to time. They have been of critical importance in the Netherlands and constitute a significant forum in Great Britain. In Belgium, national economic policy bodies produced joint agreements, usually accepted by the government. The more significant these agencies were, the greater the influence unions could have through them on their countries' policies.

The most dramatic developments in recent years involved direct union-government negotiations and often included employer associations, as in Austria, Great Britain, Italy, and the Netherlands. Austrian tripartite discussions on major economic and industrial relations issues effected through the Parity (Joint) Commission have become a well-established forum for policy-making. In Italy, the center-left governments seek union acquiescence as part of an effort to secure both broad acceptance for their programs and industrial peace. Nevertheless they acknowledge the unions' rights to criticize specific programs or the total package and even to implement their position through work stoppages. In the United Kingdom and countries with socialist leadership, government and trade unions frequently reach direct agreements on legislation to be proposed by the former.

Union influence in such instances is dependent on an identity of views between the government and unions as well as upon union economic strength and the effectiveness of unions' positions. With the upsurge in labor militancy, economic and social issues presented by unions gained greater acceptability.

Representation on governmental agencies in European countries is considered a serious responsibility. Prestigious leaders tend to be assigned to the posts. Delegations are held to strict account for their action, and their reports are submitted regularly to national conventions or responsible executive agencies.

Trade union leaders highly prize these opportunities. At a minimum, the procedure provides information and permits them to gain new expertise and possibly to influence governments. Even when governments take a centrist and conservative turn, union leaders continue to participate in these bodies, if they are continued.

Developments in the social security systems clearly demonstrated the importance of government policy. Union leaders had hoped that they would serve as a means for the redistribution of national income. But government economic, fiscal, and social policies easily thwarted these hopes.

A second problem arising from such trade union consultation and participation results from the great distance between this level of decision-making and the membership. On occasion, some unions such as the AFL-CIO, Britich TUC, CFDT, and the Dutch unions dramatically withdrew from participation to inform their followers of their disapproval of the policies of a specific body or of the government as a whole. Trade union spokesmen are ever ready to insist that they are independent of the agencies in which they participate as consultants. At times they even present their views to the public to avoid being tarred by an action that they will not endorse. Experts rather than leaders are on occasion given these consultation assignments to minimize the political consequences of cooperation. The major problem of communications with the membership remains. It is being faced in new ways by national unions as they increasingly use modern communication methods. Still not solved by the unions is the problem of proliferating representational functions and the need for personnel and the funds to cover them.

## In the Enterprise

Union representation on governmental advisory and negotiating bodies provided many opportunities for influencing national developments. But unions became increasingly aware that in all economies, many basic economic decisions are made at the enterprise level, in the setting developed by overall economic institutions policies and programs.

Nationalization of industry was the first postwar solution proposed by socialistically oriented trade union centers. This priority receded as unions recognized that even more liberal personnel and industrial relations policies did not alter the economy. Moreover, they observed that public enterprises remained subservient to governmental directives or guidance. The recent revival of interest in nationalization or governmentally financed corporations in Sweden and Great Britain derive from economic rather than trade union pressures, though the British union proposals seek to reorganize less effective industries. Demands for government financial intervention to support marginal plants are voted in Belgium and France.

The current disposition is for unions as an alternative to demand minority, or in the case of the British TUC and the German DGB equal, employee representation on the supervisory boards of corporations or variants of this arrangement. The Dutch unions prefer increased accountability of the board of directors to employees rather than direct representation. The Netherlands works council nominates candidates to be coopted by the existing boards and retains veto powers on all new selections. A basic question is which agency should select employee board members, with some favoring works councils or employee electorates, as in Austria, Denmark, Germany, and the Netherlands, and the others, unions, as in Norway and Sweden and in the British TUC proposal. Union officials are specifically permitted to hold such positions under the new German Government measure and in the British TUC proposal, but they are barred from these posts in the Netherlands. The British TUC scheme more than the others underscores the direct accountability of these representatives to the union membership. Support for the basic concept of employee representation on corporate boards is not universal in union ranks. Suspicion and opposition exist among strong leftist and communist-oriented unions, while there is lack of interest among traditionalists in union ranks.

Labor representation on boards of supervisors has had its most complete test in the co-determination system of Germany's coal, iron, and steel industries and in the minority representation system in other industries. While many German and foreign observers are critical of the operations, the DGB steadfastly supports its extension, insisting on equal-employee representation on boards of supervisors. The new Swedish system of minority employee representation on boards of supervisors envisages the current scheme as a trial effort to be reassessed. With systems now in operation in several countries (Germany, Norway, Netherlands, and Sweden) more will be learned about their respective contributions to industrial democracy.

A third variant to these efforts at greater trade union or worker participation in corporate decision-making is collectively negotiated savings plans for capital formation. This provides a formal procedure permitting all employees in an enterprise to accumulate assets in enterprises from which the individual is to receive benefits at a later date. To be financed initially or primarily by employers over and above the regular real wage increases, the plan offers employees permanent shareholdings and permits them to share in surplus profits and from accretions in capital values. As one indirect benefit, employees may acquire the right to designate representatives on the boards of directors. Some proponents see in the plan a means of freezing payments to employees in periods of inflation and releasing buying power during periods of slackness. If central national investment funds are developed, union representatives can share in the decisions. The plan has the advantage of permitting employees to enjoy the benefits of corporate self-financing and promoting a more equitable distribution of capital ownership.

Unions oppose the plans for diverse reasons. Some labor leaders prefer more direct techniques for attaining union objectives, and others point to the complexities of the schemes and the inability to project their effects. Only German unions have negotiated plans within the context of their tax laws. Union centers in Austria, Denmark, Italy, and the Netherlands are promoting them. The Danish Social Democrats introduced a 1973 bill prescribing a broader program but did not follow through on it. The German coalition government pressed a far-reaching scheme in this field for a time in 1974 but shelved it to avoid interfering with its economic policies. The trade union movements and often the governments in other countries, including Austria and Switzerland, are actively examining proposals, with the metal and watch-making unions in the latter country negotiating voluntary plans.

Other New Trade Union Guides
for Collective Bargaining

The preceding sections highlighted two major trade union developments. Consolidation and centralization are transforming the union structures to improve their operations. Both workers and unions are seeking additional channels for individual participation in both enterprise and job decision-making. Some unions are also promoting negotiated-savings plans for capital formation to share in the economic growth of the enterprise.

Complementing these aspirations and specific programs are important new guides for collective bargaining. One type deals with actual contract provisions and wage policy; a second with working conditions; a third with the rigidity of the current collective bargaining systems in their respective countries; and a fourth with the increase in the security of the union as an institution.

## Equity and Protection of Labor
## and Wage Achievements

Closely interwoven into the trade union outlook is the demand for equitable returns and treatment for all employees. From a determination to achieve this goal, there flow at least three objectives. The most pervasive one insists upon profiting from the rise in national productivity. Wage levels and standards, it is argued, could be raised and hours shortened. Equal pay for equal work by women and young people as well as the prevention and prohibition of discrimination are also included, dictated by the claims of equity.

The incomes of lower wage groups had to be raised by higher-than-average increases. The Swedish "solidary" wage movement had no equal in other countries, but most unions supported the narrowing of occupational differentials. Moreover, unions sought flat across-the-board, rather than percentage, increases to offset the

rise in the cost of living. Equalization of benefits of hourly workers
to the level of salaried employees was demanded, and substantial
progress was made in this direction. This movement was complemented by extensive white-collar organization. Protection for employees displaced for technological or economic reasons won considerable attention. Statutory, works councils, and collective bargaining protection became the norm. Thus, justification of dismissals by
employers, review by works councils and unions, prolonged notice,
and, ultimately, the payment of severance pay, where layoffs could
not be avoided, were required. Moreover, public authorities made
provisions for retraining and relocation to facilitate movements to
new locations.

Inflation led to the inclusion of escalator clauses ("threshold
agreements" in Great Britain) in collective agreements as well as
shorter contracts or specific provisions for wage reopening. Moreover, governments more freely than ever before adjusted statutory
wage standards or minimums and the pay of their employees in compensation for the rise in the cost of living. In other cases, unions
demanded subsidized prices for food or meals. But more puzzling is
the possibility and perhaps the likelihood of a decline in (if not a
negative) rate of growth in Western countries, threatening existing
living standards. The British TUC adherence to the "social contract"
implies the principle of no general rise in living standards. Prime
Minister Harold Wilson, addressing the July 1974 Socialist International Leaders Conference, declared that "We shall do well to maintain the domestic standard of living this year and for the year or two
to come." And he warned "unless governments make the right response the miseries of slump stagnation and unemployment--produc-
tion lost forever--would be loaded on the inflation we all have to
face." Urging a "voluntary consensus between government and the
citizens" based on the government's commitment to "create a fair
and compassionate society," he proposed as the guiding principle
that "what is available (should be) fairly shared." He advised first
tackling the domestic price problem and avoiding deflation, depreciation, and import restrictions. The Italian trade union movement
is already confronted by far-reaching austerity measures, and others
will be. Meeting these problems will force the economic interests
to find acceptable solutions for their countries, which in part means
those the trade union movement can accept as reasonable and equitable. Union centers with only enclaves of power in selected industries and determined to unionize the remainder of the work force
usually resist such agreements.

Even before the current crisis, individual nations faced periods
of economic sluggishness. Trade unions invariably proposed reflationary measures, hoping to attain and maintain the highest possible

levels of production, employment, and rates of growth. They also
supported industrial and geographical structural economic reforms.
In advocating these measures, they were challenging orthodox deflationary schemes, displaying a lack of confidence in the effectiveness
of the private sector on its own to correct national economic difficulties.

Should these problems be prolonged, national union centers and
the regional and international confederations will adjust their basic
tenets to these new circumstances. They will probably seek equity
in allocating the burdens of economic stagnancy and the costs of structural changes and propose new ways for governments to design and
guide the private sector by organizations in which they will seek an
active role.

Traditional wage and income controls will probably not suffice
for the trade unions. Neither are they likely to rely on the voluntary
efforts of the private sector. The German trade union movement
abandoned for a time the "cooperative wage" policy; the Dutch secured
the removal of wage controls; in other countries, the rank and file
forced the collapse of various income control systems. Systems of
restraint need redesign but not along lines suggested by neoclassical
economists, for unions will urge and insist on directly negotiated
socially equitable wage, income, and social service and economic
policies and programs. Austria, Belgium, and Norway offer now
different operative patterns in this area. The outlines of such new
systems of economic governance are in evidence in other countries.

Humanizing the Work Place and Job

Originally suspicious that the slogans for humanizing work and
the work place were redesigned catchwords of the "human relations
school" of personnel management, union leaders condemned them.
These officials, consequently, remained aloof or allowed themselves
to be only cautiously involved in specific projects. In Denmark,
Norway, and Sweden trade union leaders in the 1960s took up the
Tavistock message, cooperating on projects with small self-governing
groups within a factory. Other trade union centers reemphasized
their traditional concern with physical conditions in their special
departments on health or labor sciences or safety (Austria, Sweden,
United Kingdom, and the United States) or by demanding new contract
provisions. They perceived an active worker interest in the criticism
of qualitative job conditions but generally offered few new remedies.

German trade unions have proceeded further by sponsoring
studies toward defining a distinctive trade-union approach to the
subject. Human satisfaction on the job, they believe, is related to
the employee's social and job environments as well as to his

occupational social and political interests. Emphasis is upon group
work, the elimination of unnecessarily extended hierarchical structures and the usefulness of adequate training and promotional opportunities. The financial and nonfinancial costs of all work arrangements to the individual, enterprise, and society should be weighed in
the design of jobs and organizational structures. The practical application and import of such proposals are not yet clear, but they do
suggest new lines of development.

### Breaking through the Inflexibility of the Bargaining and Restrictive Legal Systems

        The wave of spontaneous wildcat strikes epitomizes labor's
impatience with existing systems of collective bargaining and law.
The bargaining parties responded to these outbreaks by negotiating
settlements on the immediate issues without either the employer or
the courts invoking established procedures for stopping or penalizing
strikers for such action. Unions have demanded revisions of contracts, the concepts of collective bargaining, and the law. The duration of agreements was shortened, often reducing them to one year,
particularly as relates to wages; provision was made for reopening
contracts or for regular adjustments of specific items, such as
wages. Cost-of-living indexes or measures of general wage changes
in an area, industry, or country became current tools for increasing
wages.
        But more fundamental were developments toward making agree-
ments open-ended or a "living document." In Great Britain, this has
been the practice, and the trade union movement is quite adamant
about retaining it. In Italy, labor's militancy after 1969 made this
approach a fact, and trade union leaders argued for it, though increasingly as bargaining became more stabilized and union power
more widely acknowledged, they displayed a more formal observance
of the dates for reopening discussions of items in agreements. In
France, a similar tolerance exists for the irregular occurrence of
strikes and the presentation of local demands for correction. Restraints in the "contracts of progress" were dropped. There has been
a growing understanding of the reasons for spontaneous strikes in
most countries and penalties were rarely invoked. In fact, a measure of de facto flexibility prevails, although not formalized. Most
parties involved in industrial relations avoided efforts to insert new
provisions for handling stoppages, hoping that the shortened contracts and the reopening provisions would be sufficient correctives.
Some British unions have sought restraints on change by employers
prior to an agreement.

Another major problem exists in countries like Germany where the courts have restricted the right to strike and threatened to penalize strikers. Trade union leaders followed the literal requirements on strike votes and contract approvals and otherwise limited local freedom in calling official walkouts. Leaders of more militant unions such as the IG-Metall are seeking ways to surmount these judicial constraints. The DGB recently issued more liberal rules for its own national unions. In Sweden, the "peace obligation" limited local action. Contract provisions, the so-called article 32, and court decisions provided employers with broad discretion in plant operations and deprived local unions of powers to deal directly with the issues and to use the strike weapon in their local controversies. The result has been an ongoing battle in contract negotiations and legislatures, currently reaching a new peak, to limit management's rights, and extend labor's area of bargaining rights. Similar efforts are being made by Danish unions to relax restraints on strikes and employers' authority in the shop.

The two desiderata, contract stability and the flexibility of the bargaining process to deal with and resolve complaints, are in a new stage of reexamination, with the pendulum now swinging in the latter direction.

## Growing Acceptance of State
## Regulation and Participation
## in Industrial Relations

Employers generally tend in tight labor markets to respond to the pressures for better wages, terms, and conditions of employment, but they have resisted demands for qualitative improvements and increased bargaining rights by employees and unions and labor's intervention into business operations. But as governments become more receptive to the views of trade unions, the latter turn increasingly to the responsive state and to legislation to bring them additional rights. Political swings to more conservative administrations in a number of countries such as Great Britain have at times produced restrictive laws. But the overwhelming trend was in the opposite direction. Even centrist governments followed such patterns, which explains much of the increase in liberal labor and industrial relations legislation. The state is less a mediator and outsider and more a critical force for implementing the humanistic socialistic goals of trade unions. In some countries, governments are actual partners in the annual collective bargaining package.

National union centers are fully aware of the dangers of this turn, foreseeing the possibility of restrictive legislation and conservative state action. The Swedish trade union movement in 1971 experienced such a shock when the SAP government suspended the public employees' legal rights to strike. The British TUC took a strong noncooperative position against the action of the Conservative government in industrial relations, ultimately securing the repeal of the Industrial Relations Act. American unions fought administration proposals to restrict their action. These experiences have borne down heavily on union centers and impressed them again with the need for a serious commitment to national politics.

## Trade Unions Move for
## Institutional Resources

The expansion of trade union activities and responsibilities produced a great need for operating money. In countries where unions administered social security funds (Belgium, Denmark, Sweden, and Switzerland), one informal result of fund membership is a greater inclination to join the union. But most such funds are now run by state agencies. Trade union and works councils agreements generally offer no practical inducement for membership, as their terms apply to all employees. In Germany the courts specifically forbade union negotiations of special privileges for unionists. Both in Belgium and the Netherlands, preferential benefits are now granted to union members, or unions receive funds from the management for training or similar activities. French laws assure unions facilities within the plants for the collection of dues as well as for a number of other activities. In Great Britain and Italy, payroll deduction systems (check-off procedures) are being more extensively applied. Voluntary membership is large, and dues collections are high. Nevertheless, the problem of collections remains a vital issue. Union centers wish to maintain both the principles of voluntarism and fiscal solvency.

## New Structural Developments in Collective Bargaining

Collective bargaining structures have responded to the new pressures from all three groups: workers and unions, employers and their associations, and governments. Each had its own goals, its own reaction to developments, producing in each country new compromises and diverse systems of bargaining units. Where industry-wide or economy-wide agreements prevailed, company and plant contracts multiplied, and where the latter dominated, there appears to be a trend to negotiate at higher levels.

## Movement from Economy-wide
## and Industry to Company and
## Plant Agreements

        The industrywide agreement either on a national or regional
basis is well established in all European countries as well as in older
North American local industries. It offered both employers and
unions certain advantages, such as a floor on costs and earnings.
Small employers could be saved from the whipsaw tactics of unions
and relieved of the need of developing their own expertise for dealing
with trade unions since employers' associations took over such responsibilities. Members of associations retained great freedom in
applying general agreements and conducting their internal personnel
policies.

        But a shift in emphasis took place toward the plant and company
agreement. Many large companies often favored this approach because of their distinctive systems of personnel and industrial relations, and they valued direct trade union sanction of agreements and
the code it produced. As the volume and depth of labor unrest
mounted, they sought to isolate themselves from, or at least to be
able to moderate the impact of, the general mood of restlessness. A
number boasted of their record of stability or their success in avoiding general strike action or troublesome incidents. Publicly owned
enterprises in most countries tended to act independently of the private sector.

        Workers, of course, struck for local demands and, in addition,
supported more general demands and promoted more aggressive
union positions. Unions learned to respond to these local complaints
and actions and to capitalize on them by enlarging their overall proposals and insisting on larger concessions.

        Unions also exploited local developments to underscore the
importance of allowing for their direct presence within the plant or
of supplanting the works councils in negotiations. Managements in
France, Germany, and the Netherlands were informed that they could
not be responsible for plant unrest if they were not substantially represented within it. Considerable progress occurred in this field,
and direct plant agreements were made in Belgium, Great Britain,
the Netherlands, and Italy. Where multiple unions existed covering
diverse jurisdictions or plural unions, unions increasingly entered
into cooperative bargaining arrangements for joint dealings with
management. In Italy, the process of decentralization moved most
swiftly and broadly, leading to plant and company agreements that
virtually replaced industrywide agreements in collective bargaining.
In the United States, most master company agreements allowed for
some issues to be settled through local plant agreements.

The movement for local plant and enterprise agreements had considerable government encouragement. They received legal status in France in 1971. Germany did the same through works councils agreements that grew broader in scope. The U.K. Donovan commission in its report advocated de jure recognition and integration into the bargaining structure of de facto local agreements, with those on productivity representing the most distinct evidence of the need for new forms of bargaining and instruments.

Opposition to these local contracts did exist in some union circles and among managements devoted to industry-wide agreements. The dissent was particularly strong in countries where contracts laid down national rules for general wage movements. The latter could not restrain the wage drift--that is, increases at the local level to all or a select group of employees above the general wage increases. These varied in size and scope, tending to run a third or more above the official increase. In Sweden, the parties included such concessions in the projections of wage movements and subsequently provided for comparable increases to employees who had not initially shared in them. But no country adequately coped with the independent action of employers or with pressures from local groups, including the Netherlands, which most diligently sought to restrain these local increases.

## Movements toward Master Agreements

Changes were not all in this direction. In France the government fostered national interindustry agreements between the unions and the employers' organization (CNPF), with the latter changing its constitution to provide for interindustry authority. National wage agreements served as guides rather than enforceable regulations. In Germany the IG-Metall in 1968 negotiated national agreements (with their counterpart employer organizations) pertaining to technological change and to a reduction in working hours. In the United Kingdom, the engineering unions failed in a strategy to break up a national agreement and replace it by local ones. In the United States, coalition bargaining fostered centralized master agreements with individual companies on specific issues. The long-established practice for national cross-industry agreements continued unchallenged in Belgium, Norway, and Sweden. But in the Netherlands, the parties were no longer agreeing on the terms of such pacts.

## Convergence of Bargaining Unit Systems

The experience of the 1960s clearly indicates the need for an integrated system of bargaining including units at the lower, intermediate, and national levels. Such a system allows for the widest flexibility for dealing with issues arising at all levels. Workers through their unions and managements bargain at the job and plant levels. The industry- and national-level negotiations serve important functions in stabilizing and developing industrial relations rules of conduct, standards, and changes. Necessarily, there is increasing pressure from unions in most countries to expand the subjects of consultation and to broaden the scope for negotiations, bargaining, and bilateral and multilateral decision-making.

## Government Bargaining

In recent years, there has been a significant extension of collective bargaining in the government sector. As noted above, the government as an employer has organized special bargaining agencies. In a number of countries (France, Italy, and Sweden) government employees gained formal rights to strike and exercised them. Elsewhere, they took similar action without specific legal sanction. Fundamentally, the process and outcome introduced few innovations, except that in some countries, as in Germany and Sweden, where unions participated actively in plans to improve the specific services, they developed precise procedures and the ultimate administrative form of the understanding.

## Tripartite Bargaining and Union Bargaining with Governments

One significant departure from the traditional concepts of bargaining arises in countries where employer associations and union centers work out agreements with the government as direct participants (Austria, Belgium, the Netherlands, Norway, and Italy). The resulting agreements usually embrace not only provisions affecting the terms of the employment contract but also employees and employers as citizens and taxpayers including the regulation of food prices, other prices and incomes, social security benefits, adjustments in tax rates for the lower-income groups, or rebates on some taxes. Another arrangement, in Germany, Great Britain, Italy, and Sweden, is a direct understanding between the trade union center and the administration in power upon a legislative program that affects the economic package for workers. In Great Britain, the "social contract" is an agreement of this type.

## The Multinational Corporation: A Challenge to National Bargaining Systems

The multiplication in the number and size of multinational corporations has finally aroused all national union centers, making them aware of new dimensions of their problems with management. Unionists in the home countries of the multinationals saw the multinationals exporting jobs and weakening union bargaining powers in part through their ability physically to shift production. National labor standards and programs as well as long-term economic social and industrial relations objectives could be thwarted. The receiving-country unionists might at first see multinationals as suppliers of jobs but in time would recognize them as threats to national economic and political independence depriving the nations of the ability to direct their own destinies and their independence. Industrial relations policy in these countries would be governed by officers operating at a distance from the employment sites.

Being nationally organized and divided by political, denominational, and other issues, trade unions found themselves at a disadvantage in dealing with multinationals. Unions had little experience or no rights to transcend national boundaries.

Many obstacles had to be overcome to unite trade union groups on a common program and strategy to deal with these huge international entities. Most previous contacts among national centers at the international level had been inspirational in character. But, in the last decade, the International Trade Secretariats have initiated action to meet these problems and to help national unions surmount their limitations. The secretariats established international industry and company councils seeking to bring together unions in all plants--even those in Asia. They provided information, advice, and expert negotiators to assist unions, and they use international propaganda to help in local battles. In the case of strikes, affiliates are in some places refusing to produce transferred work or engage in overtime to offset lost production in other plants of the multinationals. Unions in the corporations' home country have interceded on behalf of workers abroad and assisted in settlements; joint strike strategies have at times been evolved. In a few cases, regular consultative meetings have been arranged with the heads of the multinational company to discuss issues of concern to both, but in no case have they produced bargaining relations, an ultimate goal of trade unionists. This end was approached in the agreements with large U.S. automobile companies operating in both Canada and the United States.

Recognizing the limitations of the collective bargaining approach to control, the International Confederation of Free Trade Unions (ICFTU) organized a body to coordinate and supplement the efforts of the trade secretariats in dealing with direct trade union issues and enlist the power of socialist parties in the various nations. It seeks to reinforce international pressure for legal control of the corporations. Regarding the latter, it stresses company responsibilities toward national labor standards and International Labor Organization

(ILO) conventions and recommendations, and to permit trade unions
to operate freely. For the time being, the national and international
trade union movements are seeking ways to engage in true international bargaining. The EEC is moving to this end through the European Company law now under consideration. Union relations with
multinationals remain a foremost challenge for which the precise
structure does not exist and will probably embitter industrial relations in the years ahead.

## Appraisal of Directions in
## Western Countries

No country can illustrate the mature system of integrated and
articulated bargaining between trade unions. In European countries,
the major shortcomings prevail at the job or plant level. Recent advances are increasingly correcting this weakness, but national rates
of progress are uneven. France shows the least progress in job and
plant bargaining; in Germany, the dual system of bargaining through
works councils severely inhibits the process. In the two North American countries, the system of bargaining stops at the company level;
pattern bargaining and several industry agreements set widely accepted models. The very incompleteness of the bargaining structures
in all countries spells continued friction and wrangling, as trade
unions seek integrated and articulated bargaining structures and
relations.

## THE TRADE UNION MOVEMENT: AN INDOMITABLE
## FORCE FOR CHANGE, EQUITY, HUMANISM,
## AND OPPORTUNITY

In Western societies, the trade union, the strike, and the labor
demonstration are sanctioned channels for expressing disapproval of
existing conditions and for presenting demands for change. The
trade union is the employees' direct instrument for both communication and negotiations and redress either with management or political
leaders or both. Representing those seeking improvements in life
and work standards, unions necessarily are critical of the status quo.
In the postwar years, the rhetoric of those demanding improvements
in the life and conditions of labor may have been extreme, but the
behavior was moderate. A number of unions and unionists accented
their revolutionary intent and anticapitalistic outlook, but they really
alluded to distant goals more than to current efforts at violent change.
Communist-guided trade unions spoke in reformist terms and followed
a moderate strategy. Radical groups hardly penetrated the existing

trade union system.  When expectations are being approximately met, the unionist is likely to accent stable and responsible relations with management, hoping thereby to encourage continuing gains.  This was the prevailing attitude in the European and American trade union movement.  But a change, begun in Europe at the end of the 1960s, is currently becoming evident in Canada but is barely apparent in the United States.

Formerly acquiescent leadership has responded to the new disquiet among its following.  This restlessness is most evident among the young and especially aggrieved groups.  The response was prompt in some countries, laggard in others.  But in time leaders began to reflect the new moods, even if they were not so inclined or had been dulled to perceive such disquiet in advance of outbreaks.  Dissenters are ever present within the unions.  Though generally contained, in periods and places of minimal dissatisfaction, revolts, in one form or other, mild or sweeping, may develop and may take the form of wildcat strikes, political challenges of entrenched leaders, or support of their aggressive militant opponents.

Owing to current inflation and structural changes, decline in rates of growth and increases in numbers of unemployed, expressions of dissent will become stronger.  Employees want better terms of employment or as a minimum the retention of current real levels, improved working conditions, expanded benefits, more respect for their rights, more security and services, and participation in decision-making at all levels--from the job to the nation and then to the European region.  They seek not only equity, but also equality. The leadership is ultimately dedicated to these ends.

Trade union approaches are increasingly broad in nature and not necessarily doctrinaire, in the formal sense, in content.  They are moreover flexible in strategy and responsive to new proposals and experiments.  In periods of acquiescence these attributes often appear submerged or even occasionally subverted by the pursuit of the narrow self-interests of individual organized groups, but in times of turmoil and militancy they gain new prominence.  Since the mid-1960s the latter trend was dominant in Europe, gave the movement its buoyancy, and produced the major changes.  Trade unions test innovations and policy essentially in terms--at least when it comes down to their final choices--of human benefits and priorities.  Participation in decision-making for employees and trade unions means union presence and equality of power in making decisions on choices and the opportunity to bear heavily on the importance of these human values.

The major union vehicle is the industrial bargaining table, and unions will turn to sympathetic governments when management is resistant or turn away from governments when they are ineffective and unyielding and to the bargaining table. Trade union independence of its political allies has grown significantly in most countries so that unions have been able to press their positions even more vigorously than before. The new determination extends to industrial relations as well as broad public issues, particularly as these relate to the domestic economy. The attainment of the goal is primary; the method, secondary.

The last decade in Europe in particular reflects this inherent adaptability of the trade union movement. The national union centers have become aggressive and militant. They have secured and stimulated the granting of many important advances on the road to further gains. They have forced changes in the industrial relations and capitalist systems. Further modifications will result as they strive for even greater benefits and innovations and for a more entrenched position within the economies of some Western countries. The trade union record of responsibility is well established. But unions will probably demand a major role in assuring the appropriate priority to humanistic values to which they are dedicated and thereby seek further to modify the existing system to fashion it for survival, growth, and greater equity for the worker and low-income groups and continuing high employment.

## NOTES

1. Ronald Englehart, "The Silent Revolution in Europe: Intergenerational Change in Post-Industrial Societies," American Political Science Review 65 (December 1971): 991-1107; New York Times, May 22, 1974, p. 45.

2. Stephen Castles and Godula Kosack, Immigration Workers and Class Structure in Western Europe (London: Oxford University Press, 1973).

3. Malcolm Fisher, Measurement of Labor Disputes and Their Economic Effects (Paris: OECD, 1973), p. 135.

4. OECD Labour-Management Programme Experts Meeting 1973-74, "Absenteeism and Staff Turnover," Report on a Meeting of Management Experts, Paris, October 17-19, 1973, p. iii.

5. Ivor L. Roberts, "Trade Union Membership Trends in Seven Western European Countries, 1950-65," Industrial Relations Journal 4 (Summer 1973): 45-56.

6. Industrial Democracy Programme adopted by the 1971 Congress of Swedish Trade Union Confederation (Stockholm: LO, 1972); Ake Burstedt, Gosta Dahlstrom, Bo Jonsson, Anders Leion, Lars Ljung, Margareta Medri, and Clas-Erik Odhner, Social Goals in National Planning: A Critique of Sweden's Long-Term Economic Survey (Stockholm: Bokforlaget Prisma, 1972).

The index relates solely to the contents of Chapters 1 and 11. Its purpose is to facilitate the location of material in these two chapters which relate to the countries dealt with in individual chapters and other countries, places, and organizations discussed in these two chapters. The Table of Contents serves as an index to the subject matter.

# ABOUT THE EDITOR AND CONTRIBUTORS

SOLOMON BARKIN. M.A.; Professor of Economics, University of Massachusetts, Amherst; President, Industrial Relations Research Association (1964); Deputy to Director, Manpower and Social Affairs Directorate and Chief of Social Affairs Division, OECD, Paris (1963-68); Research Director, Textile Workers Union of America (1937-63); Author: The Decline of the Labor Movement and What Can Be Done About It, Center for the Study of Democratic Institutions, 1961; Editor: International Labor, 1968.

JOACHIM BERGMANN. Ph.D. Professor of Sociology, Darmstadt University; Thesis: "Das Soziale System von Talcott Parsons."

PIETRO MERLI BRANDINI. Dr.; Research Director, Center of Economic Studies and Planning, Rome; Secretary General, Industrial and Labor Relations Research Institute (1962-68); Member, General Council of CISL; Author: Relazioni Industriali (Industrial relations), 1969; Coauthor: I Cub: Comitati Unitari Di Base (The cub: basic unit assemblies), 1970.

JOHN F. B. GOODMAN. Ph.D.; Senior Lecturer in Industrial Relations, University of Manchester; Author: Shop Stewards, 1973.

GEORGE VICKERS HAYTHORNE. Ph.D.; Commissioner, Price and Income Commission (1969-73); Deputy Minister of Labor, 1961-69; Chairman, Governing Body of I.L.O., 1964-65; Author: Labor in Canadian Agriculture, 1960.

MARC-HENRI JANNE. Licencie en Sciences sociales; Research Associate, Institut de Sociologie Universite Libre de Bruxelles; Collaborator: Tradition et Continuite dan les societes industrielles (Tradition and continuity in industrial societies), 1973.

WALTHER MULLER-JENTSCH. Diplomsoziologe; Research Sociologist, Institut fur Sozialforschung of the Johann Wolfgang Goethe-Universitat; Coeditor: Gewerkschaften und Klassenkampf, Yearbook on labor problems and unionism.

BRAM PEPER. Ph.D.; Associate Professor of Sociology, Erasmus University, Rotterdam; Author: Vorming van welzijnsbeleid (The making of welfare policy), 1972; Editor: De Nederlandse arbeidsverhoudingen (Dutch industrial relations), 1973.

JEAN-DANIEL REYNAUD. Ph. D. ; Professor of Sociology of Labor, Conservatoire National des Artes et Metiers, Paris; President-Elect, International Industrial Relations Association; Author: Les Syndicats en France (The trade unions in France), 3d edition, 1975; Coauthor: La negociation collective en France (Collective bargaining in France), 1972.

SUMNER ROSEN. Ph. D. ; Senior Staff, Institue of Public Administration; Author: "The Unions: Making Out with the Labor Elite" in Gartner, Greer, and Riessman, eds. What Nixon Is Doing to Us, 1973.

GUY SPITAELS. Ph. D. ; Member of National Senate: Professor, Universite Libre de Bruxelles; Professor, College d'Europe a Bruges; Director of Research, Institut de Sociologie: Author: Le Mouvement syndical en Belgique (The trade union movement in Belgium), 1967; Reflexions sur la politique de Securite sociale (Reflections on social security policy), 1973; L'Annee sociale (The social yearbook).

CASTEN VAN OTTER. Ph. D. ; Senior Lecturer (sociology), Graduate School of Social Work and Public Administration, Stockholm; President, Swedish Sociological Association (1972): Coauthor: Lonebildningen pa arbetsplatsen (Plant-level wage determination), 1973.

THE SCOPE OF PUBLIC SECTOR COLLECTIVE
BARGAINING
Joan Weitzman

THE URBAN LABOR MARKET: Institutions,
Information, Linkages
David Lewin, Raymond Horton,
Robert Shick, and Charles Brecher

THE LABOR MARKET: AN INFORMATION SYSTEM
Boris Yavitz and Dean W. Morse
with Anna B. Dutka

LABOR MOVEMENTS IN THE COMMON MARKET
COUNTRIES: The Growth of a European Pressure
Group
Marguerite Bouvard

REFORM IN TRADE UNION DISCRIMINATION IN
THE CONSTRUCTION INDUSTRY: Operation Dig
and Its Legacy
Irwin Dubinsky

INTERNATIONAL MANUAL ON COLLECTIVE
BARGAINING FOR PUBLIC EMPLOYEES
edited by Seymour P. Kaye
and Arthur Marsh

LABOR IN THE TRANSPORTATION INDUSTRIES
Robert C. Lieb

TRADE UNION WOMEN: A Study of Their
Participation in New York City Locals
Barbara M. Werthheimer
and Anne H. Nelson